Introduction to SNA Networking

A Guide for Using VTAM/NCP

Other McGraw-Hill Books in Mini and Mainframe Computing

Introduction to SNA Networking
A Guide for Using VTAM/NCP

Jay Ranade
George C. Sackett

McGraw-Hill Book Company

New York St. Louis San Francisco Auckland Bogotá
Hamburg London Madrid Mexico Milan Montreal
New Delhi Panama Paris São Paolo
Singapore Sydney Tokyo Toronto

Library of Congress Catalog Card Number 89-83754

10 9 8 7 6 5 4 3 2 1

ISBN 0-07-051144-6

McGraw-Hill Book Company
1221 Avenue of the Americas
New York, NY 10020

Art by Visionquest U.S.A., Inc., Rutherford, NJ 07070
Composed in Ventura Publisher by Context, Inc., San Diego, CA

*This book is dedicated to my loving wife and friend Peggy
and our beautiful daughter Chelsea,
who have stood beside me, never behind or in front.*

George

This book is dedicated to my loving wife Ranjna.

Jay

Contents

Chapter 13   VTAM User Tables — USSTAB, MODETAB, and COSTAB   239

Part 4   NCP   261

Chapter 14   NCP Macros — PCCU, BUILD, and SYSCNTRL   263

The following table of contents gives a rough outline of what is included in the sequel to the current book.

Acknowledgments

It's been a long time coming. Over two years of research and writing, not to mention keeping up with the latest IBM announcements, have gone into this book. I hope you find it informative and helpful in your SNA networking endeavors.

Some people say you make your own opportunities and others say you take advantage of them when they knock on your door. I think that it is a little of both.

First and foremost I must thank Ildy Mandy for recommending me to Jay Ranade as a coauthor. Her thoughtfulness will always be remembered. Thanks, Ildy. Thanks to Joe Asaro, Mike Aversano, and Ed Diminno, the boys at Kwasha-Lipton, who gave a part-time security guard studying computer programming the opportunity of a lifetime. Thanks to Joe Visovsky and Tony Costa for reviewing and for their technical assistance. Last, but not least, my sincere thanks to Ruoh-Yann Huang for her expert review on several chapters. I also thank my coauthor, Jay Ranade, for his support and the special guidance only he can deliver. A special thanks to Peggy and Chelsea, for giving me time to complete the book, understanding its importance, and a never-ending love. And thanks to all those who have helped me with clarifications, undulations, and information during the writing of this book.

George C. Sackett

First and foremost I am grateful to Kyungjoo Suh for spending many hours in reading, reviewing, and criticizing all the chapters. My thanks are also due to Saba Zamir for making useful suggestions. I gratefully acknowledge the assistance provided by Kenya Sanders in typing various chapters at unbelievable speed. My very special thanks to Peggy Sackett for drawing impressive sets of line art figures.

My very special thanks to Theron Shreve, our senior editor, for his constant encouragement. My thanks are also due to Alan Rose for taking care of the production details. Finally, special thanks to Ranjna for giving me time to complete this book.

Jay Ranade

Preface

SNA is IBM's grand architecture for designing and implementing computer networks. VTAM and NCP are communications software products that are SNA-compliant and form the basis of SNA implementation. The purpose of this book is to teach you how to use VTAM and NCP to create single-host/single-domain networks. In a companion volume, entitled *Advanced SNA Networking*, you will learn about large multi-domain networks.

THE 80/20 RULE

The SNA and VTAM/NCP literature provided by IBM constitutes about 20,000 pages of reading material. This text is not a summary of the IBM manuals nor is its purpose to replace those manuals. We have applied the 80/20 rule for material to be included in this text. The material which is used 80 percent of the time constitutes 20 percent of the material available. This is what is covered in this text; the rest has been discarded. While this approach gives you sufficient knowledge to feel comfortable with the software, it does not qualify this book as a reference manual.

WHO THIS BOOK IS FOR

This book has been written with many types of readers in mind. It can be used as a primer for those who want to be VTAM/NCP systems programmers. It provides the practical aspects of SNA network implementation for those who have only a theoretical knowledge of the subject. It is ideal for CICS systems programmers who do not have a clear picture of networks and data communications. It can be easily understood by network operators who would like to gain background information on SNA networks. Network engineers will need this book to complement their hardware knowledge with communications software information.

Because the book provides sufficient information to understand logical units, InterSystems Communications (ISC), distributed systems, and a lot more, we would even go so far as to say that application programmers working in a COBOL/CICS environment would benefit from this text. As data processing evolves more and more toward distributed application/data, it will be beneficial to all levels of personnel to understand how various components of a network are interconnected.

PC users will find Parts 1 and 2 of this book especially useful. Since OS/2 Extended Edition Communication Manager has become available, PC communications are no longer limited to asynchronous protocols. The PC community will have to learn how they fit into the large SNA environments and gain insight into PC connectivity to LANs, communications controllers, and cluster controllers. They will also have to learn about APPC and LU 6.2 in the very near future.

WHAT IS THE PREREQUISITE

If you have been in data processing for a couple of years, you can understand this book. If you are only a COBOL programmer, that's fine too. If you know CICS, so much the better. If you are a systems programmer, this book will be a breeze.

The authors do not expect you to know anything about data communications; it is discussed in Part 1. The book has been structured in such a way that it may be used as a self-teaching guide. It may be used as a textbook for a 3- to 5-day in-house or public seminar on VTAM/NCP.

WHAT ENVIRONMENT THIS BOOK IS FOR

This book covers the MVS, MVS/XA, DOS/VSE, and VM operating systems environments. It is applicable to large mainframes (e.g., IBM 3090, 3084, 4381) as well as not-so-large mainframes (e.g., IBM 9370). It includes both CICS and IMS/DC installations.

A WORD ON THE STYLE USED

The authors have made extensive use of diagrams, figures, examples, and illustrations. The style has purposely been kept simple. We hope to alleviate readers' fears about the intricacies of networks. As you move from one chapter to the next, you will begin to appreciate the structure and underlying simplicity behind small and large net-works.

We do not go into too much theory. This is a practical book. As a matter of fact, this is the first and only practical guide on SNA. If you are more interested in the theory, please consult the bibliography for additional sources.

WHY THIS BOOK IS COMPLETE

You name it and it's in there. You will learn about hardware such as 3174s and 3745s; we include various protocols such as SDLC, BSC, half-duplex, and full-duplex. Telecommunications concepts and various physical transmission media are discussed, and a discussion of the various layers of SNA has been incorporated. It's only after we give you the necessary background information that we begin to talk about VTAM and NCP. In addition, this book is up-to-date as of the most recent releases of VTAM and NCP. The authors intend to revise the book if a significant IBM announcement makes it necessary to add, delete, or modify parts of the text.

WHAT IS INCLUDED

Part 1 begins with the concepts of data and telecommunications. It moves on to details about the communications hardware, software, and protocols. We also talk about SNA and its various layers. This part lays the foundation for understanding networks and their components.

Part 2 concentrates on SNA domains and networks. We also discuss defining a network topography.

After finishing Part 2, you will be ready to move onto defining the network to VTAM and NCP. This takes place in Part 3. Various VTAM start options, major nodes, path tables, user tables, and the macros needed to define them are discussed. A separate discussion of channel attached VM and VSE configurations is also included.

Part 4 illustrates the use of various NCP macros such as PCCU, BUILD, HOST, PATH, GROUP, LINE, CLUSTER, TERMINAL, etc.

WHAT IS THE NEXT STEP

This text concentrates on single-domain networks only. Single-domain networks typically involve the use of a single host. If you work in such an environment, that's all you will need to know. However, most of the computer installations that need to communicate over a network have two or more mainframes. A sequel to this text, entitled *Advanced SNA Networking: A Professional's Guide to VTAM / NCP,* is in the final stages of completion. It will include IBM 3174, IBM 3745, multi-domain networks, SNI, VTAM initialization, Low Entry Networking, IBM 9370 connectivity, network operations, NetView, NetView/PC, and performance management. We hope you find it a suitable sequel to the current text.

After reading this book, you will not only know how to use VTAM/NCP macros, but also how various networking hardware, software, and protocols fit into the whole picture. This will give you a global view of the networking components. The authors expect that after finishing this book, you will be able to design and code for single-domain networks with a high degree of confidence and competence.

Introduction and Concepts

1

Data Communications and Telecommunications

Communications is the ability to exchange information between two or more entities. When such entities are human beings and the distances involved are insignificant, communications is not a problem. Human beings have evolved over millennia to develop different language patterns and speech formats so that their brains can comprehend and analyze such information. When the distances involved were significant, the necessity to communicate resulted in the invention of other methods of information exchange. Throughout history, there have been examples of information transfer through the use of smoke signals, drum beats, mirror reflections, etc.

As the world advanced into the industrial era, the invention of wireless exchange of information was a giant step toward expediting the information transfer. The invention of telephones further made it possible to communicate quickly and conveniently over long distances. Recently, there has been widespread use of other telecommunications media such as microwave, satellite, and fiber optics. One of the most astonishing examples of communications is the transmission of images of planet Uranus by Voyager II from billions of miles away. After the shortest possible sample of communications history, let's get to the relevant topic — the computer communications.

1.1 TYPICAL IBM COMMUNICATIONS ENVIRONMENTS

To understand computer communications in an IBM environment, we will make extensive use of examples and sample environments.

The hardware and software we will be mentioning will be discussed in subsequent chapters; this section will give you a global view of what it's all about.

1.1.1 Single-Host, Local Terminals Environment

Refer to Figure 1.1 for the simplest possible communications environment. It consists of a single mainframe computer which is also called a "host processor." All the users who need to access the host applications are in the same building in which the host processor is installed. What we need in this case is a cluster controller which can be attached to the byte multiplexer channel of the host. A cluster controller is a device which controls a cluster of terminals. Terminals cannot be directly attached to a channel; they have to be hooked to this device, which is further attached to the channel. The byte multiplexer channel of a host processor is a communications link between the host and the peripheral devices such as cluster controllers, communications controllers, operating system printers, etc. Another channel type, the block multiplexer channel, is generally used to connect to Direct Access Storage Devices (DASDs), tape drives, etc.

A cluster controller can control terminal (e.g., IBM 3278) and printer devices (e.g., IBM 3268 printer). Depending upon the model of the cluster controller, you can attach anywhere from 8 to 32 printers or terminals. The link between the cluster controller and the terminal or printer device is usually a coaxial cable with proper connectors on either side which provide the physical interface. Be aware that this environment is possible only if the host, the cluster controller, and the terminals or printers are in the same building. A channel attached cluster controller cannot be more than 100 to 200 feet from the channel itself. The terminals or printers cannot be more than 500 to 1000 feet from the cluster controller.

To give you a taste of the real environment, let's look at the examples of software and hardware involved in this configuration:

• A host processor is an IBM 3090, IBM 4381, or IBM 9370.
• A channel-attached cluster controller is an IBM 3274 Model 41D or IBM 3274 Model 41A.
• A display terminal is an IBM 3278, an IBM 3290, or an IBM 3270 PC.
• A printer device is an IBM 3268 or an IBM 3287.
• The operating system is MVS/XA, MVS/ESA, or DOS/VSE.
• An application subsystem is CICS/VS, IMS/DC, or TSO.
• The communications access method is ACF/VTAM or ACF/TCAM.

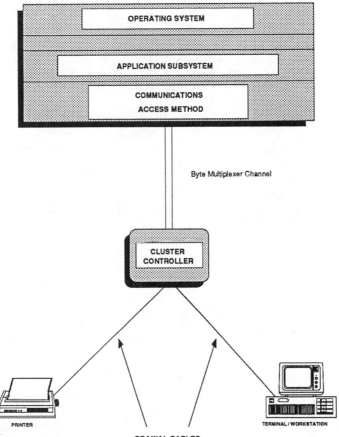

Figure 1.1 A single host with channel-attached local terminals.

If you are overwhelmed with the introduction of so many acronyms, it will console you to know that you are not expected to know
or remember them. Just try to get a global picture of different environments. Then, when we start discussing the individual components, you will know where they fit in the whole puzzle.

1.1.2 Single-Host Local and Remote Terminals

Figure 1.2 shows an environment in which you have a single mainframe but not all the attached terminals are in the same building.
Suppose that the business requirements dictate that a regional office

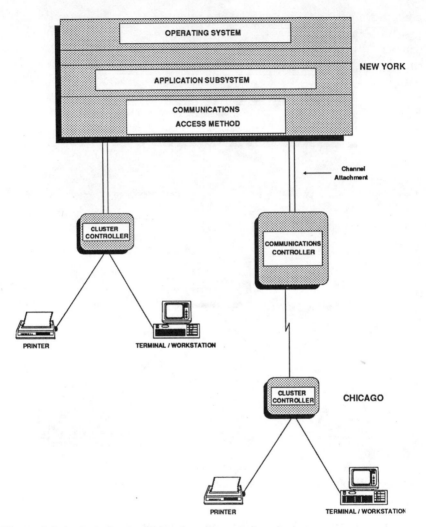

Figure 1.2 A single host with local and remote terminals.

in Chicago must access the host applications in New York. While you still need local cluster controllers to support terminals and printers in the same building, you cannot attach terminals in Chicago to the same cluster controller. What you need is a "remote cluster controller" in Chicago to which all the printer and terminal devices in Chicago will be attached.

A remote cluster controller is different from a local cluster controller. A local cluster controller attaches to a computer channel, but a remote one only has a link to the communications lines. In our case, the communications lines will be the telephone link between the Chicago and New York offices. A remote cluster controller uses the same physical connectivity media such as coaxial cables to attach to the terminal and printer devices. Therefore, as far as the end-user devices are concerned, their connectivity is the same for remote and local cluster controllers.

Furthermore, a remote cluster controller cannot be directly attached to the computer channels over the communications lines. You need a device in the middle called a "communications controller." In our sample environment, while the cluster controller is attached to the communications controller over a telephone link, the communications controller itself is hooked to the mainframe through a channel. A communications controller can control a number of cluster controllers located at multiple geographical locations.

The following are examples of the new hardware and software introduced in this section:

- A remote cluster controller is IBM 3274 Model 41C.
- A communications controller is an IBM 3745, IBM 3720, IBM 3725, or IBM 3705.
- The software running in a communications controller is the Network Control Program, or NCP.

While the communications software running in the mainframe and the communications controllers are named ACF/VTAM and ACF/NCP, respectively, the software running in the cluster controller does not have a specific name. For our purposes, we will call the cluster controller software the "Cluster Controller Load" program.

1.1.3 Single-Host Local and Remote Communications Controllers

In the previous section we talked about local and remote cluster controllers. In this section we introduce local and remote communications controllers. In our hypothetical company, the Chicago office has grown so rapidly that now they have a staff of 1500 people and an inventory of 600 terminals. All the terminals are attached to 20 different remote cluster controllers located in Chicago. The 20 cluster controllers have 20 different communications links to the channel-attached communications controller in New York. It is determined that it will be more cost effective to install a communications controller locally in the Chicago office and attach the cluster controllers to it through modem eliminators. The connectivity would be through high bandwidth communications lines between New York and Chicago. Such communications lines can be 56-kilobits-per-second (kbps) leased lines which are usually referred to as Digital Dataphone Service (DDS) lines. Figure 1.3 shows such a configuration.

Notice that the communications controller located in Chicago is *not* channel attached to the New York host. It is link-attached (through

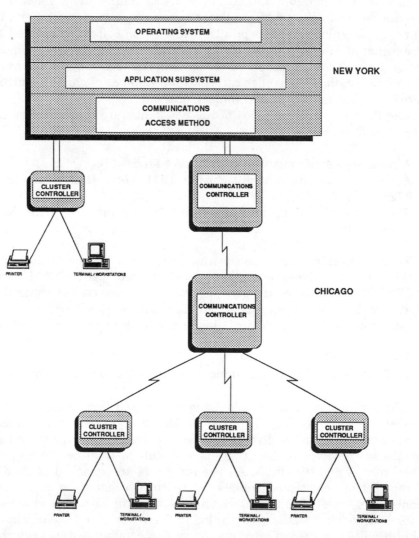

Figure 1.3 A single host with channel- and link-attached communications controllers.

communications links) to the channel-attached communications controller located in New York. The link-attached communications controller has almost the same characteristics as the channel-attached one. It is used for concentrating data from multiple cluster controllers at a remote location. Examples of such communications controllers are IBM 3745, IBM 3720, IBM 3725, and IBM 3705. The software running in a link-attached communications controller is also NCP.

1.1.4 Local Host Connectivity to a Remote Host

In our next scenario, there is a business requirement to open a new zonal office in Los Angeles. The processing requirements are such that a host is required to run new applications in Los Angeles. At the same time, the Los Angeles host would like to communicate with the New York office to exchange and access its data. The configuration would look as shown in Figure 1.4.

Notice that the Los Angeles host requires a channel-attached communications controller to have connectivity to the New York host through its own channel-attached communications controller.

Although we have not shown it in the figure, there will be channel-attached cluster controllers and communications controller-attached cluster controllers at various locations.

The communications access methods running in New York and Los Angeles hosts can be ACF/VTAM and their applications subsystems can be CICS/VS.

1.1.5 Remote Printing

In our final scenario, we have a requirement to print enormous amounts of reports in our Houston office. In the past the requirements were met by printing them in New York and then mailing them to Houston. But the urgency of those reports requires that they be printed on a real-time basis. Figure 1.5 shows a configuration in which we have installed a Remote Job Entry (RJE) device in Houston. Such a device can be attached to a printer, a card reader, a card punch, and a console. Examples are IBM 2770, IBM 2780, IBM 3777, and IBM 3780 devices. An RJE device communicates with the host through a communications link to the communications controller.

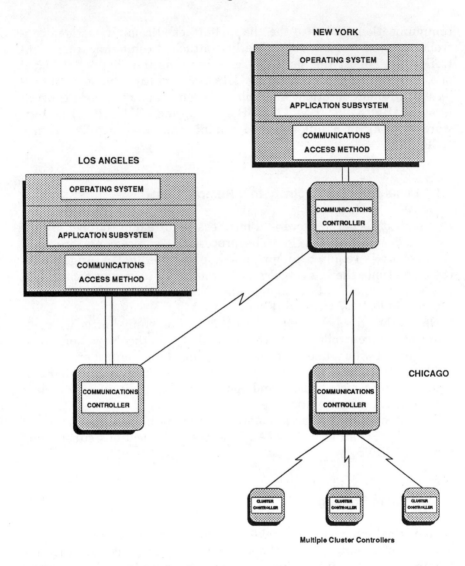

Figure 1.4 Two remote hosts having connectivity through communications controllers.

A printer attached to an RJE device is usually a high-speed printer such as an IBM 3203 or IBM 3211. An RJE device is controlled by a host subsystem such as JES2 or JES3. Don't confuse high-speed RJE printers with low-speed VTAM printers, which are attached to a cluster controller. VTAM printers are used by application subsystems such as CICS/VS or IMS/DC and not JES2 or JES3.

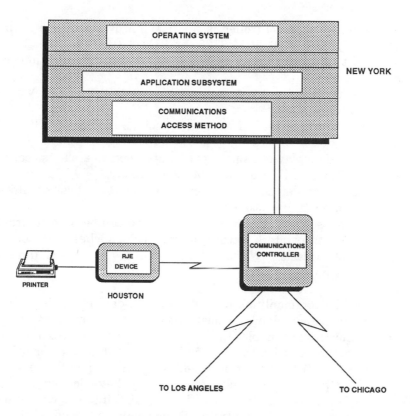

Figure 1.5 Remote printing using RJE devices.

1.1.6 Components of IBM Communications World

In the previous examples, we have seen the global picture of different IBM communication environments. We will cover each component in detail in the following chapters. When you learn about individual hardware and software components, keep in mind the global view so that you can relate them to other components. Let's summarize what we have learned about the SNA communications world so far:

- The operating systems running in the hosts can be MVS/SP, MVS/XA, MVS/ESA, VM, and DOS/VSE.
- The communications access methods running in the host can be ACF/VTAM or ACF/TCAM.
- The application subsystems running in the host can be CICS/VS, IMS/DC, TSO, etc.

- A communications controller is an IBM hardware device such as IBM 3745, IBM 3720, IBM 3725, or IBM 3705. It can be channel attached to a host or link attached to another communications controller.
- Software running in a communications controller is the Network Control Program (NCP).
- A cluster controller is IBM hardware such as IBM 3274, IBM 3276, IBM 3174, etc.
- Examples of display terminal devices attached to a cluster controller are IBM 3278, IBM 3290, IBM 3270 PC, etc.
- A cluster controller can be channel attached to a host or link attached to a communications controller.
- RJE devices such as IBM 3777 or IBM 3780 can be used to provide connectivity to printers, card readers, card punches, and consoles at a remote location. Without RJE, such devices are channel attached to a host.

Some of the commonly used names for the devices we have introduced so far are as follows. A host is also called a "mainframe" or a "Central Electronic Complex" (CEC) or a "Central Processing Unit" (CPU). A communications controller is also called a "box," or a Front End Processor (FEP), or a "front end." You will frequently hear communications programmers saying that they have loaded the box. What they mean is that they have loaded NCP into the communications controller. A cluster controller is also called a "terminal controller."

1.2 TELECOMMUNICATIONS FACILITIES AND CONCEPTS

In the previous section, we talked about connecting different hardware over communications lines. Such connectivity issues could involve the following:

- Connecting a communications controller to another communications controller.
- Connecting a cluster controller to a channel-attached or link-attached communications controller.
- Connecting a terminal device directly to the communications controller.

1.2.1 Common Carriers versus Value Added Carriers

If the distance between the devices is less than a few hundred feet and they are in the same building, they can be connected directly using proper cables and physical interfaces. Such connectivity may involve use of devices such as modem eliminators. More often than not, such devices are *not* located in the same building. They may be located in two or more different buildings in a metropolitan area. They can also be dispersed over long distances ranging from a few miles to several thousand miles. Under those circumstances, you have to use the services of a common carrier such as a telephone company. For connectivity requiring the use of equipment which falls in the domain of different regional telephone companies, you require services of a long distance carrier such as AT&T, MCI, Sprint, etc.

Common Carriers. Common carriers build the actual physical networks; e.g., they lay telephone cables. They are regulated by government regulatory authorities such as the Federal Communications Commission (FCC), and they are licensed to build their physical networks on public property. Common carriers file their tariffs with the regulatory agencies and upon approval these tariffs become legally binding upon the telephone company and the recipient of the service.

Value-Added Carriers. There is another kind of service provided by Value-Added Carriers (VACs). VACs, unlike common carriers, are not regulated by the government. VACs lease the physical networks from the common carriers and add some additional services to it. Such additional services are provided through the network of computers installed by the VACs connecting their leased physical networks. Examples of VACs are Telenet, Tymnet, and Datapac (in Canada). Services provided by VACs can be protocol conversion, code translation, and packet switching. Such networks are also called "Value Added Networks" (VANs).

In the past, the physical network used by common carriers was based on copper wires and cables, and most of the switching equipment used by them was electro-mechanical in nature. Since the advent of computer technology, most of the switching is now done by computer-controlled electronic ones rather than electro-mechanical ones. Also, because of advancements in the telecommunications technology, a lot of other physical media are used for transmission purposes. Such physical media could be microwave transmission, satellite communications, or the use of fiber optics.

1.2.2 Analog versus Digital Transmission

Before we get to know more about the physical media for data transmissions, we must understand two modes of transmission, analog
and digital.

Analog Transmission.   Analog mode of transmission is the older and
still the most widely used mode of information transmission. Since
the human voice is analog in nature, the telephone networks were
designed to meet the need of human communications. Analog transmission is waveform in nature (see Figure 1.6a.).

(a) ANALOG TRANSMISSION

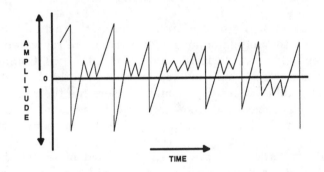

(b) DIGITAL TRANSMISSION

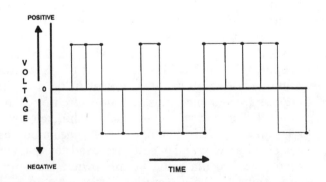

Figure 1.6 (a) Analog transmission; (b) digital transmission pulses.

Although the human voice can have a frequency anywhere from 200 to 7000 cycles per second (also called "hertz," Hz), the telephone transmission filters permit transmissions only between 300 and 3300 Hz. Analog signals can be used over copper wires, cables, and microwave and satellite transmission. Since analog signals get weak over distances, they are boosted at regular intervals using amplifiers. The boosters not only amplify the real analog signal but also the noise associated with it.

Digital Transmission.   While analog transmission consists of a continuous stream of different frequencies, digital transmission consists of separate pulses (see Figure 1.6b). Digital transmission is possible over copper wires and cables, microwave transmission, satellite transmission, and optical fiber facilities. Recall that analog transmission is not possible over fiber optics transmission media. Digital transmission pulses are also boosted at regular intervals using regenerative repeaters, which do not boost any extraneous signal associated with the digital pulses. Therefore, digital transmission is better in transmission quality than analog transmission and also has a lower transmission error rate. Examples of digital transmission services provided by common carriers are Dataphone Digital Service at 56 kbps and T1 lines at 1.544 megabits per second (mbps). While the capacity of an analog line is measured in hertz, for digital lines it is measured in bits per second.

Hosts, communication controllers, cluster controllers, and terminals generate and receive only digital signals. Computers by design are digital (and not analog) in nature. Whether you use analog or digital circuits to transmit data, it has to be ensured that proper conversion must be done at the proper place.

When you are using the analog mode of transmission, the interface equipment is called a "modem" and for a digital transmission it is called the "Data Service Unit/Channel Service Unit" (DSU/CSU).

1.2.3 Switched versus Leased Lines

When you dial a phone number and carry out a conversation, the connection between your phone and the destination phone is established for the duration of that conversation. The common carrier company charges depend on the distance, the time, and the duration of the call. Such a connection is called a dial-up or a switched connection. In a switched connection, the circuit used for establishing the call varies with each call. If you hang up and dial again, you may get a different circuit whose quality may be different from the previous one. You may also experience a circuit-busy signal and dial tone delays.

In a leased line, the circuit is assigned by the telephone company on a permanent basis. You may or may not use the line for any useful purpose, but you are paying for it and it is there when you need it. The telephone company charges a flat monthly fee that primarily depends upon the distance involved. The circuits involved in the path are known and stay the same for the duration of the lease. The circuit quality is verified at the outset and does not have to be verified later because the circuit path does not change.

Switched and leased line requirements depend upon the application needs. If you need to transmit data for only a few minutes or hours, a switched line may be more economical.

1.2.4 Point-to-Point versus Point-to-Multipoint

On a point-to-point connection, a communications link is dedicated for communication between two end objects. In our case such end objects can be a communications controller and a cluster controller. Figure 1.7a shows a point-to-point connection. In a point-to-multipoint link, multiple devices can be attached on a single link. For example, you can have up to 254 cluster controllers on a single link to a communications controller port. Figure 1.7b shows a configuration in which four cluster controllers are connected to a single link coming from a communications controller. In telecommunications terminology, point-to-multipoint is also called a "multidrop link."

In a point-to-multipoint configuration, the intelligence and control to manage the flow of information lies with the device which is at the head of the multidrop line. In our case, the communications controller controls the multiple number of cluster controller devices. It sends requests to each cluster controller, asking them if they have any data to send. This process is also called "polling." Each cluster controller has to wait for its turn to be polled before it can send any data to the communications controller.

1.2.5 Data Terminal and Data Circuit-Terminating Equipment

Terminologies of data terminal and data circuit-terminating equipment are used quite extensively by the network engineers, so it is important that VTAM/NCP systems programmers understand them.

(a) POINT-TO-POINT

(b) POINT-TO-MULTIPOINT

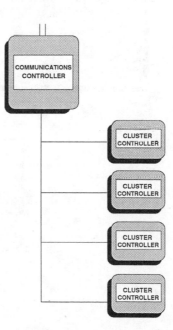

Figure 1.7 (a) A point-to-point communications link; (b) A point-to-multipoint communications link.

Data Terminal Equipment. Computer equipment which needs to communicate over communications links is referred to as "Data Terminal Equipment" (DTE). The communications controllers and link-attached cluster controllers are examples of DTE.

Data Circuit-Terminating Equipment. Data terminal equipment cannot be directly attached to the communications lines. You need hardware that interfaces between the DTE and the link lines. It also translates the digital signals generated by DTE and transmission methodology employed in the communications link. The communications links may be analog or digital in nature.

The equipment which sits between the DTE and the communications links is called "Data Circuit-Terminating Equipment," or DCE for short. Figure 1.8 shows the DTE and DCE in an IBM environment. If the communications lines are analog, the DCE is a modem.

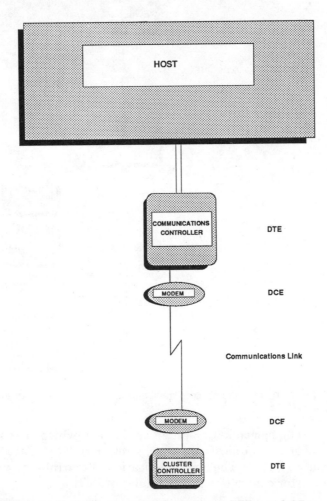

Figure 1.8 Diagram illustrating connectivity between DTE and DCE in a network.

1.2.6 Modem and DSU/CSU

Modem. Most communication lines are analog in nature because these lines were required to fulfill demand for voice communications. Since DTEs generate digital data, some kind of equipment is needed which can act as a translator of signals between the digital DTEs and analog communications lines. A device that can accomplish this is called a "modem" (modem stands for *modulator/dem*odulator).

A modem receives a binary bit stream of 0s and 1s from the sending DTE and modulates them to analog signals for transmission over the voice grade lines. On the receiving end, the second modem receives the analog signals from the communications lines and demodulates them to binary data to be passed on to the receiving DTE. Modems always work in pairs because the sending and the receiving DTE both require them. In network engineering terminology, a modem is a DCE for analog lines.

DSU/CSU. Quite recently, there has been a proliferation of digital circuits. Digital circuits are not only used for data communications but also for voice. For voice communications, the voice signals are translated into digital data, transmitted over digital lines, and reconstituted on the other end into audio frequency signals. Some of the available digital transmission services are DDS (56 kbps) and T1 lines (1.544 mbps). Most probably the prominent digital service in the future will be Integrated Services Digital Network (ISDN).

The DCE that provides an interface between the DTE and digital communications links is called "Data Service Unit/Channel Service Unit" or (DSU/CSU). It receives the binary data from DTE and translates it into digital pulse signals which can be transmitted over the communications links. It also provides the clocking function which must be in synchronization with the DSU/CSU on the receiving end.

1.3 TELECOMMUNICATIONS MEDIA

There are different media used for telecommunications. When the voice-based telephone networks were developed in the past, copper wire was used as the physical medium for transmission. Each telephone conversation required a bandwidth of 4000 Hz. Later on, the same copper wire medium was used as a digital carrier. The method used for sending voice over digital facilities is called "Pulse Code Modulation" (PCM). Although the analog carriers require a bandwidth of 4 kilohertz (kHz) for a single voice circuit, the digital voice channel requires 64 kbps of transmission speed. More recently, other modes of communications were developed which were based on microwave, satellite, and optical fiber transmission.

1.3.1 Microwave Radio Transmission

Microwave transmissions do not require any solid physical media (e.g., copper wire or optical fiber) for transmission. Therefore, it is the most widely used long-haul transmission facility in the United States. Microwave facilities require parabolic or horn microwave antennas. One of the most important requirements for this form of transmission is the need for a straight line of sight between the antennas. Any form of obstruction can cut off or degrade transmission quality.

Microwave transmission frequencies vary from 2 to 25 gigahertz (GHz). At lower frequency range, repeaters to boost the signal are required approximately every 100 miles. At a frequency above 18 GHz, you may need repeaters at every mile.

At microwave frequencies, radio waves are close in characteristics to light waves. Therefore heavy rain or heavy fog conditions can increase the transmission error rate and thus also increase retransmissions between DTEs.

Microwave transmission is used quite extensively in metropolitan areas. Rooftops of office buildings in every large city are crowded with microwave antennas. When data transmission is required between two closely spaced office buildings of a company, microwave transmission provides an economical alternative to common carrier services. Because of allocation of almost all frequency ranges, it is almost impossible to get a frequency assignment in large metropolitan areas.

A single radio channel, which consists of 30 megahertz (MHz) of bandwidth, can provide 6000 voice channels of 5000 Hz each.

1.3.2 Satellite Communications

Communications satellites have become quite popular in the last 25 years. They orbit the earth over the equator at a geosynchronous altitude of 22,300 miles. At this altitude, a satellite travels at the same speed as the spin of the earth so that its location remains the same relative to any point on earth. Three satellites can cover the entire earth's surface for broadcast transmission.

A satellite can carry an enormous transmission capability. For example, INTELSAT VI satellite can transmit 33,000 voice channels in addition to four TV channels.

Satellites are currently spaced at 3-degree intervals. However, it is possible that in the future they will be spaced at 2-degree intervals to accommodate more satellites.

The transmission frequency for a satellite has quite a wide range. The preferred frequency range, also called "C band," varies between 3700 to 4200 MHz on the down link and 5925 to 6425 MHz on the up link. At this frequency range, impairment of transmission quality by rain and fog is insignificant. C band frequencies are almost unavailable these days because of congestion.

The available frequency range consists of 11.7 to 12.2 GHz on the down link and 14 to 14.5 GHz on the up link side. This frequency range is called "Ku band." Because of high frequency (hence small wave length), you require a smaller and more economical earth station antenna to receive the signal. However low reliability of Ku band because of rain attenuation is a serious problem. A still higher frequency range called "Ka band" is also available, but the rain factor does not make it a popular choice.

Advantages. Satellite transmission is more desirable for certain applications for the following reasons:

- While terrestrial communication is a factor of the distance involved, satellite communications cost is independent of such distance.
- Satellites have enormous bandwidth. They are more suitable for applications requiring large data transfers.
- Using satellite transmission facilities, you can directly reach your destination, thus bypassing the telephone companies.
- Satellite transmission is excellent for broadcast purposes. If data has to be transmitted from a single source to multiple destinations, satellite is much more economical. For example, there could be applications in which a brokerage house's central location in New York must transmit stock prices on a real-time basis to its 200 branch offices. While this could be accomplished by a single satellite broadcast, an alternative would be to have 200 terrestrial links between the central office and the branch offices.
- Earth stations, after transmitting data to a satellite, can verify the accuracy of their transmission by listening back to the return signal.
- Satellite communications are suitable for those areas which are difficult to reach because of their rough terrain. They are also more

economical for those far away areas where it will be uneconomical to install and maintain terrestrial transmission facilities.

Disadvantages. Satellite transmission comes with some inherent problems as follows:

- Satellite transmission takes a trip of 22,300 miles from transmitting earth station to the satellite and 22,300 miles from the satellite to the receiving earth station. Even though radio signals travel at the speed of light, they impose approximately 1/2 second(s) delay in transmission. This delay can cause severe performance problems for those link level transmission protocols which have to send an acknowledgment on each transmission. Such protocols are ARQ and BSC. It is recommended to change link level protocols to SDLC under those circumstances or otherwise not to use satellite transmission.
- At higher frequencies of Ku and Ka band, the rain attenuation factor can cause data errors and hence retransmission delays.
- Because of the higher reliability of C band, there is more crowding in that frequency range. This can cause interference from the terrestrial microwave transmission facilities operating on the same frequency.

1.3.3 Fiber Optics Communications

Fiber optics communications makes use of light (also called "photons") as a transmission object as compared to radio frequency signals used by microwave and satellite communications. The transmission media used by it is an optical fiber which is a hair-thin fine strand of pure quartz glass. Optically transmitted data transmits at the speed of 125,000 miles through these strands.

Fiber optics is the fastest growing transmission technology. It seems that it will be the predominant voice and data communications media in the near future. One of the long distance communications carriers, US Sprint, has 100 percent of its network based on optical fiber.

Advantages. Fiber optics has the following advantages over other communications media:

- Because the technology is based on light wave transmission, it is immune from Radio Frequency Interference (RFI) and Electromagnetic Interference (EMI). Thus optical cable can run in any environment without the risk of generating or receiving such interference from other sources.

• With the advancement of technology, optical fiber can carry enormous bandwidth.
• Optical fiber can withstand temperatures of up to 1800 degrees Fahrenheit.
• Transmission is highly reliable. Optical fiber has a Bit Error Rate (BER) of one in a trillion (a trillion is a thousand billion or 10^{12}).
• Since there are no electromagnetic emissions involved, optical transmission is highly secure. Therefore it is particularly useful for military purposes.
• It is lightweight. While a mile of optical cable weighs about 50 pounds (lbs), a mile of other types of cables weighs about 325 lbs.

Thus we see that optical fiber is superior in usefulness over copper wire cables which have been in use over the last century or so. Moreover copper is a limited natural resource, and its prices fluctuate. Optical fibers are made from sand or silica which are the most abundant natural resource on earth.

The only hazard against which an optical fiber must be protected is water because ice can damage a cable. Ice can also create attenuation and thus affect transmission quality.

1.4 SUMMARY

In this chapter we discussed various environments involving networking of IBM hardware and software. Although the detailed discussion of each of the discussed components is the subject matter for the rest of the book, it gave us a global view of typical networking environments. We also introduced a lot of commonly used telecommunications facilities and transmission media. A lot of telecommunication terminologies introduced in this chapter will be referred to in the subsequent chapters. Therefore it is important that you understand them thoroughly before proceeding further. And now, on to the next chapter on communications hardware.

2

Communications Hardware — Cluster Controllers and Communications Controllers

SNA gives the underlying architecture for connecting various communications hardware and software. Although this book is primarily oriented toward learning VTAM and NCP, it is essential to understand the hardware that comprise the physical network. First we will get a global picture of all the hardware components involved. After learning the basic function of each one, we will get more detailed information about some of them.

2.1 GLOBAL VIEW OF THE COMMUNICATIONS HARDWARE

Normally, an end user, whether an application programmer or a nontechnical user of the application systems, is only aware of the physical existence of a terminal. In addition, an application programmer will also be aware of the presence of a computer at the other end. The existence of the complex network hardware in the middle is usually transparent to them. Here is an overview of each component:

Terminal. A device through which the end user communicates with the host computer. Usually, a terminal is connected to a cluster controller through a coaxial cable.

Cluster controller. It sits between the terminals and the host for a channel-attached configuration and between terminals and the communications controller for a link-attached configuration. Depending upon the model, it can control a cluster of 8 to 32 terminals.

Communications controller. It runs NCP software which performs the network control functions. Link-attached cluster controllers, RJE/RJP devices, and asynchronous terminals are attached to the communications controller.

Network controller. An IBM 3710 network controller acts as a protocol converter and line concentrator for start/stop and BISYNC lines and devices. It is connected to a communications controller.

Network conversion unit. An IBM 3708 provides for the linking of ASCII devices to an SNA network.

RJE/RJP device. It handles batch as well as remote job entry functions for the console: printers, card readers, and card punches.

Physical interfaces. Physical interfaces define the physical connectivity and electrical interface between a Data Terminal Equipment (DTE) such as a communications or cluster controller and Data Circuit-Terminating Equipment (DCE), such as a modem. Most common examples of such interfaces are RS-232-C, V.35, and RS-449.

Modem. It is a device that acts as an interface between the DTE device, such as communications or cluster controllers, and the analog communications links, such as voice grade telephone lines.

Patch panels. Although you can directly connect a DTE and a DCE over a physical interface (e.g., RS-232-C), usually it is done via a patch panel. Patch panels make moving DTE devices from one place to another less cumbersome. They are also used to connect terminal devices to the cluster controllers. Such patch panels have coaxial links coming from the terminals and the cluster controllers. Any time a terminal device is moved from one office to another, patch panel links make it easy to establish a connection.

Multiplexers. They are used whenever multiple links are concentrated over a single link to use the single link as a transmission media. On the other end, the single link is further split into multiple link connections. Individual links on either side seem to have a direct connectivity between them. Multiplexers on each side of the link do the necessary conversion for the multiple links on either side. A T1 multiplexer is used to split the bandwidth of 1.544 mbps into multiple line speed channels. A coaxial multiplexer (e.g., IBM 3299) is used to concentrate up to eight terminal lines on a single coaxial cable.

We have reviewed almost all the hardware devices that will be referred to in this book. Now, let's discuss the cluster controllers and communications controllers in more detail. Other hardware components will be discussed in the next chapter.

2.2. CLUSTER CONTROLLERS

2.2.1 Functions

As the name suggests, cluster controllers are used to control a number (cluster) of terminals. Depending upon the model, you can attach anywhere from 8 to 32 terminals or printers to it. A cluster controller can be directly attached to a host computer channel or can be link attached to a communications controller (Figure 2.1).

A channel-attached cluster controller is linked to the byte or block multiplexer channel of a mainframe. Its interface is the bus and tag interface to the host channel. A link-attached cluster controller is linked to the communications controller through a communications link. The hardware that links it to the communications link is called "DCE." DCE can be a modem for analog lines or a DSU/CSU for digital circuits. The physical interface between the cluster controller and the modem depends upon the line speed and communications controller port considerations. Some examples of such interfaces are RS-232-C, RS-449, V.35, etc.

At the other end of the cluster controller are a number of coaxial cable connector ports. You can attach a 3270-family terminal or a printer to each port. The number of such ports depends upon the model and can be 8, 16, 24, or 32. The physical media used to connect a cluster controller port and a terminal or printer is usually a coaxial cable.

2.2.2 Different Types

Depending upon the link level protocol used, cluster controllers can be of two types — BSC or SNA/SDLC. The end-user terminal or printer is *always* the same whether it is connected to a BSC or an SNA/SDLC controller. The host software VTAM defines those two types in its tables using different sets of macros. It has to be ensured that the VTAM definition, the NCP definition, and the cluster controller type refer to the same protocol.

Any channel-attached cluster controller model which ends in D (e.g., IBM 3274 Model 41D) is a channel-attached non-SNA controller. If it ends in A (e.g., IBM 3274 Model 41A), it is a channel-attached SNA controller. A link-attached cluster controller model ends in C (e.g., IBM 3274 Model 41C). Any C-model controller can be

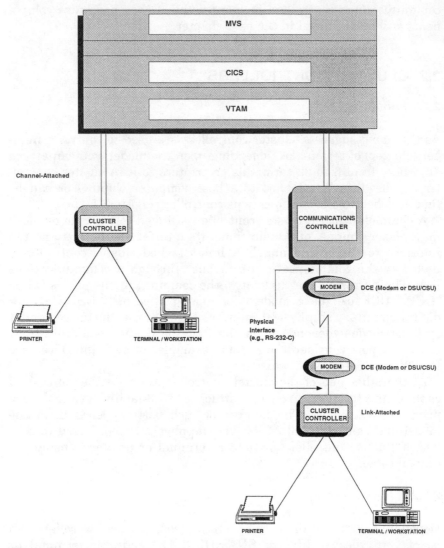

Figure 2.1 An example of cluster controller configuration — channel attached and link-attached.

either BSC or SNA/SDLC depending upon the software used to configure it. All the cluster controllers, channel attached as well as link attached, come with configuration disks to do port assignments and configure them for different types of printers or terminals.

How do you know whether the IBM 3278 terminal you have is attached to a BSC or an SNA/SDLC controller? Look at the lower left-hand corner of the terminal. If you have the character A, it is a

BSC controller. Otherwise, the presence of character B indicates an SNA/SDLC controller.

The devices that can be attached to a cluster controller are grouped into two categories, A and B. Type A devices are the new models of terminals and printers. They support extended attributes such as highlighting, reverse video, and color capability (e.g., in IBM 3279 display terminals). In addition, they also support user-defined character or graphic symbols. Category B terminals do not have such capabilities. You can mix category A and B terminals in an IBM 3274 cluster controller. A list of such devices is given in Figure 2.2.

An SNA/SDLC cluster controller is known as Physical Unit Type 2, or PU Type 2. A display device (e.g., IBM 3278) attached to a PU Type 2 is known as Logical Unit 2, or LU 2. A printer device attached to a PU Type 2, depending upon the device and the definition, can be LU 1 or LU 3. The meaning and significance of these acronyms will be discussed in a later chapter. However, we will start introducing the terminology now to enhance your understanding of them later on.

2.2.3 Models and Their Capacities

Cluster controllers can be broadly categorized into two groups, the *old* IBM 3274 family and the *new* IBM 3174 family of controllers.

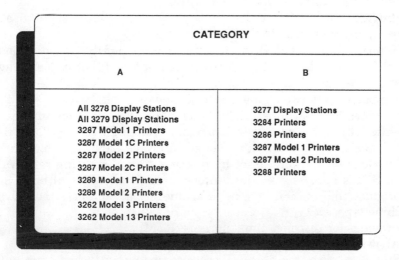

CATEGORY	
A	B
All 3278 Display Stations All 3279 Display Stations 3287 Model 1 Printers 3287 Model 1C Printers 3287 Model 2 Printers 3287 Model 2C Printers 3289 Model 1 Printers 3289 Model 2 Printers 3262 Model 3 Printers 3262 Model 13 Printers	3277 Display Stations 3284 Printers 3286 Printers 3287 Model 1 Printers 3287 Model 2 Printers 3288 Printers

Figure 2.2 Category A and terminals in the 3270 family of display and printer devices.

IBM 3274 controllers come in various capacities and characteristics and still have a huge installed base in IBM shops. However, as the industry moves slowly from a dumb end-user terminal environment to an intelligent workstation, these controllers will be replaced by an IBM 3174 or a similar device.

IBM 3274 Cluster Controllers.   Some of the widely used IBM 3274 controllers are explained as follows:

- IBM 3274 Model 41A is an SNA channel-attached controller and can support up to 32 category A and B devices.
- IBM 3274 Model 41D is a non-SNA channel-attached controller which can support up to 32 category A and B devices.
- IBM 3274 Model 41C can be a link-attached BSC or SNA/SDLC controller which can support 32 terminal devices. IBM 3274 Models 51C, 61C, and 31C can be BSC or SNA/SDLC controllers which can support 8, 16, and 24 terminal devices, respectively.

IBM 3174 Subsystem Control Units.   Notice that 3174 cluster controllers are called "Subsystem Control Units" (SCUs) in IBM lingo. The capabilities of IBM 3174 SCUs are far beyond what is possible with the IBM 3274s. Some of their prominent features are listed below:

- Provides for customizing disks of remote sites at a central site location and maintains them in a library.
- Provides for electronic distribution of microcode or customization parameters for remote IBM 3174s.
- Supports Intelligent Printer Data Stream (IPDS) which supports All Points Addressability (APA) to position text, bar codes, images, and vector graphics on a page.
- Supports up to two 20 megabyte (Mb) fixed disk drives.
- Provides for IBM token ring attachment and host communications either through a gateway feature or through an IBM 372X or 3745 communications controller's Token Interface Card (TIC) feature.
- Provides for network asset management by supporting retrieval of an SCU's hardware product information from a central host. Such product information can be machine serial number, model, machine type, etc.
- Provides for response time monitor (RTM).
- Allows for expansion of SCU's main storage to 3 Mb.
- Supports one or more ASCII host access to its attached terminals.

Various models of IBM 3174s and their characteristics are explained as follows:

3174 Model 1L. This model is a channel-attached SCU which can be SNA or non-SNA. As a general convention all 3174 SCUs having the suffix L are local (channel attached) while those having the suffix R are remote (link attached) cluster controllers. You can attach up to 32 terminals to it. The basic configuration comes with 1 Mb of main storage and a 1.2-Mb high-density disk drive. Some of the optional features you can install are the IBM Token Ring Adapter and the Token Ring 3270 Gateway. It also supports an Asynchronous Emulation Adapter, which can support up to 24 ASCII devices.

3174 Model 1R. It is a link-attached SCU that can be SNA/SDLC or BSC. You can attach up to 32 terminal devices to it. The basic configuration comes with 1 Mb of main storage and a 1.2-Mb high-density disk drive. It supports ASCII terminals through the installation of an optional Asynchronous Emulation Adapter feature. You may also install the Token Ring Adapter and the Token Ring 3270 Gateway feature. In fact a 3174 Model 1R with the Token Ring attachment features is called "3174 Model 3R." The SCU supports a multitude of physical interfaces for DCE connectivity. Such interfaces are EIA-232-D, V.24, and V.35 and are discussed in Chapter 3.

3174 Model 2R. This model has the same characteristics and capabilities as the 1R except that the physical interface is an X.21 (CCITT V.11). It can also be upgraded (like Model 1R) to a Model 3R for token ring connectivity.

3174 Model 3R. This model is in fact a Model 1R or 2R with a Token Ring attachment. All other features and capabilities are the same as the other models. Model 3R can also be converted back to Model 1R or 2R by installing Type 1 communications adapter for Model 1R conversion and Type 2 communications adapter for Model 2R conversion. Remember, although Model 3R has a Token Ring connectivity, it *cannot be* a Token Ring 3270 Gateway.

3174 Model 51R. This model has the same capabilities as Model 1R except that it supports a maximum of 16 terminal devices instead of the 32 supported by 1R. This model can have a Token Ring attachment and can also be a Token Ring 3270 Gateway. Its physical interface with DCE can be EIA-232-D, V.24, and V.35.

3174 Model 52R. This model has the same capabilities as Model 2R except that it supports a maximum of 16 terminal devices instead of the 32 supported by 2R. This model can have a Token Ring attachment and can also be a Token Ring 3270 Gateway. It has an X.21 (CCITT v.11) interface.

3174 Model 53R. This model has the same capabilities as Model 3R except that it supports a maximum of 16 terminal devices instead of 32 supported by 3R. This model can have a Token Ring attachment but *cannot* be a Token Ring 3270 Gateway.

3174 Model 81R. This model can attach to a maximum of eight terminal devices. Its physical interface with DCE can be an EIA-232-D, V.24, or V.35. It *cannot* have a Token Ring attachment.

3174 Model 82R. This model can attach to a maximum of eight terminal devices. Its physical interface is X.21 (CCITT V.11). It *cannot* have a Token Ring attachment.

2.2.4 3174s and Token Ring Features

In the previous section we mentioned the Token Ring attachment and Token Ring Gateway features. Let's see what these features do to enhance connectivity.

Token Ring is an implementation of local area network (LAN) for the IBM environment. An LAN enhances connectivity between multiple scattered devices (e.g., between the floors of a single building) and helps them share their resources, such as files, printers, programs, etc. LANs are normally used to connect microcomputers (e.g., IBM PCs and PS/2s) for sharing resources and to communicate with each other. IBM has gone one step further to provide connectivity between IBM 3174 SCUs over a Token-Ring-based LAN.

How do 3174s fit in an LAN? Under normal circumstances, a cluster controller is either directly attached to a host channel or to a communications controller's port over a communications link. You can also multidrop a number of cluster controllers over a single link. Token Ring LAN provides an alternative to the multidrop approach for cluster controllers housed in a single building location.

Devices such as IBM PCs, PS/2s, and 3174 SCUs can be attached to a Token Ring LAN through a MultiSystem Access Unit (MSAU). When we talk about upgrading a 3174 to support Token Ring features, we are referring to the hardware, microcode, software, and physical interface needed to support Token Ring protocols and physical connectivity to MSAU. MSAU looks like a wall-mounted plate with 10 physical interfaces. Two of the interfaces connect to other MSAUs (i.e., MSAU-in and MSAU-out) and the other eight interfaces are used by the devices needing connectivity to the LAN.

Token Ring Connectivity versus Token Ring 3270 Gateway. The Token Ring connectivity feature enables an IBM 3174 SCU to be connected to a Token Ring through an MSAU port. Token Ring 3270 Gateway feature enables a single IBM 3174 SCU to act as a gateway to the SNA network for *all* the IBM 3174 SCUs attached to the Token Ring network through the Token Ring connectivity feature.

While the connectivity feature provides for physical connectivity to the Token Ring, the 3270 gateway feature proves the means to be connected to the outside world. A single 3270 gateway IBM 3174 can provide connectivity to a number of LAN-attached 3174s (see Figure 2.3).

We have a channel-attached IBM 3174 SCU with the Token Ring 3270 Gateway feature. It provides connectivity for itself and the

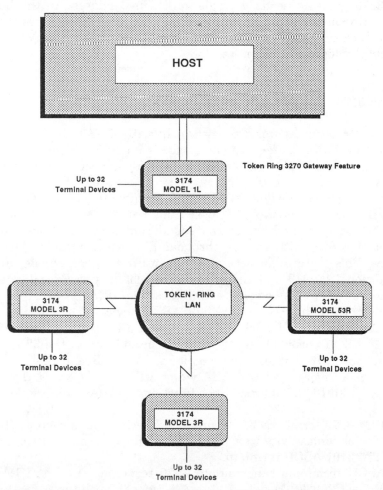

Figure 2.3 An example of a single IBM 3174 SCU with a Token Ring 3270 Gateway feature providing connectivity for itself and a number of other IBM 3174 SCUs on a token ring LAN.

other three IBM 3174s through the Token Ring connectivity feature. The gateway SCU does not have to be channel attached; it can be remote (link-attached).

Only IBM 3174 Models 1L, 1R, 2R, 51R, and 52R support the 3270 gateway feature. Models 3R and 53R can only support connectivity to a Token Ring LAN but can not act as gateways. Models 81R and 82R neither support LAN connectivity nor the 3270 gateway feature.

We can define a maximum of 140 Token Ring-attached devices to VTAM in a host. The channel-attached IBM 3174 Model 1L acting as a 3270 gateway needs a single subchannel address to the host. A link-attached IBM 3174 acting as a 3270 gateway requires a single SDLC station address. More on this when we talk about VTAM and NCP in subsequent chapters.

2.2.5 3174s and ASCII Terminal Support

The IBM terminal world consists primarily of 3270-like devices. For non-IBM hosts, the equivalent device is an ASCII terminal. Earlier, if you worked in an environment in which you needed connectivity to IBM as well as non-IBM hosts, you had no choice but to have two separate display terminals. Now, it is possible to have connectivity to an IBM as well as an ASCII host from a single terminal device. Figure 2.4 gives an architecture for such a configuration. What you need is a 3174 SCU with an Asynchronous Emulation Adapter (AEA) feature. This feature consists of a hardware card, microcode, and an additional 1.2 MB disk drive. It can be installed on a local (channel-attached) as well as a remote (link attached) IBM 3174 SCU.

Each AEA supports up to eight ASCII devices. You can install up to three AEAs for Model 1L, 1R, 2R, and 3R to support a maximum of 24 ASCII ports. These 24 ports are in addition to the 32 terminal ports for 3270 devices. However for models 51R and 52R, you may not install more than one AEA which will support 8 ASCII ports in addition to 16 3270 ports. Three functions of AEAs are as follows:

- IBM 3278 terminals can emulate ASCII terminals such as the VT-100 for connectivity to a DEC/VAX host. They can also emulate an IBM 3101 ASCII terminal.
- ASCII terminals can emulate 3270 terminals such as IBM 3178 Model C2, 3279 Model 2A, or a 3287 Model 2 printer.
- ASCII terminals rather than emulating 3270 devices can have a straight pass through to an ASCII host or a Public Data Network (PDN).

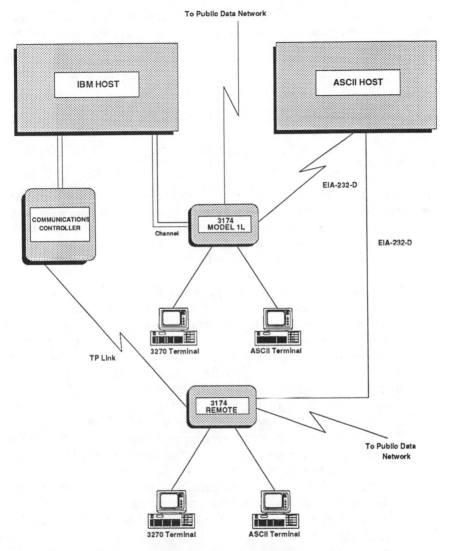

Figure 2.4 Interconnectivity between the IBM 3270 and ASCII terminals to the IBM and ASCII hosts.

2.2.6 Additional Considerations

Different ports on a cluster controller can be configured from a 3270 terminal attached to port 00 (first port). Later on, the same port can be used for a regular host session. The configuration considerations depend on whether a port is to be used for a printer, a monochrome display device, or a colored display device and the model of the terminal. The port configurations must be in synchronization with the VTAM and NCP definition for that port address.

2.3 COMMUNICATIONS CONTROLLERS

2.3.1 Function

The communications controllers are intelligent systems which are dedicated to the control of communications lines and devices. Any device which cannot be channel attached because of the distances involved has to be connected through a communications controller, which can be split into the following three functional categories:

1. *Front End Processor (FEP).* It is attached to the channels of one or more host systems, and it accepts data from its host processors for subsequent transmission to the appropriate devices. It also accepts data from the terminal devices or other communications controllers for routing it to the proper host system. In Figure 2.5, CC-1 and CC-2 are the FEPs. In this case, CC-2 is attached to two different hosts.
2. *Concentrator.* A communications controller acting as a concentrator controls a number of cluster controllers, terminals, RJE/RJP devices, and other communications devices. In Figure 2.5, CC-4, CC-5, and CC-6 provide the concentrator function in a communications controller.
3. *Intelligent switch.* An intelligent switch is an intermediary node which provides switching and routing functions between other communications controllers. CC-3 in Figure 2.5 is an intelligent switch.

Remember that we are classifying the communications controllers by the functions they perform. Such functions can be overlapping. For example, CC-3 in our example can be an intelligent switch and a concentrator at the same time. The communications controllers run under the control of the Network Control Program, or NCP.

Channel-Attached and Link-Attached. A communications controller can either be attached to the host channel or can be link-attached to another communications controller. In Figure 2.5, CC-1 and CC-2 are

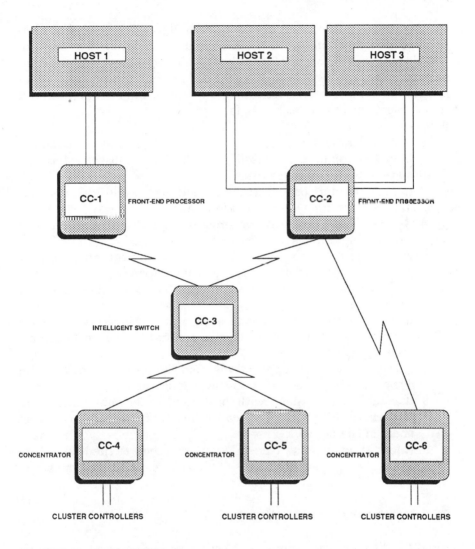

Figure 2.5 A sample network in which different communications controllers perform the functions of a front end processor, a concentrator, and an intelligent switch.

channel-attached while CC-3, CC-4, CC-5, and CC-6 are the link-attached ones. Some of the top-of-the-line communications controllers (e.g., IBM 3745 Model 410) have the capability of having up to 16 channel attachments.

Major Functions. A communications controller offloads communications related functions from the host and thus leaves it to perform what it was meant for — running application systems. Without communications controllers, a host would be interrupted every time data is transmitted or received from another source. Major functions of a communications controller are as follows:

1. It provides data buffers for temporary storage of data coming from the communications lines or host for subsequent transmission to the target location.
2. It controls and corrects transmission errors and ensures that data is retransmitted if it is erroneous.
3. It controls the physical transmission and receiving of data on various communications lines.
4. It controls message pacing to ensure that it regulates the flow of data to devices depending upon their capacity.
5. It selects appropriate routes for the data depending upon its destination.
6. It sequences the messages to ensure that the receiving device can reconstruct it from the sequence numbers assigned to message segments.
7. It frees up the host applications from the burden of polling the devices having a session with that application.
8. It establishes sessions with hosts and other communications controllers to provide logical connectivity between various nodes of the network.
9. It logs and transmits transmission error data to the host.
10. It provides concentrator and intelligent switching functions.

2.3.2 Architecture

Although different communications controllers are architected in different ways, they basically consist of three subsystems:

1. Control
2. Transmission
3. Maintenance and operator

Figure 2.6 gives a very simple architectural view of such a communications controller.

The control subsystem is the brain of the system. Its channel adapter interface receives and drives channel signals in a channel-

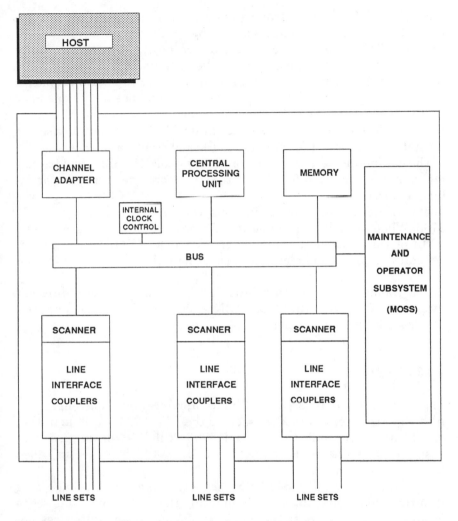

Figure 2.6 A simplified version of the architecture of a communications controller.

attached FEP. The memory component provides temporary buffers for data coming from or going to the channels or the transmission subsystem. The CPU provides the necessary cycles to perform these functions.

The transmission subsystem is the primary interface with the communications lines. It is a three-tiered architecture. Scanners, which are powerful microprocessors, provide for the control of a number of line interface couplers. A line interface coupler controls a line set consisting of a number of transmission lines. Line speeds of the communications lines determine how many of them can be used in a coupler. Finally, the speed of a scanner determines the ultimate transmission load a scanner can handle. The underlying principle is that every time a bit of data comes on the line, the scanner should be ready to grab the bit and pass it over the bus to its memory buffers. Load balancing of communications lines over multiple scanners is a design issue and a subject in itself. Readers are advised to consult appropriate IBM manuals to become more familiar with it.

The Maintenance and Operator Subsystem (MOSS) provides the maintenance functions for the controller. It provides an operator interface through a console and a keyboard. The MOSS feature was not provided in old communications controllers such as the IBM 3705. When used, it helps in online diagnostics, Initial Program Load (IPL) of the controller, Initial Microcode Load (IML) of a scanner, generating alarms and alerts, and isolating failures to a specific component.

The communications controllers family consists of four different models — IBM 3705, IBM 3725, IBM 3720, and IBM 3745. They are discussed in the next section.

2.3.3 IBM 3705

The IBM 3705 is the largest selling communications controller ever. Although its successor models such as the IBM 3725, 3720, and 3745 are advanced controllers, the IBM 3705 still has the largest user base. It is estimated that there are over 48,000 units installed throughout the world.

IBM announced this model in November 1975 and started shipping it in the middle of 1976. After dominating the communications scene for over a decade, it is at the end of its life cycle, and IBM does not market it anymore. It is being discussed here because of its large user base.

This is the *only* IBM communications controller which does not have an attached MOSS console and therefore depends upon a host for control and diagnostics. In a network, it can function as a front-end processor, a concentrator, an intelligent switch, or a combination of these. It can support line speeds anywhere from 1200 bps to 230.4 kbps and can accommodate BSC, SDLC, or ASCII protocols. It can also emulate the old IBM 2701, 2702, and 2703 hard-wired controllers.

IBM 3705 comes in two models. Model 80, which was announced in March 1981, is the low-end model, supports 256 Kbytes of mem-

ory, up to 128 communications lines, and up to two channel interfaces. Model II is the high-end model, supports up to 512 Kbytes of
memory, up to 352 communications lines, and eight channel-attached
host processors.

2.3.4 IBM 3725 and 3720

The IBM 3725 controller was announced in March 1983 and was
meant to replace the aging 3705 equipment. It comes in two models.
Model 1 supports eight channel-attached hosts, up to 256 communications lines, and up to 3 Mbytes of main storage. Model 2, the low-
end IBM 3725, supports up to four channel-attached hosts, up to 80
communications lines, and up to 2 Mbytes of memory. Although the
high-end 3725 supports 256 lines compared to the high-end IBM
3705, which supports 352 lines, the IBM 3725 is architected to support full-duplex communications on a single communications port.
The IBM 3705 requires two adjacent ports to support this. In 1986,
IBM also provided support for an IBM 3725 attachment to a Token
Ring network.

The IBM 3720 was announced in May 1986 and was primarily
meant for small or medium-size enterprises. It was also helpful as a
low-cost concentrator for remote regional and branch offices of a company. It makes sense to use a low-cost IBM 3720 as a front end to
the 9370 family of processors. Otherwise, an IBM 3725 could cost
more than the IBM 9370 host itself. The IBM 3720 comes in four
models. Model 1 is for channel attachment and can support a maximum of 28 lines. Model 2 is the remote attachment model and can
also support 28 lines. A 3721 expansion unit can enhance Model 1 or
2 and provide for 32 additional lines. Models 11 and 12 are channel-
attached and link-attached models, respectively, which support two
IBM Token Ring attachments also. These Token Ring Interface Couplers (TICs) reduce the number of lines supported from 28 to 16.
Models 1 and 2 can be upgraded to Models 11 and 12, respectively.

Now that we are familiar with some of the capabilities of the IBM
3725 and IBM 3720, let's look at some of the terminology that is
used to refer to their various components.

2.3.5 Line Attachment Base (LAB) and Line Interface Coupler (LIC)

LAB provides interface between the communications controller's
CPU and the scanners. Depending upon its type, am LAB can interface with one or more scanners. On the other end an LAB interfaces

with multiple LICs. LIC ports are the ones which have direct physical interface with the communications lines. Although you are aware
of the LABs and LICs, scanners are basically invisible entities. Let's
look at these elements from a hierarchical perspective.

- A communications controller has a number of LABs. Each LAB can
  be of a different type.
- Each LAB can control a number of LICs. There are various types
  of LICs too. Some LICs can be attached only to certain types of
  LABs.
- Communications lines are attached to various ports of an LIC.
- Physical ports on an LIC signify different physical interfaces and
  determine the LIC type. Examples of a physical interface are RS-
  232-C, V.35, etc.

Figure 2.7 gives the characteristics of various types of LABs.

CLAB stands for Channel and Line Attachment Base. Each CLAB
comes with one channel adapter and up to 32 line attachments (via
LICs of course). In case of an IBM 3725 Model 1, two CLABs come
with the box. LAB A is generally meant for low-speed lines with a
maximum of 19.2 kbps. LAB B is used for high-speed lines and can
support up to 256 kbps. LAB C is used for Token Ring attachment. A
3725 Model 1 can have a maximum of eight LABs while the Model 2
can have only three.

TYPE	NUMBER OF SCANNERS USED	TYPE OF LICS SUPPORTED	MAXIMUM LINE ATTACHMENTS
CLAB	1	1 or 4A	32
LAB A	1	1 or 4A	32
LAB B	2	1, 2, 3, 4A, or 4B	32
LAB C	1		4 Token Interface Couplers (TICs)

Figure 2.7 Characteristics of various types of LABs for the IBM 3725.

Communications Scanner Processors (CSP). A CSP is actually a microprocessor. While an LAB provides interface between the communications controller's CPU and the CSP, the CSP provides interface between the LAB and the LICs. There is only one type of CSP. An IBM 3725 Model 1 can have a maximum of 14 CSPs, while for Model 2 the limit is 4. CSP also provides one integrated clock controller (ICC) per LAB. ICC is required for direct attachment to nonclocking modems, e.g., asynchronous modems. In other words, an ICC when used with a special cable acts as a modem eliminator.

2.3.6 Types of Line Interface Couplers

While a single LAB supports multiple LICs, a single LIC may support one or more communications lines. Various types of LICs provide different capabilities and features. Figure 2.8 gives a summary of various LIC types and their characteristics.

Although lines at T1 speeds (1.544 mbps) are not supported, a Request for Price Quotation (RPQ) has been available since June 1987 to support T1 lines on an IBM 3725. Such an alteration can use six scanners. However, one might like to consider an IBM 3745 which supports such line speeds more efficiently.

2.3.7 LIC Weight for IBM 3725

You cannot connect communications lines to the IBM 3725 ports at random. Connection is strictly controlled by considerations for LIC weight for the scanner that controls that line. The basic principle is as follows: No scanner can have an LIC weight of more than 100 units. If an LAB is a single scanner LAB (i.e., CLAB, LAB A, and LAB C), that LAB cannot have an LIC weight of more than 100 units either. If the LAB is a two-scanner LAB (i.e., LAB B), it can have a weight of up to 200 units. Now how do you determine the LIC weight? IBM supplies a table (Figure 2.9) which gives the LIC weight based on LIC type, line speed, and link level protocol used.

Now make a chart of the LICs within an LAB and the physical lines within an LIC. Put the weight of each line from Figure 2.9 into that table. Determine the line with *maximum* value within each LIC. Determine such maximum values for each LIC in the LAB. Add them up. The sum should not be more than 100 for a single scanner LAB and 200 for a double scanner LAB. Figure 2.10 gives an example; it is an LAB A with eight LICs. Each LIC could have a maxi-

LIC TYPE	INTERFACE	PROTOCOL	LINE SPEED (BPS)	LIC WEIGHT
LIC 1	RS-232-C	BSC EBCDIC or SDLC (HDX)	9600	12
	V.24	BSC ASCII or SDLC (FDX)	4800	12
	X.21 BIS	BSC ASCII or SDLC (FDX)	9600	25
		BSC EBSDIC or SDLC (HDX)	19200	25
		BSC ASCII or SDLC (FDX)	19200	50
	RS366 or V.25	AUTOCALL		12
		Burst Mode ASYNC (S/S)	1200	12
		Burst Mode ASYNC (S/S)	2400	25
		Burst Mode ASYNC (S/S)	4800	50
		Burst Mode ASYNC (S/S)	9600	100
		Burst Mode ASYNC (S/S)	19200	100*
		Character Mode ASYNC (S/S)	300	12
		Character Mode ASYNC (S/S)	600	18
		Character Mode ASYNC (S/S)	1200	37
		BSC Tributory	1200	42
		BSC EBCDIC or SDLC (HDX)	14400	20
LIC 2	Wideband 8751, 8801, or 8803	BSC EBCDIC or SDLC (HDX)	64000	25
		BSC ASCII or SDLC (FDX)	32000	25
		BSC ASCII or SDLC (FDX)	64000	25
		SDLC (FDX/HDX)	128000	50
		SDLC (FDX/HDX)	230000	100
LIC 3	V.35	BSC EBCDIC or SDLC (HDX)	64000	25
		BSC ASCII or SDLC (FDX)	32000	25
		BSC ASCII or SDLC (FDX)	64000	25
		SDLC (FDX/HDX)	256000	100
		SDLC (FDX/HDX)	128000	50
LIC 4A	X.21	SDLC (HDX)	9600	12
		SDLC (FDX)	4800	12
		SDLC (FDX)	9600	25
LIC 4B	X.21	SDLC (HDX)	64000	25
		SDLC (FDX)	64000	25

HDX = Half Duplex   FDX = Full Duplex
* Only Two Points Usable per LIC

Figure 2.8 Characteristics of various types of LICs for the IBM 3725.

mum of four physical ports. LIC-1 has four lines each with an LIC weight of 12. Thus LIC weight for LIC-1 is 12. *Remember that LIC weight is the maximum value within an LIC and not a sum of all the values.* LIC-2 has two ports of weight of 12 each and a third of 25. Thus the maximum value is 25. Notice that the fourth port in LIC-2 is not used. If we were to add another full-duplex line at 9600 bps (weight 25), LIC-2's empty port would be the right choice because it

LIC TYPE	PHYSICAL INTERFACE	MAXIMUM LINE SPEED (KBPS)	NUMBER OF PORTS
LIC 1	RS 232 / V.24	19.2	4
	RS 366 / V.25		
	X.21 BIS		
	Direct	19.2	
LIC 2	Wideband for 8801, 8803, or 8751 Service	64 (BSC) 230.4 (SDLC)	1
LIC 3	V.35 Direct	256 240	1
LIC 4A	X.21 Direct	9.6 9.6	4
LIC 4B	X.21 Direct	64 56	1

Note: X.21 is not available in U.S.A.

Figure 2.9 Table showing relationship between LIC weight and LIC type, line speed, and link level protocols for an IBM 3725.

would not affect the LIC weight at all. Similarly in LIC-3 and LIC-5, the maximum value is 12 each. In LIC-4, the maximum value is 37. The sum total of all such values up to LIC-5 is already 98. Therefore we cannot use LIC-6, LIC-7, and LIC-8 because LAB A, being a single-scanner LAB, has an upper-limit LIC weight of 100.

LAB A

PORT	SCANNER							
	LIC 1	LIC 2	LIC 3	LIC 4	LIC 5	LIC 6	LIC 7	LIC 8
1	12	25	12	18				
2	12	12	12	12				
3	12	12		37	12			
4	12							
Maximum Value	12	25	12	37	12			

Total LIC Weight = 12 + 25 + 12 + 37 + 12 = 98

Figure 2.10 An example to determine LIC weight for a scanner.

Configuration Rules. LIC weight considerations and other configuration rules are summed up as follows:

1. Total LIC weight on a scanner cannot exceed 100.
2. Given the total scanner capacity of 307,200 kbps, calculate the LIC capacity as follows:

$$\text{Total LIC capacity} = \frac{\text{total scanner capacity}}{\substack{\text{number of last LIC position physically} \\ \text{installed on the scanner.}}}$$

3. After finding out the LIC capacity from 2 above, the maximum line speed for an LIC is calculated as follows:

$$\substack{\text{Maximum line speed} \\ \text{for a LIC}} = \frac{\text{total LIC capacity}}{\text{number of ports per LIC}}$$

The above rules must be strictly followed for the communications controller to function properly. If the rules are not followed properly, the Physical Unit (PU) activation fails after NCP load and corrupted data is transmitted over the line.

Line Weight for 3720. The IBM 3720 communications controller's configuration is not based upon LIC weight but rather on line weight. Since the rules for an IBM 3745 are also based on line weight, refer to the discussion in Section 2.3.9 of this chapter.

2.3.8 IBM 3745

Announced in January 1988, the IBM 3745 is IBM's latest and most powerful communications controller. It comes in two models. Model 210, available since March 1988, has a single Central Control Unit (CCU). Model 410, available since September 1988, has two CCUs each capable of running a separate NCP. The following are the salient features of the IBM 3745.

1. Model 210 is field upgradable to Model 410.
2. Each CCU supports up to 8 MB of memory.
3. It supports up to eight high-speed scanners with interfaces for up to 16 T1 lines.
4. It can have up to 512 full-duplex lines.
5. It supports up to 16 host attachments and up to eight Token Ring adapters.
6. Each model comes with a 45 Mb hard disk for storage of NCP load modules. This helps in automatic restart, thus avoiding the necessity of downloading NCP from the host.
7. It supports local and remote consoles.

Model 210 is twice as powerful as IBM 3725 while Model 410 has 4 times the capacity of an IBM 3725. The IBM 3745 also supports twice as many ports as the IBM 3725. Model 410, with its two CCUs, can be configured to run in the following three modes:

• *Twin dual mode.* Each CCU acts as a separate communications controller. Therefore you can run two independent NCPs. It is just like having two separate Model 210 controllers standing side by side. It is important to note that the two NCPs in Model 410 have no internal link. For them to communicate with each other requires an external connectivity aid such as a channel adapter or a communications link.
• *Twin standby mode.* In this mode there is one active NCP while the second one is in a standby mode. This allows quick recovery from storage-related failures and from the CCU's hardware check.

Note that the idle CCU is totally inactive unless a failure is detected.

- *Twin backup mode*. In this mode, each CCU is approximately half the network. Each CCU is half full. It is like having two 3725s each running one-half of the network load. If one CCU fails, the other CCU can assume the load of the failed CCU. It also allows for easy recovery from storage-related failures and the CCU's hardware check.

2.3.9 Line Weight for the IBM 3745 and 3720

While an IBM 3725 was configured using LIC weight considerations, an IBM 3745 and 3720 are configured using line weights. While configuring an IBM 3725, we took the *maximum* LIC weight value from each LIC and added them up for a specific LAB. We also made sure that the total of all LIC weights does not exceed 100 for a single-scanner LAB and 200 for a dual scanner LAB. While configuring an IBM 3745 and 3720, we take the line weight from each port of an LIC within an LAB and add them together. Such line weight cannot exceed 100 for each scanner.

Characteristics and types of different LABs and LICs are the same as discussed before for an IBM 3725. You may refer to Figures 2.8 and 2.9 because the tables are applicable to IBM 3745/3720 as well. Figure 2.11 gives line weights based upon line speed, link level protocol, and scanner considerations. While configuring an IBM 3720 and 3745, line weights are considered to have a cumulative effect. Thus you add up the line weights for each active port on an LIC and add up cumulative line weights of each LIC within an LAB. For example, Figure 2.12 shows an LAB with eight LICs. Each LIC could have a maximum of four physical ports. LIC1 has four physical ports each supporting an SDLC (HDX) at 9600 bps. Thus each line has a line weight of 3.1. LIC2 has two ports each having SDLC (FDX) lines at 19,200 bps with a line weight of 12.5 each. LIC3 uses a single port for SDLC (FDX) with a line speed of 14,400 bps, thus having a line weight of 9.4. LIC4 has four ports each having a line weight of 0.8 because they are BSC EBCDIC with a line speed of 2400 bps. We add all the line weights up and it comes to a total of 50. We can install more lines on other LICs up to a maximum line weight of 100. Notice that we took higher line weights from the table in Figure 2.12 because LAB A is a single-scanner LAB.

PROTOCOL	LINE SPEED (BPS)	LINE WEIGHT
SDLC (FDX)	256000**	100
	64000**	25
	57000**	22.3
	19200**	7.5
	19200	10/12.5*
	14400	7.5/9.4*
	9600	5/6.2*
	4800	2.5/3.1*
SDLC (HDX) and BSC EBCDIC	256000**	60
	64000**	15
	57000**	13.5
	19200**	4.5
	19200	5.6/6.2*
	14400	4.2/4.7*
	9600	2.8/3.1*
	4800	1.4/1.6*
	2400	0.7/0.8*

HDX = Half Duplex
FDX = Full Duplex
* Lower Line Weights are for Double Scanner LABs and the Higher Line Weights are for Single Scanner LA
** One Port LICs

Figure 2.11 Table showing relationship between line weight, line speed, and link level protocols used for IBM 3720 and 3745.

Configuration Rules. Line weight considerations and other configurations rules are summed up as follows:

1. Total line weight of *active lines* on a scanner cannot exceed 100. Notice that while in the case of an IBM 3725 we consider the *installed lines*, for an IBM 3745 we only take *active lines* into account. It increases your responsibility to ensure that you do not activate more lines than a scanner can accommodate. Since line speed in the case of an IBM 3745 can be changed from a MOSS console, you could inadvertently exceed the line weight limit. Be very careful.

LAB A

PORT	SCANNER							
	LIC 1	LIC 2	LIC 3	LIC 4	LIC 5	LIC 6	LIC 7	LIC 8
1	3.1	12.5	9.4	0.8				
2	3.1	12.5		0.8				
3	3.1	12.5		0.8				
4	3.1			0.8				

Total LIC Weight = 12.4 + 25.0 + 9.4 + 3.2 = 50

Figure 2.12 An example for determining the line weight for a scanner in an IBM 3720 and 3745.

2. Maximum line speed per line must meet the following criterion:

$$MLS = \frac{307200}{NAL \times NAP}$$

where MLS = maximum line speed
NAL = total number of active LICs
NAP = number of ports on that LIC

2.4 SUMMARY

In this chapter we discussed various communications hardware equipment such as cluster controllers and communications controllers. We also gave a global view of other communications hardware such as terminals, network controllers, network conversion units, physical interfaces, modems, patch panels, multiplexers, etc. When we start learning about the software, we will commonly refer to cluster controllers as PU Type 2 and communications controllers as PU Type 4. In the authors' next book titled *Advanced SNA Networking*, we will devote a full chapter to IBM 3174s and 3745s each. In the next chapter we will learn about some additional communications devices.

3

Communications Hardware — Miscellaneous

We learned about cluster controllers and communications controllers in the previous chapter. Although that takes care of the major components of communications hardware equipment, there are many other components to properly understand VTAM/NCP-based network configurations.

Such components are described in this chapter.

3.1 PROTOCOL CONVERTERS AND CONCENTRATORS

The IBM 3270 family of terminals has the largest installed base in the mainframe environment. In the non-IBM environment, most popular terminals are the asynchronous ASCII devices. IBM PC, PS/2, and IBM 3101 are also asynchronous ASCII devices. ASCII terminals are generally far less expensive than the IBM 3270 family of terminals. Protocol converters provide for connecting such ASCII terminals to the SNA hosts and having them *emulate* IBM 3270 terminals.

3.1.1 IBM 3708 Network Conversion Unit

The IBM 3708 is a protocol converter that comes with 10 ports. One or two of these ports provide connectivity to one or two hosts through a communications controller (IBM 3725, 3720, or 3745). Other ports (the eight or nine remaining ones) provide direct connectivity to the asynchronous ASCII terminals. The protocol conversion software in the IBM 3708 makes the ASCII devices look like IBM 3270 terminals. Besides protocol conversion facilities, it also provides a pass-through mode in which the ASCII devices communicate directly with an ASCII host. In this case, the IBM 3708 only redirects the data without any conversion. Figure 3.1 shows a configuration in which some of the terminals are emulating in the IBM 3270 mode while others are accessing ASCII hosts.

Three terminals, T1, T2, and T3, have direct sessions with the ASCII host. Here, the IBM 3708 is acting in the pass-through mode.

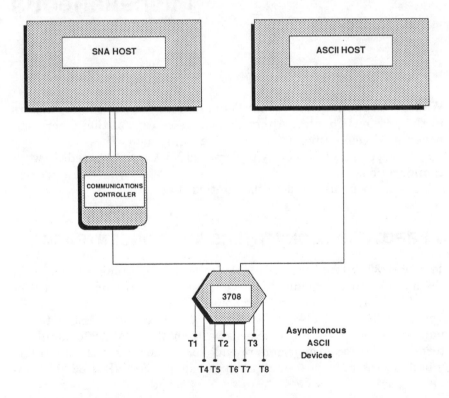

- ASCII Terminals T1, T2, and T3 are Communicating with the ASCII Host

- ASCII terminals T4, T5, T6, T7, and T8 are Emulating as 3270 Devices and Communicating with the SNA Host

Figure 3.1 A sample configuration using an IBM 3708 network conversion unit.

Five terminals, T4 through T8, have sessions with the SNA host. Here, the IBM 3708 is working as a protocol converter.

An IBM 3708 is defined as a Physical Unit Type 2 (PU Type 2) to VTAM/NCP. An emulating terminal appears as 3278 Model 2, 3178, 3179, or 3279. An ASCII printer appears as a 3287 Model 1 or 2 and looks like Logical Unit 1 (LU1) or Logical Unit 3 (LU3) to VTAM/NCP. An IBM 3708 supports line speeds up to 19,200 bps to the SNA host and the ASCII host.

3.1.2 IBM 3710 Network Controller

The IBM 3710 provides the functions of a line concentrator and a protocol converter. As a line concentrator, it can concentrate up to 31 lines onto a single SDLC link going to the host. As a protocol converter, it can attach up to seven 8-Port Communication Adapters (8PCAs). Each 8PCA can have up to eight ASCII terminals attached to it. Thus as a protocol converter it can support up to 56 ASCII terminals. In addition, 8PCAs provide for attachment to a maximum of five SNA hosts.

The IBM 3710 supports line speeds up to 19.2 kbps on an RS-232-C and up to 64 kbps using a V.35 interface. The IBM 3710 itself is defined as a PU Type 2 to VTAM/NCP and is directly attached to a communications controller.

3.1.3 IBM 7171 Protocol Converter

While the 3708 and 3710 provide 3270 emulation capabilities for remote sites, the IBM 7171 provides similar features for a channel-attached local environment. The IBM 3708 and 3710 need a communications controller for host connectivity. The IBM 7171 is directly attached to a block multiplexer channel of an SNA host. Up to 64 ASCII terminals can be attached to it in increments of eight. Figure 3.2 shows a configuration with an IBM 7171 in it.

An IBM 7171 with up to 32 ASCII devices looks like a channel-attached cluster controller 3274 Model 1D. An IBM 7171 with more than 32 devices (maximum up to 64) looks like two IBM 3274 Model 1D cluster controllers. The ASCII devices are attached to it using the RS-232-C physical interface in the United States and the V.24/V.28 interface elsewhere. Only full-duplex transmissions between ASCII devices and the IBM 7171 are supported. Some of the popular ASCII terminals supported are IBM 3101, IBM PC, IBM PS/2, DEC VT100, and Televideo 912/920/950.

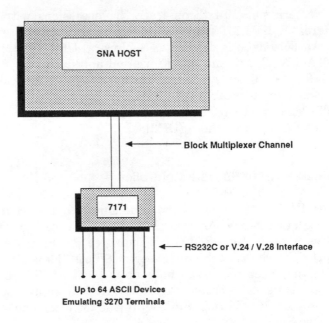

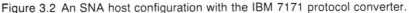

Figure 3.2 An SNA host configuration with the IBM 7171 protocol converter.

Since an IBM 7171 is attached to a block multiplexer channel, there is the possibility of attaching other devices on the same channel as well. Be aware that tape devices may adversely affect the IBM 7171's operation and therefore should not be put on the same channel.

3.2 PHYSICAL INTERFACE STANDARDS

Physical interfaces provide the connectivity between Data Terminal Equipment (DTE) and Data Circuit-Terminating Equipment (DCE). As discussed in Chapter 1, an example of a DTE is a cluster controller or a communications controller. A DCE could be a modem. The physical interfaces between such equipment have long been established and are governed by standards organizations. The standards define the electrical characteristics of and the mechanical specifications for the interface. The electrical characteristics include voltage levels, current levels, and grounding requirements. The mechanical specifications include cable length (between DTE and DCE), design of the pin connector, etc. Examples of some of the physical interfaces are RS-232-C, RS-449, V.24, X.21, and V.35.

Different organizations are instrumental in setting up these standards. In the United States, Electronic Industries Association (EIA) controls some of the most widely used standards such as the RS-232-C and RS-449. Founded in 1924 by the Radio Manufacturers Association, EIA has over 200 technical committees. Although EIA is primarily based in the United States, Geneva-based Comité Consultatif Internationale de Télégraphique et Téléphonique (CCITT) provides such standards at the international level. CCITT consists of 15 study groups. Some of the well-known interface standards provided by it are V.24, V.35, X.21, etc. Let's now look at some of the widely used physical interfaces in more detail.

3.2.1 The RS-232-C and EIA-232-D

RS-232-C. Electronic Industry Association's Recommended Standard 232C (EIA RS-232-C) is the most widely used DTE-to-DCE interface standard in the United States. It defines the electrical and mechanical characteristics of the interface. It is functionally compatible with the CCITT's recommended standard V.24. Some salient features of RS-232-C are:

* It supports asynchronous (start/stop) as well as synchronous (e.g., BSC or SDLC) transmissions.
* It supports data speeds up to 19,200 bps.
* It is applicable to point-to-point or multipoint configurations.
* It supports private as well as common carrier lines. In common carrier circuits it supports switched as well as dial-up lines. Lines can be two-wire or four-wire.
* Transmission can be half duplex or full duplex.
* The mechanical interface consists of a 25-pin connector.
* The recommended cable length between the DTE and the DCE is 50 feet. However, larger cable lengths are supported in case of low data rates or low capacitance cables.

The standard defines the 25 pin assignments and each pin has a specific function. The connector has 13 pins in the top row and 12 pins in the bottom row to make it difficult to make a wrong connection. Figure 3.3a shows the pin assignments and Figure 3.3b gives the function of each pin.

Each pin has a specific function and one has to follow the rules to be universally compatible. For example, pin 22 always transmits a *ring indicator* signal. In Figure 3.3b, you will also see the V.24

(a)

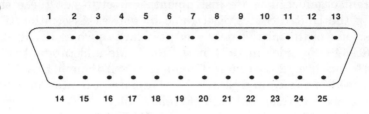

(b)

PIN NUMBER	PIN FUNCTION	V.24 EQUIVALENT
1	Protective Ground	101
2	Transmitted Data	103
3	Received Data	104
4	Request to Send	105
5	Clear to Send	106
6	Data Set Ready	107
7	Signal Ground / Common Return	102
8	Received Line Signal Detector	109
9	Reserved for Testing	-
10	Reserved for Testing	-
11	Not Assigned	-
12	Secondary Received Line Signal Detector	122
13	Secondary Clear to Send	121
14	Secondary Transmitted Data	118
15	Transmitter Signal Element Timing	114
16	Secondary Received Data	119
17	Receiver Signal Element Timing	115
18	Not Assigned	-
19	Secondary Request to Send	120
20	Data Terminal Ready	108.2
21	Signal Quality Detector	110
22	Ring Indicator	125
23	Data Signal Rate Selector	111 / 112
24	Transmitter Signal Element Timing	113
25	Secondary Clear to Send	-

Figure 3.3 (a) RS-232-C pin assignments; (b) RS-232-C pin functions.

equivalent for the RS-232-C pin functions. V.24 is the CCITT equivalent for RS-232-C.

Since RS-232-C has limitations on the transmission speed and cable length, EIA came up with a new standard in 1977 called RS-449. Although RS-449 will be covered in a later section, it is important to know that you can use an "interface converter" to make an RS-232-C compliant equipment compatible with an RS-449 compliant equipment.

EIA-232-D. RS-232-C was revised in November 1986 and the new standard was called "EIA-232-D." Notice that it is prefixed with EIA and not RS. With the introduction of EIA-232-D, the standard is in line with the CCITT V.24 and V.28. It is also equivalent to the International Standards Organization (ISO) IS 2110 standard. In addition to including RS-232-C functions, it supports the following new features:

• Local loopback
• Remote loopback
• Test mode

3.2.2 RS-449

Since RS-232-C could only support data rates up to 19,200 bps and also had cable length limitations, EIA came up with the RS-449 standard in 1977. This standard can support data rates up to 2 million bps which is 100 times the maximum data rate for RS-232-C. RS-449 was developed in cooperation with ISO and CCITT; therefore, it is compatible with CCITT's V.24 and ISO's 4902 standards.

RS-449 comes with a 37-pin connector. The electrical characteristics are specified with two additional standards — RS-422-A for balanced circuits and RS-423-A for unbalanced ones. In 1980 the RS-449-1 standard was issued, which differed from the previous one in specifying changes to pin 34.

RS-449 is compatible with RS-232-C if an interface converter is used. However, you must not exceed the limitations imposed by RS-232-C in that case; i.e., the data rate must not exceed 19,200 bps and the cable length between DTE and DCE must not exceed 50 feet.

RS-449 did not become a very popular standard. For data speeds below 19,200 bps vendors still use RS-232-C. For data speeds above 19,200 bps, V.35 is the more commonly used interface.

3.2.3 Additional Standards

V Series Interfaces. Besides RS-232-C, EIA-232-D, and RS-449, there are other standards that define the physical interface between DTE and DCE. Figure 3.4 gives the salient features of V series interfaces developed by CCITT. Currently they are the most widely used standards in the world. They were last revised in 1984.

EIA-530. The EIA-530 uses the 25-pin mechanical connector of EIA-232-D and is intended to replace the RS-449 standard. It was ap-

NUMBER	LINE SPEED	FDX / HDX	ASYNCHRONOUS / SYNCHRONOUS	SWITCHED LINE SUPPORT
V.21	300	FDX	Both	Yes
V.22	1200	FDX	Both	Yes
V.22 BIS	2400	FDX	Both	Yes
V.23	1200	HDX	Both	Yes
V.26	2400	FDX	Synchronous	No
V.26 BIS	1200	HDX	Synchronous	Yes
V.26 TER	2400	Both	Both	Yes
V.27	4800	Both	Synchronous	No
V.27 TER	4800	HDX	Synchronous	Yes
V.29	9600	Both	Synchronous	No
V.32	9600	FDX	Synchronous	Yes
V.35	48000	HDX	Synchronous	No

Figure 3.4 CCITT's V series interfaces for DTE-to-DCE connectivity.

proved in 1987 by EIA. It is used for data rates from 19,200 bps to 2 mbps.

EIA-366-A. The EIA-366-A defines the interface for a DTE, DCE (modem), and Automatic Call Unit (ACU). It is a dial and answer system which gets the phone number from DTE and makes sure that the DCE is in operable condition. It also scans the call on a continual basis and determines when to disconnect.

3.2.4 X.21 Interface

In traditional DTE-to-DCE interfaces, each pin has a specific function to perform. Therefore they are called pin-per-function interfaces. Examples of such interfaces are RS-232-C, CCITT's V.24, and RS-449. CCITT's X.21 interface uses coded character strings for each function. The pin-per-function technique puts a limitation on the number of functions supported because of the size of the mechanical connectors involved. However, a coded character string approach can help in assigning unlimited functions.

The X.21 interface was developed and approved by CCITT in 1972. It was last modified in 1980. The X.21 is the designated interface for X.25 based packet switching networks. Examples of packet switching networks in North America are Tymnet, Telenet, and Datapac. The X.21 can also be used in environments which are not related to packet switching. Because of the extreme popularity of RS-232-C the in United States, X.21 has not really gained wide acceptance. Another reason for its lack of acceptance is the cost factor. It needs an intelligent device to interpret the character strings.

X.21 bis is the interim solution for X.25 packet switching networks. X.21 bis is compatible with RS-232-C and V.24 interfaces. Instead of pins, it defines 25 interchange circuits between DTE and DCE.

3.3 TERMINALS

Terminals provide the visual interface between human beings and the computer. Information requested is transmitted from the host to the terminal via the communications controller, modems, communications lines, and cluster controller. Display or printer terminals are attached to the cluster controller via a coaxial cable.

For the mainframe environment, IBM terminals can be classified as two categories:

1.   IBM 3270 family of terminals
2.   ASCII terminal devices

3.3.1 The IBM 3270 Family of Terminals

The IBM 3270 family of terminals is the most widely used set of terminals in the SNA environment. It offers the user many choices and models to select from, each having different shapes, sizes, screen display capacity, color features, and other characteristics.

In an SNA environment, a terminal uses the IBM 3270 Data Stream protocol. An SNA/SDLC display terminal looks to VTAM like a Logical Unit 2 (LU2) while a BSC terminal looks like a 3270 device. A printer terminal in an SNA/SDLC environment looks like LU1 or LU3 and in BSC environment, like a 3286. In fact, a 3270 display terminal or printer does not know about SNA/SDLC or BSC protocols. It is the cluster controller that makes it look like one. You may disconnect a 3278 terminal from a 3274 Model 41D (channel-attached non-SNA) and connect it to a 3274 Model 41A (channel-attached SNA/SDLC device) without any hardware consideration. Thus a terminal device is independent of the link level protocols; all the intelligence to interpret them lies in the cluster controller. The following are some of the widely used IBM 3270 terminals:

IBM 3270 Display Station. This comes in five models. Model 1 displays 12 lines by 80 columns. Model 2 is the most widely used display terminal and comes in a 24-row by 80-column display. Model 3 displays 32 lines while Model 4 displays 43 lines, both on 80-column screens. Model 5 gives a 27-row by 132-character display.

IBM 3178 Display Station. This is functionally equivalent to 3278 Model 2 and provides a 24-row by 80-column display. Models C1, C2, C3, and C4 differ only in keyboard capabilities. A 3178 is less expensive than the 3278.

IBM 3180 Display Station. This is functionally equivalent to 3278 Models 2 through 5. It comes in two models. Model 1 has four operator or program selectable screen formats. They provide the same capabilities as 3278 Models 2, 3, 4, and 5, respectively. Model 2 is used for connectivity to the System/36 and System/38.

IBM 3279 Color Display Station. This comes in three standard models. Model S2A has a 24-line by 80-column screen and supports base color mode. Model S2B also supports extended color mode and extended highlighting. Model S3G is the top of the line and supports 32 lines by 80 columns, extended highlighting, extended color mode, and programmed symbols. Base colors are red, green, blue, and white. The extended colors are yellow, pink, and turquoise. Extended highlighting includes reverse video, blinking, and underscoring.

IBM 3179 Color Display Station. This comes in four models. Model 1 can function in the 3279 Model S2A and S2B mode. The configuration depends upon how the cluster controller (e.g., the 3274) is configured. Model 2 works with System/36 and System/38. Models G1 and G2 have Model 1 characteristics and also support All-Points-Addressable (APA) graphics. In the graphics mode an eighth color, black, is also supported.

IBM 3191 Display Station. This comes in four models. Models A10 and B10 display green phosphor characters while Model A20 and B20 provide amber-gold phosphor characters. All models display 24 lines by 80 columns.

IBM 3193 Display Station. This comes in two models. Both models support the equivalent of 3278 Model 2 (24X80), Model 3 (32X80), and Model 4 (43x80). In addition, they also support a display of 48 lines by 80 columns. A 3193 can also act as two logical terminals. It supports APA capability.

IBM 3194 Color Display Station. This comes in two models. Both models support seven colors with 24-row by 80-column display. It supports up to four host sessions and two local notepad sessions. Various sessions can be displayed simultaneously by manipulating the windows.

IBM 3270 Personal Computer. This can run up to four host sessions, one PC-DOS session, and two notepad sessions. Multiple sessions can be displayed simultaneously by using the windows. The 3270 PC is defined as a Distributed Function Terminal (DFT) when required to create multiple host sessions.

IBM 3290 Information Panel. This is a flat gas plasma display panel which has the capacity to display up to four host sessions in four different quadrants of the panel. Each quadrant can display a 24-row by 80-column screen. Although a 3270 PC can also display four host sessions simultaneously, they overlap each other as far as the display is concerned. In 3290, you can have concurrent viewing of up to four 3278 Model 2 screens or two 3278 Model 3 screens or two 3278 Model 4 screens or two 3278 Model 5 screens. It can also display 62-row by 132-column full-resolution graphics. A 3290 is defined as a DFT terminal (four sessions maximum) rather than a Control Unit Terminal (CUT) to the VTAM. A CUT-mode terminal can have only one host session. Figure 3.5 summarizes the characteristics of 3270 display terminals.

3.3.2 The IBM 3270 Family of Printers

The 3270 family of printers communicates with the host via a cluster controller. They are defined to VTAM as LU1 or LU3 and are called VTAM printers. Their physical interface to the cluster controller is through a coaxial cable. They are different from the high-speed JES printers which are completely under the control of a spooling software such as JES2 or JES3. In comparison, JES printers are either channel attached to a host or are connected via an RJE/RJP device through a communications controller to the host. Printouts to a VTAM printer are sent by a VTAM application such as CICS or IMS/DC. Printouts to a JES printer are sent by JES2 or JES3 and are controlled through MVS JCL statements. The following are some of the commonly used VTAM printers.

IBM 3268 Matrix Printer. This prints at a speed of 340 characters per second (cps) and can support six-part paper. It can look like an LU1

TERMINAL	COLOR	SCREEN SIZE ROWS x COLUMNS	GRAPHICS SUPPORT	DFT / CUT *	COMMENTS
3278	Green	12 x 80, 24 x 80, 32 x 80, 43 x 80, 27 x 132	No	CUT	• Large User Base • Comes in 5 Models
3178	Green	24 x 80	No	CUT	• Functionally Equivalent to 3278 Models 2 thru 5
3180	Green	24 x 80, 32 x 80, 43 x 80, 27 x 132	No	CUT	• Equivalent to 3278 Model 2
3279	Multicolor	24 x 80 32 x 80	Optional	CUT	·
3179	Multicolor	24 x 80	No	CUT	·
3191	Green or Amber	24 x 80	No	CUT	·
3193	Black / White	24 x 80, 32 x 80, 43 x 80, 48 x 80	Images	CUT	• Can Be Two Logical Terminals
3194	Multicolor	24 x 80	No	CUT	• Can Also Be Monochrome
3270 PC	Multicolor	24 x 80	Yes	DFT	• One PC-DOS Session • Two Notepad Sessions
3290	Amber	24 x 80, 32 x 80, 43 x 80, 27 x 132	Yes	DFT	• Flat Gas Plasma Display • Each Session is in a Different Quadrant

* CUT = Control Unit Terminal; Single Host Session
DFT = Distributed Function Terminal; Up to Four Host Sessions

Figure 3.5 Characteristics of IBM 3270 display terminals.

or LU3 to VTAM. Maximum line length is 132 characters. IBM 3268 Model 2C is a color printer which supports base colors (black, red, blue, and green) and extended colors (pink, yellow, and turquoise). The base colors are selected at the field level, which may consist of many characters. Extended colors can be selected at the individual character level.

IBM 3262 Line Printer. These are relatively fast printers and their speed can range from 12 to 650 lines per minute (lpm). They do not come in color models.

PRINTER	COLOR / MONOCHROME	WIDTH IN CHARACTERS	SPEED MAXIMUM	COMMENTS
3268	Both Models	132	340 CPS	-
3262	Monochrome	132	650 LPM	-
3287	Both Models	132	120 CPS	-
4250	Monochrome	-	-	All Points Addressable with 600 dots per inch resolution

CPS = Characters Per Second
LPM = Lines Per Minute

Figure 3.6 Characteristics of IBM 3270 printers.

IBM 3287 Matrix Printers.   These are the desktop models and are relatively low-speed printers. Model 1 operates at 80 cps while Model 2 supports a 120-cps print speed. Both can print up to 132 characters on a line. Models 1C and 2C are the color models but they support colors from position 1 through 120 only. Positions 121 through 132 can only be printed in black.

IBM 4250 APA Printer.   This is a very high-resolution APA printer with a resolution of 600 dots per inch (dpi). It supports multiple fonts, typefaces, and graphics objects. Figure 3.6 summarizes the characteristics of the IBM 3270 family printers.

3.3.3 ASCII Terminals

While the most widely used terminals in the IBM environment are the 3270-family terminals, for other vendors they are the ASCII terminals. While the 3270 terminals are connected to a cluster controller via a BNC connector and a coaxial cable, the ASCII terminals are usually connected through an RS-232-C interface. IBM entered the ASCII terminal market in 1979 with the introduction of the 3101 terminal. Other popular vendors for ASCII terminals include TeleVideo, Wyse Technology, and Qume. Characteristics of ASCII terminals are as follows:

IBM 3101 Terminal. This is a TTY-compatible terminal which comes in two models. Model 13 supports character mode transmission while Model 23 supports character as well as block mode. In the latter case, either mode is switch selectable. It supports both the RS-232-C and RS-422-A communications interfaces, and is also switch selectable. With the introduction of the 316X family of ASCII terminals in 1985, it looks like IBM is phasing out the 3101 models.

IBM 316X Family Terminals. This series consists of four models. The IBM 3151 supports 24-row by 80-column display and comes in green or amber character display. The 3162 supports 24-row by 80-column or 80-row by 132-column display and also comes in green or amber character display models. The 3163 supports 24-row by 80-column display and has memory for 7680 characters. The 3164 is a color model. All models support RS-232-C and RS-422-A physical interfaces. They emulate certain well known and established ASCII terminals such as DEC's VT52, VT100, and VT220, Lear Sieglar, ADDS Viewpoint, Hazeltine 1500, TeleVideo 910, WYSE, and few others.

Figure 3.7 summarizes the characteristics of IBM ASCII terminals.

TERMINAL	COLOR	SCREEN SIZE	GRAPHICS SUPPORT	EMULATION
3101	Green	24 x 80	No	TTY
3161	Green / Amber	24 x 80	Line Drawing Set	Televideo 910, Hazeltine 1500, Leer Siegler, ADDS Viewpoint, ADM3A
3162	Green / Amber	24 x 80 80 x 132	Line Drawing Set	WYSE, Hazeltine 1500, ADDS, Televideo, VT52, VT100, VT220, Lear Siegler
3163	Green / Amber	24 x 80	Line Drawing Set	VT52, VT100
3164	Multicolor	24 x 80	Line Drawing Set	VT52, VT100

Figure 3.7 Characteristics of IBM ASCII terminals.

3.3.4 IBM 3299 — The Terminal Multiplexer

To provide physical connectivity between a terminal and a cluster controller, you need a coaxial cable. If the cluster controller can provide attachments for 32 devices, you need to run up to 32 individual coaxial cables between the controller and the devices. The cost of running cables under these circumstances can be fairly high. The problem is more severe if the controller and the devices are on different floors. Old buildings in metropolitan areas do not have risers large enough to accommodate the cable requirements for increased use of terminals. Under these circumstances you need a device which can concentrate data from multiple terminals in one physical location of a floor and provide connectivity to the cluster controller on a single cable. The IBM 3299 terminal multiplexer provides such capabilities. It can concentrate data from up to eight category A devices and transmit over a single cable to the controller (Figure 3.8).

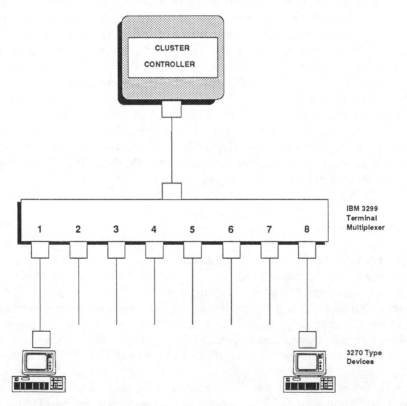

Figure 3.8 Use of an IBM 3299 terminal multiplexer.

As shown in Figure 3.8, there are up to eight cables going from the terminals to the 3299 but only a single cable going from the terminal multiplexer to the cluster controller. Thus you can run only four cables from four different terminal multiplexers to provide connectivity for up to 32 terminals. The IBM 3299 comes in two models, 2 and 3. Model 2 can use a coaxial cable as well as the IBM cabling system. Model 3 can be used to attach terminals using twisted-pair wire. Since the terminals have a coaxial connector at their end, you need a coax-to-twisted-pair adapter for terminal-to-3299 connectivity. An IBM 3274 Model 51C is *not* supported by the terminal multiplexers.

3.4 MODEMS AND MULTIPLEXERS

For the computer equipment to communicate with each other, there must be a physical media over which the data can travel. We learned in Chapter 1 that such computer equipment is Data Terminal Equipment, or DTE for short. The physical media can be copper wire, optical fiber, microwave, or any other possible media. The media can be owned by the enterprise, or the services for such media can be provided by a common carrier such as AT&T, MCI, Sprint, and Bell holding companies. In either case, the transmission technology can be based on analog or digital transmission. The equipment that provides the interface between the DTE and the communications media is Data Circuit Terminating Equipment, or DCE for short. In case of analog transmission lines, the DCE is a modem. For transmission media that provides digital facilities, the DCE is DSU/CSU. Figure 3.9 gives a pictorial representation of this.

3.4.1 Modems

Transmission Speed. The data transmission speed of a modem is measured in bits per second (bps). It signifies the number of bits that can be sent over the transmission media in 1 second. Generally, the term "baud" is also used to represent the bits per second rate for a modem. Technically, it is inaccurate. Baud denotes the number of signal changes per second. Generally, analog lines can accommodate 2400 signal changes per second. If each signal change can be translated into 1 bit, the baud rate and the bit rate will be the same; i.e., the baud rate will be 2400 and the bit rate will also be 2400 bps. If you can represent 8 bits on each signal change, the baud rate will still be 2400 but the bit rate will be 8 times 2400, or 19,200 bps.

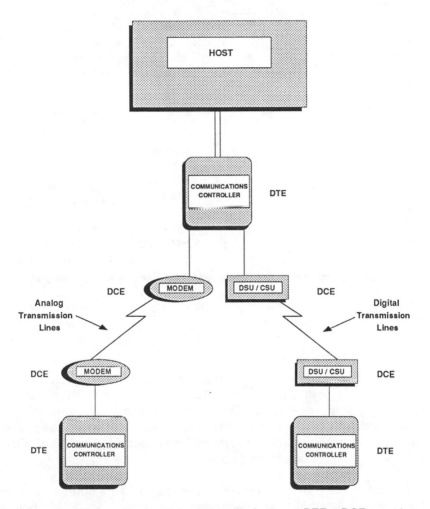

Figure 3.9 A diagram showing the relationship between DTEs, DCEs, modems, and DSU/CSUs.

Generally speaking, 2400 is the highest baud rate and 19,200 is the highest line speed you can achieve on analog lines. It should also be noted that the line speed depends upon the pair of modems used on each end of the transmission line. You do *not* order lines with a certain speed from a common carrier. It is the same four-wire line which, depending upon the modem used, may transmit at 110 or 19,200 bps. However, for higher line speeds you do ask the carrier company to give you a conditioned line.

NAME	TRANSMISSION RATE (BPS)	ASYNCHRONOUS / SYNCHRONOUS	OTHER CHARACTERISTICS
103	300	ASYNCHRONOUS	POINT-TO-POINT
212	1200	BOTH	POINT-TO-POINT
201B,C	2400	SYNCHRONOUS	POINT-TO-POINT
208A,B	4800	SYNCHRONOUS	POINT-TO-POINT MULTIPOINT (for 208A)
209	9600	SYNCHRONOUS	POINT-TO-POINT MULITPOINT CONDITIONING REQUIRED

Figure 3.10 Some of the more commonly used AT&T standards for modem specifications.

Line Conditioning. At higher speeds, modems may not function properly because of transmission line problems such as noise, phase jitter, or amplitude distortion. The telephone company can supply a conditioned line at additional cost. Such a line will have less severe transmission problems. A conditioned line generally involves the use of amplifiers and attenuation equalizers.

Modem Standards. In the predivestiture era, AT&T's standards were the most widely used modem standards in United States. Although this is changing very rapidly, they are still being used quite extensively. Conforming to such standards ensured that two different modems from two different vendors would work with each other without any problems. AT&T's modem specifications define standards for data rates varying from 300 to 9600 bps. Figure 3.10 outlines the characteristics of such modem specifications.

CCITT's modem standards, though biased toward European telephone facilities, are more international in nature. Generally known as V standards for modem specifications, they specify line speeds from 200 to 14,400 bps. Figure 3.11 outlines some of the commonly used specifications and their characteristics. Any suffixes of "bis" or "ter" signify second or third iteration of the standard, respectively.

NAME	TRANSMISSION RATE (BPS)	ASYNCHRONOUS / SYNCHRONOUS	OTHER CHARACTERISTICS
V.22	300	BOTH	POINT-TO-POINT
V.22 BIS	1200	BOTH	POINT-TO-POINT
V.26	2400	SYNCHRONOUS	POINT-TO-POINT MULTIPOINT (for 208A)
V.26 BIS	2400	SYNCHRONOUS	POINT-TO-POINT
V.27, V.27 BIS	4800	SYNCHRONOUS	POINT-TO-POINT MULTIPOINT (for 208A)
V.27 TER	4800	SYNCHRONOUS	POINT-TO-POINT
V.29	9600	SYNCHRONOUS	POINT-TO-POINT MULTIPOINT (for 208A)
V.32	9600	SYNCHRONOUS	POINT-TO-POINT
V.33	14400	SYNCHRONOUS	POINT-TO-POINT

Figure 3.11 Some of the commonly used CCITT standards for modem specifications.

Limited Distance Modems (LDMs). Also called short haul modems, they are used to transmit data over short distances. Both the DTEs for such transmissions are usually in the same location. LDMs cost less than regular modems and are used to bypass the telephone company's transmission facilities for short distance communications.

Modem Eliminators. When distances between DTEs are less than 1000 feet, you may replace two LDMs with a single modem eliminator. A modem eliminator sits midway between the DTEs. By using low-capacitance cable, you may increase the distance between DTEs to more than a thousand feet.

Line Drivers. They act as repeaters and can drive a signal from a few hundred feet to several miles. Generally, they are used to connect DTEs within the same premises.

3.4.2 Data Service Units/Channel Service Units (DSU/CSU)

DSU/CSUs are to digital lines what modems are to analog lines. They are required for AT&T's Dataphone Digital Service (DDS) and Accunet T1.5 Service. DDS is available at line speeds of up to 56 kbps. Accunet T1.5 supports digital signals at 1.544 million bps. Such service is also commonly known as T1 lines.

For digital services, modems are not required at all. All the necessary interface functions such as timing, control signals, signal translation, and data regeneration are supplied by the DSU/CSU. The physical interface between the DTEs and DSU/CSU for 56 kbps DDS services is the CCITT's V.35. Recall from Chapter 2 that V.35 interface exists on LIC Type 3, which is supported by LAB Type B.

3.5 SUMMARY

In Chapter 2, we learned about the communications controllers and cluster controllers. In this chapter, we discussed data communications and telecommunications equipment. IBM 3708 and 3710 are used for concentration and protocol conversion. Physical interfaces such as RS-232-C, RS-449, and V.35 provide interface between DTEs and DCEs. We also discussed various terminal types available in the 3270 and ASCII family. In the end we talked about modems for analog lines and DSU/CSUs for the digital lines. Modems and DSU/CSUs provide the DCE function in a network. Now that we have the necessary background in some aspects of the IBM SNA environment, let's find out in the next chapter what SNA really is.

4

SNA and Telecommunications Access Methods

4.1 SYSTEMS NETWORK ARCHITECTURE CONCEPTS

The advent of the expanding thirst for quick and accurate retrieval of information by government, business, and the general public has necessitated rules to govern the interaction of components within the information network. A hierarchical structure composed of seven layers has become the cornerstone for handling the information demand. It was developed by IBM and is known as Systems Network Architecture (SNA).

4.1.1 Network Components

A communications network comprises hardware and software components. As seen in Figure 4.1, these components include the processor, communications controller, cluster controller, workstation, distributed processor, and printer. These components make up the hardware portion of the network. The software components are found in the two main components of the hardware. The cornerstone of all communication software executes on the main processor and is known as the telecommunications access method. It is this software that correlates and manages the entire network. To allow the expansion of a network to remote end users, a network control program was developed and executes in the communications control unit. The

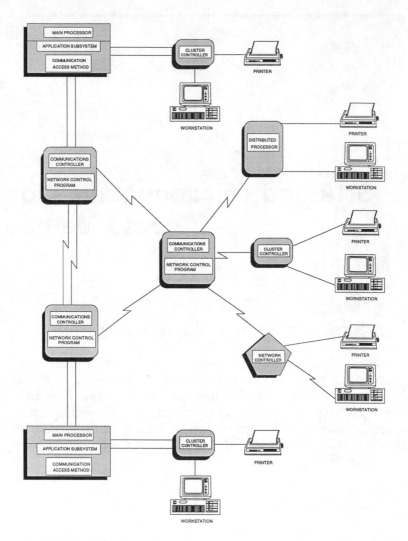

Figure 4.1 Network components.

network control program defines to the telecommunications access method the topology of the remote end-user network. The last and most important piece of SNA software to the end user is the application subsystem. It executes on the main processor and uses the other two components of SNA software to communicate to the end user. The consistency of data integrity between the end user and the application subsystem must be provided by an addressing scheme that addresses the individual end-user workstations and the corresponding requested information from the application subsystem.

4.1.2 Nodes

As we discussed, an SNA network consists of hardware and software components. The hardware and its associated software components that implement the functions of SNA are called "nodes." In SNA there are three types of nodes: (1) host subarea nodes, (2) communications controller subarea nodes, and (3) peripheral nodes, as depicted in Figure 4.2.

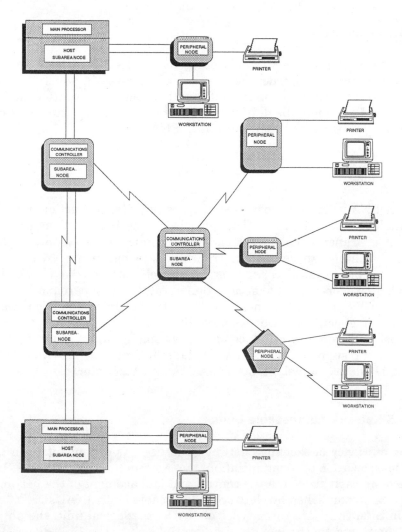

Figure 4.2 SNA nodes.

Host subarea nodes control and manage the network. The combination of hardware and software components that make up this node is the main processor and the telecommunications access method. The communications controller subarea nodes route and control the flow of data through a network. This node is an association of the communications controller and a network control program.

All other hardware and software components and their respective associations are peripheral nodes. This includes cluster controllers, distributed processors, workstations, and printers.

4.1.3 Subareas

A subarea is a designated address given to a subarea node and its attached peripheral nodes. This address informs SNA which subarea node is the originator of the information being transmitted and is also used to denote the destination subarea node of the transmission. Figure 4.3 diagrams subarea nodes in SNA.

4.1.4 Links

Since SNA nodes are separate entities, a physical connection must be established between them. This physical connection is the actual medium of transmission. A telephone wire, microwave beam, or fiber optic medium can be used to transmit data between SNA subarea nodes. This physical connection by any of these media is called a "link." One or more links can connect adjacent subarea nodes, as seen in Figure 4.4. The media constitute the link connection. Each link connection has two or more link stations. The link stations transmit the data over link connections using data link control protocols. SNA supports the following data link control protocols: System/370 data channel, SDLC, BSC, S/S, and X.25 interface.

4.1.5 Network Addressable Units

The efficiency of exchange between end users is dependent upon the synchronization of communication, management of the resources that make up each node, and the control and management of the network. This is accomplished by Network Addressable Units (NAUs).

In SNA there are three types of NAUs: the logical unit, the physical unit, and the system services control point. The first allows the

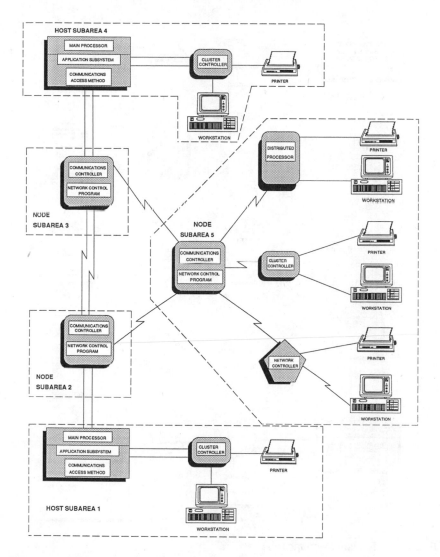

Figure 4.3 SNA subareas.

end user access to the network. This NAU is a Logical Unit (LU). The LU manages the exchange of data between end users. It is the port to the network. In other words, it is not a one-to-one connection between end users and LUs.

For end users to communicate with each other a mutually agreed upon relationship must be established. This relationship is called a "session." When a session connects two LUs, it is called an "LU-LU"

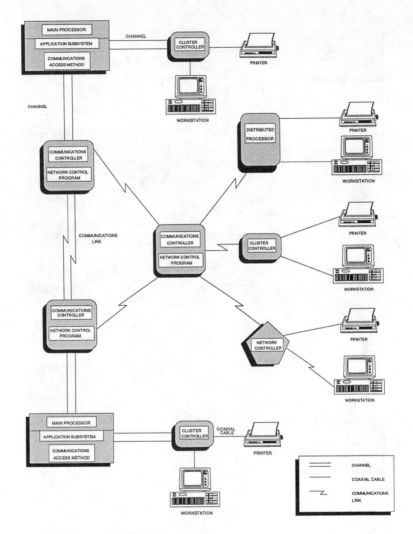

Figure 4.4 Transmission facilities.

session. If multiple, concurrent sessions occur between the same two LUs, they are called "parallel LU-LU" sessions. LU-LU sessions can exist only between LUs of the same type. SNA defines nine types of LUs as can be seen in Appendix C.

The LUs are managed by a Physical Unit (PU). The PU represents a processor, communications controller, and cluster controller and presents the LUs to the links that connect its node to adjacent nodes. As described in Appendix C, there are four types of physical units, one representing each type of SNA node. PUs are implemented by a combination of hardware and software components that describe to the PU its own node.

The third NAU, System Services Control Point (SSCP), lies within the telecommunications access method. The SSCP is found only in host subarea nodes. Each SSCP in a network activates, controls, and deactivates network resources that have been defined to that SSCP as being in its domain. When there is one SSCP in a network, it is called a "single-domain" network. If there is more than one SSCP in a network, it is called a "multiple-domain" network.

4.1.6 Network Addressing

This leads us to the actual assignment of addresses for network resources. Each NAU is assigned a unique address within a network based on the subarea to which the peripheral node is assigned and an element address for each NAU of that subarea node. The unique subarea address is assigned to each host subarea node and communications controller subarea node during the telecommunications access method definition process. This subarea number is assigned to the subarea address field of the network address. All network resources in that subarea and any peripheral node attached to that subarea, along with the link and link stations that connect adjacent subareas, will be assigned this unique subarea number.

Now that each node has a subarea address, each NAU within that node must have a unique address. This is the element address of the network address. The element address is assigned by the SNA access methods and network control programs during the resource definition process, dynamic reconfigurations, switched SDLC link resource activation, and the initializing of parallel LU-LU sessions. These element addresses are assigned in sequence according to the order in which the resource definition statements are read by the SNA access method or the network control program.

Now that we have seen how the network address is derived, let's take a look at the three formats for the network address. In Figure 4.5, we see a 16-bit network address format and two extended formats, 23-bit and 31-bit network address formats. The 16-bit address format allows from 1 to 255 subareas. However, the subarea address field length is variable according to the maximum number of subareas that are defined to the SNA access method. For example, if we defined the maximum subarea address as 63 in our network, the size of the subarea address field will use 6 of the available 16 bits for the

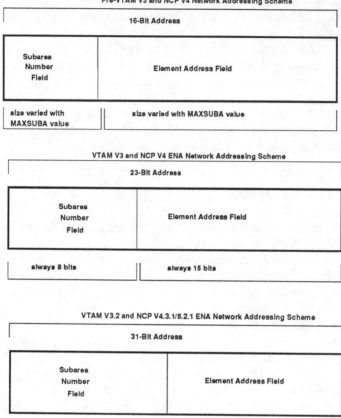

Figure 4.5 SNA network addressing schemes.

network address. This limits the size of the element address field to 10 bits. The highest element address that can be assigned to any NAU in any subarea node for this example is therefore 1023. Likewise, if the maximum subarea address is defined as 31, 5 bits are used for the subarea address field, leaving 11 bits for the element address field. This translates into 2047 elements or NAUs available for any one subarea. This address split has to remain constant throughout the network and many large shops quickly exhaust their element address limits. Because of this limitation of network resources on large networks, IBM announced Extended Network Addressing (ENA).

At first, ENA added 7 bits to the network address format and removed the network address split. This allowed for 255 subareas, which is the same as the 16-bit format, but it created a constant element address field size of 15 bits. This provided each subarea node with a maximum of 32,768 addressable NAUs, thus allowing for virtually unlimited growth for large networks.

In September 1988, IBM announced network addressing enhancements that break all bounds by adding 8 more bits to the subarea addressing field of the network address. Now with VTAM V3.2, NCP V4.3.1, and NCP V5.2.1 we can have 65,535 subareas with 32,768 elements in each subarea.

Addressing within peripheral nodes is also necessary. Local addresses are assigned to each NAU in each peripheral node. These local addresses are unique only within that peripheral node. These addresses are translated into their corresponding network addresses by the boundary function of the host and communications controller subarea nodes.

During the access method definition process the NAUs can be assigned network names. These network names must be unique within the network and are used by the network operator, workstation operator, and application programs. A directory is built during the definition process and the SSCP uses this directory to translate the network name to the network address.

4.1.7 SNA Routes

In the previous section we discussed how each NAU in a network is assigned a unique network address which consists of a subarea number and an element number. This addressing scheme has fostered the need for a technique to route information through the network. This routing technique is designed to maximize the amount of data being transmitted, data security, and route availability as well as minimize transmission time, transmission errors, traffic congestion, and cost. Although these are the objectives, not all can be equally satisfied. If one is favored, another will be at loss. The choice of which objective takes priority depends upon what type of session is more important to the corporation's service goals.

As we discussed in Section 4.1.4, links connect adjacent subarea nodes. In SNA, if two or more links may connect adjacent subarea nodes, they are called "parallel" links. Each link or group of links between two adjacent subarea nodes is called a "Transmission Group" (TG). A transmission group appears to the path control component of SNA as a single link. So that a TG can be addressed, a transmission group number is assigned to the TG. A TG with parallel links has more availability than a TG with one link assigned. Usually, similar transmission characteristics govern which links are mapped to a TG. An example would be links that have the same transmission speed.

For SNA to follow a specific route, a path for that route must be defined. This path consists of the nodes, links, path control, and data link control components that are used for the transmission of data between two NAUs. A path is defined to SNA by an Explicit Route (ER) and a Virtual Route (VR) along with the TG.

An explicit route is the physical connection between two subareas. Each explicit route is mapped to a transmission group. However, you can define more than one ER to the same TG. This will increase the probability that a path will be available for transmission between two nodes. ERs are bidirectional. They have a forward and reverse path. The ER Number (ERN) assigned to the forward path can be different from the ER number assigned to the reverse path. The only requirement is that the ER pair must traverse the same set of subarea nodes and transmission groups.

The virtual route of a path is the logical connection between two subarea nodes. Each VR is mapped to an ER. One or more virtual routes can be assigned to an explicit route, again providing greater availability for transmission of data through the network. Each VR takes on the characteristics of the ER it is mapped to. The primary usage of VRs in SNA is the assignment of transmission priority to a session over an ER. The correlation of VR with a transmission priority is accomplished through the Class of Service (COS) table. During an LU-LU session initiation, a class of service is requested. It is this COS that determines the transmission priority of the session. More discussion about the definition and usage of the class of service table will follow in Chapter 11.

One more important point of SNA routing should be mentioned. SNA distributes the responsibility of defining paths between subarea nodes to all the subarea nodes. Each subarea node needs only the information to pass data to the next adjacent subarea node, even if that adjacent subarea node is not the intended destination of the information. For example, Figure 4.6 shows data that needs to be routed from Node A to Node D. The path definitions in Node A define a route to Node D but there are no physical links that connect Node A to Node D. However, Node A transmits the data to Node D via an Intermediate Networking Node (INN) which in turn transmits the data over TG 5 ER 2. Node D then sends the data to the destined logical unit.

4.1.8 SNA Layers

Each of the seven layers of SNA are well defined to perform a specific SNA function in the architecture. The layers have been designed to be self-contained, allowing for autonomy between the layers. Although each layer is autonomous from the other, each layer performs services for the next higher layer, requests services from the next

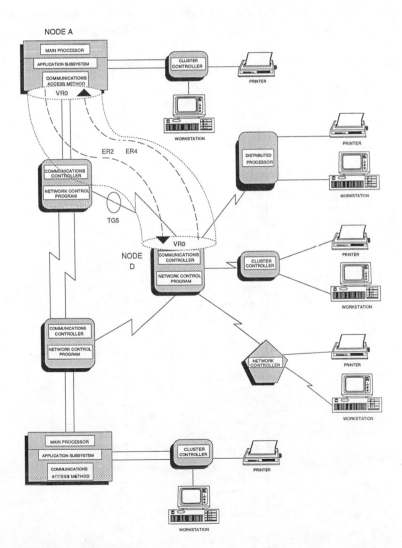

Figure 4.6 SNA routing example.

lower layer, and allows peer-to-peer communication between equivalent layers.

As seen by the end user (Figure 4.7), the first layer involved with communications is the Transaction Services Layer. This layer allows the end user access to the network by providing application services and requests services from the Presentation Services Layer. The Transaction Services Layer also has the function of providing services to control the network's operation through three components (Figure 4.8).

The Configuration Services component controls resources associated with the physical configuration during the communication ac-

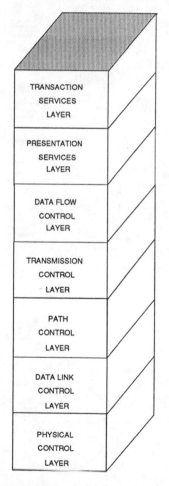

Figure 4.7 The seven layers of SNA.

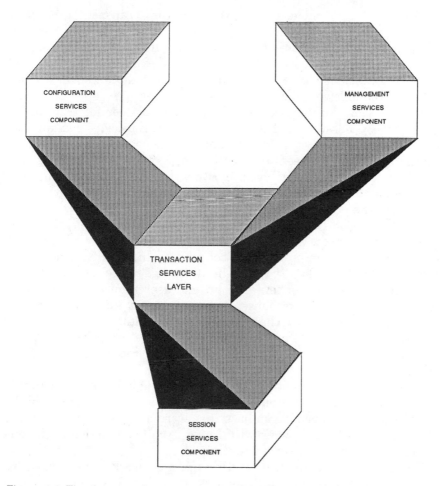

Figure 4.8 The three service components of the Transaction Services Layer.

cess method's System Services Control Point (SSCP) to a Physical Unit (PU) session. This is known as a SSCP-PU session. These services are used for activation and deactivation of communication links, loading same-domain software, and assigning network addresses if dynamic reconfiguration is being used.

The establishment of an LU-to-LU session is a function of the session services component. It is during SSCP-SSCP and SSCP-LU sessions that these services are invoked. Session services perform translation of network names to network addresses. User passwords and user access authority are verified here, as is the selection of session parameters.

The third component that makes up the Transaction Services Layer operational control of the network is the Management Services component. These services perform the monitoring, testing, tracing, and recording of statistics for network resources for SSCP-PU and SSCP-LU sessions. SSCP, PU, and LU will be discussed in further detail in the following section.

The Presentation Services Layer provides services for transaction programs by defining and maintaining the protocol of communications. Presentation Services also controls the conversational level of communications between transaction programs by providing the function for loading and invoking other transaction programs, enforcement of correct verb parameter usage and sequencing restrictions, and the processing of transaction program verbs.

LU-LU session flow is controlled by the next SNA layer, the Data Flow Control Layer. Communication of data between two LUs must be transmitted in an orderly and cohesive fashion. The services provided by this layer do just that. The units of data being transmitted are given sequence numbers and an end-user request is correlated with the transactions response. Related request units are grouped into chains and related chains are grouped into brackets of data. This layer enforces the protocol and coordinates which session partner can send and which session partner can receive at any given moment.

The Transmission Control Layer is responsible for the synchronization and pacing of session-level data traffic. It does this by checking the session sequence numbers that were assigned to the request units from the Data Flow Control Layer. Another function is the enciphering and deciphering of end-user data.

The routing of the data units through a network is performed by the Path Control Layer. All types of sessions use this layer. Its main function is to route the unit of data to the desired destination in the network, be it a terminal or an application program executing on a mainframe computer. The function is performed in subarea nodes. The Path Control layer consists of three sublayers as seen in Figure 4.9. The inner layer, the Transmission Group Layer, provides the transmission group connections between subarea nodes. The middle layer, Explicit Route Control, determines which of the transmission group connections information is to be passed between two end subarea nodes of a path. Finally, the third sublayer is the Virtual Route Control sublayer. It is considered the outer sublayer of the three sublayers. Virtual Route Control provides the explicit route(s) that can be used to route information during a session.

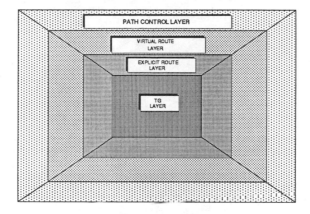

Figure 4.9 The sublayers of the Path Control Layer.

The sixth layer of control in SNA is the Data Link Control Layer. This layer performs the scheduling and error recovery for the transfer of data between link stations of two nodes. The Data Link Control Layer supports the link level flow of data for both SDLC and System/370 data channel protocols.

The last layer in SNA provides the description of the physical interface for any transmission medium. It defines the electrical and transmission signal characteristics necessary to establish, maintain, and terminate all physical connections of a link. This layer is called the Physical Control Layer.

The seven layers of SNA are grouped into two distinctive functional groups as seen in Figure 4.10. The first four layers are grouped into the Network Addressable Unit and Boundary Function classification. If you review the previous discussion, you will see this classification is accurate. Remember, it is the first four layers that enable the end users to send and receive data through the network by providing the definition of the logical unit functions in each node. The last three layers of SNA are grouped as the Path Control Network Functions. As discussed previously, it is in these three layers that the data is actually routed and transmitted between network addressable units.

4.1.9 SNA Sessions

In SNA there are four session types that occur in the network: (1) SSCP-SSCP, (2) SSCP-PU, (3) SSCP-LU, and (4) LU-LU. Each ses-

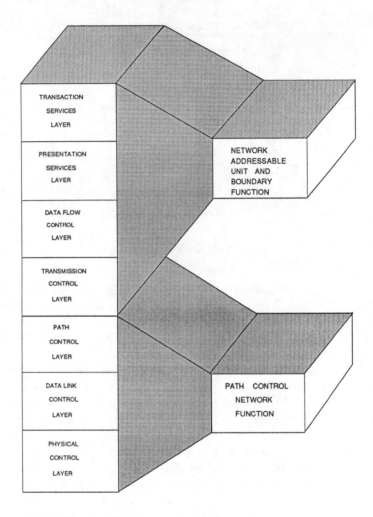

Figure 4.10 The two functional groups of SNA.

sion is used for a specific purpose in SNA. Figure 4.11 illustrates the four SNA sessions.

The SSCP-SSCP session is used by SSCP to communicate with another SSCP in another VTAM. This session is primarily used to set up cross-domain LU-LU sessions in a multidomain network and cross-network LU-LU sessions in an SNI network.

The SSCP-PU session determines the boundaries of the SSCP's domain. The PU is seen as being owned or controlled by the SSCP it is in session with. The session occurs when the SSCP receives the PU's acknowledgement of the SSCP's activation request. This session is

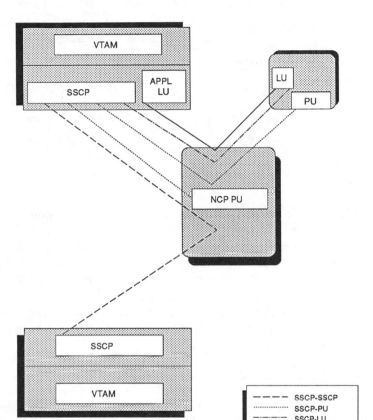

Figure 4.11 Diagram depicting the four SNA session types.

used primarily for activating the LUs associated with the PU and for request and response network management data that flows on the SSCP-PU session.

The SSCP-LU session occurs when the LU acknowledges the SSCP's activation request. It is this session that allows an end user to request a session with an application. The request for the application flows on the SSCP-LU session. The SSCP in turn passes the request to the application over the application's SSCP-LU session. Once the two LUs have agreed on session protocols, the LU-LU session is established. It is this session with which most end users are familiar.

LU-LU sessions come in two types. Applications such as CICS and IMS can have multiple and parallel LU-LU sessions. As seen in Fig-

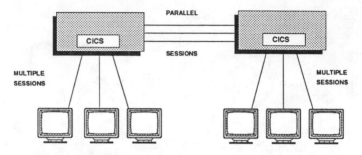

Figure 4.12 Example of multiple and parallel LU-LU sessions.

ure 4.12, multiple sessions can occur concurrently between CICS and several end users. However, from the end user's point of view, he or she is the only session partner. The distinction here is that each of the end users are in session with the same network addressable unit. That is, CICS uses the same network address for all multiple sessions. Parallel sessions on the other hand can also occur concurrently between LUs. The distinction here is that the sessions are occurring between the same two LUs, but each session partner of each session is assigned a unique network address.

4.1.10 Open Systems Interconnection and SNA

So far we have discussed IBM's architecture for data communications, SNA. But other companies and organizations are in the process of developing, or have developed, alternative data communications architectures. One group, the International Standards Organization (ISO), has developed a standard for exchanging information between different architectures, Open Systems Interconnection (OSI).

Unlike SNA, OSI is designed to exchange information between autonomous systems by standardizing the communication protocols between the architectures. SNA, however, is designed solely to standardize communications protocols between IBM products. Although no direct correlation of the layers between the two architectures can be drawn, the functions provided by each layer are quite similar.

If we look at Figure 4.13, we can see the similarities of the two distinct architectures. The table shows that the SNA path control layer functions are found in the OSI network and transport layers. Likewise, the OSI physical layer and the SNA physical control layer both describe to the architecture the physical characteristics of the transmission medium.

It is important to remember that although there are many similarities between the two architectures, the purpose of each is distinct.

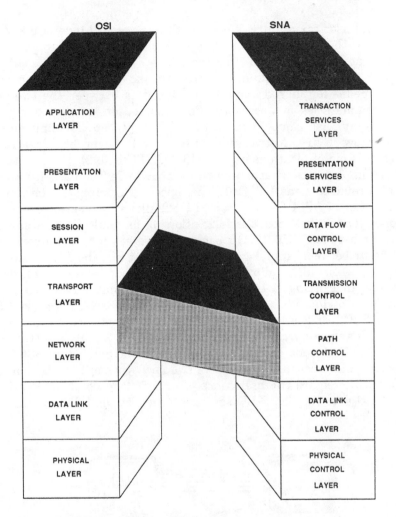

Figure 4.13 The OSI and SNA architectures.

SNA was designed specifically for IBM networks using IBM products. OSI was designed to provide communications between unlike
network architectures. IBM has acknowledged the ISO OSI standard
and is pursuing APPC/LU6.2 as the OSI standard for OSI's peer-to-
peer communications.

4.1.11 SNA/LEN and APPC/LU6.2

The rapid expansion of distributed office processors dedicated to specific applications has brought a dramatic change in SNA. The distributed processors provide local access to the majority of the applica-

tions end-user community; however, there may still be end users attached to the host processor that need periodic access to the data located at the distributed processor. The distributed processor and host processor are frequently hardware and software incompatible and a means for shared applications and data between the two end-user communities is necessary. For this reason a new concept of "any-to-any" has come forth in SNA. This concept is implemented using Low Entry Networking (LEN) and Advanced-Program-to-Program Communications using LU6.2 (APPC/LU6.2).

LEN implements what is known as SNA Node Type 2.1, from here on also referred to as PU T2.1. This special PU supports the unique capabilities of APPC/LU6.2. Each LU6.2 allows for peer-to-peer communications with another LU6.2, allowing for multiple and parallel sessions between LU6.2s. On each of these sessions a conversation can occur between application programs that use the LU6.2 session (Figure 4.14). LEN allows these peer-to-peer sessions to occur through an existing SNA network providing that VTAM V3.2 and NCP V4.3 and/or V5.2 are implemented in the SNA network. LEN with APPC/LU6.2 allows any resource of any network to communicate with any resource of any other network.

The PU T2.1 node does not necessarily participate in an SSCP-PU session. This is because it supports two new types of LUs. Dependent LUs (DLU) require the assistance of an SSCP to establish sessions. The DLU uses the SSCP-LU session to request the SSCP services to

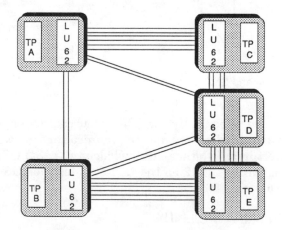

Figure 4.14 The multiple and parallel session capabilities of APPC/LU 6.2. Note that VTAM is not involved in the session configuration.

establish an LU-LU session. These are historically the most common LU Types 0, 1, 2, and 3. In this case, the PU T2.1 supports an SSCP-PU session on behalf of the DLUs. However, the second type of LU, Independent LUs (ILU) can request and establish an LU-LU session without the services of an SSCP. LU Type 6.2 is an ILU. The PU T2.1 that is supporting ILUs therefore does not participate in an SSCP-PU session. See Chapter 8 for more information on Low Entry Networking (LEN).

4.2 SNA/SDLC FORMAT SUMMARY

From the previous discussions, we now know how SNA addresses and routes data to different types of processors, communications controllers, cluster controllers, workstations, and printers. In this section we will see how this information is relayed to the nodes and NAUs of the network by using SNA frames. These SNA frames are created using SDLC protocol. There are three types of frames. The information frame passes SNA commands and responses, and user data requests or responses, and acknowledges information frames (I-frames). The supervisory frame acknowledges I-frames and reflects the status of the NAU as being Ready-to-Receive (RR) or Receive-Not-Ready (RNR). The final frame is the unnumbered frame, which passes SDLC commands and is used in data link management.

4.2.1 Message Unit Formats

In SNA, each message unit along the route is given a specific format. This format is directly related to the location of the message unit on the SNA route. If we look at Figure 4.15, there are three types of message unit formats. Each one correlates to a specific layer within the SNA architecture.

Network addressable units use the Basic Information Unit (BIU) format to exchange information with other NAUs. The BIU is created as a function of the LU when the LU prefixes a Request Header (RH) to the Request Unit (RU). Only NAUs use request headers. The LU then passes the BIU to the path control element for that NAU.

The path control elements for NAUs prefix a Transmission Header (TH) to the BIU. This transmission header denotes a Path Information Unit (PIU). As its name implies, the PIU is used by the path control layer to route the message unit to the appropriate destination.

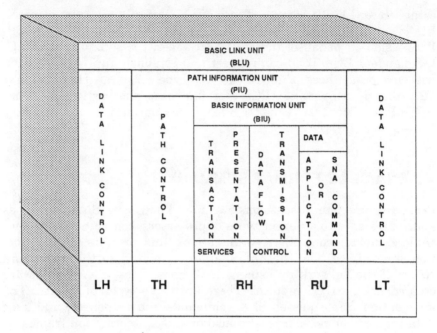

Figure 4.15 Message units and their relationship to the SNA layers.

Path control then passes the PIU to data link control for prepara-
tion to transmit the PIU. Data link control prefixes a Link Header
(LH) and appends a Link Trailer (LT) to the PIU before transmission. As is suggested from their names, the LH and LT contain information that concerns the functions of the data link layer of SNA.
The addition of LH and LT to the PIU makes up a SDLC frame, also
known as Basic Link Unit (BLU).

4.2.2 Link Header

The format of the link header can be seen in Figure 4.16. The link
header contains three fields. The first field, the flag, is always a hexadecimal value of 7E. This notifies the data link control element that
this is the start of a new SDLC frame.

The second field is the SDLC station address. This address can be
a specific station address or a group address. It can also reflect a
broadcast address. This broadcast address is always a hexadecimal
value of FF and is mostly used by link level protocol for NAU notifi-

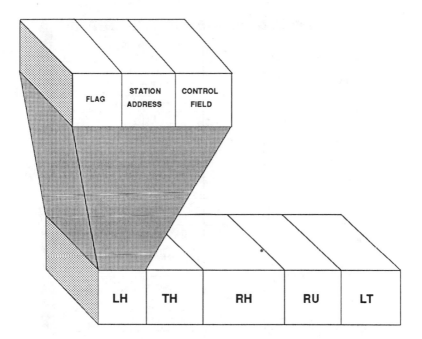

Figure 4.16 Format of the SDLC Link Header.

cations. One more address may be found in this field, a "no stations" address which is reserved and is a hexadecimal 00 value.

The third field of the link header is the control field. This field describes to the data link control elements the frame format being used. The frame format may be an unnumbered, supervisory, or information frame. The unnumbered frame dictates the SDLC link level command being issued. The supervisory frame denotes if the station is in the RR or the RNR state or if the previous frame transmitted is rejected. The information frame basically keeps track of the sequence frames sent and frames received. This is used for synchronization of BLUs.

4.2.3 Transmission Header

Because SNA supports different types of nodes in a network, the transmission header has five formats. These formats are identified by the first byte in the transmission header. It is the Format Identification Field, or FID. The FID type depends on the type of node

NODE TYPE	FID TYPE	TH LENGTH	USAGE
Non-SNA	0	10 bytes	Non-SNA traffic between adjacent subarea nodes not supporting explicit and virtual route protocols
PU5 PU4	1	10 bytes	SNA traffic between adjacent subareas not supporting explicit and virtual route protocols
PU5 PU4 PU2 PU2.1	2	6 bytes	SNA traffic between a subarea node and an adjacent peripheral node
PU4 PU1	3	2 bytes	SNA traffic between an NCP subarea node and a peripheral node type 1
PU5 PU4	4	26 bytes	SNA traffic between adjacent subarea nodes supporting explicit and virtual route protocols
PU5 PU4	F	26 bytes	Specific SNA commands between adjacent subarea nodes supporting explicit and virtual route protocols

Figure 4.17 Relationship of SNA PU node types to SDLC FID types.

involved with the transmission. If we look at Figure 4.17, we can see the relationship of FID type to the corresponding node type. We can also see that the length of the TH varies with the FID type. The evolution of SNA networks and the dominance of node Types 2 and 4 being used as the backbones of these networks has promoted the use of FID Types 2 and 4 in the majority of transmission formats.

It is important to remember that the purpose of the TH is for path control (Figure 4.18). In the TH we can find the origin address field, the destination address field, the sequence number of this PIU in relation to other PIUs for this request or response, the length of the RU, and whether it is the only, first, middle, or last in the transmission. For FID Type 4, explicit and virtual route information is found along with the originating subarea and element addresses and the destination subarea and element addresses. The FID Type 4 is also used to indicate if the PIU is from a non-SNA device (FID Type 0) by

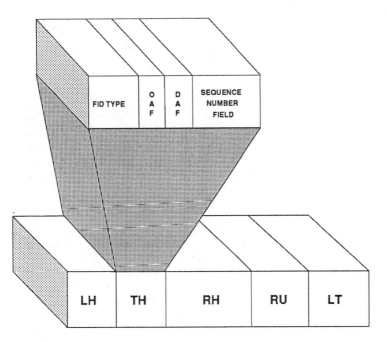

Figure 4.18 The common fields of transmission header FID types.

setting a bit in the transmission header. The diagram in Figure 4.19 depicts the flow of FID types through a network.

4.2.4 Request/Response Header

Following the transmission header is a 3-byte header that describes the actual information being transmitted (Figure 4.20). This header is called the Request/Response header (RH). The basis of the RH is to describe the data that follows. The header type is indicated by bit 0 of the header. If bit 0 equals a 0, the header is a request header; if it is a 1, it is a response header.

The request header provides information on the format of the data and the protocol that governs the session. It describes to the PU if a definite response is indicated for this transmission, if brackets are being used, where in the chain of data this BIU is positioned, and if a pacing request is indicated for this transmission.

The response header provides the appropriate information to the requester in regard to the requested protocol. The response header is chiefly responsible for returning a positive or negative response to

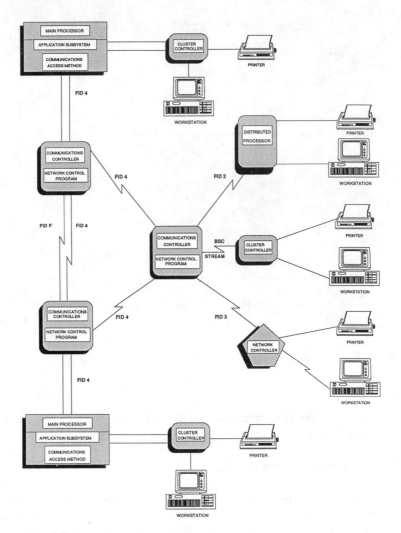

Figure 4.19 FID flows through the SNA network.

the requester. If a negative response is transmitted, a sense data indicator bit is set to 1, which indicates to the requester that sense data follows that explains the negative response to the request.

4.2.5 Request/Response Units

Request units follow request headers (Figure 4.21). These units are variable in length and may contain end-user data or an SNA com-

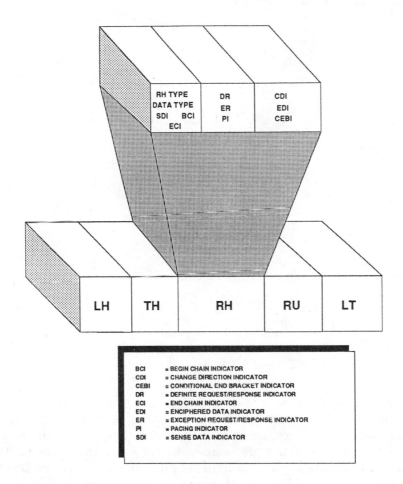

Figure 4.20 Request and Response Header fields.

mand. The data RUs contain the information that is to be exchanged between end users. The command RUs control the operation of the network by issuing appropriate SNA commands. Although the request unit is variable and in theory is infinite, the restriction of a 2-byte field in the TH, the Data Count Field (DCF), allows for a maximum RU size of 64K bytes. However, most logical units only support an RU size of 256 bytes. This is because the data link buffer in most PUs is only 256 bytes. The number 256 has been chosen as the prime size for a link buffer because of tests that were performed on telephone lines. These tests showed that 256 bytes can be transmitted with the lowest percentage of transmission error. The re-

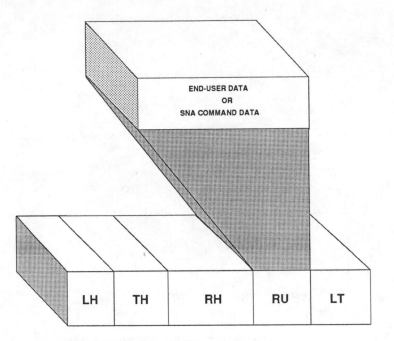

Figure 4.21 Request and Response Unit.

sponse unit in the case of a positive response to a data request unit is null; there is no response. However, in the case of an SNA command response, the response unit is generally 1 to 3 bytes in length. Negative response units are usually 4 to 7 bytes long. The first 4 bytes indicate the sense code data that describes the reason for the negative response. This could be protocol violation, transmission error, or a possible path outage. Three more bytes may be sent to identify the rejected request.

4.2.6 Link Trailer

The final field in the SDLC frame format is the Link Trailer (LT). The link trailer has two fields: the Frame Check Sequence (FCS) field and the link trailer flag as seen in Figure 4.22.

The FCS field is used to check the received frame for transmission errors. The transmitting link station executes an algorithm based on Cyclic Redundancy Checking (CRC). The data for the computation is inclusive of the link header address field through the RU. The receiving link station performs the similar computation and checks its re-

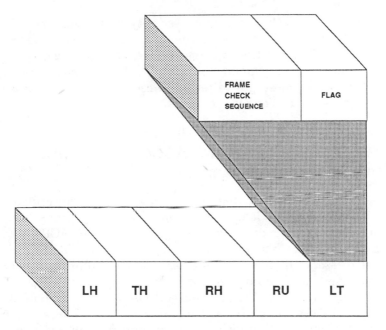

Figure 4.22 Link Trailer Format.

sults against the FCS field. If the results are not acceptable, a transmission error sense code is sent to the originating link station stating that retransmission is necessary.

The link trailer flag indicates to the receiving data link control element that the frame has ended and a new frame should be expected. The flag is also defined as a hexadecimal 7E.

4.3 BASIC TELECOMMUNICATIONS ACCESS METHODS

One of the first telecommunications access methods is Basic Telecommunications Access Method (BTAM). This provides the user with support for input operations from the end user. BTAM can be regarded as the basis for subsequent access methods. It provides routines to manage buffers, and detect and handle some transmission errors, switched line support, leased line support, and control of network resources. However, since BTAM's function is to control the lines to the end user, each line is dedicated to an application and, unlike workstations, cannot share the same line. The user is responsible for providing code to BTAM to perform queuing and routing of messages, any additional error analysis and recovery above that which BTAM supplies, and system security and integrity. The biggest drawback to BTAM is that the user must supply the control program. This includes keeping lines active, adding or removing line control characters, assembling blocks of data into completed messages, translating messages to terminal code, and editing messages. This is extensive and complex coding.

4.4 TELECOMMUNICATIONS ACCESS METHODS (TCAM)

TCAM is a queued access method. It has a high-level control program called Message Control Program (MCP). By using supplied TCAM macro instructions, the user can direct the MCP to queue messages received from or sent to remote terminals. TCAM can transfer messages from one remote terminal to another and between terminals and application programs. TCAM supports SDLC, BSC, and Asynch terminals. The advantage TCAM has over BTAM and VTAM is its message control and queuing abilities. These two functions greatly increase the user's security and data integrity by preventing loss of data. Most brokerage houses, banks, and institutions whose loss of data can cause a loss of millions of dollars, use TCAM's message control and queuing to the fullest extent. With TCAM came full control of network resources. In conjunction with TCAM is the IBM Network Control Program, which extends the access methods ability to control and maintain telecommunications lines. TCAM operates under an MVS or OS/VS1 operating system environment. It supports both SNA and non-SNA devices concurrently.

The most recent version of TCAM V3 has been stripped of access method responsibilities but has kept the message control and queuing capabilities intact. This version executes on a host processor as an application under VTAM.

4.5 VIRTUAL TELECOMMUNICATIONS ACCESS METHOD (VTAM)

VTAM is an access method that controls communications between logical units. It directly controls the transmission of data to and from channel-attached devices and uses the IBM Network Control Program (NCP) to forward and receive data from remotely attached devices over telecommunication links. Unlike TCAM, VTAM is not a queuing access method. Its main function is to route data to its desired destination. The VTAM user is concerned only with logical units. Non-SNA devices must be handled by an emulation program or a protocol converter of some type, be it hardware or software. The only exception to this is that VTAM does support 3270 BSC devices. An emulation program or protocol converter can be included in the NCP as a partitioned emulation program (PEP). We may also use IBM's Network Terminal Option (NTO) or Non-SNA Interconnect (NSI) in conjunction with the NCP. VTAM operates in MVS, OS/VS1, VM, and VSE operating system environment.

4.6 VTAM EXTENDED (VTAME)

VTAM extended operates only under a VSE operating system environment. It provides all the functions of VTAM plus the support for non-SNA devices, other than BSC 3270 terminals, attached by a loop adapter. VTAME also provides intermediate-node routing functions that versions of VTAM prior to VTAM version 2 did not provide.

4.7 SUMMARY

In this chapter we learned about various network components like nodes, subareas, links, and NAUs. Considerations for routing data such as explicit route, virtual route, and transmission group were discussed. Functions of various SNA layers and their relationship to the OSI model were considered. SNA sessions consist of four different types: SSCP-SSCP, SSCP-PU, SSCP-LU, and LU-LU. APPC/LU 6.2 forms the basis of distributed processing in an SNA environment. LEN provides for peer-to-peer sessions without the participation of SSCP. Finally we learned about various headers such as RH, TH, LH, and LT and different information unit formats such as BIU, PIU, and BLU. Now that we feel comfortable with SNA components, let's move on to the next chapter on communications protocols.

5

Communications Protocols

Protocols define a set of rules which two or more participating entities must follow for proper exchange of information among them. In a computing environment such protocols become more important because of the complexities of modern day networks. The protocols must ensure that the information is accurate and exchanged in an orderly fashion. In this chapter we will first discuss the link level protocols such as SDLC and BSC. Thereafter, we will talk about the session level protocols such as half duplex and full duplex.

5.1 LINK LEVEL PROTOCOLS

In wide area networks, most of the communications takes place over long distances. The physical media to carry information from one point to the other is provided by common carriers such as AT&T, MCI, Sprint, and local telephone companies. Such physical media could also be located in the same building or campus and may be owned by the enterprise itself. One of the inherent shortcomings of long-distance data communications is the erroneous information which could be transmitted to the receiving node. Such errors could be caused by communications equipment, electro-magnetic interference, weakening of signal, and many other reasons. The common carriers cannot totally eliminate such communications errors. It is the responsibility of the Data Terminal Equipment (DTE) to ensure that the transmitted and received data is the same. DTEs can be the communications controllers and cluster controllers.

The protocols which ensure *accurate and orderly* exchange of information between two or more DTEs are the link level protocols. Such protocols logically connect the Data Link Control layers (DLC) of SNA. The DLC layer is one level above the physical control layer. One such protocol that was developed in 1965 was Binary Synchronous Communications, or BSC for short. Although still in use, it is being rapidly replaced by a more advanced protocol, Synchronous Data Link Control (SDLC). SDLC was introduced in 1973 and is the recommended protocol for SNA networks.

5.1.1 DTEs and Link Level Protocols

When the DTEs are two communications controllers, the preferred link level protocol is SDLC. Since such devices exchange relatively large amounts of data, they need to exchange information simultaneously. Later in this chapter we will learn that such simultaneous exchange is called "full duplex" which is only supported by SDLC.

If one of the DTEs is a communications controller and the other one is a cluster controller, the protocol can be BSC or SDLC. The most widely used remote cluster controller is the IBM 3274-41C. Any cluster controller model having a suffix of *C* is a remote one. A remote cluster controller can be BSC or SDLC depending upon the microcode disk which is used to configure it. Examples of other remote cluster controllers are 3274-51C (8 ports) and 3274-61C (16 ports).

Remember that link level protocols ensure end-to-end data integrity between DTEs only. Although there are also DCEs (modems and DSU/CSUs) involved in the middle, they do not participate in such protocols. However, SDLC and BSC protocols do require synchronous modems. Asynchronous modems *cannot* be used for BSC or SDLC protocols and devices.

5.2 SYNCHRONOUS DATA LINK CONTROL (SDLC)

SDLC is the preferred link level protocol for SNA networks. Introduced in 1973, it is very widely used in the IBM networking environment. It is equivalent to a similar protocol developed by International Standards Organization (ISO) and adopted by many non-IBM vendors. ISO's link level protocol is called "High-Level Data Link Control" (HDLC).

SDLC protocol ensures that the DTEs exchange information accurately and in an orderly fashion. There are two entities involved in data transmission — the sender and the receiver. Communications controllers and the cluster controllers can both be senders and receivers in a data exchange.

5.2.1 Primary and Secondary Stations

In a point-to-point configuration, there is one primary and one secondary station. In a point-to-multipoint configuration, there is still one primary but many secondary stations (Figure 5.1).

a) Point-to-Point Configuration

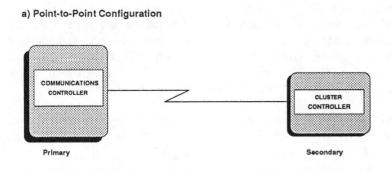

b) Point-to-Multipoint Configuration

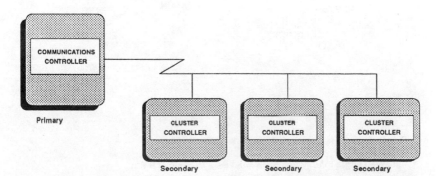

Figure 5.1 Primary and secondary stations in an SDLC environment.

In other words, there is one and only one primary station on an SDLC line. The primary station is aware of the transmission status of different secondary stations all the time. A primary station can send data to a secondary station at any time but the reverse is not true. A primary station has to *invite* the secondary station to send data.

In a point-to-multipoint environment, a primary station usually operates in full-duplex mode while the secondary stations operate in half-duplex mode.

5.2.2 SDLC Frames

DTE breaks down the transmission data into a number of small pieces of information. Each chunk of information is enclosed within transmission control fields before it is sent over the communications lines. Such a transmission unit is called an "SDLC frame." Figure 5.2 gives various fields constituting an SDLC frame. Let's look at the contents and functions of each field in the frame.

Flag Field.   There are two flags in an SDLC frame — at the beginning and at the end. Each flag is 8 bits (1 byte) in size and always

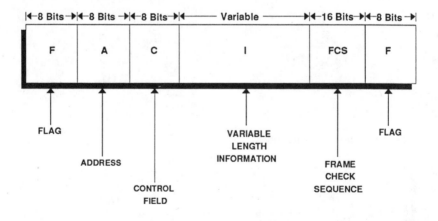

* Flag Is Always Hexadecimal 7E or Binary 01111110.

* Variable Length Information Field Must Be a Multiple of 8 Bits.

Figure 5.2 Format and contents of an SDLC frame.

contains a binary value of 01111110 or hexadecimal 7E. A set of six 1s following a binary 0 indicates an SDLC flag. Any data contained between the flag fields may not contain six consecutive 1s because that implies an end-of-frame status. Since in reality an information field may contain any combination of bits, a technique called "bit stuffing" is used to get around this problem. Bit stuffing is discussed later in this section.

Address Field. *This field always identifies the secondary station on a line.* When the primary station is inviting the secondary station (polling) to send data, it identifies the station being polled. When the secondary station is sending data to the primary station, it identifies the sender's own address. In a point-to-point configuration, this field may contain only one address because there is only one secondary station. In point-to-multipoint, it can identify up to 254 secondary station addresses. Although an 8-bit address can have 256 addresses, the remaining 2-bit configurations are used for different purposes as follows:

• All binary 0s are used for testing only.
• All binary 1s are used to send a broadcast message from the primary station to all secondary stations.

It is also worthwhile mentioning that the address hexadecimal FD is used by IBM modems. Therefore, if multiple cluster controllers are multidropped on a line, the logical limitation is 253 such devices.

Control Field. A control field is an 8-bit field which can have three different formats. Figure 5.3 gives contents for each format. Notice that the leading bit of the transmission has been shown in the extreme right position. The logic for determining what format the control field belongs to is as follows:

• If the leading bit is 0, it is an information format.
• If the leading bit is 1, it is a supervisory or unnumbered format. If the second bit is 0, it is a supervisory format; otherwise it is an unnumbered format.

The significance of each format is explained as follows:

• *The information format* shown in Figure 5.3a indicates that the frame contains application-specific data. The source of such data could be from VTAM applications such as CICS/VS, IMS/DC, TSO, VM/CMS, etc.

(a)

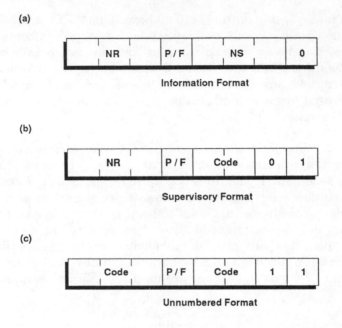

Information Format

(b)

Supervisory Format

(c)

Unnumbered Format

- NR = Number of Error Free Frames Received Since Last Acknowledgment
- NS = Number of Frames Sent Since Last Acknowledgment
- P = Poll Bit from Primary Source
- F = Final Frame Bit Sent by Secondary Station
- Code = Supervisory and Unnumbered Command Codes

Figure 5.3 Format and contents of the control field in an SDLC frame.

- *The supervisory format* shown in Figure 5.3b contains a 2-bit code field which can yield four different combinations. A value of 00 indicates that the station is ready to receive data (RR). A value of 01 means it is not ready to receive data (RNR). Finally, 10 indicates a reject (REJ) and requests retransmission of the frame.
- *The unnumbered format* shown in Figure 5.3c contains a 5-bit code field and can have up to 32 different values. So far, only 15 different commands have been devised and used. Readers are advised to refer to the appropriate IBM literature to get details about such commands.

Now let's talk about NR and NS. Simply put, NS indicates the number of frames sent and NR represents number of correct frames received. The primary and secondary stations exchange NR and NS values to know how many frames they have sent the other and what is the last correct frame received. The primary station maintains the NS value for each secondary station and keeps track of NR information coming from every secondary station based on the address field.

The 3-bit NR and NS field can contain a maximum value of 7. Therefore, in SDLC protocol the sending node (station) can send up to seven frames (NS = 7) before expecting a response for the first one. In contrast, the BSC protocols would not allow transmission of a second frame unless a response has been received regarding the first one.

There is another thing you should know. NR specifies the number of error-free frames received. *If a particular frame has had a transmission error, every frame following that number is retransmitted.* For example, if the second frame is found to be in error, all the frames from the second to the seventh will be retransmitted. This will be done even though all the frames after the second were transmitted without errors.

Because of the advent of high-speed communications links such as DDS lines and T1 lines, it was found that the maximum limitation of seven transmissions was inadequate. The satellite-based network further aggravated the problem with long transmission delays. With the release of NCP Version 3, you have a choice of keeping the limit to 7 or increasing it to 127. It is controlled by the MAXOUT parameter (MAXOUT = 127) during NCP generation. When the network is handling the capability of transmitting up to 127 unconfirmed frames, NS and NR values are contained in 7 bits each. Thus, the control field under those circumstances is a 16-bit field. This feature also permits the retransmission of a selected erroneous frame rather than having to retransmit all the frames following the frame in error.

Finally, let's talk about the P/F bit in the control field. When the frame is being transmitted from the primary to the secondary station, this bit means a poll. It indicates that the secondary station can send more data. When the frame is being transmitted from the secondary to the primary, it means the final frame. In other words, the secondary station indicates that it is the final frame and it has nothing more to send.

Information Field.   The information field is a variable-length field and contains application specific information. In most cases, this is the real data you intend to transmit. It is always a multiple of 8 bits. It is an optional field since control fields containing unnumbered commands do not transmit application data in the frames.

Frame Check Sequence (FCS). The FCS is a 16-bit field and is used to verify whether the data is error free or not. It contains the *Cyclic Redundancy Check (CRC)* value. The sending station computes the FCS and appends it as a 2-byte field after the information field. The receiving station uses the same formulas to calculate the CRC constant and compares it with the value it received. If they are identical, the data is correct. The fields used to calculate the CRC constant are address, control, and information.

5.2.3 Bit Stuffing

Bit stuffing is also referred to as "zero insertion." Since the presence of six 1s indicates a flag field, the presence of this bit combination can give a false indicator of the end of frame. To overcome this problem, bit stuffing is used to ensure that the address, control, information, and FCS fields do not contain contiguous six 1s anywhere. Figure 5.4 shows how this is done. Wherever the sending station detects five contiguous 1s in an SDLC frame, it inserts a 0 after it. This

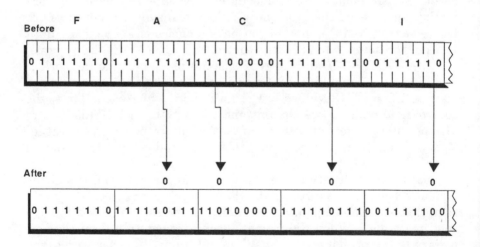

* Frame Size Before Bit Stuffing Is 40 Bits.

* Frame Size After Bit Stuffing Is 44 Bits.

Figure 5.4 An example of bit stuffing in an SDLC frame.

way, you will not see six contiguous 1s except in the flag fields. The receiving station takes out the single zero after it detects five 1s. Although bit stuffing increases transmission volume, it ensures data transparency for any bit combination. In general, bit stuffing adds about 5 percent overhead to the transmitted data.

5.2.4 Other Characteristics

SDLC is a full-duplex protocol. The primary and the secondary stations can send data to each other at the same time. Each station can send up to 7 (or 127) frames before waiting for an acknowledgment. Since SDLC is a bit oriented protocol, it is insensitive to code which may be ASCII or EBCDIC. The acknowledgment for the data is usually sent with the data itself, while in other protocols, such as BSC, it is a separate transmission. This feature of SDLC reduces unnecessary transmissions between the stations. In general, SDLC is a better protocol with more efficient transmissions and lesser amount of overhead.

5.3 BINARY SYNCHRONOUS COMMUNICATIONS (BSC)

BSC protocol, announced in the mid-sixties, is being rapidly replaced by the new and powerful SDLC protocol. We will give minimal coverage to this protocol because of its antiquity. The following are some of the highlights of its characteristics.

Batch Orientation.   When this protocol was designed, there were very few online applications. Most of the transmissions were batch oriented and involved the use of remote job entry stations. The terminals which used BSC for batch transmissions were IBM 2770, IBM 2780, and more recently the IBM 3780. Although these batch terminals are still in existence, the new RJE/RJP stations use SDLC protocols.

Propagation Delays.   While SDLC protocol is full duplex, BSC only supports half-duplex transmissions. The sending station must get an acknowledgment for the data it sent before sending another batch. Therefore, BSC is not suitable for those environments in which the physical transmission media can cause long propagation delays. An example of such media is satellite transmission.

Although BSC is a half-duplex protocol, it can be used over full-duplex channels. In the case of full duplex, synchronization is maintained in either direction at all times. This reduces the turnaround time and increases the transmission efficiency.

Point to Point versus Multipoint. As in the case of SDLC, BSC supports point-to-point as well as point-to-multipoint transmissions. Point-to-point transmissions can occur over leased as well as dial-up (switched) lines.

Error Checking. In the case of SDLC, the error checking is done by the Cyclic Redundancy Check (CRC). In BSC protocols, the same methodology is used if the data being transmitted is EBCDIC. If the data is ASCII, there are two techniques applied to do the error checking. Vertical Redundancy Check (VRC) is applied to check each ASCII character while Longitudinal Redundancy Check (LRC) is used to check the entire block.

Byte-oriented Protocol. While SDLC is a bit-level protocol, BSC deals at the byte level. In SDLC, all the control information, flags, and data fields are dealt with at the bit level. The bit stuffing takes into account only consecutive 1s irrespective of the fact that they may span over 2 bytes. In contrast, BSC deals with the transmission at the byte level. The control characters are all interpreted at the byte field only. Individual bits within the characters do not hold any special significance.

5.3.1 SDLC versus BSC

Figure 5.5 outlines the comparison between SDLC and BSC protocols. Most of the characteristics have already been discussed before in the previous sections. In SDLC protocols, an invitation from the primary station (polling) to the secondary station to send data is included in the control field of the frame. In BSC, it is a separate sequence with its separate transmission. Similarly, acknowledgment for the data is included in the SDLC frame itself and is represented by NR. Again, in BSC it is a separate sequence. In other words, SDLC protocol provides for performing multiple functions in the same transmission. In BSC, each transmission usually performs only one function.

The BSC protocol is ill-suited for physical transmission media having substantial propagation delays. Thus BSC is not recommended for satellite-transmission-based networks.

SDLC protocol guarantees textual transparency and deals with the occurrence of end-of-frame flags by using bit stuffing techniques. In BSC, you have an *option* to use the transparency feature with the

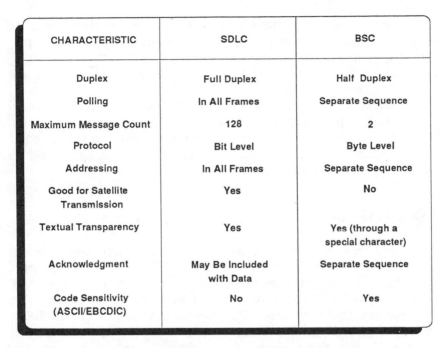

CHARACTERISTIC	SDLC	BSC
Duplex	Full Duplex	Half Duplex
Polling	In All Frames	Separate Sequence
Maximum Message Count	128	2
Protocol	Bit Level	Byte Level
Addressing	In All Frames	Separate Sequence
Good for Satellite Transmission	Yes	No
Textual Transparency	Yes	Yes (through a special character)
Acknowledgment	May Be Included with Data	Separate Sequence
Code Sensitivity (ASCII/EBCDIC)	No	Yes

Figure 5.5 Comparison between SDLC and BSC link level protocols.

use of a Data Link Escape (DLE) character before the occurrence of an End of Text (ETX) character within the text. In EBCDIC transmissions, ETX is a hexadecimal 03 while the DLE is a hexadecimal 10.

Since SDLC is a bit-level protocol, it is basically code insensitive. It does not care whether the information being transmitted is ASCII or EBCDIC. Since BSC is a byte level protocol, it is code sensitive. There is a different set of control characters for ASCII and EBCDIC transmissions.

SDLC protocols are the same irrespective of the type of device used. The only difference in an SDLC environment is whether the maximum message count value before acknowledgment is 127 or 7. In the first case there will be 2 control bytes while in the latter case there will be 1. In contrast, there are many types of BSC protocols. Two of the most popular BSC protocols are 2780 BSC and 3270 BSC. The first is oriented toward batch transmissions while the latter is designed for interactive communications.

5.4 ASYNCHRONOUS COMMUNICATIONS

Asynchronous communications was developed in the 1950s and is a primitive protocol compared to SDLC and BSC. It is still a very widely used mode of communications for the PC environment. Its widespread use can be attributed to the low-cost asynchronous modems that support this kind of communications. On the other hand, SDLC and BSC protocols require synchronous modems which are more expensive.

Another name for this protocol is start-stop communications. According to this protocol, only one character is transmitted at a time. In SDLC and BSC communications, a block of data is transmitted at a time. Even the error detection is done at the character level in asynchronous communications.

5.4.1 Data Stream

Figure 5.6 shows the bit structure of a single character transmission in asynchronous communications. The first bit is called the "start bit." The next 7 bits include the real data that is to be transmitted. Since each ASCII character set consists of 7 bits, each transmission can send one ASCII character. The eighth bit is used for error checking and is generally referred to as the parity bit. Parity can be odd or even. If the parity is even, all the binary 1s in the data and the parity bit must be an even number. If the parity is odd, the number must be odd. Since the communications software at either end can choose even or odd parity, you must ensure that both ends use the same parity. The last bit in the transmission is a stop bit.

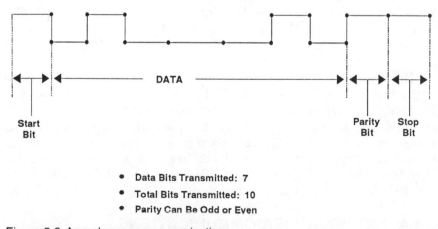

- Data Bits Transmitted: 7
- Total Bits Transmitted: 10
- Parity Can Be Odd or Even

Figure 5.6 Asynchronous communications.

5.4.2 Error Checking

The odd or even parity checking methodology employed by asynchronous communications does not ensure complete data integrity. If one of the 7 data bits in an ASCII character is altered, the parity bit can detect the error. If 2 bits are altered during transmission, it is not possible to detect the error. Two such scenarios are given as follows:

• If a binary 1 is altered to 0 and a binary 0 is changed to 1, parity will remain the same.
• If two binary 1s are both changed to 0s or two binary 0s are both changed to 1s, parity will still remain the same.

In either example, erroneous data will be transmitted, but the error detection procedures will not be able to detect it. For these reasons, asynchronous communications is not recommended for applications where data integrity is a must.

5.4.3 Performance

As shown in Figure 5.6, there are 3 bits of overhead for every 7 bits of data transmission. In other words, the superfluous data bits add approximately 43 percent more volume to the data. In SDLC protocols, there are about 6 bytes of overhead for each frame. If an average frame is 200 bytes, the overhead comes to approximately 3 percent. Add another 5 percent for bit stuffing and the total SDLC overhead comes to 8 percent. It is significantly lower than 43 percent, however. BSC protocols have an overhead which may be slightly more than that of SDLC.

5.4.4 Eight-bit ASCII Code

Seven-bit ASCII code allows for a maximum character set of 128. Some vendors use an extended ASCII character set in which 8 bits are used to represent each character. In such cases, it is not possible to use the eighth bit for error checking. Parity checking is turned off under these circumstances.

Asynchronous communications is generally used by devices which have no buffers. It is also used for reasons of economy because asynchronous modems are inexpensive. However, it is pertinent to add that some communications protocols use asynchronous modems but use better error checking techniques to ensure high data integrity. Some of these protocols are Xmodem, Kermit, and Crosstalk.

5.5. FULL DUPLEX AND HALF DUPLEX

There are two ways in which data can be transmitted between nodes. In the full-duplex mode, two nodes send and receive data at the same time. In half-duplex mode, only one node can transmit at one time. Only after one node is done with the transmission is the second node allowed to initiate a transmission back to it.

5.5.1 Transmission versus Application Data Flow

The terms "full duplex" and "half duplex" are generally misunderstood. When these terms are used by communications engineers, they are usually associated with the *transmission* media. Physical transmission between two devices can be half or full duplex. Such transmission is associated with the data communications equipment. When they are used by communications systems programmers, they refer to the data flow between applications. *One has nothing to do with the other*. While a physical transmission could be taking place in full-duplex mode, the applications could be communicating in half-duplex mode.

The term "duplex" for transmission flow is link based and refers to the data link control layer of SNA. This layer is the second layer of SNA as shown in Figure 4.7. It is controlled by the data link control protocols such as SDLC and BSC. The term "duplex" for flow control refers to the data flow control layer of SNA. This layer is the fifth layer of SNA as shown in Figure 4.7.

5.5.2 Full Duplex

Figure 5.7a illustrates a full-duplex environment. It represents data flow control between Logical Units (LUs). An example of an LU in this case is an LU6.2, which could be a CICS running as a VTAM application in a host. Such a CICS could be communicating with another CICS running in a different host. In this case either CICS could send a message at any time. Therefore both the participating LUs should be ready to receive and send data at any time. Usually, recovery in a full-duplex data flow control environment is more complex. This is because various LUs (CICS in our example) should be able to correlate the requests they send and the responses they get from multiple sources on an ongoing basis.

Data flow control between Network Control Programs (NCPs) running in different communications controllers is also full duplex. However, the transmission between the NCPs controlled by data link control could be half duplex. Notice the difference. In the first case it is the logical transmission of data between two entities and in the latter case it is the physical transmission of data between the same two entities.

5.5.3 Half Duplex

Figures 5.7b and 5.7c illustrate the concept of half duplex. Each of the LUs in a session take turns to be the sender and later on to be the receiver of data. But they cannot be both at the same time. This protocol is relatively less complex and ensures easy recovery.

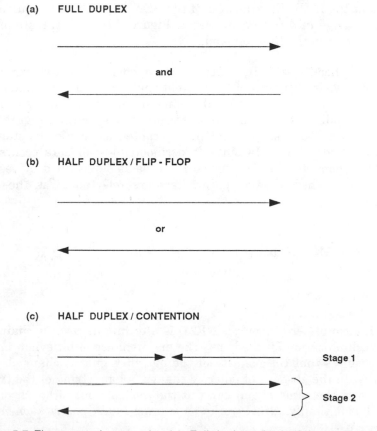

Figure 5.7 Flow control protocols. (a) Full-duplex; (b) half-duplex/flip-flop; (c) half-duplex/contention.

Data flow control between an intelligent LU (e.g., CICS) and a terminal LU (e.g., 3278) is half duplex. In this case it is an LU6.2 and an LU2 communicating with each other. Also, the link level communications between NCP and a single 3274 cluster controller is also half duplex. This is irrespective of whether you define it as full or half duplex. The only time you can take advantage of full-duplex communications in an NCP to cluster controller setup is when these are multiple 3274s on a line. As we already learned, such a setup is called "point-to-multipoint" configuration.

Flip-Flop Half Duplex. In a flip-flop mode of half duplex, the LUs take their turns in sequence. The sender of the message gives a change of direction indication to tell the receiver that it can send data now. When a session is established between two LUs, the BIND indicates who will initiate the first dialogue. For example, in the CICS environment the INVITE parameter of the SEND command is equivalent to the change in direction indicator. Figure 5.7b illustrates half-duplex protocol in the flip-flop mode.

Contention Half-Duplex. In a contention mode, either LU can send data at any time. If both of them do at the same time, it results in a contention. At the time of establishing the session, the session parameters indicate who will win in a contention situation. Figure 5.7c illustrates half-duplex protocol in the contention mode. In stage 1, the contention occurs. In stage 2, a smooth flow of data occurs depending upon who the first speaker will be as determined by session parameters. These session parameters are referred to as the bind image.

5.6 NRZI AND NRZ

5.6.1 NRZI

Non-Return-to-Zero-Inverted (NRZI) is a technique used to maintain bit synchronization for modems. The maintenance of bit synchronization requires that the polarity of the modem signal is changed periodically. In the absence of polarity change, a long string of the transmission of the same signal can put the modems out of synchronization. Put it simply, NRZI works as follows: *Invert polarity when you see a zero.*

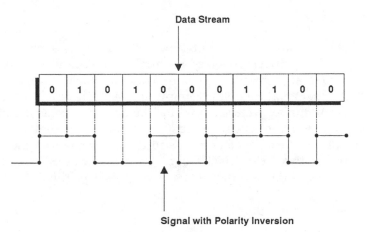

Data Stream

Signal with Polarity Inversion

Figure 5.8 An example of polarity inversion using NRZI.

Figure 5.8 illustrates the use of NRZI. Notice that every time a zero is encountered, the polarity is changed. Different combinations of 1s and 0s work as follows:

• If a 1 is followed by a 1, keep the same polarity.
• If a 1 is followed by a 0, change polarity.
• If a 0 is followed by a 0, change polarity.
• If a 0 is followed by a 1, keep the same polarity.

Basically, NRZI is used for those modems that do not provide timing. In other words, if the DCE (modem) cannot provide its own timing, the DTE (communications controller/cluster controller) must provide it. An example of such a modem is the IBM 3872. For those modems which do provide timing signals, NRZI need not be used. However, you must ensure that if NRZI is used on a single DCE on a data link, it must be used by all the DCEs on the same data link.

5.6.2 NRZ

Many people confuse NRZ with NRZI and think that it is a different kind of communications protocol. Remember that NRZ has nothing to do with data communications. NRZ is used for tapes.

5.7 SUMMARY

In this chapter we talked about link level protocols such as SDLC and BSC. SDLC, SNA's preferred protocol, is replacing BSC. We also learned about asynchronous communications which is very heavily used by the personal computer community. We discussed the full-duplex and half-duplex protocols used for the data link control and data flow control layers of SNA. It must be emphasized that one deals with the physical exchange of data and the other deals at the logical level between two LUs. NRZI technique was discussed; it provides timing signals in DTEs if they do not have this capability.

6

Communications Software — VTAM and NCP

Designing an SNA-based communications network requires various considerations of hardware, protocols, and software. We discussed hardware in Chapters 2 and 3. We also learned about various communications protocols in Chapter 5. In this chapter we will talk about the software products which are SNA compliant and therefore help in the implementation of an SNA network.

6.1 SNA SOFTWARE PRODUCTS

SNA software products can be divided into two broad categories:

- Base software for SNA networks
- Application software for end-user applications

The *base software* is the required software which helps in defining and implementing an SNA network. Examples of IBM's base software products are ACF/VTAM and ACF/NCP; we will call them VTAM and NCP. VTAM runs in the host computer and NCP runs in the communications controller. Examples of host processors that run VTAM are IBM 3084, 4381, and 3090. The communications controllers that run NCP are IBM 3705, 3720, 3725, and 3745. The base software does not perform any applications-specific function, but teleprocessing applications (e.g., CICS) need the services of such base software.

The *application software* for teleprocessing applications uses the services of base software to create an environment for end-user applications. Examples of such software are CICS/VS, IMS/DC, TSO, and VM/CMS. They provide the framework for creating real end-user applications such as accounts payable, airline reservation systems, etc.

Since different terms are used by various communications professionals for the same product, let's summarize them to avoid confusion. VTAM, the foundation of SNA software, runs in the host processor as an operating system (e.g., MVS) application. CICS runs in the host processor as a VTAM application. VTAM provides the necessary communication services to CICS to create a networking environment. The end-user applications run within the CICS address space and are the real business applications. VTAM/NCP systems programmers generally use the term "application" to refer to a CICS region or any other teleprocessing software which uses the services of VTAM. CICS systems programmers use the same term to refer to business applications running within the CICS address space. So be aware that these terms may have different meanings depending upon who is using them. Even the IBM manuals use them inconsistently.

Before getting into more details about various communications software, we need to understand the concept of Logical Units (LUs) and Physical Units (PUs). In the SNA world, various functions and responsibilities are assigned to the logical and physical units rather than to hardware and software. It is the characteristics of those LUs and PUs which are implemented in the software and hardware. But first of all let's see what these LUs and PUs really are.

6.2 PHYSICAL AND LOGICAL UNITS

6.2.1 Physical Unit

An SNA network is composed of various logical and physical units. A physical unit may be a physical device, but it does not have to be. As a matter of fact, a PU may be a combination of hardware, software, and microcode. A PU may use and handle many resources. In that respect it may be called a "resource manager." If we visualize a network as consisting of a collection of interconnected nodes, a PU is the operating system that runs in those nodes.

SNA defines various types of physical units. Figure 6.1 lists all the physical units that may comprise SNA nodes. Notice that VTAM running on an IBM (or compatible) host is a Physical Unit (PU) Type 5. NCP running in a 37X5 or 3720 communications controller is a PU Type 4. An SNA cluster controller is a PU Type 2. Be aware that PU Type 3 is not defined by SNA, at least not yet.

SNA-, VTAM- and NCP-related literature makes extensive use of the acronyms PU and LU. Getting used to their terminologies will make you feel more comfortable in the subsequent chapters.

6.2.2 Logical Unit

Logical units are the entities through which an end user can communicate with another end user. The end user does not have to be a human being. It can be a terminal, a piece of code, a printer, or another entity. As a matter of fact, the real purpose of an SNA network is to facilitate and manage interaction among various logical units. Physical units provide the means, but the logical units provide the end purpose of networking.

Figure 6.2 shows various LUs supported by SNA. Note that a logical unit is further split into two categories — Primary Logical Unit (PLU) and Secondary Logical Unit (SLU). When a session is established between two LUs, one of them is called a PLU and the other

NODE TYPES				
PU 1	PU 2	PU 2.1	PU 4	PU 5
3271	3174	S/36	NCP	VTAM
6670	3274	S/38	37X5	4300
3767	3276		3720	308X
	PC	PC		3090
	3770	TPF		
	AS/400	AS/400		

Figure 6.1 Physical units defined by SNA.

is called an SLU. A PLU is usually more intelligent than an SLU but not always. For example, if a CICS (LU6.2) is communicating with a 3278 terminal (LU2), the CICS is a PLU and 3278 is an SLU. It is also possible for two LUs to have the same processing intelligence. For example, a CICS (LU6.2) can communicate with another CICS (LU6.2). However, although both CICSs have the same rank, one has to be designated a PLU and the other an SLU at session establishment. Whether an LU will be primary or secondary is determined during the BIND process when a session is established between two LUs. PLU is usually responsible for recovery management in case of a session failure. In Figure 6.2, the logical units 0 through 7, as shown in the box on the top of each chart, represent the SLUs on the right-hand side of that chart. Products listed on the left side of the chart represent the PLUs that can establish session with the respective SLUs.

Now let's talk about some of the more popular LUs. A 3278 is an LU2. A printer attached to a cluster controller (PU T.2) can be LU1 or LU3. A CICS looks like LU6.1 or LU6.2. Notice that LU5 has not been defined by SNA — again, at least not yet.

6.3 VTAM

Virtual Telecommunications Access Method (VTAM) is the strategic and most versatile communications access method of IBM. It runs in the host processor in a separate address space. It is supported to run under various IBM mainframe-based operating systems such as MVS/SP, MVS/XA, MVS/ESA, DOS/VSE, VM, etc. Although the capabilities of VTAM may differ from one operating system support to another, the underlying characteristics remain the same. Various components of a network have to be identified and defined to VTAM. Such definitions are done through the use of VTAM macros. Part 3 of this book covers these definitions and macros in detail.

6.3.1 SNA and VTAM Services

SNA provides the architecture and protocols for a communications network. One of the SNA-defined network components called "System Services Control Point" (SSCP) provides the facilities to control the network. The most important objective of VTAM is to provide the services of SSCP. There is one and only one SSCP in each VTAM address space. In general, we can say that there is only one SSCP in

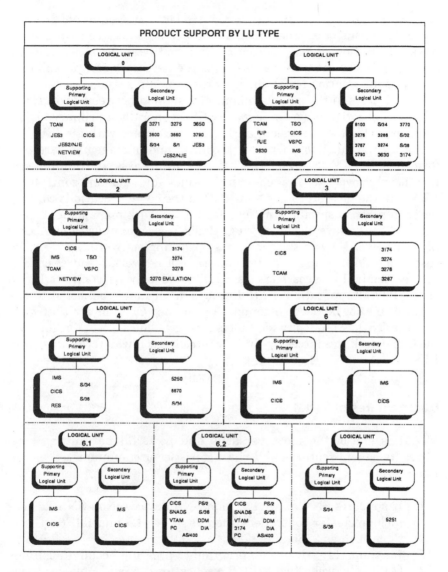

Figure 6.2 Logical units defined by SNA.

a host node. An SSCP looks like a Physical Unit Type 5 (PU T.5) in an SNA network.

A network may have multiple host processors and each of them may have its own VTAM. Therefore, a network in general has multiple SSCPs. VTAM provides the facility to communicate across SSCPs. For example, a terminal connected to a host via a cluster controller and a communications controller may communicate with the applications of another host. The other host may be in the same physical location or may be across the continent. In this case, the SSCP that owns the terminal provides the necessary control and connectivity information to establish a cross-domain session.

VTAM helps in the establishment of a session between two LUs. A VTAM application program (e.g., CICS) is generally a primary logical unit. In an LU-to-LU session, a PLU communicates with an SLU.

Not all the functions of network control and management are performed by VTAM. Some of the network awareness and intelligence has been moved to the communications and cluster controllers. VTAM in the host processor and NCP in the communications controller each perform specific functions for the network management.

In the early days of networking, Basic Telecommunications Access Methods (BTAM) was the popular networking software. As a predecessor of VTAM, it did *not* allow sharing of network resources. Each of the terminal devices such as 3278 could only be connected to a single BTAM application. In those days, a terminal connected to one CICS could not be used to connect to another CICS or for that matter to a TSO. VTAM provides for sharing of the network resources. Such network resources include controllers, lines, terminals, and LUs.

6.3.2 Features of VTAM

VTAM is one of the most versatile and powerful networking software. Its salient features and characteristics are summarized as follows:

1. It supports SNA as well as non-SNA devices. Non-SNA devices include cluster controllers such as 3274-41D and RJE/RJP stations such as 2780 and 3780.
2. It supports advanced program-to-program communications (APPC) between two LU 6.2 applications. APPC makes the two participating LUs look like peers.
3. VTAM provides for network operations control through a software product called "Network Communications Control Facility" (NCCF). NCCF is now a component of NetView.
4. It supports both channel-attached (local) and link-attached (remote) communications controllers. Examples of such controllers are 3270, 3725, and 3745.

5. It supports channel-attached (local) and link-attached (remote) cluster controllers. Examples of local cluster controllers are 3274-41A and 3274-41D while the remote cluster controllers are 3274-41C and 3274-61C.

6. It provides for sharing of network resources among applications. Such resources may be links, terminals, and other communications facilities.

7. Since version 2, VTAM supports cross-host (technically cross-domain) communications. Prior to version 2, the same facility was provided by an add-on called "Multi-System Networking Facility" (MSNF).

8. In general, VTAM is functionally compatible between DOS/VSE, MVS, and VM.

9. With some recent enhancements, it allows for dynamic network configuration and recovery.

10. Network changes and enhancements require minimal changes to the host applications.

11. Host applications are independent of the data link control protocol. Such a protocol may be SDLC or BSC.

12. VTAM architecture is based upon distribution of communications functions between host-based VTAM and communications-controller-based NCP. This results in optimum utilization of the communications controller and minimal dependence on more expensive host CPU cycles.

13. It supports a wide variety of communications requirements which include batch and interactive processing needs.

14. It allows for coexistence of other access methods such as Telecommunications Access Method (TCAM) in the same SNA network. It also provides for running TCAM version 3 under VTAM. This allows for using VTAM as an access method and TCAM as a message handler, thus using the best characteristics of both VTAM and TCAM.

6.3.3 VTAM Application Programs

A VTAM application program is a communications program that uses the services of VTAM macros to communicate and to use its services and facilities. Thus the application program can transfer data to and from other LUs such as LU 6.2 and LU2. All the complexities of network awareness and networking usage are hidden from the application. Thus most of the complexities of polling, scanning, pacing, and device-dependent characteristics are handled by

VTAM rather than the application itself. Some of the requirements and characteristics of VTAM applications are as follows:

1. A VTAM application runs in a host under the operating system. Even though the application uses the services of VTAM, both of them are subservient to the host operating system.
2. A VTAM application looks like an LU to VTAM.
3. The interface between the application and VTAM must be written in assembler language.
4. A VTAM application can communicate with other VTAM applications.
5. It uses macros to communicate with VTAM. As in the case of CICS, a command-level interface does not exist between an application and VTAM.

You do not have to write VTAM applications. As a matter of fact, the majority of the business community uses the VTAM applications already written by IBM and third party software companies. Such applications include CICS and IMS/DC. The user only writes the interaction with those VTAM applications to create business applications. In other words, the user writes application programs to run under a VTAM application (CICS or IMS/DC) and thus creates the business applications.

6.3.4 VTAM and Other Access Methods

Other telecommunications access methods used in the IBM mainframe environment are Basic Telecommunications Access Methods (BTAM) and Telecommunications Access Methods (TCAM). BTAM is gradually moving toward extinction. It communicates with a telecommunications control unit (TCU) (e.g., 270X), channel-attached, and communications-controller-attached (emulation mode) terminals. One of the major drawbacks of BTAM is that it does not provide for sharing of network resources. For example, a terminal (e.g., IBM 3278) connected to an application (e.g., CICS) can only have a session with that application. It *cannot* log off and connect to another application (e.g., TSO). The BTAM application has exclusive control of the terminal.

TCAM, although being used less often, is still an access method of choice for environments with very large terminal networks. Pooled TCAM allows for control of very large terminal networks without having to define every terminal in the CICS Terminal Control Table

(TCT). This saves considerable amounts of virtual storage in a system. VTAM does not provide for any such comparable feature. TCAM version 3 runs as a VTAM application program, thus using the features of VTAM as a superior access method. At the same time, it retains the features of TCAM as a message handling subsystem for which there is no VTAM equivalent. Thus it provides the best of both access methods for large terminal network installations.

TCAM, VTAM, and BTAM can run and operate concurrently in an MVS system.

6.3.5 Diagnostic and Recovery Aids

In conjunction with the operating system, VTAM provides a number of diagnostic and recovery aids. They are briefly described as follows:

Diagnostic Aids.

Trace Facility. Provides trace information on flow control, buffer contents, transmission group (TG), SDLC line, I/O activity, storage management services, and many other facilities. Under MVS, trace data is collected using Generalized Trace Facility (GTF). It can be printed using the Trace Analysis Program (TAP) or print dump (PRDMP) utility. In DOS/VSE environment, trace records are collected in a trace file. They can be printed using TAP or VTAM trace print utility.

TOLTEP. The Teleprocessing Online Test Executive Program (TOLTEP) provides for online testing of communication devices. These tests are conducted while such equipment is performing normal operations. TOLTEP is not supported for releases subsequent to VTAM 2.1.

Formatted Dumps (MVS only). Available through the services of MVS operating system. ABDUMP is provided by the ABEND or SNAP macro. Such dumps can be formatted using the VTAM formatted-dump program. This program prints VTAM control blocks and also provides information on broken control block chains or invalid addresses. SDUMP is provided if an error occurs during the processing of a VTAM request. However, SYS1.DUMP must exist beforehand. MVS provides for a service aid AMDSADMP to dump the contents of main storage to a printer or a tape. This dump, called the "Service-Aid Dump," does not produce formatted control blocks.

NCP Dump. The contents of the NCP can be dumped at the operator's request or automatically if an NCP failure is detected.

In addition VTAM provides other diagnostic aids such as hardware error recording, SDLC link test, printing error records using error recording edit and print (EREP) program, route verification, and LU connection test. More on this is in *Advanced SNA Networking*.

Recovery Aids. Recovery aids facilities provide for restart of a communications controller and network configuration establishment. They try to restore a domain as soon as a failure is detected. This can be done automatically or can be at the operator's intervention. In addition, multiple SDLC links, called a "Transmission Group" (TG), can operate concurrently between communications controllers. Failure of one or more links in a TG does not interrupt the data flow because the data traffic is diverted to other links.

6.4 NCP

The Network Control Program (NCP) is the operating system of the communications controller. It supports various host environments such as MVS/SP, MVS/XA, MVS/ESA, DOS/VSE, VM, etc. The NCP is generated on the host system and then loaded in the communication controller from the host NCP load libraries. Various parameters specified to generate NCP fall in the following two categories:

• NCP-only parameters
• NCP- and VTAM-specific parameters

Such parameters are discussed in detail in Part 4 of this book. Just as the SSCP component of VTAM looks like a PU Type 5 in SNA networks, an NCP looks like a PU Type 4.

6.4.1 Functions of NCP

One of the major functions of NCP is to off-load some of the communications related routine tasks from the host and run them on a dedicated processor such as a communications controller. NCP interacts with the host access method such as VTAM or TCAM. It controls the cluster controllers (e.g., 3174) and terminal nodes attached to its various ports. It routes data to adjacent NCPs running on other communications controllers if the destination LU is not within its own subarea. It does the polling for stations and dialing and answering for switched lines. It maintains records of errors occurring in the links, NCP, and the controller itself. It allocates buffers for the data coming from and going to the host and other stations.

6.5 RELATED SOFTWARE

VTAM and NCP alone are not enough to perform all the functions required for network support, operations, and management. IBM supports a host of related software to support various functions.

6.5.1 NTO

The Network Terminal Option (NTO) supports certain non-SNA terminals in an SNA network. It supports start and stop terminals such as IBM 2741 and IBM 3767. NTO translates SNA session protocols and commands into a format which can be interpreted and used by such terminals. It runs in the communications controller along with NCP.

6.5.2 NPSI

The NCP Packet Switching Interface (NPSI) is a program that runs in the communications controller with NCP. It provides interface to the networks that conform to the X.25 standard. Examples of packet switching networks in the United States are Telenet and Tymnet; in Canada such services are provided by Datapac. NPSI allows application programs (e.g., CICS) and link-attached devices (e.g., IBM PC) to have sessions over an X.25 packet switching network.

6.5.3 EP/PEP

As Emulation Program (EP) runs in a communications controller and provides functional capabilities of the transmission control units (TCUs). Examples of TCUs are 2701, 2702, and 2703. They were the predecessors of communications controllers. EP runs as a separate entity and has no interaction with NCP. In order to run EP and NCP in different partitions as two mutually exclusive programs, you need the services of Partitioned Emulation Program (PEP).

6.5.4 NPM

Network Performance Monitor (NPM) helps in managing the growth and performance of a network. It provides for analysis of historical, as well as real-time data. It dynamically updates network data and identifies network bottlenecks. It comes in handy as a tool for capacity planning. NPM has now been brought under the NetView umbrella and is called NetView Performance Monitor.

6.5.5 SSP

System Support Program (SSP) consists of utilities and support programs that help in the generation, load, and dump of NCP. It runs in the host. It consists of a Configuration Report Program (CRP), NCP/EP Definition Facility (NDF), dump utility, Trace Analysis Program (TAP), loader utility, and Configuration Control Program (CCP).

6.5.6 NetView

NetView is a program that helps perform operator, information, and hardware problem analysis functions. Previously, the same functions were provided by a set of different products such as NCCF, NPDA, NLDM, and others. NetView is discussed in detail in *Advanced SNA Networking*.

NCCF. The Network Communications Control Facility (NCCF) component is a VTAM application program such as CICS or IMS/DC. It provides a set of services for the network operators and other network management programs such as NPDA and NLDM. An operator may execute VTAM commands, receive network messages, and perform network-related functions from the NCCF terminal. In a nutshell, NCCF provides a window to the network. Under NetView NCCF is called the Command Facility.

NPDA. The Network Problem Determination Aid (NPDA) is used to collect and display error data about different communications components. It collects data and error counts on communications controllers, SDLC lines, BSC lines, modems, cluster controllers, terminals, and start and stop lines. It works in conjunction with the NCCF component of NetView. It also provides suggested operator action for each error occurrence. NPDA is called the Hardware Monitor under NetView.

NLDM. The Network Logical Data Manager (NLDM) collects data pertaining to SNA sessions. While NCCF runs as a VTAM application, NLDM runs as a program under NCCF. The collected session data may be stored in the disk files for subsequent analysis. NLDM can collect data for single-domain as well as multiple-domain networks. Data collected by NLDM can be displayed on the NCCF terminal. NetView has incorporated NLDM and it is now called the Session Monitor.

6.6 VTAM APPLICATIONS

The end purpose of communications networks and networking software and hardware is to support applications and end users. VTAM supports a number of applications such as CICS, IMS/DC, JES2/JES3, and TSO. All such communications subsystems are VTAM applications.

6.6.1 CICS

The Customer Information Control System (CICS) is a general-purpose teleprocessing monitor and database/data communications system. It supports a wide range of terminals and SNA logical units. It supports database management systems such as IMS/DB, DOS DLI, DB2, and SQL/DS and access methods such as VSAM and BDAM. Business-related end-user applications can be created using high-level languages such as COBOL and PL/1. CICS is supported under MVS, DOS/VSE, and VM.

6.6.2 IMS/DC

Information Management System/Data Communications (IMS/DC) is a transaction-oriented teleprocessing monitor. It supports database management systems such as IMS/DB and DB2. IMS/DC runs only under MVS and is not supported by DOS/VSE and VM. It also supports a wide range of terminal devices. User applications can be written in high-level languages such as COBOL and PL/1.

6.6.3 TSO

Time Sharing Option (TSO) is an MVS-only subsystem and primarily gives programming personnel a general-purpose time-sharing capability. It supports SNA and non-SNA terminals. Although some computer installations use TSO as a production-oriented subsystem, it is better to use it only in an application development environment. Unlike CICS, each TSO user is a separate address space under MVS.

6.6.4 JES2/JES3

Job Entry Subsystems (JES) provide various operating system controls, batch processing facilities, and spooling capabilities for print devices and card readers. JES2/JES3 also provide Remote Job Entry (RJE) facilities where a remote workstation such as an IBM 3777 or an IBM 3780 can be used for submitting jobs and printing reports, as well as for remote console operations. JES2 is generally used in a single-host environment. JES3 can perform job scheduling for up to eight channel-attached MVS hosts.

6.7 SUMMARY

In this chapter, we discussed various communications software to support SNA networks. VTAM running in the host and NCP running in the communications controller provide the basis for SNA networking. TCAM and BTAM are other communications access methods. Some of the sundry but specialized functions are performed by software such as NTO, NPSI, EP/PEP, and NPM. Network control and management is supported by NetView, an IBM product previously consisting of software such as NCCF, NPDA, NLDM, and others. SSP provides the basis for generating, loading, and dumping NCP. Various VTAM applications such as CICS, IMS/DC, and TSO provide the platform for end-user application development. JES2 and JES3 perform the essential function of spooling, job scheduling, and management and support for RJE/RJP stations.

Now that we have laid the foundation by learning about SNA hardware, software, protocols, telecommunications, and SNA layers, we are ready to learn about SNA networks. This chapter completes Part 1 of this book. In Part 2, we will concentrate on SNA domains, and networks and on defining network topography.

SNA Networks

7

SNA Domains and Networks

In SNA there are four basic networking environments that use the various components of SNA. The simplest of these is the single-domain network. A more complex configuration is created when several single-domain networks are combined into one. This type of network is called a "multiple-domain" network. Within the multiple-domain network the Job Entry Subsystems (JES) can have their own networking facility to direct job output and job execution. Both the single- and multiple-domain networks can participate in a multinetwork configuration using SNA Network Interconnection.

7.1 DOMAINS

Under SNA there are single and multiple domains. A domain can be defined as the SNA resources that are controlled by an SSCP. This ability to control the resources is accomplished by the SSCP issuing an activate and/or deactivate request to the resource. These resources include the application programs, communications control units, lines, cluster controllers, terminals, and printers; in essence, the access method SSCP, PUs, LUs, links, and link stations. Once a resource issues a positive response to an activate request by an SSCP, that resource is owned and controlled by that SSCP only. However, a PU Type 4 can be shared by up to eight SSCPs, but the PU Type 4 peripheral resources can have only one SSCP controlling it.

7.1.1 Single Domain

The single-domain network consists of one SSCP and all the SNA resources in this network. Theoretically, a single-domain network can have 255 subareas (65,535 subareas with VTAM 3.2 and NCP V4.3.1/V5.2.1), of which 254 can be PU Type 4 subarea nodes that contain the Network Control Program (NCP). However, reality will dictate the actual number of PU Type 4 subareas controlled by this SSCP. Since there is only one SSCP in a single-domain network, all the resources defined in VTAM resource definition list (VTAMLST) are owned and controlled by this SSCP. Figure 7.1 is an example of a single-domain network with three PU Type 4 subarea nodes. Note that each subarea node has two SDLC links between each adjacent subarea node. These links are associated with routes that are defined in VTAM and NCP. The routes detail the possible paths that can be taken during session establishment. Chapters 11 and 15 contain more information on defining routes and paths to VTAM and NCP.

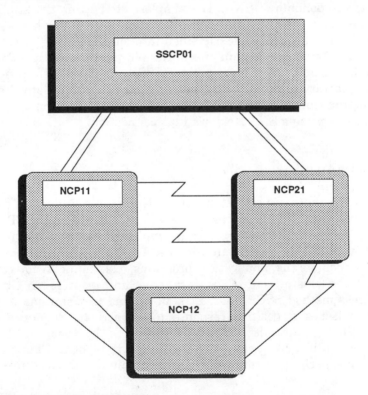

Figure 7.1 A single-domain network.

7.1.2 Multiple Domain

A configuration that consists of one or more SSCPs is considered to be a multiple-domain network when resources of one SSCP can communicate with resources of another SSCP via LU-LU sessions or when an NCP is being shared among SSCPs.

Figure 7.2 illustrates a simple multidomain environment between two SSCPs. In Figure 7.1, SSCP01 owns and controls NCP11, NCP21, and NCP12. In Figure 7.2, SSCP02 also activates these NCPs. NCP12 is channel attached and NCP11 and NCP21 are remotely activated by SSCP02. All three NCPs are shared by SSCP01 and SSCP02. Both SSCPs have the same NCP major node defined in their respective VTAMLST. However, the ISTATUS operand of the resource definition statements in the NCPs may be defined differently to designate the controlling SSCP.

The NCP resources determine their ownership by responding to the first activate request received. Hence, by defining the ISTATUS operand conversely to the opposing SSCP, the individual domains can be obtained. Another option to this is the use of the OWNER operand. *Advanced SNA Networking* contains a discussion on using the ISTATUS and OWNER operands in NCP.

7.2 MULTI-SYSTEM NETWORKING

To take full advantage of a multiple-domain network you must implement the Multi-System Networking Facility (MSNF) of VTAM. This facility was incorporated into VTAM with VTAM V2 but can still be purchased as a separate product for VTAM V1 and TCAM. This facility provides the mechanism for cross-domain communications between SSCPs and LUs.

7.2.1 Cross-Domain Resource Manager

In order for an SSCP to control initiate and termination requests for resources out of its domain, a Cross-Domain Resource Manager (CDRM) function is provided. The CDRM communicates with CDRMs of other SSCPs in a multiple-domain network. The CDRM is defined to VTAM in a major node of VTAMLST by the CDRM definition statement. When a resource of this CDRM requests a session with a target resource of another CDRM, the CDRM sends a cross-domain initiate request to the target resource CDRM on behalf of the

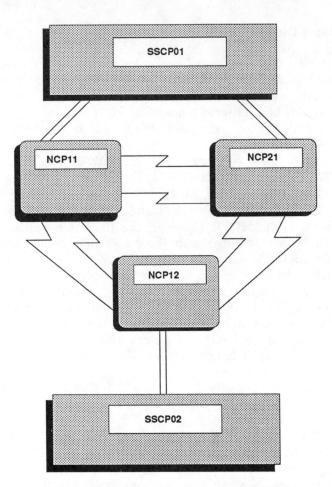

Figure 7.2 A multidomain network.

originating resource and likewise for termination. The CDRMs communicate over an SSCP-SSCP session.

7.2.2 Cross-Domain Resources

The resources owned by CDRMs can be explicitly or dynamically defined to other CDRMs. These resources are known as Cross-Domain
Resources (CDRSC). A CDRM knows a cross-domain resource by its
network name and associated CDRM. In large multidomain networks
it is best to use dynamic definitions for the CDRSCs. This simplifies

synchronizing network updates and naming convention modifications. For cross-domain acquires, however, the resource to be acquired must be explicitly defined to the CDRM. To define cross-domain resources to VTAM the CDRSC definition statement is used in a CDRSC major node in VTAMLST.

7.2.3 Cross-Domain Sessions

There are two types of cross-domain sessions, SSCP-SSCP and LU-LU. The SSCP-SSCP sessions are established by the CDRMs of the respective VTAMs when the CDRM major node that defines another PU Type 5 subarea CDRM is activated. VTAM knows that a CDRM major node being activated is not the CDRM for this domain because the SUBAREA operand value found on the CDRM definition statement does not match the subarea number specified in VTAMLST for this VTAM. A cross-domain LU-LU session is established when an LU of one domain requests a session with a resource that this VTAM does not recognize. At this point the SSCP calls upon the CDRM function to locate the owning CDRM of the target resource to satisfy the session request.

7.3 SNA NETWORK INTERCONNECTION

The accelerated growth of SNA networks in the late 1970s and early 1980s prompted the need to connect two or more totally independent networks. Multiple-domain SNA networks were quickly reaching their subarea address limits but needed to expand to provide access for a growing number of users. SNA Network Interconnection (SNI), incorporated into VTAM V2R2, provides the capability to have two or more independent SNA networks communicate with each other. Each gateway NCP can support up to 255 interconnections.

SNI should be considered when your network (1) has reached its limits for providing adequate service to end users, (2) does not implement Extended Network Addressing (ENA) and the number of subareas has drastically reduced the number of elements per subarea, (3) you want to combine ENA functionality with releases of VTAM and NCP that do not support ENA, and (4) a need has arisen to connect two or more independent SNA networks (e.g., corporate mergers). Figure 7.3 lists SNI functionality with releases of VTAM and NCP.

	MVS	VM	NOTES FOR BACK-LEVEL
VTAM V3	ALL	R1.1	
VTAM V2R2	ALL	N/A	
NCP V3	ALL	N/A	
NCP V4/V5	ALL	R2	
NCP V1R2.1			Not supported by VTAM V2R2 or higher. Must be owned by VTAM V2R1 or lower.
NCP V1R3			Must be supported by VTAM V2R2 or lower.
NCP V2			Back-level NCP does not support SNI but supports all VTAMs.
TCAM V2R4			Needs MSNF for SNI support.
VTAM V1R3			Same as NCP V1R3 and TCAM V2R4. Needs a PTF for autologon with VTAM V3, V2R2 resources.
VTAM V2R1			Needs a PTF for autologon with VTAM V3, V2R2 resources.
NCP V4 SUBSET			No SNI support.

Figure 7.3 SNI functionality of VTAM and NCP.

7.3.1 Single Gateway

SNI provides access to other SNA networks through gateways. A single-gateway configuration comprises a gateway SSCP and a gateway NCP. This configuration is also sometimes known as a "simple" gateway. The gateway VTAM must have the following start options defined in order for it to be a gateway VTAM: SSCPID, SSCPNAME, NETID, and GWSSCP. The presence of these four options denotes that a VTAM is at least gateway capable. A gateway NCP is defined by the following NCP definition statements: GWNAU and NETWORK.

In Figure 7.4 a simple gateway is configured. NETA01 is the sole gateway SSCP. As a gateway-SSCP, VTAM can initiate, terminate, take down, and provide session outage notification for cross-network sessions. The gateway SSCP provides network name translation and assists the gateway NCP in assigning alias network addresses for cross-network resources. Note that the box depicting the gateway NCP has two labels. When NETA01 resources communicate with NETB01 resources, they are actually addressing that function of the NCP that is acting as the gateway (GW-NCP11). Likewise, when NETB01 resources communicate with NETA01 resources, they address the GW-NCP11 function of the NCP. This gateway function of the NCP acts like a pseudo-CDRM.

7.3.2 Multiple Gateway

Several gateways can be configured to connect the same two independent SNA networks for cross-network sessions. In Figure 7.5 we see that NCP21 is also a gateway NCP. The rationale for defining NCP21 as a gateway NCP in this scenario is two-fold: (1) backup and recovery for the gateway NCPs can easily be implemented and executed and (2) distribution of the cross-network session flows and volume. Networks are considered adjacent networks when the session path flows through only one gateway NCP. These networks are said to be nonadjacent when the session flow is through multiple gateway NCPs.

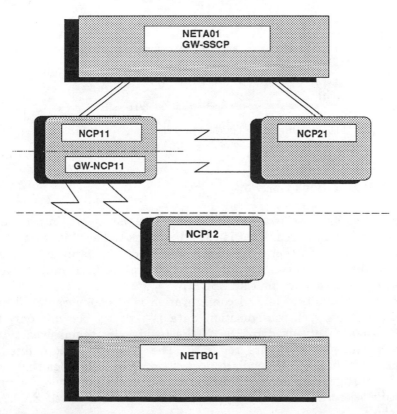

Figure 7.4 Single-gateway configuration.

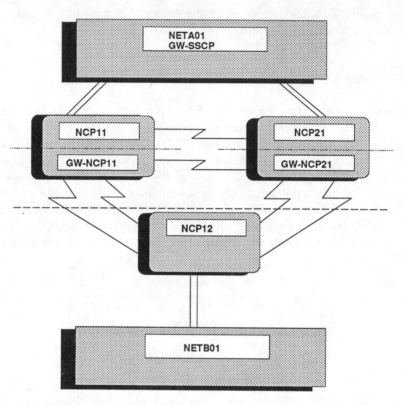

Figure 7.5 Multiple-gateway configuration.

7.3.3 Back-to-Back Gateway

When two or more gateway NCPs are connected, an intermediate network is configured. This is called a "back-to-back" gateway (Figure 7.6). In NETX there is no SSCP involved. The gateway functions of the three NCPs can actually be considered to be a null network; that is, a network without an SSCP.

Actually, this type of SNI configuration is most favorable. The exchange of network configuration data is reduced because only the subarea numbers used by the NCPs to identify themselves to the intermediate network are required. The numbers that define the routes within the intermediate network are the only ones that need to be changed. All other routes can remain in effect. For a more detailed description and analysis of SNI consult *Advanced SNA Networking*.

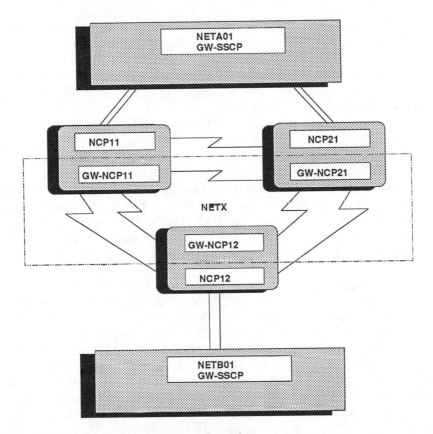

Figure 7.6 Back-to-back gateway configuration.

7.4 EXTENDED NETWORKING

Although SNI supplied an answer to growing network resource requirements, it is not the solution for every network. For some networks the task of migrating to SNI may be too disruptive for normal operations to exist. To allow growth in these types of networks, Extended Network Addressing (ENA) was introduced with VTAM V3 and NCP V4. ENA provides an effective means for network resource growth on the existing network configuration.

With ENA the network addressing scheme allows from 1 to 255 subarea nodes, each subarea with a maximum of 32,768 Network Addressable Units (NAUs) also known as "network elements." Before ENA, the network address was 16 bits long. The subarea-element split varied according to the MAXSUBA value specified in the VTAM start options. For instance, if the MAXSUBA value is set to 63, the maximum number of elements addressed in any subarea in this network is reduced to 1023. This is because the subarea-element split allows for 6 bits for the subarea number and 10 bits for the element addresses. In ENA the network addressing scheme provides 23 bits for the network addresses. The subarea field is always 8 bits and the element address field is always 15 bits.

In the most recent releases of VTAM and NCP this network addressing scheme has been expanded to a maximum of 65,535 subarea nodes. Each subarea node can have a maximum of 32,768 elements. In VTAM V3.2, NCP V4.3.1, and NCP V5.2.1 the 23-bit network address has been expanded to 31-bit addressing. This allows for 16-bit addressing used for the subarea address and 15-bit addressing used for the element address. VTAM V3.2, at the time of this writing, needs a Program Temporary Fix (PTF) to accommodate this new addressing scheme. Figure 7.7 illustrates the various SNA addressing schemes.

Not all levels of VTAM and NCP can participate in an ENA network. Releases of VTAM prior to VTAM V3 and NCP V4 cannot have full participation in an ENA network. A PTF must be installed on VTAM V2s and NCP V3s to allow ENA participation. If these pre-ENA nodes communicate with ENA nodes in the same network, the ENA nodes must specify the MAXSUBA values in the VTAM and NCP. This MAXSUBA value must match the value specified for the back-level VTAM and NCPs that reside in the same network as the ENA nodes. Although MAXSUBA is not required for ENA, it is required when ENA nodes communicate to pre-ENA nodes. The ENA nodes need this information to translate the pre-ENA 16-bit addresses when communicating with pre-ENA nodes.

Problems do occur when ENA node elements try to access pre-ENA nodes. If an ENA element address exceeds the maximum element address for a pre-ENA node, the ENA element cannot establish a session with any pre-ENA element. These restrictions can be overcome by implementing SNI to separate the network into back-level nodes and ENA nodes.

7.5 LEN AND APPC/LU6.2 NETWORKS

Low Entry Networking (LEN) is an advanced SNA network that allows connection of any resource of any network to participate in an LU-LU session through an SNA network using APPC/LU6.2 session protocols. Figure 7.8 details a sample LEN network configuration.

Pre-VTAM V3 and NCP V4 (NON-ENA)

# of Subareas	Max. # of Elements/Subarea
3	16,384
7	8,192
15	4,096
31	2,048
63	1,024
127	512
255	256

VTAM V3 and NCP V4 ENA

# of Subareas	Max. # of Elements/Subarea
3	32,768
7	32,768
15	32,768
31	32,768
63	32,768
127	32,768
255	32,768

VTAM V3.2 and NCP V4.3.1/V5.2.1 ENA

# of Subareas	Max. # of Elements/Subarea
65,535	32,768

Figure 7.7 Non-ENA and ENA element tables' effect on MAXSUBA operand.

The implementation of LEN requires VTAM V3.2, announced June 1987, and NCP V4.3 for an IBM 3725 communications controller and NCP V5.2 for the IBM 3720 or IBM 3745 communications controllers. VTAM V3.2 incorporated APPC/LU6.2 basic functions. This allows for LU6.2 applications under VTAM to take full advantage of the APPC protocols. This release also includes the Boundary Function (BF) SNA request and response commands from NCP for establishing and tearing down peer-to-peer sessions through the network. NCP V4.3 and V5.2 provide the PU Type 2.1 boundary function necessary to allow peer-to-peer sessions through the SNA backbone net-

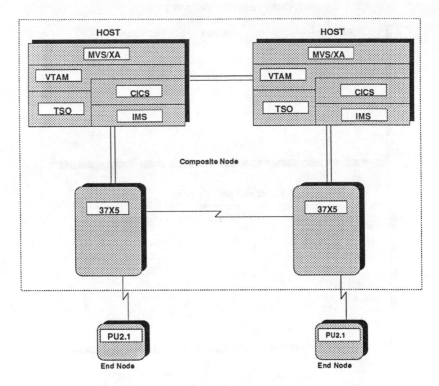

Figure 7.8 Low Entry Network configuration.

work. The VTAM V3.2 and NCP V4.3 or V5.2 are seen from the End Node T2.1 (EN T2.1) as a Composite Node Type 2.1 (CN T2.1).

7.6 SUMMARY

In this chapter we discussed SNA domains and networks. SNA provides for establishing a single-domain or a multiple-domain network. In order to have cross-domain sessions, the MSNF must be implemented. CDRM plays a major role in having cross-domain sessions. SNI provides connectivity between two or more separate SNA networks. We discussed single-gateway, multiple-gateway, and back-to-back gateway possibilities in SNI. Finally, we briefly talked about LEN and APPC/LU 6.2. Now that we are familiar with the concept of domains and networks, it is time to learn about defining network topography in the next chapter.

8

Defining Network Topography

The task of designing a viable and useful communications network is not easy. There are many factors that will dictate and direct the topography of a network. These factors should be identified by the communications systems programmer and the network designer. It is their responsibility to translate management's business needs, objectives, and requirements for end-user access to the network. This could mean restricting end-user access to specific applications or entire domains or restricting access to all applications in all domains of the network. Evaluation and documentation of the current network should be performed. How large is the network? Does management anticipate steady or rapid growth? Is the communications control unit storage size adequate for current and future needs?

Figure 8.1 outlines the major issues of concern for the communications systems programmer. The first issue listed, service level agreement, is a proviso between the communications systems programming staff and the end-user community. This accord should describe an acceptable level of service for the end-users to meet their objectives. The second issue, host processor configuration, is a network concern in that multiple hosts within the same network may need network accessibility. This can be accomplished by using MSNF. Another possibility is access to applications executing on host processors that reside in another network. We may choose to use the SNI facility for this connectivity. The third issue, communications controller configuration, is of great importance because it is directly related to the network topography. The size of the network, the end-user population, and the number of telecommunications lines influ-

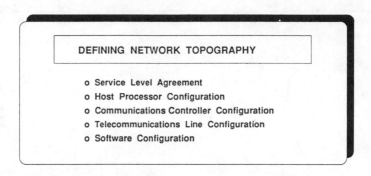

Figure 8.1 Network definition issues.

ence the hardware requirements for the communications controller. The fourth issue, telecommunications line configuration, is a major factor in complying with the service level agreement. The speed of the lines, the number of end-users associated with the lines, and the use of leased and switched lines must all be considered. The final issue listed, software configurations, plays a significant role in defining the network. The various levels of software must all be synchronized. Some of the end-user requirements may constitute the acquisition of new software to support their needs.

We must remember to view the network as a vehicle that delivers information to applications and end-users. Any modifications or enhancements suggested by the communications systems programmer and network designer must be reviewed with great scrutiny. Changes designed for end-user accessibility may prove to be detrimental for the delivery of information. For example, providing additional workstations on a link may allow more end-users to access an application simultaneously, but the increase in traffic can decrement end-user performance by increasing response time. This change in response time may negate the original objective of allowing greater accessibility for the end-user. An important factor in the final decision of this type of trade-off is the end-users' overall requirements.

8.1 END-USER REQUIREMENTS

Many organizations develop network requirements and objectives from the end-user community. This community is usually regarded as the recipients of the services provided by the applications that execute on the host processor. They can be the accounting, inventory, or sales departments or in some instances the public at large.

The matrix in Figure 8.2 presents the relationship between the end-user requirements and their effects on the network configuration. The volume of the end-users' applications affect all the configurations. The processing capacity of the host processor may have to be increased or even offloaded to another host processor for effective throughput. The communications controller storage size may have to be increased to support the abundance of traffic to the remote network. Telecommunications lines may need a broader bandwidth to support the peak volume periods. This, in turn, can affect the hardware configuration of the communications controller by necessitating a comparable line interface coupler or line set. The operating system software may need more storage to accommodate a larger application address space to sustain the volume of applications. The types of applications that use the network have a measured effect on the network configuration. For some applications, a dedicated host processor may be necessary to achieve acceptable performance, in particular

END USER REQUIREMENTS	HOST PROCESSOR	COMMUNICATIONS CONTROLLER	LINE CONFIG	SOFTWARE CONFIGURATION
Peak Application Volume	*	*	*	*
Application Types	*		*	*
User Grouping & Dispersion		*	*	
Response Time	*	*	*	*
Recovery	*	*	*	*
Number of Users	*	*	*	*

Figure 8.2 User requirements and affected network configurations.

for online inquiry and updating applications. The use of dedicated or switched telecommunications lines should be addressed. Remote data entry using a store and forward type of operation may be used with switched lines, whereas online scientific or accounting applications can use leased lines. The operating systems' Job Entry Subsystem (JES) may need modification specifically for remote job processing. The degrees of software levels should be scrutinized for incompatibilities and functionality to meet the end-user requirement. VTAM's routes may need reconfiguration to balance the application mixture along with the application load. The grouping of the users can again affect the communications controller hardware configuration. Higher-capacity LICs may need to be installed, which may dictate a line attachment base expansion or installation. The telecommunications line may be set up for point-to-point or multipoint. A configuration like this can determine if full-duplex or half-duplex transmission can be used. Response time and the user population are both heavily weighed factors for all the configurations. The ability of the host processor, communications controller, telecommunications line, and the software to provide acceptable response time and to support the user population is proportional to the other end-user requirements. Recovery of the networks is dependent upon the corporation's ability to function during a down period. The importance of recovery in most institutions comes down to the bottom line. Recovery can be quite expensive. Mirror-image data centers, duplication of telecommunication lines, software license fees, and added personnel can be an extremely costly insurance policy. The methodology of network recovery can be a book in itself.

The representatives of the end-user communities must supply present and future objectives to the communications systems programmer and network designer. Several institutions relay this information by use of a service level agreement.

8.1.1 Service Level Agreement

A service level agreement between user communities and the network programmers and network designers outlines the objectives and requirements for network service. It should cover some if not all of the following information:

1. Recoverability of network resources. State the minimum time of outage and identify back-up procedure.
2. Availability of network resources. An example would be an agreement to a specified uptime percentage for lines, workstations, communications controllers, and cluster controllers.

3. Accessibility to network resources. A proviso stating path availability to host applications.
4. Serviceability of network resources.

Here is where we define end-user response time and throughput. This agreement is probably the most visible out of all the previous points. The end-user is always at the mercy of network service to execute his or her transaction as quickly as possible. End-user performance is determined by network performance. Figure 8.3 is an example of a service level agreement.

NETWORK SERVICE LEVEL AGREEMENT

Application Name: CICSP01

Estimated Volume: 10,000 TRANS/DAY

Estimated Number of Users: 1000

MINIMUM OUTAGE TIME

    Lines: 30 min

    FEP: 15 min

    Clusters: 30 min

RECOVERY PROCEDURES

    Lines: 1) Modem testing
                2) FEP port swapping
                3) Matrix switching
                4) Dial back-up services

    FEP: 1) Matrix switching to direct lines to back-up FEP

    Clusters: 1) IML of failed cluster
                2) Inactivate/Activate of failed resource
                3) Contact field support

AVAILABILITY: 92-98%

ACCESSIBILITY: 98.2%

SERVICEABILITY:

    Average Response Time @ Peak Periods: 4 seconds
    Transmission Volume @ Peak Periods: 4000 transactions

Figure 8.3 A network service level agreement.

In reality, all the above mentioned points have their roots in network performance. The performance is based on several factors, some of which are device types in the network, the applications using the network, and the number of domains and/or networks connected.

8.1.2 Device Types

The data terminal equipment used in networks varies greatly. Usually based upon application or end-user requirements, the device types in a network determine other network factors. Most devices are developed with specific protocol usage, such as binary synchronous, SDLC, or start/stop and their ability to operate in half-duplex or full-duplex mode. Line speed may be a restriction of the device because of its configuration. For example, IBM 3274 model 61C operates in half-duplex mode using SDLC protocol and can support 56 kbps but in most cases is configured for 9.6 bps. This automatically dictates how a point-to-point line is defined for this device in the NCP. By knowing the device types connected to the network, the communications systems programmer knows the basic VTAM or NCP definition. In our first network example (Figure 8.4), we will be using both BSC and SDLC remote IBM 3274 cluster controllers, a channel-attached non-SNA 3274, and an SNA/SDLC 3274, also channel attached.

8.1.3 Multi-System Networking Facility (MSNF)

Requirements for cross-domain sessions concerning end-users and their applications must be determined. Does the network use MSNF now? How will management objectives affect its use? Should a dynamic cross-domain resource definition be in effect or should specific cross-domain resource definitions be used? Are there any facilities provided by MSNF that need closer review and possible consideration, such as the adjacent SSCP table? These are just some questions that should be asked by the communications systems programmer on planning the use of MSNF.

8.1.4 SNA Network Interconnect (SNI)

Some SNA networks have tens of thousands of terminals with perhaps 50 domains all connected in the same network. To meet

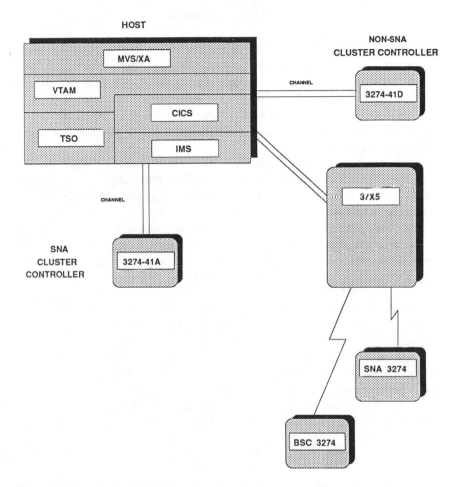

Figure 8.4 A sample single-domain network.

management's objectives and provide desirable service to the end-user, the communications systems programmer and network designer may suggest the use of SNA Network Interconnect (SNI). Your corporation may have recently acquired several companies, each with its own SNA network. Accessibility to all the networks may be a requirement. However, to incorporate several networks into one large network would be an incredibly long and drawn-out process taking several months to possibly several years to coordinate and implement. SNI can alleviate this problem, allowing for network autonomy and a rapid implementation with little end-user involvement.

8.1.5 RJE, NJE, and RJP JES3 Networking

Many end-user applications don't require fast information retrieval. These applications usually execute in the background or batch processing modes. Yes, the information is important but does not have a high processing priority. Usually, this information is in the form of a printed report for management or customer use. The communications systems programmer must provide a path for submission and transmission of this data.

In our scenario, several remote end-users have offline processing. That is, there is no need for computer center facilities to compile data. However, applications on the host processor use this data as input for management reports. Figure 8.5 depicts an RJE scenario configuration. The data is forwarded via Remote Job Entry (RJE) in a JES2 environment or by Remote Job Processing in a JES3 environment. Basically, these facilities allow end-users to start a session with the appropriate Job Entry Subsystem (JES) to execute a batch program in the host processor that uses the remote's forwarded data. The report from this batch program can be routed to other networks for printing by using JES2/Network Job Entry (NJE) or JES3 Networking. Both these facilities use application-to-application sessions to route the report to one or more destined network printers. The device types used for RJE and RJP vary. In our primary network JES2 will be the job entry subsystem and the users have a need for an RJE station at a remote site. This RJE workstation will be an SNA 3770 device and it will have two printers and an operator's console attached to it.

8.1.6 Switched Lines

One more end-user requirement that needs to be considered is dial-in or switched line support. This support is accomplished by the end-user or the network operator making a telephone call which establishes a communications line for the transmission of data. We place switched line support under end-user requirements for two reasons. One is the amount of time the end-user needs access to the host processor facility. Many end-users, such as the previous RJE/RJP scenario, need very little line time to accomplish their functions. These groups are prime candidates for switched line service. The second reason is for use as a back-up procedure. Some networks are all point-to-point. An example would be one cluster control unit per line. Since cluster controllers are mostly used for interactive applications,

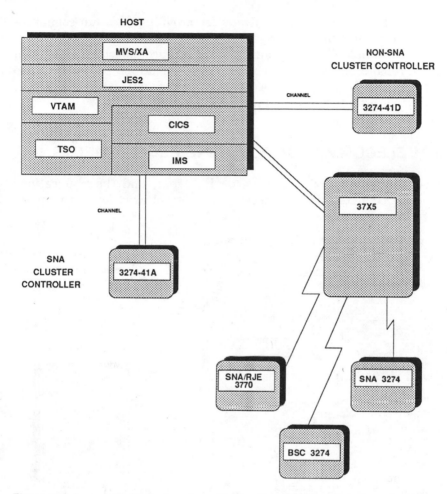

Figure 8.5 A sample single-domain network with an RJE workstation attached.

the importance of availability is great. If the line to the cluster controller should fail, switched line support will allow access to the host processor. The communications systems programmer and/or network designer should determine if the network has the proper configuration to support switched lines. Does the communications controller have switched line support? Do the modems support switched lines? If not, what hardware features are required? Is the proper software in place for switched line support? If not, determine the software required to support the hardware.

One more note of special interest to the network designer. VTAM V3.1.2 and NCP V4.3 or V5.1.2 include support for switched subarea links. This is important specifically for providing back-up communications links for subarea connectivity.

In our sample single-domain network (Figure 8.6), the corporation has a remote site that uses an IBM S/36 for offline processing. The data entered during the work day is to be transmitted to the host at night over a switched line using SDLC protocol.

8.2 TELECOMMUNICATIONS LINE REQUIREMENTS

The requirements of end-users, device types, and the applications can directly determine the speed and protocol used for the network

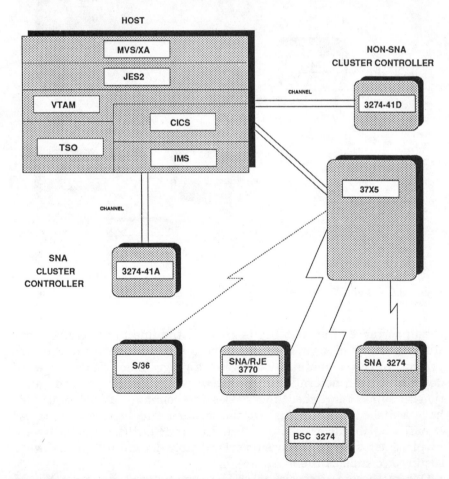

Figure 8.6 A sample single-domain network with a switched line to an S/36.

telecommunications lines. Not only is the type of communications facility of concern, but also the positioning of end-user cluster controllers and terminals on each telecommunications line. An accounting of the amount and type of data that traverses these lines must be gathered for use by the network designer to determine line saturation thresholds. This data can be found by the use of several different types of monitoring software that are used at the application, host, and network levels. Once the data is compiled, it can be used to determine such factors as line speed and actual line configurations.

8.2.1 Line Speed

Many communications systems programmers and network designers believe that line speed may prove to be the quickest and easiest solution to increasing end-user response time and throughput. However, several points must be considered when deciding on line speed for your network.

Remember that links are composed of physical connections. Communications controllers, cluster controllers, modems, and telecommunications lines are all part of the link. As a communications systems programmer or network designer, you should research each of these components and determine if the communication facility support is available for each component. For example, Figure 8.7 shows links connected to an IBM 3725 communications controller. One of these links connects a 3725 communications controller, and the other connects a 3274 cluster controller. As you can see, the link speed between the 3725 communications controllers is designated at 56 kbps. while the 3274 cluster controller link is 9.6 bps. If line speed is be-

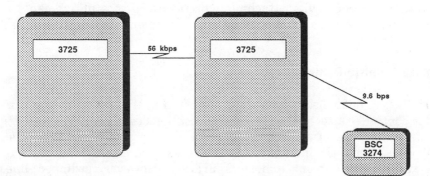

Figure 8.7 Line speeds and device restrictions.

lieved to increase response time, why not increase the 3274 cluster controller link to 56 kbps? This is a sound and logical question which deserves a logical but simple answer. This 3274 cluster controller is using BSC protocol, and there is a restriction of line speed of 9.6 bps for this device. If, however, this device were a remote 3274 SNA cluster controller with the proper hardware features, it would be able to handle a line speed of 56 kps. Here is just one example where research about the hardware configuration of the device and the line configuration must be compared and assessed carefully.

8.2.2 Multiplexing

A different approach to line configurations allows the use of high-speed lines to devices that have a speed restriction. This is called "multiplexing." Multiplexing is a means of breaking down a high-speed line into several lower-speed lines. For example in Figure 8.8, the backbone of the network is a T1 carrier. The communications control unit has defined to it four 256 kbps dedicated links to remote 3725s. To use the large bandwidth of the backbone link, a multiplexer unit can be used to concentrate and then expand the bandwidth to the appropriate speeds.

Take a look at Figure 8.8. The front-end processor has four 256 kbps lines connected to a multiplexer. The multiplexer concentrates these lines to a bandwidth of 1.44 million bits per second (mbps). At the receiving end of the link another multiplexer reduces the incoming data to 256 kbps and directs the data to the designated destination. The same holds true for the reverse route. Thus, high-speed transmission is accomplished by multiplexing down the speed to lower speeds for several devices attached to the front-end processor. This brings us to another factor of line requirements, the line configuration for one device attachment or several device attachments to the line. These are point-to-point and multipoint configurations, respectively.

8.2.3 Point-to-Point

In the previous discussions we described a configuration of one cluster controller attached to the communications controller. We also discussed the use of a switched line for cluster controllers and other devices which use dial-up access to the network. Both scenarios illustrate a point-to-point line configuration. However, switched lines may never be used for more than one remote controller at a time. In an SNA network it is safe to view a point-to-point configuration as

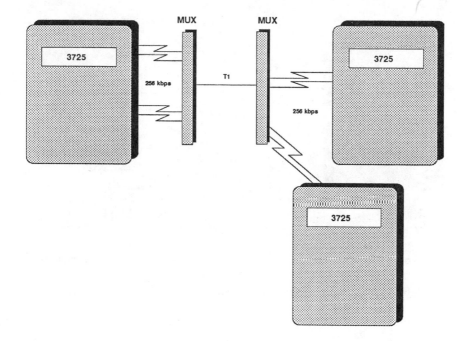

Figure 8.8 The use of a multiplexer device.

having one PU attached to each link. Reasons for the use of point-to-point configurations are many. Response time, control of the type of data, security, and ease of recovery are all viable objectives, to name a few.

In Figure 8.9, we can clearly see the point-to-point configuration. Remember when we use the term "point-to-point" we are describing the physical connection of the link and its end points, the local end point, and the remote end point. There is no intervening point between them. Links with more than one remote end point are multipoint links.

8.2.4 Multipoint

Like a point-to-point line configuration, a multipoint line describes the physical connection of the remote end points. In this configuration, more than one remote point shares a single telecommunications line.

The concept of a multipoint line is not difficult if you can see the configuration. Figure 8.10 draws the picture clearly. What we see is

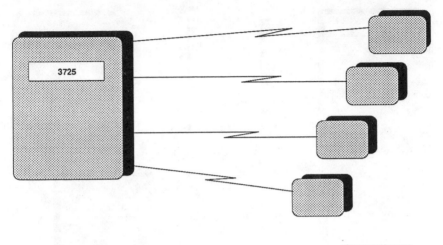

LOCAL POINT   REMOTE POINTS

Figure 8.9 A point-to-point line configuration.

one dedicated link with four remote points or drops attached to the
link in a perpendicular arrangement. This design will allow any of
the remote links that tap into the dedicated link to fail without affecting the other drops. It can also be cost effective to the company
because it decreases the number of dedicated links necessary to support the end-users. A careful study of the application mix and volume will assist you in determining if a multidrop or multipoint line
is sufficient. There are two factors of interest in multipointing. The
first is the use of full-duplex transmission. Even if the remote device
cannot function in full-duplex mode, the line can be defined to NCP
as having a send and receive address. This will allow one remote
point to send data while another remote point on that multipoint line
is receiving data. An example of this is multipointing 3274 cluster
controllers. These cluster controllers operate in half-duplex transmission protocol only. The second factor is that the link protocol must be
the same for all points on the line. No mixture of BSC, SDLC, or S/S
is functional. This is because the network control programs line configuration must be aware of the link protocol.

   An advanced multipoint configuration is available with VTAM
V3.1.2 and NCP V4.2 and higher. These levels allow a multipoint
link to be used in conjunction with subarea SDLC links. This configuration will allow the network designer to use cost-effective link configurations for large SNA backbone networks.

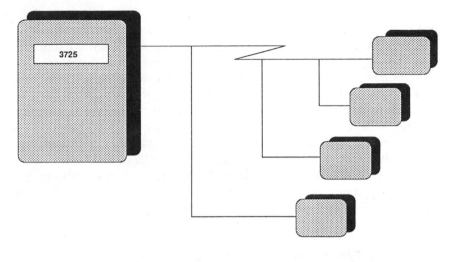

LOCAL POINT   REMOTE POINTS

Figure 8.10 A multipoint configuration.

8.3 LINK PROTOCOLS

The devices and applications that use a telecommunications line dictate the link protocol. Again, we see that hardware dependencies of a device for a specific link protocol can affect the design of a network. Some applications are designed for specific protocols and therefore also affect the network topography. There are two categories of link protocol to discuss. One is non-SNA link protocols, which includes S/S, BSC, and X.25. The second category is SNA link protocol, which is SDLC.

8.3.1 Start/Stop Link Protocol

Asynchronous protocols in today's networks are used for such devices as an IBM 3767, IBM 3101, TWX model 33/35, or WTTY-type devices. In Chapter 4 we discussed VTAM and how it supports SNA. You should also take note from that discussion that VTAM does not support asynchronous link protocol. Therefore, the asynchronous data being transmitted must be converted to a format that is sup- ported by VTAM. This can be accomplished by the use of an IBM program called Network Terminal Option (NTO). NTO resides in the communications controller with the network control program (Figure

8.11). A main function of NTO is to allow asynchronous devices access to the VTAM host by converting the start/stop commands to an SNA format. Another and more recent means of allowing asynchronous devices to access VTAM is by using protocol converters. One such protocol converter has already been previewed, the IBM 3710 network controller. This device can have several start/stop devices attached to it. In turn, the 3710 provides the protocol conversion function and passes the data to the network control program in SDLC format, eliminating the need for protocol conversion software residing in the communications controller. The 3710 can also be used for BSC protocol conversion. It is up to you, the communications systems programmer or network designer, to determine if either of these is feasible in the design of your network.

8.3.2 Binary Synchronous Link Protocol

BSC has been by far the most widely used link protocol since 1966. Because of this large user base, VTAM supports only one type of non-SNA device: IBM 3270 BSC. All other non-SNA devices must either emulate an IBM 3270-type device or have a software package of some type to provide the emulation for the device. We have already discussed the NTO program product in the previous section for S/S devices. NTO can also be used for BSC devices as well.

More often than not, another IBM software package, the Emulation Program (EP) (Figure 8.12), is used for non-SNA BSC devices.

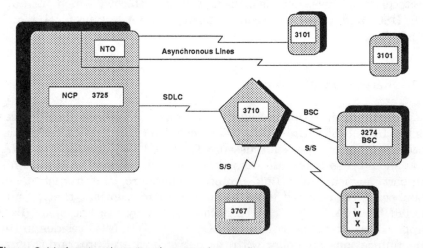

Figure 8.11 A network protocol conversion configuration.

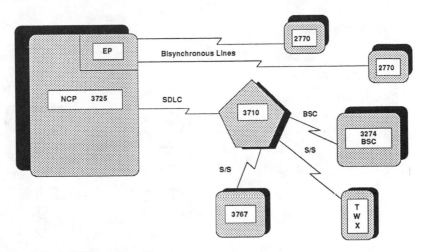

Figure 8.12 A PEP configuration.

This emulation program executes with the NCP in the communications control unit. It provides the proper interface for BSC devices to their respective applications that are executing on the main processor. When both NCP and EP are loaded into the communications controller, it is a Partitioned Emulation Program (PEP). An example of a non-SNA BSC device is the IBM 2770 remote workstation. This workstation is used for RJE processing. Like all non-SNA devices, NCP and VTAM have no knowledge of these devices. This includes data transmission and session setup. It is all provided by EP.

One other program that is worth mentioning here is the Non-SNA Interconnect (NSI) program offered by IBM (Figure 8.13). This program allows BSC RJE networks and BSC NJE networks to use SNA by enveloping the BSC data with SNA headers. This is done in the communications controller where NSI executes with the NCP.

8.3.3 X.25 NPSI

Packet switch data networks allow several telecommunications users to transmit their specific data over public telephone circuits. This idea came about as a way to reduce a corporation's line costs by using existing communications lines rather than having to pay large installation and maintenance fees for private circuits.

NPSI, executing with the NCP in the communications controller, provides the interface and link procedures needed for transmission of data through the public switched data network (Figure 8.14). It does

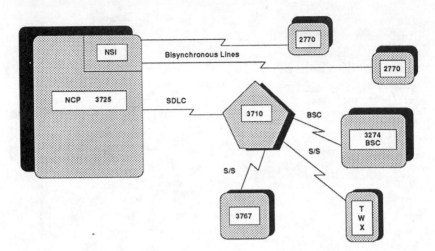

Figure 8.13 An NCP/NSI network configuration.

this by creating a packet and then affixing the X.25 linkage headers. If your company is either planning to use a PSDN or looking at other cost-effective communications, serious consideration should be given to X.25 NPSI.

8.3.4 SDLC

Of all the communications link protocols being used today, SDLC for the greatest part has become the industry standard for network link protocols. In part because of the emergence of SNA, SDLC gives the user improved problem determination capabilities over the previous

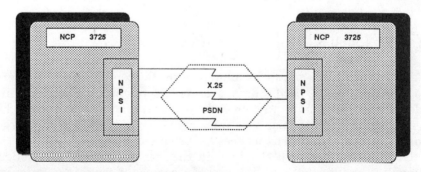

Figure 8.14 An X.25/NPSI network configuration using a Public Switched Data Network (PSDN).

protocols, BSC and S/S. Also, SDLC is a more efficient protocol for data transmission and transmission recovery. Its ability to transmit data with great integrity at high speeds has brought it to the forefront of telecommunications. If the opportunity arises to redesign or create a new network, indicate to management the uses of SDLC and how it is incorporated into SNA. Remember, any SNA device uses SDLC link protocol and therefore no emulation program is required for the device to access the network.

We have seen how the various telecommunications line requirements are affected by the devices attached to the lines and how these different device types may require additional software in order for them to be supported. But also to be considered is the operating system software, the communications system software, and the subsystem software.

8.4 SOFTWARE

All software in an effective system must be carefully selected and evaluated. The different levels of software available may not provide the support needed for you to implement your network. The pieces to the puzzle must fit in such a way that proper support is maintained. As you will see later on, many different levels of software may or may not provide the support you design for your network.

8.4.1 Operating System Software

Much consideration has to be given to the operating system that controls the main processor. Any channel-attached communications controller or cluster controller or any EP devices must be defined to the operating system. If an EP device is used in the network, as a requirement, the communications controller that defines that EP device must be attached to a byte multiplexer channel. A byte multiplexer channel sends data to the main processor 1 byte or multiple bytes at a time. This yields a maximum transfer rate of 1.5 megabytes per second. The importance of the transfer rate is related to the processing speed of your channel-attached front-end processor. The newest communications controllers can execute 1 million instructions/second (mips) and to let the controller lay idle at that instruction speed is not cost effective. However, if your network configuration will allow for the front-end processor to be channel attached via a block multiplexer channel, the data transfer rate may reach a maximum of 4.5 megabytes/sec. The size of the block that is transferred is dependent on application device buffer sizes. This high volume of data transfer is important not only for the network response time, but also the performance of the operating system. So, consideration of network device types can influence the operating system's I/O configuration, which in turn can affect the overall response time and throughput of the operating system.

The three major operating systems, MVS, DOS/VSE, and VM, must be generated properly when considering the telecommunications system hardware and software. The different versions and release levels of the operating system software can affect the functions and features of the communications software. The chart in Figure 8.15 describes the functions that are unique to each operating system. As you can see in the figure, not all the operating systems have unique functions. The majority of the communications software functions are available to each operating system. Some functions, how-

FUNCTION	MVS	MVS/XA	VSE	VM
31-Bit Addressing		*		
Direct Link-Attached Devices, Hosts, NCPs				*
VSCS Display Capability FORCE Command Internal Trace				*
Extended Recovery Facility (XRF)		*		
Programmable Operator Message Exchange (PMX)				*
Symptom String Subset		*		

Figure 8.15 Unique function support for operating systems.

ever, are available only if the proper version and release of related communications software is installed.

8.4.2 Communications System Software

During the development of VTAM, each new version and release provides an increase in function of different VTAM components as well as the addition of new ones. Associated with this growth is the natural creation of communications network management (CNM) software. As VTAM's capabilities increased, so too did the abilities of management software. We should point out to you that although VTAM executes under MVS, VM, and VSE operating systems, some functions of VTAM do not cross operating systems. You as the communications systems programmer must be aware of the differences between the versions of VTAM, NCP, and CNM products and how they differ between operating systems. Figure 8.16 illustrates the various components of VTAM.

For instance, there are differences between VTAM versions executing on an MVS system as compared to a VM system. An example is SNI which is supported in an MVS system from version 2, release 2 of VTAM but not incorporated for a VM operating system until VTAM version 3, release 1.1. This, however, is dependent upon the level of NCP executing in the communications controller. In order for SNI to function, the NCP must be, at a minimum, version 3. So you can see how this software-level dependency can cascade. This software compatibility not only affects the communications software functions, but it can have a great effect on the subsystem applications that request these functions.

8.4.3 Subsystem Software

The final piece of the software puzzle is the application software. The different types of application software can and will affect the performance and makeup of the network. One of the most popular interactive subsystems being used today is IBM's Customer Information and Control System (CICS). This software package has become the industry standard for use in information retrieval and updating. Under CICS, a company may execute several different applications at the same time, all sharing the same address space in the host computer. Accounts receivables, name and address applications, inventory, and order entry applications may all execute under the

FUNCTION	VTAM					NCP						
	V2.1	V2.2	V3.1	V3.1.1	V3.2	V2	V3	V4.1	V4.2	V4.3	V5.2	V5.2.1
Channel-attached cross-domain NCPs		*	*	*	*							
CTC attached hosts	*	*	*	*	*							
ENA (MVS, MVS/XA)			*	*	*			*	*	*	*	*
ENA (VSE, VM)				*	*			*	*	*	*	*
SNI (MVS, MVS/XA)		*	*	*	*		*	*	*	*	*	*
SNI (VM)			*		*		*	*	*	*	*	*
XRF (MVS, MVS/XA)			*	*	*			*	*	*	*	*
PORT SWAP (37X5, 3720)							*	*	*	*	*	*
Dynamic PATH reconfiguration					*					*	*	*
Dynamic TABLE reconfiguration					*					*	*	*
Dial-up SDLC subarea links					*					*	*	*
Mixed Multipoint line support					*					*	*	*
Token-ring subarea links										* (V4.3.1)		*

Figure 8.16 Functional components of VTAM/NCP in relation to version and release levels.

same CICS subsystem. Two other very popular database software products may also execute under CICS. One is IBM's Information Management System (IMS), the other is Cullinet's Information Database Management System (IDMS). A coordinated effort by both the communications systems programmer and the CICS and/or the database systems programmers will result in smooth network implementation and a satisfactory performance curve for the end-user.

One other major software package that is a primary development tool for most computer shops is IBM's Time Sharing Option (TSO). This software facilitates the development and systems programmers' throughput by providing increased productivity for maintenance and development by using TSO's powerful commands and command list facility. Along with its own features, TSO has an extensive offering of programming tools that can execute in the TSO subsystem. Some of these are ISPF/PDF, a menu-driven development facility; online compiler program products for COBOL, FORTRAN, and PL/I; a graphics display product called GDDM; and many more.

8.5 SUMMARY

This chapter has covered the basis for network design. This included the analysis of user requirements and its effect on network requirements, the research needed on device types and how they will interface with the network, and the interdependency of the software levels and this effect on available functions to complete the network design. All these points are necessary in order to evaluate and implement your network. There are of course many other variables that need to be discussed. We will bring them to your attention as we proceed to the next chapters which concern the actual coding of VTAM and NCP parameters that are needed to map a network.

3

VTAM

9

Defining a
Single-Domain Network

In this chapter we will lay the foundation for all VTAM network definitions, including multiple-domain and SNI networks. No matter what type of configuration your network may have, all networks consist of a base design. That basis is the definition of a single-domain network. But, before we start coding the VTAM definition statements, we must introduce you to the format of definition statements used in this book and the "sift-down" effect.

9.1 DEFINITION STATEMENT FORMAT AND SIFT-DOWN EFFECT

All definition statement formats in this book will follow standard assembler language rules (Figure 9.1). The NAME field assigns a symbolic name that identifies the definition statement or minor node.
   The NAME field has the following format:

1. The field must be one to eight characters.
2. The first character must be uppercase alphabetic (A to Z) or the national characters @, #, or $.
3. The second to eighth characters must be uppercase alphabetic (A to Z), numeric (0 to 9), or the national characters @, #, or $.
4. The field must start in column 1 of the definition statement and must be followed by at least one blank.

1 - 8	10 - 17	19 - 71
NAME	DEFINITION OPERANDS	STATEMENT

Figure 9.1 Definition statement format.

The DEFINITION STATEMENT field identifies the definition statement. It must be preceded and followed by one or more blanks.

The OPERANDS field contains the required and optional definition statement operands. Some of these operands are called keyword operands. They are denoted by being followed by an equal (=) sign which is followed by the keyword value or values. Required keywords will be identified in **bold type**, the default operands will be underlined, and the optional keywords will be surrounded by brackets ([ ]). If more than one keyword is possible, the "or" bar (|) will be used.

All definition statements are coded in columns 1 through 71 of a statement. The continuation of a statement is accomplished by placing a nonblank character in column 72. The continued part of the statement must begin in column 16 of the following card. Comments can appear after the last operand field or by placing an asterisk (*) in column 1 of the statement.

The sift-down effect (Figure 9.2) relieves the communications systems programmer from repetitive operand coding. This is done by coding the operand on a higher-level node, and the following lower-level nodes will use this value. However, the lower-level node may override the sifted value by coding the same operand, and this value will be used instead.

```
        GROUP      USSTAB=USSSNA
        LINE
        PU
          LU       (uses USSSNA)
        PU
          LU       USSTAB=USSRMT        uses USSRMT
          LU       (uses USSSNA)
        PU         USSTAB=,
          LU       (uses IBM supplied default)
          LU       USSTAB=USSRMT        uses USSRMT
          LU       USSTAB=USSSNA        uses USSSNA
```

Figure 9.2 Example of sift-down effect.

9.2 VTAM START OPTIONS LIST ATCSTR00

The start options list in VTAM is used at initialization time to define to the SSCP the initial topology of the network. The start list is found in a member of the MVS library named SYS1.VTAMLST. This default member name is ATCSTR00. This member is always read at initialization time. It may, however, be overridden by an operator command during start up. Figure 9.3 lists the start options that should be assessed for a single-domain network.

```
SSCPID=n,
NETID=name,
SSCPNAME=name,
GWSSCP=YES|NO,
[,bufpoolname=(baseno,bufsize,slowpt,F,xpanno,xpanpt)]
[,COLD/WARM]
[,CONFIG=xx|00|name]
[,CSALIMIT=0|n|nK|nM]
[,CSA24=0|n|nK|nM]
[,DLRTCB=n|32]
[,HOSTPU=name of VTAM PU|ISTPUS]
[,HOSTSA=n|1]
[,IOINT=n|180]
[,ITLIM=n|0]
[,LIST=xx]
[,MAXSUBA=n|15]
[,MSGMOD=YES|NO]
[,NODELST=name]
[,PPLOG=YES|NO]
[,PROMPT|NOPROMPT]
[,SONLIM=([m|60][,t|30])]
[,SUPP=NOSUP|INFO|WARN|NORM|SER]
[,TNSTAT[,CNSL|NOCNSL][,TIME=N|60]|NOTNSTAT]
[,TRACE|NOTRACE,ID=nodename,TYPE=BUF|IO|[,EVERY]]
[,TRACE|NOTRACE,ID=linename,TYPE=LINE[,COUNT=n|ALL]]
[,TRACE|NOTRACE,ID=nodename,TYPE=SIT[,COUNT=n|ALL]]
[,TRACE|NOTRACE,ID=VTAMBUF,TYPE=SMS]
[,TRACE,TYPE=VTAM[,MODE=INT|EXT][,SIZE=n|2]
     [,OPTION=ALL|option|(option,option,...,option)]]
[,NOTRACE,TYPE=VTAM]
[,USSTAB=tablename]
```

Figure 9.3 VTAM start options for VTAM.

9.2.1 Required Start Parameters

The SSCPID=n parameter is used when VTAM constructs a 48-bit identification sequence that is sent to a PU during session establishment using the SNA command ACTPU. The n value is a decimal integer from 0 to 65,535 and must be unique within its own network and interconnected networks.

For our sample network we will use the decimal value 2. Therefore we will code in SYS1.VTAMLST member ATCSTR00:

```
SSCPID=2,                                                              *
```

The NETID=name parameter assigns a network name to this VTAM. It is a required statement for VTAM V3.2 only. In pre-VTAM V3.2, this parameter is optional and is used for specifying gateway SSCP capabilities in an SNI network. The name contains one to eight alphanumeric characters. In VTAM V3.2 it is used as a prefix to all network resource names. This name is used for all VTAMs in a single SNA network.

The SSCPNAME=name parameter is a network unique name for the SSCP of this VTAM. It is also a required parameter in VTAM V3.2. For pre-VTAM V3.2 networks the parameter along with the NETID parameter specifies that this VTAM can participate in gateway SSCP responsibilities for cross-network sessions over an SNI network. The name can be one to eight alphanumeric characters in length, and it is highly recommended that the name specified here match the CDRM name assigned to this VTAM when defining a multisystem network. For more on defining a multi-system network consult *Advanced SNA Networking*.

The final required parameter under VTAM V3.2 is the GWSSCP=YES|NO parameter. This parameter is required because unlike pre-VTAM V3.2, the NETID and SSCPNAME parameters do not denote gateway SSCP capabilities. It is used specifically for SNI networks. More information on SNI can also be found in *Advanced SNA Networking*.

9.2.2 Buffer Pool Start Options

These options define to VTAM the buffer pool allocations to use for the holding of data and building of control blocks. The format of the buffer pool start option is:

```
bufpoolname=(baseno,bufsize,slowpt,F,xpanno,xpanpt)
```

POOL NAME	USAGE
CRPLBUF	Request parameter list (RPL) copy pool in page-able or virtual storage
IOBUF	Input/output message pool in fixed storage
LFBUF	Large buffer pool in fixed storage (also serves as message pool)
LPBUF	Large buffer pool in pageable or virtual storage
SFBUF	Small buffer pool in fixed storage
SPBUF	Small buffer pool in pageable or virtual storage
WPBUF	Message-control buffer pool in pageable or virtual storage

Figure 9.4 VTAM buffer pools for MVS.

The *bufpoolname* value is one of the names listed in Figure 9.4. It identifies which buffer pool the following options apply to. The *baseno* option defines the initial number of buffers VTAM is to allocate at start up. The range is 1 to 32767. The *bufsize* option defines to VTAM in bytes the size of the buffer being defined. This value is applicable only to the fixed-storage message pools IOBUF and LFBUF. It is ignored for all other buffer pools. It is a requirement for this *bufsize* value to match the UNITSZ operand of the HOST statement defined in the resource definition list for a channel-attached NCP definition. If these two values do not match, the NCP will not be activated and VTAM will issue an error message. The *slowpt* value will determine when VTAM is to perform slow-down mode. Slow-down mode occurs when the number of available buffers in this buffer pool is equal to or less than the value specified for *slowpt*. VTAM will then only honor priority requests, such as reads from a channel-attached device, until the available buffer number rises above the *slowpt* value. Note that if you choose a *slowpt* value that is too high, VTAM may never come out of slow-down mode, thus affecting network performance tremendously.

The F stands for fixed. It defines to VTAM that this buffer pool is to be fixed in storage on our MVS system. In other words, the buffers are always resident and in the CPU memory versus being paged from storage every time a buffer is requested. This greatly increases your performance specifically for the IOBUF pool. The *xpanno* value is the amount of buffers VTAM will expand this buffer pool if the initial allocation from the *baseno* value has been exhausted and all buffers are allocated. This is performed by VTAM dynamically. If, however, a value of 0 is coded, VTAM will not perform dynamic buffering, which may very well lead to slow-down mode. The range for this value is 0 to 32767. The value you pick is rounded upward to the nearest whole page of storage. A page of storage is 4096 bytes. If your value for expansion causes the number of buffers times the bufsize to go over one page by only a few bytes, VTAM will allocate two pages. Therefore, care should be taken when estimating the expansion number. The *xpanpt* value is directly related to *slowpt* and *xpanno*. This value defines to VTAM at what point of free buffers for this pool should the buffer pool be expanded to avoid slow-down mode. This value should be larger than *slowpt*.

The buffer pool of most concern is the IOBUF. We will code an appropriate size for any VTAM system before capacity analysis has been determined. The remaining pools will be defaulted. Figure 9.5 shows ATCSTR00 with the buffer pool defined.

9.2.3 CONFIG Start Option

This option identifies to VTAM the location of the list of major nodes to be activated at initialization time. The format is:

```
CONFIG=xx|00|name
```

The xx value is a one to two alphanumeric character value that is appended to the SYS1.VTAMLST member named ATCCONxx. VTAM upon start up will access ATCCONxx for a list of major nodes that should be made active to VTAM. If xx is coded, this value will override the default appendage of 00. The member ATCCON00 is always accessed by VTAM unless xx is coded or the operator overrides the list with the CONFIG option during VTAM start up. The name value specifies the three- to eight-character file name (DD name) of the VSAM configuration restart file. This file contains a list of all the major nodes that were active and the dynamic recovery data set files and the PATH statements that were applicable at the

```
SSCPID=2,                                              *
IOBUF=(32,256,4,F,16,8),                               *
```

Figure 9.5 ATCSTR00 after defining buffer pools.

time of failure or deactivation of VTAM. The name value should be coded on the NODELST option also to include updating of major node activation after VTAM is active. The file must have been used prior to failure or deactivation for the configuration restart facility to execute. If the file is empty, VTAM does not activate any major nodes during initialization.

In our sample start list we are going to append the value 01 to the ATCCONxx member name. Figure 9.6 now shows the start list after adding the CONFIG start option.

9.2.4 CSALIMIT Start Option

This option defines to VTAM the maximum amount of the MVS operating system Common Service Area (CSA) that VTAM will use. The format for this option is:

```
CSALIMIT=0|n|nK|nM
```

The 0 value is the default value and tells VTAM there is no limit to the amount of CSA it can use. In an MVS/370 system the maximum is 16 million bytes (16 Mb) and in an MVS/XA system the maximum is 2 billion bytes, or 2 gigabytes (2 Gb). Taking the default could seriously impede the operating system if VTAM were to take advantage of being nonconstrained from CSA usage. The n|nK value denotes the number of 1000-byte (1 Kb) areas of storage in decimal that VTAM will use as the CSA maximum. This value is rounded to the next multiple of 4. The nM value is the number of 1-million-byte (1 Mb) areas of storage VTAM will use as the CSA limit. If just the n value is coded, kilobytes is assumed. If you code a value that is greater than the real available CSA storage, no limit is used. If a CSALIMIT is coded, you should carefully define the LPBUF values so there is no buffer expansion. If LPBUF must be expanded but the CSALIMIT is reached, VTAM may enter a locked condition and cause messages to be lost or session initiation and termination failures.

```
SSCPID=2,                          *
IOBUF=(32,256,4,F,16,8),           *
COLD,CONFIG=01,                    *
```

Figure 9.6 ATCSTR00 for MVS after defining CONFIG start option.

After conferring with the MVS systems programmer for our sample network, we are going to code a CSALIMIT of 512 Kb. Figure 9.7 shows the start list after adding the CSALIMIT start option.

9.2.5 CSA24 Start Option

Prior to the MVS/XA operating system, a 24-bit addressing scheme was in use with the MVS operating system, allowing the highest address of storage to be 16 Mb. With the 31-bit extended storage addressing scheme provided by MVS/XA, the highest available storage address was moved up to 2 Gb. Because of the VTAM architecture for such VTAM elements as IOBUF, some VTAM code must execute in the 24-bit addressing mode. MVS/XA has provided an area of CSA storage below the 16-Mb line for programs to use the CSA in 24-bit addressing mode. This start option determines the amount of CSA storage VTAM may use below the 16-Mb line. The format for this option is:

```
CSA24=0|n|nK|nM
```

The 0 value is the default value and tells VTAM there is no limit to the amount of CSA it can use. The maximum is 16 million bytes (16 Mb). The default for CSA24 is usually taken. This is caused by the new structure of VTAM's buffers. In VTAM V3, only the IOBUF pool is below the 16-Mb line. All the other pools are above the line. The $n|nK$ value denotes the number of 1000-byte, or 1 Kb, areas of storage in decimal that VTAM will use as the CSA maximum. This value is rounded to the next multiple of 4. The nM value is the number of 1-million-byte, or 1 Mb areas of storage VTAM will use as the CSA limit. If just the n value is coded, kilobytes is assumed.

In our sample network the operating system is MVS/XA and we will be taking the default value of 0. It is not necessary to code the option, but for documentation purposes we will enter it into the start list. Figure 9.8 shows the start list after the addition of the CSA24 option.

```
SSCPID=2,                              *
IOBUF=(32,256,4,F,16,8),               *
CONFIG=01,CSALIMIT=512,                *
```

Figure 9.7 ATCSTR00 after defining CSALIMIT start option.

9.2.6 HOSTPU Start Option

Remember that VTAM's SSCP is a PU Type 5 and like other PUs in the network is given a name. This option allows the communications systems programmer to assign a name to VTAM's PU that should be network unique. It is highly recommended that you use this option to specify a unique PU name for ease of debugging purposes or if you are using the IBM program products NetView or NLDM. This name should not be the same as this VTAM's cross domain manager name or the SSCP name assigned to this VTAM if you have a multidomain or SNI network. The format for this start option is:

```
HOSTPU=VTAM PU name|ISTPUS
```

If the VTAM PU name or this option is not coded, the default name ISTPUS will be used. For our network we will assign the name VTAM01 to the VTAM PU.

9.2.7 HOSTSA Start Option

This option assigns the subarea number to this VTAM. This number is between 1 and 255 decimal. In VTAM V3.2 with the help of a Program Temporary Fix (PTF) this value can range from 1 to 65,535. It is a good idea to always code the subarea number for VTAM. This number is the unique address for this VTAM in a network and is important for multidomain or SNI networks. Any duplication of sub-area numbers in a multidomain network will result in one of the subareas not being activated. The format is:

```
HOSTSA=n|1
```

The default value is always 1 if the option is not coded. The n is the number you assign to the VTAM subarea.

For our network, we will use the default value of 1 as the subarea number for VTAM. Again, for documentation purposes, we will code the option in the start list as is shown in Figure 9.9.

```
SSCPID=2,                                              *
IOBUF=(32,256,4,F,16,8),                               *
CONFIG=01,CSALIMIT=512,CSA24=0,                        *
```

Figure 9.8 ATCSTR00 for MVS/XA after defining CSA24 start option.

```
SSCPID=2,                                                         *
IOBUF=(32,256,4,F,16,8),                                          *
CONFIG=01,CSALIMIT=512,CSA24=0,HOSTPU=VTAM01,                     *
HOSTSA=01,                                                        *
```

Figure 9.9 ATCSTR00 for MVS/XA after defining HOSTPU and HOSTSA start options.

9.2.8 MAXSUBA Start Option

It is important for us to keep in mind the direct relationship of the different version levels of VTAM and NCP and how they relate functionally to each other. For this option, if we are using VTAM version 3 or higher, we have the capability of using the Extended Network Addressing facility (ENA). However, ENA can only be used on an MVS or MVS/XA system if (1) all other VTAMs in the network are version 3 or higher and (2) the version of NCP is version 4 or higher. If either one of these factors is not found in your network, you should code the MAXSUBA option. The one requirement when coding MAX-SUBA is that all VTAMs in the network must specify the same MAXSUBA value. See the discussion on ENA in Chapter 4 for more information on ENA and non-ENA addressing. Remember, in a non-ENA network this value dictates the number of resources address-able in the network. The format is:

MAXSUBA=n|15

where n is the value of the maximum subarea defined in the net-work. The range for this value is 3 to 255. The default value is 15 and for our sample network this value will give us more than enough addressable resources. But, since our single-domain network consists of VTAM V3 and NCP V4 or V5, the MAXSUBA option is not needed since VTAM will be using extended network addressing.

9.2.9 NODELST Start Option

This option defines the file or DD name VTAM is to open to main-tain a list of currently active major nodes. This list is accessed if the CONFIG option is coded with the name operand. If the names on the CONFIG and NODELST options match, VTAM will activate all the major nodes that were active prior to failure or deactivation of the network. This NODELST data set is updated whenever a major node is activated or deactivated. This assists in recovery of major nodes that need to be active after start up from a failure. If the name operands of the CONFIG and NODELST options differ, the NODELST data set is erased before any major nodes are activated. Since we have already chosen the CONFIG=01 option, we need not use the NODELST option for our sample network start list.

9.2.10 PPOLOG Start Option

This option is valid only for VTAM V3R1.1 and higher. It refers to the primary program operator log that interfaces with VTAM to capture VTAM commands and messages. The format is:

```
PPOLOG=YES|NO
```

The default NO means that VTAM commands, messages, and responses entered on the systems' console will not be recorded on the primary program operator's log. The value of YES means recording will be in effect and also that NetView is executing on the system, since this option is also only valid if NetView is installed on the system. For our sample network in its early stages we will use the default value of NO.

9.2.11 TNSTAT Start Option

In the beginning of this chapter we briefly discussed the different buffer pools VTAM uses. This option tells VTAM to keep records of the buffer pools and the amount of CSA storage that is being used during VTAM's execution. This is the only way you can track the buffer pool and CSA usage. If TNSTAT is not specified at start-up time, it is not possible to keep statistics on these storage uses. The format is:

```
TNSTAT[,CNSL|NOCNSL][,TIME=n|60]|NOTNSTAT
```

The default value is NOTNSTAT and is not recommended. If you take this default, you will not be able to start tuning statistics at a later time by using the operator MODIFY command. However, if TNSTAT is coded, you may stop the tuning statistics at a later time

```
SSCPID=2,                                                        *
IOBUF=(32,256,4,F,16,8),                                         *
CONFIG=01,CSALIMIT=512,CSA24=0,HOSTPU=VTAM01,                    *
HOSTSA=01,ITLIM=0,PPOLOG=YES,PROMPT,                             *
TNSTAT,CNSL,TIME=60
```

Figure 9-10 ATCSTR00 for MVS/XA pre-VTAM V3.2 after defining all the appropriate start options. Note the absence of the continuation character in the last line denoting the end of the start list.

and restart them if you wish. The CNSL operand denotes recording of tuning statistic records to the system console as well as the MVS Systems Management Facility (SMF). NOCNSL specifies recording only to the SMF data set. The TIME operand specifies the time interval for recording the tuning statistics records. The default is 60 minutes, which can be modified using the MODIFY command if greater determination of storage usage is desired. For our network we will use the TNSTAT,CNSL,TIME=60 option.

9.2.12 TRACE Start Option

It is our recommendation that the TRACE options not be used and allowed to default to NOTRACE. This is because of the heavy burden placed upon VTAM to trace. The fact is that trace should only be turned on if it is needed to perform problem diagnosis. This can be accomplished by using the operator MODIFY command. In our start list all traces will be allowed to default to NOTRACE. Figure 9.10 is the completed ATCSTR00 start list for our sample VTAM single domain.

9.3 SUMMARY

In this chapter we discussed the fundamentals of single-domain, multiple-domain, and SNI networks. We learned about the sift-down effect when coding the VTAM macros for network definition. VTAM start options list, coded in the ATCSTR00 member of SYS1.VTAMLST library, helps SSCP in defining the initial network topology at the initialization time. Some of the important start options parameters discussed were SSCPID, buffer pool, CONFIG, CSALINIT, CSA24, HOSTPU, HOSTSA, MAXSUBA, NODELST, PPOLOG, TNSTAT, and TRACE. In the next chapter, we will learn about VTAM major nodes.

10

VTAM Major Nodes — Application, Non-SNA, and SNA

10.1 APPLICATION PROGRAM MAJOR NODE

During our research of the topography of the network, we discussed some of the applications and subsystems that may be employed on the host computer. These interactive programs use VTAM functions to communicate with the end user. The interface that the application will use to VTAM and consequently to the end user is defined in the application program major node. This major node differs from our previous discussion on nodes in Chapter 4. In that discussion we were concerned with the nodes of an SNA network. In this discussion and several to follow, the nodes are VTAM symbolic names that represent resources to VTAM. The major node name is actually the member name found in VTAM's definition library called SYS1.VTAMLST. The VTAM major node consists of a set of resources that can be activated or deactivated by VTAM as a group. These major nodes contain a set of related minor nodes. The minor node is a uniquely defined resource within the major node and is also assigned a symbolic name.

The major node may contain one or more or all of the applications in your network. It is recommended that an application major node be coded for each application. This gives you greater control and flexibility in your network when you have to activate or inactivate major nodes because of problems with the application. This way only the

187

```
name     VBUILD    TYPE=major node type
                   [,CONFGDS=ddname]
                   [,CONFGPW=password]
                   [,MAXGRP=n]
                   [,MAXNO=n]
```

Figure 10.1 VBUILD statement and applicable operands.

users on the application experiencing the problem will be affected
and not the entire user community.

10.1.1 VBUILD Statement

For every major node defined, a VBUILD statement must appear as
the first definition statement. This statement defines to VTAM the
type of major node VTAM is to build from the minor nodes that follow. Figure 10.2 shows the possible operands in VTAM for a
VBUILD statement. The major node type field is any of the column
names from Figure 10.2. The purpose of each operand is as follows:

TYPE=APPL defines to VTAM that this is an application major
node definition. There are no other optional operands applicable
when defining an application major node. APPL is also the default
type if the TYPE operand is not coded. However, we have denoted
the format with the TYPE operand as a required operand.

TYPE=LOCAL defines to VTAM that this is a local SNA device
major node. The applicable optional operands are CONFGDS and
CONFGPW.

The CONFGDS operand is the Data Definition statement name
(DDname) that is assigned to the configuration restart data set from

OPERANDS	VBUILD TYPE=							
	APPL	LOCAL	CDRM	CDRSC	CA	DR	SWNET	ADJSSCP
CONFGDS=		•	•	•	•		•	
CONFGPW=		•	•	•	•		•	
MAXGRP=							•	
MAXNO=							•	

Figure 10.2 VBUILD types and applicable operands.

the VTAM start procedure that is to be used for this major node. Refer to Section 9.2.3 for more information on this data set.

CONFGPW is the password for the VSAM configuration restart data set referred to by the CONFGDS operand. This operand is only coded if CONFGDS is coded. If a password is not supplied here, the VTAM operator is prompted for the correct password whenever VTAM accesses the configuration restart data set. In our example we will not be using the configuration restart data set.

TYPE=CDRM tells VTAM that this major node contains the cross-domain manager definitions for this VTAM. CDRM is discussed in greater detail in *Advanced SNA Networking*. The valid optional operands are CONFGDS and CONFGPW.

TYPE=CDRSC tells VTAM that this major node contains the list of cross-domain resources for this VTAM. The CDRSC is discussed in *Advanced SNA Networking*. The valid optional operands are CONFGDS and CONFGPW.

TYPE=CA tells VTAM that this major node contains the definitions for a channel-attached major node. Examples include a channel-to-channel attachment between VTAMs and a channel-attached NCP major node. Again, the optional operands are CONFGDS and CONFGPW.

TYPE=DR tells VTAM that this major node contains the definitions for dynamic reconfiguration. There are no optional operands for this VBUILD type.

TYPE=SWNET tells VTAM that this major node contains the definitions for a switched communications resource. Besides the CONFGDS and CONFGPW optional operands, the MAXGRP and MAXNO optional operands are also applicable. This major node provides a list of switched resources that can gain access to the network over switched lines.

The MAXGRP operand is coded only if a switched PATH statement is coded. The maximum value is 32,767. This value is the number of unique path group names defined by the GRPNM operand of the PATH statement for this switched major node.

MAXNO is coded only if a switched PATH statement is coded. Its maximum value is 32,767. This value is the number of unique telephone numbers defined by the DIALNO operand of the PATH statement in this switched major node.

TYPE=ADJSSCP tells VTAM that this major node contains the adjacent SSCP table. This table is used by VTAM to search for unknown resources controlling SSCP. We will discuss this major node in greater detail in *Advanced SNA Networking*.

10.1.2 APPL Statement

One APPL definition statement is required for each application that is to be identified to VTAM (Figure 10.3). The name field is used to assign the minor node name to the application. The assigned name must be unique within a network. This name is also referred to as the applications network name. An example would be CICSP01 or IMSP01.

The ACBNAME=acbname operand is also the minor node name for this application. ACB stands for application control block. This is a VTAM control block that contains all the information VTAM needs to know about the applications characteristics. Again, this acbname must be network unique. If the ACBNAME operand is not coded, the name of the APPL definition statement is used as the ACBNAME. In our network configuration, we will assign the name to the acbname. Having the APPL statement name and the ACBNAME the same

```
name    APPL        [ACBNAME=acbname]
                    [APPC=YES|NO]
                    [,AUTH=([ACQ|NOACQ]
                            [,CNM|NOCNM]
                            [,PASS|NOPASS]
                            [,PPO|SPO|NOPO]
                            [,TSO|NOTSO]
                            [,VPACE|NVPACE])]
                    [,DLOGMOD=default logmode name]
                    [,EAS=n|491|509]
                    [,ENCR=SEL|REQD|OPT|NONE]
                    [,HAVAIL=YES|NO]
                    [,MAXPVT=0|n|nK|nM]
                    [,MODETAB=logon mode table name]
                    [,PARSESS=YES|NO]
                    [,PRTCT=password]
                    [,SONSCIP=YES|NO]
                    [,SPAN=(NCCF or NetView spanname)]
                    [,SRBEXIT=YES|NO]
                    [,SSCPFM=USSNOP|USSPOI]
                    [,USSTAB=name]
                    [,VPACING=n|0]
                    [,VTAMFRR=YES|NO]
```

Figure 10.3 APPL definition statement format.

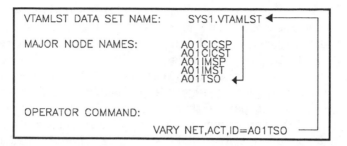

```
VTAMLST DATA SET NAME:      SYS1.VTAMLST

MAJOR NODE NAMES:           A01CICSP
                            A01CICST
                            A01IMSP
                            A01IMST
                            A01TSO

OPERATOR COMMAND:
                            VARY NET,ACT,ID=A01TSO
```

Figure 10.4 Relationship of VTAM operator command to VTAMLST and major nodes.

helps to avoid confusion as to what the application's acbname really is.

The APPC=YES|NO operand is specific to VTAM V3.2. This operand tells VTAM V3.2 that the application defined here may wish to use the basic functions of LU6.2 that VTAM V3.2 supplies. This is denoted by specifying APPC=YES. The default is APPC=NO.

Let's take a look at Figure 10.4, which illustrates how VTAM activates and uses the various operands defined for an application major node. In Figure 10.4 we see how VTAM correlates the major node name in VTAMLST to an operator activate command for the major node A01TSO. Actually, upon initialization, VTAM has created a Major Node Table (MNT) that contains pointers to the specific ACBs for each application in its domain. Let's look at the minor node definition of each of the listed major nodes in SYS1.VTAMLST.

For each CICS subsystem only one application statement is necessary, even though the subsystem can have several different applications under its address space (Figure 10.5). Each application task

```
Major Node Name: A01CICSP
Minor Node Name:
                VBUILD      TYPE=APPL
     CICSP01    APPL        ACBNAME=CICSP01,                    X
                           AUTH=(ACQ,PASS,VPACE),               X
                           MODETAB=MTLU62,EAS=100,              X
                           PARSESS=YES,VPACING=4,SONSCIP=YES
```

Figure 10.5 Application major and minor nodes for a production CICS address space.

shares CICS resources with the other application tasks executing in the CICS address space. Two of the coded operands indicate this. The EAS operand has defined 100 concurrent estimated active sessions. The PARSESS operand tells us that this subsystem can have multiple sessions with other applications on an LU-LU session. The AUTH operand defines this subsystem to have the ability to acquire an LU (ACQ) and to pass session establishment requests to other applications (PASS) and specifies that this subsystem will adhere to the methodology of VPACING to LUs (VPACE). The SONSCIP operand tells VTAM that it can terminate sessions with the SLU on behalf of the application.

The test CICS example in Figure 10.6 is quite similar to the production CICS example. The only differences are in the naming convention for the application and the estimated number of active sessions. One operand not discussed for Figure 10.6 is the MODETAB operand. This operand defines to VTAM the logon (logmode) mode table VTAM is to search for locating the LOGMODE that is to be used by the application when it participates as an SLU. This mode table contains entries that define session parameters for SLUs. The default LOGMODE operand (DLOGMOD) is where you can specify the name of the default session parameter entry name that is to be used with this application. The session parameters are coded in a LOGMODE entry of the logon mode table in VTAM. These session parameters pertain to the application only when the application is acting as the secondary logical unit, for instance, during an application-to-application session where this application is the SLU. If DLOGMOD is specified, VTAM will search the value given from the MODETAB operand. If the LOGMODE entry is not found in the specified MODETAB, VTAM will select the first entry from the default logon mode table supplied by IBM. If MODETAB is specified and DLOGMOD is not coded, the first LOGMODE entry in the specified MODETAB table will be used. If either DLOGMOD or MOD-

```
Major Node Name:    A01CICST
Minor Node Name:
                    VBUILD      TYPE=APPL
        CICST01     APPL        ACBNAME=CICST01,                    X
                                AUTH=(ACQ,PASS,VPACE),              X
                                MODETAB=MTLU62,EAS=25,              X
                                PARSESS=YES,VPACING=4,SONSCIP=YES
```

Figure 10.6 Application major and minor nodes for a test CICS address space.

```
Major Node Name:  A01IMSP
Minor Node Name:
                  VBUILD      TYPE=APPL
      IMSP01      APPL        ACBNAME=IMSP01,                    X
                             AUTH=(ACQ,PASS,VPACE),              X
                             MODETAB=MTLU62,EAS=20,              X
                             PARSESS=YES,VPACING=4
```

Figure 10.7 Application major and minor nodes for a production IMS address space.

ETAB is not coded, the first entry in VTAM's default logon mode table will be used. For more information on session parameters and LOGMODES see Chapter 13.

In both the CICS minor nodes a logon mode table name of MTLU62 has been specified. This tells VTAM to search in the logon mode table named MTLU62 for a LOGMODE entry to use for application-to-application sessions. However, a default LOGMODE (DLOGMOD) was not specified. VTAM will select the first LOGMODE entry in MTLU62 mode table.

Just like the CICS examples, the IMS production address space can acquire LUs, pass session establishment requests to other applications, and follow the rules for VPACING. However, the IMS subsystem is not expected to be used by as many users as the CICS subsystem. This is apparent from the EAS operand value of 20 (Figure 10.7). However, the application program must handle failure termination since the operand SONSCIP was not coded and the default is SONSCIP=NO.

We see in Figure 10.8 that the number of estimated active sessions is reduced to 10. Can you determine what the name of the ACB for this application is? If you remember our discussion on the ACBNAME operand, the acbname value will be taken from the net-

```
Major Node Name:  A01IMST
Minor Node Name:
                  VBUILD      TYPE=APPL
      IMST01      APPL        AUTH=(ACQ,PASS,VPACE),             X
                             MODETAB=MTLU62,EAS=10,              X
                             PARSESS=YES,VPACING=4
```

Figure 10.8 Application major and minor nodes for a test IMS address space.

```
Major Node Name:    A01TSO
Minor Node Name:
                    VBUILD   TYPE=APPL
        TSO01       APPL   AUTH=(PASS,NVPACE,TSO),           X
                           EAS=1,ACBNAME=TSO
        TSO01001    APPL   AUTH=(PASS,NVPACE,TSO),           X
                           EAS=1,ACBNAME=TSO0001
        TSO01002    APPL   AUTH=(PASS,NVPACE,TSO),           X
                           EAS=1,ACBNAME=TSO0002
        TSO01003    APPL   AUTH=(PASS,NVPACE,TSO),           X
                           EAS=1,ACBNAME=TSO0003
        TSO01004    APPL   AUTH=(PASS,NVPACE,TSO),           X
                           EAS=1,ACBNAME=TSO0004
        TSO01005    APPL   AUTH=(PASS,NVPACE,TSO),           X
                           EAS=1,ACBNAME=TSO0005
```

Figure 10.9 Application major and minor nodes for the TSO subsystem.

work unique name (the name of the APPL statement) for this application minor node. The name for the ACB is IMST01.

As you can see from Figure 10.9, the TSO application definition is quite different from the previous examples. This is because TSO is actually part of the operating system control program. TSO primarily consists of two components, the Terminal Control Address Space (TCAS), which is a component of the operating system, and the VTAM Terminal I/O Coordinator (VTIOC), which is a component of VTAM. The TCAS component accepts the end user's logon and creates an address space for each user that requests a TSO/VTAM session, hence the extra APPL definition statements, one for each user that logs on to TSO. TCAS is represented by the first application definition statement. Its ACBNAME must always be TSO. No substitutes are allowed. The VTIOC component coordinates the interface between TSO and VTAM.

Two operands coded on the application definition statement should stand out to you. One is the coding of the TSO parameter for the AUTH operand. This should tell you immediately that this APPL statement is for the definition of a TSO application. The other major difference is the EAS operand. Because TSO users are allocated their own address spaces, coding an EAS greater than 1 would waste valuable storage in the host's Common Storage Area (CSA).

There is just one more requirement for coding TSO application definition statements. The APPL statements that define the user's TSO application must have an ACBNAME in the format of TSOnnnn. The nnnn value must be a decimal integer and the first value coded must start with 0001, with the remaining APPL ACBnames ascending sequentially as depicted in Figure 10.9.

When a user issues a logon to TSO, the next available user application will be attached to that user by TCAS. Suppose one user is logged onto TSO and the name of the application statement (applid) assigned to the user is TSO01002. Then the next user logging on will be assigned TSO01003, even if TSO01001 is available.

This concludes our discussion on defining applications to VTAM. Remember that it is important for you as the communications systems programmer to converse with the systems programmer responsible for the applications to obtain any necessary information on how the application will interface with VTAM.

Now that we have defined the applications, we need to describe to VTAM the locally attached terminals and logical units the end user will use to access the applications.

10.2 LOCAL NON-SNA DEVICE MAJOR NODE

There are two types of locally attached (channel-attached) terminal devices the user can use to access the network. One is the non-SNA device and the other is an SNA device. The non-SNA device terminal is defined to the operating system as an addressable unit unto itself. The cluster controller the terminal is attached to is not defined to VTAM. Therefore each terminal, although attached to different cluster controllers, may be grouped into a major node based on location or perhaps by application. This may be an approach you may wish to pursue in your shop. An advantage of this is that not all users attached to a local non-SNA cluster controller will be affected if the major node is inactivated. Figure 10.10 diagrams the attachment of local cluster controllers.

10.2.1 I/O GEN Considerations

For all local attached devices, the host control program for input/output services must be aware of the device channel and unit address. This is accomplished by the operating systems programmer when he or she performs an I/O generation (GEN) process. For most local non-SNA channel-attached terminals the I/O GEN parameters should resemble the example in Figure 10.11.

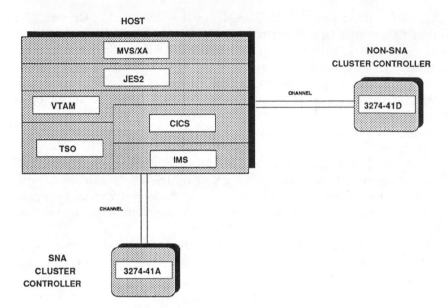

Figure 10.10 Local attached cluster controllers.

In Figure 10.11, we can see that the cluster controller being defined is attached to channel 2. The 3274 cluster controller is defined
to have 30 3278-2 type terminals and 2 3286-2 type printers. From
the IODEVICE macro we can determine that the terminals will be
attached to Channel Unit Address (CUA) 220 to 23D, which correlates to ports 0 to 30 of the cluster controller. The second IODEVICE
defines two printers for the cluster controller on ports 31 and 32,
which correlates to channel unit addresses 23E and 23F, respectively.

```
CONSOLE    MCONS=221,ROUTCDE=ALL
CHAN1      CHANNEL ADDRESS=2,TYPE=BLKMPXR
CNTLUNIT   CUNUMBR=210,UNIT=3274,PATH=(02),                 X
           UNITADD=((20,32)),SHARED=N,PROTOCL=D
IODEVICE   UNIT=3278,MODEL=2,ADDRESS=(220,30),              X
           FEATURE=(EBKY3277,DOCHAR,KB78KEY),               X
           CUNUMBR=210
IODEVICE   UNIT=3286,MODEL=2,ADDRESS=(23E,2),               X
           CUNUMBR=210
```

Figure 10.11 MVS I/O GEN parameters for local non-SNA cluster controller.

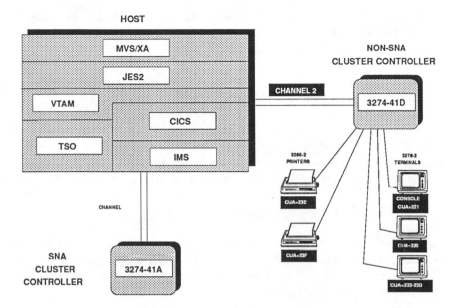

Figure 10.12 The physical connection of a local non-SNA cluster controller.

We added the CONSOLE macro here to make you aware of an important factor when considering non-SNA major and minor node definitions. Assume, for a moment, that the host is an IBM 3090-180 mainframe. On these host computers and all the 30xx mainframe computers IBM makes, the main operator console and all secondary operator consoles will take a port on the non-SNA locally attached cluster controller. In this example, the main console will be attached to channel unit address 221, which will correlate to port 1 on the cluster controller. Figure 10.12 gives you a pictorial representation of this addressing.

There are two important distinctions between local non-SNA and SNA cluster controllers. The first point is the protocol. The local non-SNA cluster controller uses channel protocol. The local SNA cluster controller uses SDLC protocol. The second distinctive characteristic is the addressing scheme. Each local non-SNA terminal and/or printer is assigned a unique channel unit address. Therefore, each device is polled individually by VTAM. The operating I/O subsystem has complete control of each device. On a local SNA cluster controller, there is only one polling address for all the attached devices. Consequently, the I/O subsystem has control over this one address. Unfortunately, if this one address is brought offline by the I/O subsystem, all the end users connected to the local SNA cluster controller are brought offline. The use of this one channel unit address is discussed in the following sections.

10.2.2 LBUILD Statement

Now that we know the non-SNA device addresses, we can begin to code the local non-SNA major node. To tell VTAM that this major node is for local non-SNA devices we must code the LBUILD definition statement. The format of this statement is:

```
[name] LBUILD [CONFGDS=name][,CONFGPW=password]
```

As you can see from the format, the name parameter is optional. If it is coded, it is purely a symbolic name that VTAM ignores. The CONFGDS and CONFGPW operands have the same function here as they do on the VBUILD statement

10.2.3 LOCAL Definition Statement

For each local non-SNA terminal that is to be in VTAM's domain, we must code a LOCAL definition statement. The format of the LOCAL definition statement is outlined in Figure 10.13. An explanation of it follows:

The name operand defines to VTAM the network unique symbolic name for this locally attached non-SNA terminal. This name is also the minor node name assigned to this network resource.

```
name     LOCAL    CUADDR=channel unit address
                  ,TERM=3277|3284|3286,
                  [,DLOGMOD=default logmode entry name]
                  [,FEATUR2=([EDATS|NOEDATS][,MODEL1|MODEL2]
                  [,ISTATUS=ACTIVE|INACTIVE]
                  [,LOGAPPL=application program name]
                  [,LOGTAB=interpret table name]
                  [,MODETAB=logon mode table name]
                  [,SPAN=(NCCF or NetView spanname)]
                  [,USSTAB=USS definition table  name]
```

Figure 10.13 Format of the LOCAL definition statement.

The CUADDR is the actual channel unit address for this device. The CUAs defined in Figure 10.12 are the values that should be coded for the local non-SNA device on the CUADDR operand.

The TERM operand tells VTAM what type of station is being defined for this CUA. Only those values specified on the TERM operand can be coded. Any other value will cause an error.

The DLOGMOD operand is optional and defines the default LOGMODE entry name to be used for this device. This name will refer VTAM to what session parameters this device will use for session establishment. See Chapter 13 for more information on the LOGMODE entry.

The FEATUR2 operand identifies the specific features for this device. The EDATS|NOEDATS parameter tells VTAM if this device supports the extended data streaming feature. The default is NOEDATS. The MODEL1|MODEL2 parameter tells VTAM the default screen and buffer size. MODEL1 denotes a size of 480 bytes and MODEL2 denotes a size of 1920 bytes. The default is MODEL1 despite the fact that the majority of 3270 family type displays and printers have screen and buffer sizes of 1920 bytes and greater.

The ISTATUS operand tells VTAM if this device should be activated when the major node is activated. The default is ACTIVE. If INACTIVE is coded, it can be overridden with an operator command, which is:

```
VARY NET,ACT,ID=major node name,SCOPE=ALL
```

The SCOPE=ALL operand tells VTAM to activate all the minor nodes associated with this major node. The LOGAPPL operand tells VTAM that when this device is activated, automatically begin a LOGON to the specified application program coded on this operand. This application becomes the controlling primary logical unit for this device. You can verify this by displaying the LUname for this device and searching for the CONTROLLING PLU= field in the displayed output.

The MODETAB operand defines the name of the LOGON mode table to be used for this device when searching for session parameters.

The SPAN operand is only coded if NCCF or NetView is be used to manage the network.

The value coded in the USSTAB operand tells VTAM to look in the USS definition table named by this operand. Usually, this name is the name assigned to a user-created Unformatted System Services (USS) table. If you omit this operand, VTAM will search a default

USS table. See Chapter 13 for more information on the USS table and how to create your own USS definition table.

All of the above mentioned optional operands have the same function for an SNA device. The exception to this is the FEATUR2 operand. It is applicable to non-SNA devices only.

Figure 10.14 shows how we coded the example non-SNA channel-attached cluster controller from the example in Section 10.2.2. Notice that we did not code CUA 221 for the console in this major node. Since the operating system owns that device, VTAM will not be able to activate it.

In summary, remember for non-SNA local devices that each device is assigned a specific channel unit address. Each address is associated with a unique minor node name. The non-SNA terminals and printers need not be grouped into the same major node. Although they are physically attached to the same cluster controller, they can be logically defined in different VTAM major nodes that describe local non-SNA devices.

```
MAJOR NODE NAME:   L01TERMS
MINOR NODE NAMES:
                LBUILD
   L01T220   LOCAL   CUADDR=220,TERM=3277,DLOGMOD=L3270,         X
                     MODETAB=MT01,FEATUR2=(NOEDATS,MODEL2),      X
                     USSTAB=USSNSNA
   L01T222   LOCAL   CUADDR=222,TERM=3277,DLOGMOD=L3270,         X
                     MODETAB=MT01,FEATUR2=(NOEDATS,MODEL2),      X
                     USSTAB=USSNSNA
                "
                "
                "

   L01T23D   LOCAL   CUADDR=23D,TERM=3277,DLOGMOD=L3270,         X
                     MODETAB=MT01,FEATUR2=(NOEDATS,MODEL2),      X
                     USSTAB=USSNSNA
   L01P23E   LOCAL   CUADDR=23E,TERM=3286,DLOGMOD=L3270,         X
                     MODETAB=MT01,FEATUR2=(NOEDATS,MODEL2),      X
                     USSTAB=USSNSNA
   L01P23F   LOCAL   CUADDR=23F,TERM=3286,DLOGMOD=L3270,         X
                     MODETAB=MT01,FEATUR2=(NOEDATS,MODEL2),      X
                     USSTAB=USSNSNA
```

Figure 10.14 Coding of the non-SNA cluster controller from Section 10.2.2.

10.3 LOCAL SNA DEVICE MAJOR NODE

Locally attached SNA devices are defined to VTAM using a local PU statement for each physical unit SNA cluster controller and a local LU statement for each logical unit that is associated with the physical unit. There can be more than one PU statement in a local SNA major node, but each LU associated with a specific PU must be defined after the associated PU in the same major node. This is in contrast to the non-SNA terminal definitions in which the cluster controller is not even defined and each terminal definition associated with a cluster controller can be coded in a different non-SNA major node for the locally attached cluster controllers. This difference between the two cluster controllers is because the SNA terminal definitions are logically connected to the cluster controller. There is no physical connection to the cluster controller by means of a channel unit address for each terminal. Instead, there is only one channel unit address, and that address represents the cluster controller address.

10.3.1 I/O Generation Considerations for Local SNA

From our discussion in Section 10.2.1, we must define all channel-attached devices to the operating system. This is done by assigning a channel unit address. Figure 10.15 outlines a sample coding for a local SNA cluster controller attached to an MVS operating system.

In this example, we can see that the cluster controller being defined is attached to channel 3. The unit being described is a 3791L cluster controller, though the actual device is a 3274-41A. The cluster controller's channel unit address is 320. The individual terminal addresses are assigned during configuration of the cluster controller. Notice that there is no operating system console support on a locally attached SNA cluster controller. Figure 10.16 depicts both non-SNA and SNA channel-attached cluster controllers.

```
CHAN3        CHANNEL ADDRESS=3,TYPE=BLKMPXR
CNTLUNIT     CUNUMBER=310,UNIT=3791L,PATH=(03),  X
             UNITADD=((20,1))
IODEVICE     UNIT=3791L,ADDRESS=(320,1)
```

Figure 10.15 MVS I/O GEN parameters for a local channel-attached SNA cluster controller.

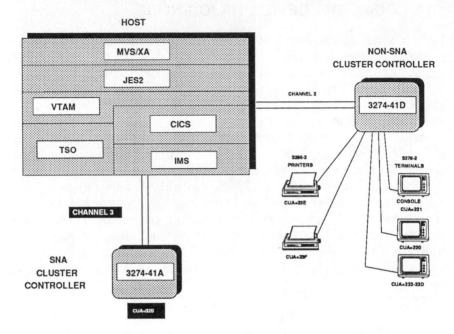

Figure 10.16 The physical connection of both non-SNA and SNA local cluster controllers.

There are two important distinctions between local non-SNA and SNA cluster controllers. The first point is the protocol. The local non-SNA cluster controller uses channel protocol. The local SNA cluster controller uses SDLC protocol. The second distinctive characteristic is the addressing scheme. Each local non-SNA terminal and/or printer is assigned a unique channel unit address. Therefore, each device is polled individually by VTAM. The operating I/O subsystem has complete control of each device. On a local SNA cluster controller, there is only one polling address for all the attached devices. Consequently, the I/O subsystem has control over this one address. Unfortunately, if this one address is brought offline by the I/O subsystem, all the end users connected to the local SNA cluster controller are brought offline. The use of this one channel unit address is discussed in the following sections.

10.3.2 PU Definition Statement for Local SNA Major Node

Prior to coding the PU definition statement, a VBUILD statement must be coded specifying TYPE=LOCAL to notify VTAM that the following statements are defining local SNA devices. More than one PU can be defined under this VBUILD statement, but this reduces the flexibility of operation.

A PU definition statement must be coded for each physical unit that is to be included in this local SNA major node definition. Figure 10.17 has the complete format of the PU definition statement.

The name parameter is required and assigns the minor node name to this physical unit. This name must be network unique. The operand CUADDR is the hexadecimal value of the channel unit address for this PU. Remember that in Section 10.3.1 we assigned a channel unit address of 320 to this PU. Code this hexadecimal value for this operand. If you do not code CUADDR, the ISTATUS value must be INACTIVE and the operator must supply the channel unit address in the VARY active command. The DISCNT operand defines how to terminate the SSCP-PU and SSCP-LU sessions when the last LU-LU session on this PU is terminated. The YES|NO tells VTAM which option to use. If YES is coded, VTAM terminates all SSCP-LU sessions and the SSCP-PU session when the last LU-LU session is terminated. IF NO, the default is coded, then VTAM terminates the SSCP sessions after normal session terminations from the PU and all the associated LU-LU sessions on that PU. The F|NF tells VTAM to flag this PU in final-use status when deactivating the PU if DISCNT=YES has been coded. This operand is not used if DISCNT=NO is coded. The F is the default and indicates "final-use" status. The NF indicates "not-final-use" status. You should consult the appropriate device publication on the use of the DISCNT operand. The ISTATUS tells VTAM if this PU should be activated when the associated major node is activated. The default is ACTIVATE. This operand can also be used to sift down to the PU's associated LUs. The MAXBFRU value defines to VTAM the maximum number of buffer

```
name      PU    [CUADDR=channel unit address]
                [,DISCNT=([YES|NO][,F|NF])]
                [,ISTATUS=ACTIVE|INACTIVE]
                [,MAXBFRU=n|1]
                [,PUTYPE=2]
                [,SECNET=YES|NO]
                [,SPAN=(spanname)]
```

Figure 10.17 Complete format of the PU definition statement for local SNA major node.

units from the IOBUF buffer pool that can be used to receive or send data from or to the physical unit. The n value is a decimal integer with a range of 1 to 65,535. The PUTYPE operand describes to VTAM the type of PU attached. The default value of 2 is the only valid PU type that can be coded in a local SNA major node. The SECNET operand should be coded only if you have the IBM 3710 network controller in your network. It tells VTAM that this PU is associated with a secondary network. The resources in this secondary network are not defined to VTAM. If YES is coded, the PU data requires special problem determination considerations when a communications management application receives the data. The SPAN operand value is the span name from NCCF or NetView that is associated with this PU.

The PU definition statement in Figure 10.18 tells us that the PU will be made active when the SNA major node is activated. The definition also tells us that this is not a 3710 resource. Now that the PU has been defined, we must define the LUs associated with this PU.

10.3.3 LU Definition Statement for Local SNA Major Node

The LU definition statements must follow the associated PU definition statement within this local SNA major node. There must be one LU definition statement for each LU defined for this physical unit. Figure 10.19 has the complete format of the local LU definition statement.

The name parameter is required and assigns the minor node name to this logical unit. This name must be network unique. The operand LOCADDR is also required. This value is the logical unit's local address that is assigned at this physical unit. The n value is a decimal integer from 1 to 255. This is the address assigned to the LU being

```
LS320      PU      CUADDR=320,                          X
                   DISCNT=NO,                           X
                   ISTATUS=ACTIVE,                      X
                   MAXBFRU=1,                           X
                   PUTYPE=2,                            X
                   SECNET=NO
```

Figure 10.18 Sample coding for PU definition statement for local SNA major node.

```
name       LU    LOCADDR=n
                 [,DLOGMOD=default logon mode entry name]
                 [,ISTATUS=ACTIVE|INACTIVE]
                 [,LOGAPPL=autologon application name]
                 [,LOGTAB=interpret table name]
                 [,MODETAB=logon mode table name]
                 [,PACING=n|0|1]
                 [,SPAN=(spanname)]
                 [,SSCPFM=FSS|USSSCS]
                 [,USSTAB=USS table name]
                 [,VPACING=n|0|1]
```

Figure 10.19 Complete format of the LU definition statement for local SNA major node.

defined by this statement. The LOCADDR need not be consecutive and an LU statement is not required for every possible local address.

According to the IBM 3274 architecture for a 3274 cluster controller, 128 logical units can be defined, even though the address range is from 1 to 255. However, the actual maximum number of LUs a local SNA IBM 3274 PU TYPE 2 device can have assigned to it is 125 logical units. This is a restriction of the 3274 and not SNA. The restriction is because of port 0 of the 3274. Port 0 may not have more than one LOCADDR value assigned to it because this port is used for the 3274 configuration process. Therefore, instead of having 128 (32 ports times 4 LUs per port), the maximum is 3 LUs fewer, or 125 logical units. There is one more requirement for the IBM 3274 SNA cluster controller. The locaddr value must start at 2. Therefore, the maximum LOCADDR value that can be coded for the SNA 3274 is 127. The LOCADDR values are assigned to the ports during the customization process for SNA cluster controllers.

The SSCPFM operand tells VTAM if this logical unit supports the SNA character string coded messages (USSSCS) or formatted messages (FSS) during SSCP communications. For LU statements defining terminals, the default FSS is used. For LU statements defining SNA printers, the USSSCS parameter is used.

The PACING operand defines how VTAM will pace data flowing to the logical unit during a LU-LU session from the channel-attached host for this LU's physical unit. The default value of 1 means that VTAM will send one message to the LU and not send any more messages until VTAM receives a pacing response from the LU. This default value and any other n value are ignored if the LU-LU session is in the same domain. The range for n is 1 to 63. The value 0 means no pacing is to be performed.

```
MAJOR NODE NAME:   L01SNA20
MINOR NODE NAMES:
                 VBUILD   TYPE=LOCAL
   LS320     PU    CUADDR=320,DISCNT=NO,ISTATUS=ACTIVE,          X
                   DLOGMOD=D4A32782,MAXBFRU=10,USSTAB=USSSNA,     X
                   PACING=0,VPACING=0
   LS320T02 LU     LOCADDR=02
   LS320T03 LU     LOCADDR=03
   LS320T04 LU     LOCADDR=04
                "

                "


   LS320P32 LU     LOCADDR=32,LOGMODE=DSC4K,USSTAB=ISTICNDT,     X
                   PACING=1,VPACING=2,SSCPFM=USSSCS
```

Figure 10.20 Coding of the local SNA major node with the PU and LU definition
statements.

The VPACING value determines the number of messages the primary logical units owning VTAM can send to the secondary logical units owning VTAM before waiting for a pacing response. This type of pacing is called two stage and is between VTAM hosts. If the LU-LU session is in the same domain, the value specified for the PACING operand is ignored and the value of the VPACING operand is used. This is called one-stage pacing.

Usually, the pacing values are set to 0 for locally attached SNA devices unless the device receives large amounts of data, such as printers or graphic terminals. In this case, a PACING value of 1 and a VPACING value of 2 should be adequate for initial trials.

The remaining operands not discussed here have been reviewed in Section 10.2.3. Turn to this section if you need to review their meaning and purpose. All the operands for an LU definition statement may be coded on the PU definition statement to use the sift-down effect. The exception is the LOCADDR and SPAN operands. These must be coded for each LU definition statement.

From the sample local SNA major node definition in Figure 10.20, we can see that we are using the sift-down effect. All the LUs defined will use the same default LOGMODE entry name of D4A32782, the same USS table name of USSSNA, the formatted system services (FSS), and a PACING and VPACING value of 0. This is true for all the LUs except the last one that is defined. This LU was created to define a SNA printer. The LU name tells us that from its format LS320P32, where the P denotes a printer for this LU definition. The pacing values of PACING=1 and VPACING=2 were coded so that the printer does not monopolize the PU during large volumes of print destined for this LU. Finally, the DLOGMOD was overridden to DSC4K and the SSCPFM=USSSCS tells us that this LU uses USS SNA character string mode when communicating with the SSCP.

10.4 SUMMARY

We have defined all the applications, local non-SNA devices, and local SNA devices. In the next chapter, we will define devices to VTAM that are not channel attached but are remotely attached through an NCP using switched lines. These resources are defined to VTAM in a switched major node.

11

Switched Major Nodes and Path Tables

11.1 SWITCHED MAJOR NODE

This major node is used to define SNA resources that gain access to the network by using dial-up facilities, that is, a phone call from either the network control center operation facility or from the remote end user's facility. This dial arrangement can provide a number of remote sites with access to the network without the added expense of using a private dedicated telecommunications line. The link protocol used is SDLC. Each switched SDLC line must have a switched line definition in the NCP. For products such as NTO, that use virtual physical and logical units, these NCP switched line definitions are also needed. The switched major node is defined using a VBUILD statement, a PU (switched) statement, a PATH statement for dial-out operations, and an LU (switched) statement. Figure 11.1 diagrams a switched connection.

In our discussion of switched lines in Section 8.1.6, we had determined that a remote System/36 (S/36) processor will transmit data to the host over a switched line during the night production shift. This will be accomplished by the S/36 emulation of an SNA/RJE 3770. We will now define to VTAM this remote switched SNA device in a switched major node.

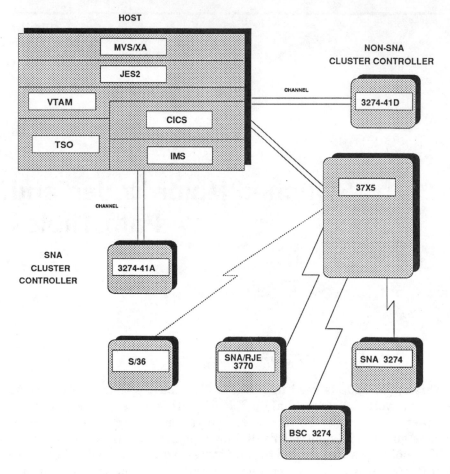

Figure 11.1 Single-domain network with a switched line to a remote System/36 processor.

11.1.1 Switched PU Definition Statement

Prior to the switched PU definition statement, a VBUILD definition statement must be coded that defines this switched major node. See Section 10.1.1 for more on the VBUILD definition statement.

A PU definition statement must be coded for each physical unit that is to be included in this switched major node. Figure 11.2 has the complete format of the switched PU definition statement.

The name parameter is required and assigns the minor node name to this physical unit. This name must be network unique. The oper- and ADDR is the hexadecimal 1-byte value of this PU's SDLC sta-

```
name         PU    ADDR=physical unit SDLC station address
                   ,IDBLK=identification block number
                   ,IDNUM=identification number
                   [,DISCNT=([YES|NO][,F|NF])
                   [,IRETRY=YES|NO]
                   [,ISTATUS=ACTIVE|INACTIVE]
                   [,MAXDATA=size|261|265]
                   [,MAXOUT=n|1]
                   [,MAXPATH=n|0]
                   [,PASSLIM=n|1]
                   [,PUTYPE=n|2]
                   [,SECNET=YES|NO]
                   [,SPAN=(spanname)]
```

Figure 11.2 Complete format of the switched PU definition statement for a switched major node.

tion address. This address must match the SDLC station address that was assigned to the PU during the configuration process of the control unit. This value does not need to be enclosed in quotes or apostrophes.

An identification structure that is unique to a switched PU is the station ID. This station ID is used during the exchange identification (XID) command during the dial procedure. The station ID must also be network unique. Figure 11.3 shows the format of the station ID.

The PU TYPE operand defines to VTAM the type of physical unit. The default is PU TYPE 2. But notice here, in a switched PU definition statement, you may code something other than a Type 2 device. You should consult the device's component description manual to determine the value for this operand. The IDBLK operand is required. This value is a three digit hexadecimal number that represents the device type. Each device type has a unique identification block num-

```
BITS:        0 - 3        Reserved
             4 - 7        PUTYPE value
             8 - 15       "00"
            16 - 27       IDBLK value
            28 - 47       IDNUM value
```

Figure 11.3 Station ID format for the XID command.

ber. Again, consult the component description manual for the device you are defining. The final piece of the station ID is the IDNUM operand. It is also a required operand. The value coded here can be any five digit hexadecimal value. Some shops use the serial number of the device, others devise their own number. This part of the station ID format is where the station ID uniqueness is derived. Make sure no switched PUs in your network have the same IDNUM value. Although the DISCNT operand was covered in the local PU definition statement, it acts differently for a switched PU. For a switched PU, the YES|NO value determines if the actual physical connection is to be disconnected after the last LU-LU session has terminated for that PU, literally hanging up the phone. This will save telephone costs, especially if a user's session is timed out by the system but the dial connection is not broken. However, the switched PU and LU status in VTAM remains active. This will allow a new dial connection to be reestablished immediately. The default NO will keep the switched link connected. It is advisable for you to code YES for this parameter. The IRETRY operand pertains to the switched PU's connecting NCP. If YES is coded, the NCP will retry a polling sequence immediately following an Idle Detect Timeout for the device. The MAXDATA is the largest Path Information Unit (PIU), in bytes, that can be received by the physical unit. The maximum value you can code is 65,535 bytes. If MAXDATA is not coded, the default is 261 for a PU Type 1 and 265 for a PU Type 2 device. The MAXOUT operand value supplies the maximum number of PIUs that can be sent to the PU before requesting a response from the PU. The value range for n is a decimal integer from 1 to 7. The MAXPATH operand value is the number of dial-out paths available to the PU. A value range of 0 to 256 is valid. The default value 0 signifies that only dial-in paths are available for this PU. The final operand is PASSLIM. This value will determine the number of PIUs that the NCP will send to the PU in one transmission. The valid range is 1 to the value of MAXOUT for switched PUs. The remaining operands not discussed can be reviewed in the previous section for local SNA major node definition.

11.1.2 Switched LU Definition Statement

The switched LU definition statements must follow the associated PU definition statement within this switched major node. There must be one LU definition statement for each LU to be defined for this physical unit. Figure 11.4 shows the complete format of the switched LU definition statement.

```
name        LU    LOCADDR=n
                  [,BATCH=YES|NO]
                  [,DLOGMOD=default logon mode entry name]
                  [,FEATUR2=LOWERCSE|DUALCSE]
                  [,ISTATUS=ACTIVE|INACTIVE]
                  [,LOGAPPL=autologon application name]
                  [,LOGTAB=interpret table name]
                  [,MODETAB=logon mode table name]
                  [,PACING=n|0|1]
                  [,SPAN=(spanname)]
                  [,SSCPFM=FSS|USSSCS|USSNTO|USS3780|USS3270|
                           USS3275]
                  [,TERM=terminal type]
                  [,USSTAB=USS table name]
                  [,VPACING=n|0|2]
```

Figure 11.4 Complete format of the switched LU definition statement for a switched major node.

The name parameter is required and assigns the minor node name to this logical unit. This name must be network unique. The operand LOCADDR is also required. This value is the logical unit's local address that is assigned at this physical unit. The n value is a decimal integer. Its range varies depending on the PU type for the physical unit. A PU Type 1 allows the range to be 0 to 63; PU Type 2 has a range of 1 to 255. Consult the device's component description manual for the correct value range. The LOCADDR need not be consecutive and an LU statement is not required for every possible local address.

The BATCH operand provides the LU's processing priority for service by the NCP. If NO is coded, the LU will have a high priority. This is particularly important if the LU is used for interactive applications. If YES is coded, NCP assigns the lowest possible priority for service. The FEATUR2 operand is used for NTO devices. This operand tells VTAM how to send the data coded with the TEXT operand of the USSMSG macro coded in the USS table for non-SNA terminals during the SSCP-LU session. The LOWERCSE operand tells VTAM to send only lowercase characters to the terminal. The DUALCSE means that VTAM send the characters as they are coded on the USSMSG macro to non-SNA terminals. DUALCSE is the default. The values for the SSCPFM operand are self-explanatory, determining device type SSCP-LU session support. The TERM operand is for virtual LUs supported through the NTO program product. It identifies the device data stream compatible characteristics. The

VPACING value on a switched LU is different from the local LU definition in that the default for a switched LU is 2. Otherwise, all the operands in Figure 11.4 are the same as those defined for a local LU definition statement.

11.1.3 Switched PATH Definition Statement

The switched PATH definition statements must immediately follow the associated PU definition statement within this switched major node. The PATH statement is used to define dial-out paths to the PU. Some of the operands are exclusive to X.21 switched protocol. You can code up to 256 PATH statements for each switched PU definition statement. The search for a path is performed in the order of the coded PATH statements by VTAM. Figure 11.5 outlines the format of a PATH definition statement.

The name parameter is optional and is not used by VTAM. The DIALNO operand is the telephone number used to call the PU over a switched link. Special characters can be coded in the phone number. A vertical bar can be used as a separator character or a dialing pause character. An underscore can be a separator character, and An *, %, or @ can be an end-of-number character. The length of this operand can be up to 32 characters. For autocall or address call with X.21 switched lines, a unique end-of-number character must follow the digits. However, you do not need to code this. VTAM will supply the unique end-of-number character for the X.21 service. If an NCP/Token Ring Interconnection (NTRI) is used, the DIALNO must be in the following format: DIALNO=xxyy4000cccccccc where xx is the Token Ring Interface Coupler (TIC) number of the communications controller. This value must be between 00 and 99. The yy value is the system access point address of the terminal. This value must be a multiple of 4. Finally, zzzzzzzz is the last four digits of the

```
[name]      PATH  [DIALNO=telephone number|LINENM=linename]
                  [,GID=n]
                  [,GRPNM=groupname]
                  [,PID=n]
                  [,REDIAL=n|3]
                  [,SHOLD=YES|NO]
                  [,USE=YES|NO]
```

Figure 11.5 Complete format of the switched PATH definition statement for a switched major node.

terminal's ring-station address. The first digit must be between 0 and 7. Each zz represents 1 byte. All the x, y, z values are decimal numbers. The LINENM option of the DIALNO operand is mutually exclusive with DIALNO. LINENM is a VSE-only operand. The line name specified must be defined as a direct call line by the common carrier facility. The GID operand identifies a group of paths that exists between all the PUs in the switched major node. The value may be 0 to 255. The GRPNM operand value is the symbolic name assigned to the NCP GROUP definition statement to which this switched line is associated. This parameter is required if you code the SHOLD=YES parameter for this PATH definition. The SHOLD parameter is applicable to VSE operating systems only. If you code YES, VTAM is aware that the path is an X.21 Short Hold Mode/Multiple Port Sharing (SHM/MPS) path. Also, the DIALNO and GRPNM operands must be coded. This feature is available on VTAM V3R1. See the GROUP statement for channel-attached major nodes in Chapter 12 for VM and VSE operating systems. The PID operand is a unique identifier for the path being defined. The REDIAL operand defines to VTAM the number of dialing retries before a dialing error is issued to VTAM. The minimum value is 0. This means there are no dial retries. The maximum is 254 retries. The final operand is the USE operand. This operand is similar to the ISTATUS operand for PUs and LUs. It tells VTAM if this path is made usable at activation of the switched major node.

In the sample switched major node, Figure 11.6, the remote SNA RJE station can be dialed by using the phone number supplied by

```
MAJOR NODE NAME:   SWS36RJE
MINOR NODE NAME:
                VBUILD   TYPE=SWNET,MAXGRP=1,MAXNO=1
   SWS36PU   PU     ADDR=C1,IDBLK=016,IDNUM=19874,PUTYPE=2,    X
                    DLOGMOD=BATCH,MAXPATH=1,MAXDATA=265,        X
                    MAXOUT=7,SSCPFM=FSS
   SWPATH    PATH   DIALNO=15551212,GID=1,GRPNM=SWRJEGRP,       X
                    PID=1
   SWRJEL01  LU     LOCADDR=01,PACING=1,LOGAPPL=JES2RJE,        X
                    ISTATUS=INACTIVE
   SWRJEL02  LU     LOCADDR=02,PACING=1,LOGAPPL=JES2RJE,        X
                    ISTATUS=INACTIVE
```

Figure 11.6 Coding of the switched major node for dial-up S/36 emulating an SNA/3770 3777 multiple logical unit.

the DIALNO parameter from the PATH statement. When the operator activates the switched major node, the logical unit will remain inactive. The operator may activate the LU with a VARY NET,ACT,ID=SWRJEL01 command after the PU has been activated or by using the SCOPE=ALL operand of the VARY ACT command when activating the major node or the PU. The IDBLK value is the coded ID of the 3777 multiple logical unit that the S/36 had configured for the SNA/3770 emulation. The two other operand values that must agree between the switched major node definition and the SNA/3770 emulation configuration are the ADDR and IDNUM operands. Both must be entered into the emulation configuration. These three values will be used in the XID command to verify the device. If the values do not match, VTAM denies the session request.

11.2 DYNAMIC RECONFIGURATION MAJOR NODE

In VTAM and NCP, you can dynamically reconfigure the network without the need for NCP generation by using the dynamic reconfiguration statements. These statements let the communications systems programmer add or delete network resources without affecting an entire NCP subarea node. Dynamic reconfiguration is available to SNA resources only. As with other VTAM major nodes, a VBUILD definition statement must be coded describing the type of major node being defined. See Section 10.1.1 for more on the VBUILD statement.

11.2.1 ADD Definition Statement for Dynamic Reconfiguration

The ADD definition statement defines to VTAM the name of the resource that is to have lower level resources added to it (Figure 11.7). The name operand is optional. But, if it is coded, VTAM will use this name in error messages if the ADD fails. The resource name is the higher level of the resource(s) being added. For adding an LU, this is the name of the LU's associated PU. For the addition of a PU, this is the name of the PU's associated line.

```
[name]    ADD   TO-resource name
```

Figure 11.7 Format of the ADD statement for dynamic reconfiguration.

```
ADDPU01     ADD   TO=PU01
LUT11       LU    LOCADDR=11,USSTAB=USSSNA,PACING=0
LUP12       LU    LOCADDR=12,PACING=1,VPACING=2
ADDLN02     ADD   TO=LN02
PU02        PU    ADDR=C2,MAXDATA=265,USSTAB=USSSNA1
LUT03       LU    LOCADDR=03
LUT04       LU    LOCADDR=04
```

Figure 11.8 Sample ADD statements for dynamic reconfiguration.

In Figure 11.8, two LUs are to be added to physical unit PU01.
The LUs will be assigned the LOCADDR of 11 and 12, respectively.
LUT11 is a terminal and will not be paced. Its USSTAB is named
USSSNA. LUP12 is a printer and it is assigned to LOCADDR 12.
Since the LU is a printer, we will pace the data transmitted to the
LU.

The second ADD statement defines LN02, line 2, as the higher
level resource. LN02 will have a PU (PU02) and two LUs (LUT03,
LUT04) added to it by using dynamic reconfiguration. The USSTAB
operand on the PU statement will be sifted down to the LUs that are
being added along with this PU to LN02.

You can code all VTAM-only operands on the PU and LU definition statements that are to be added dynamically. For a PU, however, you must code the MAXDATA operand. For an LU, you must
code the LOCADDR operand. All other VTAM-only and NCP-related
operands will default if you do not include them in the dynamic
reconfiguration major node definition.

11.2.2 DELETE Definition Statement for Dynamic Reconfiguration

The DELETE definition statement defines to VTAM the name of the
resource whose lower-level resources are to be disassociated from the
named resource (Figure 11.9).

The name operand is optional. But, if it is coded, VTAM will use
this name in error messages if the DELETE fails. The resource name
is the resource whose associated lower-level resources are to be deleted. For deleting an LU, this is the name of the LU's associated
PU. For a PU, this is the name of the PU's associated line.

```
[name]    DELETE FROM=resource name
```

Figure 11.9 Format of the DELETE statement for dynamic reconfiguration.

```
DELPU01    DELETE FROM=LN01
PU01       PU
DELLUS     DELETE FROM=PU02
LUT11      LU
LUP12      LU
```

Figure 11.10 Sample DELETE statements for dynamic reconfiguration.

In Figure 11.10, two LUs are to be deleted from physical unit PU02: LUs LUT11 and LUP12. PU PU01 is to be deleted from line LN01. Note that there are no PU or LU operands required to delete a resource and that if a PU is deleted, all of its associated LUs are also deleted.

In summary, dynamic reconfiguration provides the flexibility for reallocating network resources. The addition or deletion of resources can be accomplished without executing an NCP generation to change the network configuration. It can also allow the communications systems programmer to change VTAM-only operands on SNA resources dynamically. However, if a session exists for the resource, the session must be broken before the dynamic updates take place. Dynamic reconfiguration allows you to make these VTAM-only changes without affecting the entire network community. Remember, for dynamic reconfiguration a DRDS DD statement is needed in the VTAM start procedure. The DRDS data set can be the VTAMLST with a member defined for DR. The sift-down effect from the original NCP definitions does not take effect on the dynamically added resources. Any operands that you do not want defaulted to the IBM standard default should be coded. However, sift down does take effect within the ADD definition statements of the dynamic reconfiguration major node.

The second ADD statement defines LN02, line 2, as the higher level resource. LN02 will have a PU (PU02) and two LUs (LUT03, LUT04) added to it by using dynamic reconfiguration. The USSTAB operand on the PU statement will be sifted down to the LUs that are being added along with this PU to LN02.

11.2.3 Enhanced Dynamic Reconfiguration

Dynamic reconfiguration prior to VTAM V3.2 uses preallocated control blocks in NCP V2 to V4.2. These control block allocations are created by the NCP PUDRPOOL and LUDRPOOL definition statements. When deleting resources, these control blocks and consequently the network addresses associated with them are not reusable. The dynamically reconfigured resources are assigned their network addresses from the predefined DRPOOLs. This limits the number of reconfigurable resources if several deletions and additions are performed, leading to unavailable network addresses. This limitation has been removed by VTAM V3.2 and NCP V4.3 or NCP V5.

Under VTAM V3.2 there are two types of dynamic reconfiguration for resources, explicit and implicit definitions. Using the explicit definitions is quite similar to pre-VTAM V3.2 as discussed in Section 11.2.2. However, there have been modifications to the definition statements for dynamic reconfiguration major node. A new statement called MOVE has been added to alleviate the necessity of issuing a DELETE and then an ADD definition statement to actually relocate a PU's definition to a new line. The MOVE command is only valid for moving resources within the same NCP; that is, you cannot use this command to move a resource from one NCP to another. The old method of deleting and adding must still be used to perform this type of reconfiguration. The format of this statement is:

```
MOVE TO=linename,FROM=linename
```

Additionally, the PU definition statement in the dynamic reconfiguration major node has two new operands and the ability to modify the PU SDLC station address. The format of the new PU dynamic reconfiguration definition statement is:

```
puname      PU   ACTIVE=(NO|YES),
                 ADDR=SDLC station address,
                 DATMODE=(HALF|FULL)
```

The ACTIVE operand tells VTAM to issue an activation request for the PU after the MOVE has been completed. NO is the default value if ACTIVE is not coded. The ADDR operand now allows you to change the SDLC station address used by the physical unit when responding to the SSCP. This is not available in pre-VTAM V3.2. The final operand is DATMODE. This operand tells VTAM and the NCP whether this PU can receive and transmit data concurrently. The default is HALF, meaning that the PU can only send or receive and does not possess the capabilities of concurrent send and receive data transmission.

This new functionality of dynamic reconfiguration leads to interesting possibilities. Because we can change the PU SDLC station address, we can now move a PU to a line that was previously defined as a point to point. However, if this is going to be done, the SERVICE statement of the NCP for this line must have the MAXLST and MAXPU operands coded with sufficient values to handle extra PUs. Unlike pre-VTAM V3.2, the PU and its associated LUs carry with them all the definitions that are currently defined to them.

A new VTAM operator command is also available under VTAM V3.2 to explicitly reconfigure the network resources. The MODIFY NET, DR operator command will allow you to dynamically reconfigure the network without having a predefined DRDS member in VTAMLST. The format of the command is:

```
MODIFY procname,DR,
      TYPE=(MOVE|DELETE),ID=(puname|luname),
      FROM=(linename|puname),[TO=linename),
      ACTIVE=(NO|YES),ADDR=SDLC station address)]
```

Note that this command is only performing moves and deletions of network resources. Care should be taken by the VTAM operator when implementing this command.

The new implicit dynamic reconfiguration lets the communications systems programmer add PUs to defined lines and LUs to PUs through the NCP source definition statements. Prior to this, activation of the NCP would fail because the NCP source did not match the NCP load module defined resources. This implicit reconfiguration of VTAM V3.2 removes this restriction.

In Figure 11.11 you can see that we are moving the PU that was added to line LN02 in Section 11.2.2. The move incorporates a delete and an add in one step. All the LUs associated with the PU are also moved to the new line. You should note, however, that the resource

```
           VBUILD    TYPE=DR
           MOVE      TO=LN01,                              C
                     FROM=LN02,                            C
PU02       PU        ACTIVE=YES,                           C
                     ADDR=C1,                              C
                     DATMODE=HALF
```

Figure 11.11 Sample format of the new MOVE statement in the dynamic reconfiguration major node.

names are the same after the move. This can lead to confusion if your resource names are based on line and SDLC station addresses.

There are also new dynamic path table updates and dynamic table reconfiguration functions provided with VTAM V3.2 and NCP V4.3 and V5.2. Details of their formats and usage capabilities are found in *Advanced SNA Networking*.

11.3 PATH TABLE

Communications between SNA subarea nodes is made possible by the defining routes between each adjacent subarea. In SNA, each subarea must have a map of subareas that can be reached. These are called the "destination" subareas. This mapping of destination subareas provides the possible routes a message may use to reach its destination. The actual mapping of the routes is accomplished by coding PATH definition statements.

The PATH definition statement consists of a destination subarea operand, DESTSA; an explicit route operand, ERn; a virtual route operand, VRn; and a virtual route pacing window size operand, VRPWSnn. Review Chapter 4 for a more detailed description of a subarea, ER and VR.

```
name      PATH       DESTSA=n|(n1,n2,n3...)
                     [ER0=(adjsub[,tgn])]
                     [ER1=(adjsub[,tgn])]
                             .
                             .

                     [ER7=(adjsub[,tgn])]
                     [ER8=(adjsub[,tgn])]
                             .
                             .

                     [ER15=(adjsub[,tgn])]
                     [,VR0=er#]
                     [,VR1=er#]
                             .
                             .

                     [,VR7=er#]
                     [,VRPWSvr#tp=(min#,max#)]
```

Figure 11.12 Format of the PATH definition statement.

11.3.1 PATH Definition Statement

More than one PATH definition statement may be coded in the PATH major node. For this table the VBUILD statement is not used. The name operand (Figure 11.12) assigns a name to the PATH statement being defined. Its value is used during a definition error or a warning message during this path's activation.

The DESTSA operand defines what subareas this VTAM can communicate with over this path. The value specified for n is the subarea number of the destination subarea. For example, in our single domain network, all of our remote devices are attached to a single NCP/3725. This NCP has been assigned a subarea number of 2. Therefore, this operand is coded as:

DESTSA=2

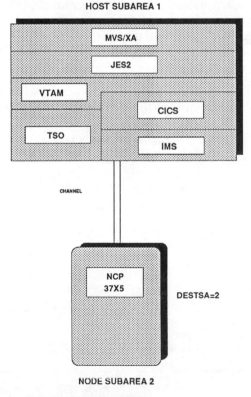

Figure 11.13 Single domain subarea nodes.

Since our single-domain example (Figure 11.13) has only one NCP, we code only one destination subarea in the PATH statement. However, later on when we discuss multiple NCPs in the network, you will see that more than one destination subarea may be coded on the DESTSA operand.

The ER0...ER15 operand identifies the adjacent subarea that VTAM can use to route data to the destination subarea. ER8 to ER15 can only be used with VTAM V3.2 when the adjacent NCP is NCP V4.3.1/V5.2.1. Each Explicit Route (ER) can have a transmission group number assigned to it. For channel attached subareas, VTAM always uses transmission group number 1.

In Figure 11.14, subarea 2 is reached by VTAM via Explicit Route 0 (ER0) over Transmission Group Number 1 (TG#1). The ER statement is coded as:

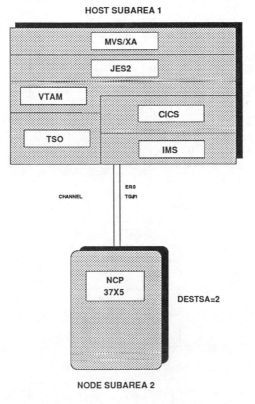

Figure 11.14 The use of explicit routes to the destination subarea 2.

```
ER0=(2,1)
```

where the adjacent subarea is 2 and the transmission group to which this subarea is attached is transmission group number 1.

The VR0...VR7 operand associates the explicit route to an adjacent subarea to a virtual route. The virtual route in VTAM is a logical route whereas the explicit route is a physical route. Figure 11.15 diagrams virtual route to subarea 2. Virtual route 0 will be mapped to ER0. The VR statement is coded as:

```
VR0=0
```

The final operand is the virtual route pacing window size. The VRPWS*vr#tp* statement defines to VTAM the number of messages

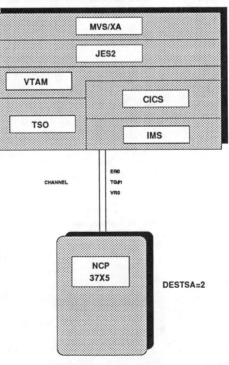

Figure 11.15 The use of virtual routes to the destination subarea 2.

that can be sent through this virtual route at any given time. The *vr#* is the virtual route number associated with this window. The tp is the transmission priority for this virtual route. The transmission priority ranges from a low priority of 0 to a high priority of 2. This means that we can have up to 24 VR pacing window size statements, from VRPWS00 to VRPWS72.

The *min#* defines the minimum window size for this VR. This value must be greater than 0 but less than or equal to the maximum window size. The *max#* is the maximum window size for this VR. The value coded here must be greater than the minimum window size and less than or equal to 255. If either the *min#* or *max#* is not coded, the VRPWS is ignored by VTAM.

If you do not code the VRPWS operand, VTAM will determine the *min#* and *max#* of the window size by:

1. Setting the *min#* to the number of subareas associated with the ER (ER length).
2. Setting the *max#* to 3 times the ER length.
3. If the VR ends in an adjacent subarea to VTAM, the *max#* is set to the larger of the following values:

   A. 15

   B. 255 minus (16 x *n*) where *n* is the number of ERs that originate in this VTAM host and pass through the adjacent subarea.

These options allow VTAM to increase or decrease the window size accordingly. For the most part, you are better off letting VTAM decide on the size of the window.

In conclusion, the PATH definition statement for our single domain network is coded as in Figure 11.16.

```
PATH12   PATH        DESTSA=2,
                     ER0=(2,1),
                     VR0=0
```

Figure 11.16 Format of the coded PATH definition statement for our single-domain network.

11.4 SUMMARY

We have now reviewed and coded all the major and minor nodes that are configured into our single-domain network in an MVS/XA operating system environment. All the operands discussed are valid for an MVS, MVS/XA, VM, and VSE operating system environment except as noted. The following chapter reviews the VTAM operands that are unique to both the VM and VSE environment but are not used in an MVS or MVS/XA environment.

12

VM and VSE Channel-Attached Configurations

The VM and VSE operating systems need special consideration when defining a VTAM network. The channel-attached SNA devices are defined to the operating systems as switched or nonswitched lines and the coding resembles that used in NCP. These VTAM resource definitions are used with either the Integrated Communications Adapter (ICA) of the IBM 4361 host processor or the Telecommunication Subsystem Controller (TSC) of the IBM 9370 host processor. For the VSE operating system, this is really the only consideration for you to remember. However, on the VM operating system we must point out the considerations in more detail.

As the name "VM operating system" implies, all devices addressed by VTAM are defined as virtual addresses rather than real addresses like those used in MVS. The virtual addresses you code for the VTAM devices must be used with the following VM commands:

1. DEDICATE statements coded in the VM directory.
2. CP ATTACH commands coded for PROFILE GCS EXECs for the VTAM and VSCS virtual machine.
3. CP ATTACH command entered from the operator console.
4. CP DEFINE commands entered on the VTAM operator console or used in a profile.

One other requirement on a VM operating system that affects VTAM definitions is the VM userid. All logical unit device names that will log onto VM cannot be the same as any VM userids in the system.

12.1 SDLC NONSWITCHED CHANNEL-ATTACHED MAJOR NODE

This major node defines to the VM/VTAM and VSE/VTAM all the characteristics and number of PUs and LUs that are grouped into this major node.

12.1.1 The GROUP Definition Statement

For SDLC nonswitched channel-attached devices, this GROUP statement defines line characteristics for the lines defined following the GROUP statement and if you desire for the PUs and LUs associated with each line. Figure 12.1 contains the operands used for the GROUP definition statement.

As you can see from Figure 12.1, the statement is not extensive. The name parameter assigns the minor node name for the line group. It can be one to eight alphanumeric characters but cannot begin with a $. The LNCTL operand is the only required operand. In this case, it defines the line control for this group as SDLC protocol. The DIAL=NO operand identifies this line group as a nonswitched line group. If switched network backup is provided, this operand is still coded as DIAL=NO. The last operand is the SPAN operand. It defines to NCCF or NetView an operator's span of control for this VTAM resource.

12.1.2 The LINE Definition Statement

The LINE statement is actually describing the channel to which the physical units are attached. A LINE statement is coded for each SDLC nonswitched line in your VM/VTAM channel-attached network. Figure 12.2 outlines the operands for the LINE definition statement.

```
name      GROUP      LNCTL=SDLC
                     [,DIAL=NO]
                     [,SPAN=(NCCF or NetView spanname)]
```

Figure 12.1 GROUP definition statement format for SDLC nonswitched channel-attached devices.

```
name      LINE        [ADDRESS=cua|030]
                      [,ACTIVTO=t]
                      [,MAXBFRU=([norm|1|2][,max|2|8])]
                      [,PAUSE=t|0.1]
                      [,REPLYTO=n|1]
                      [,SERVLIM=n|4]
                      [,ISTATUS=ACTIVE|INACTIVE]
                      [,SPAN=(NCCF or NetView spanname]
```

Figure 12.2 LINE definition statement format for SDLC nonswitched channel-attached devices.

Both the name and the SPAN operand have been discussed under the GROUP statement and their meanings also apply to the LINE statement. The ADDRESS operand is the channel unit address for the SDLC nonswitched line. The default address is 030. You may override the address by specifying the U= parameter on the VARY NET,ACT operator command. The ACTIVTO operand defines the interval that the communications adapter is to wait without detecting an SDLC frame from another NCP or VTAM.

The MAXBFRU operand defines the number of buffers VTAM will use for normal channel program reads and writes. This value must be coordinated with the IOBUF pool for VM and the LFBUF pool for VSE. These pools define the size of VTAM's message buffers. You must determine the average or normal PIU size and the maximum or largest PIU size being transmitted on this line. Once this determination has been made, you can code an appropriate value for MAX-BFRU based on the message buffer size and the average and maximum PIU sizes. The *norm* value should result in a final message PIU size that is 1 to 2 message buffers larger than the normal PIU size. The default for PU Type 1 and 2 devices is 1 and for PU Type 4 and 5 devices it is 2. The *max*imum value coded should be large enough to hold the largest PIU that is to be transmitted over this line. The default for PU Type 1 and 2 is 2 and for PU Type 4 and 5 is 8.

The PAUSE operand controls the polling to the SDLC PU. The value specified is the time to wait before sending another poll if the PU had no data to send after receiving the first poll. The default is 0.1 second. The valid range is 0 to 25.5 seconds. This operand is not used with PU Type 4 (NCP) devices.

The REPLYTO is the time-out value for the line when it is the primary station. If a response to a poll has not been received in the interval specified, an idle time-out is detected. VTAM will retry the poll up to the limit specified by the RETRIES operand of the PU statement. The range is 0.1 to 25.5 seconds. The default is 0.1 second.

The SERVLIM operand sets the ratio value of data polls to contact polls for PUs on the line. This means that all PUs that have been contacted and are active will be polled as many times as specified by the SERVLIM value before trying to contact PUs that have not responded to the contact request. This provides more service to PUs with active sessions rather than being concerned with contacting non-productive PUs. The range is from 0 to 255. The default is 4.

The ISTATUS operand tells VTAM if this resource should be made active when the major node is activated. The default is ACTIVE.

12.1.3 The PU Definition Statement

In the VM or VSE environments, a PU statement is coded for each physical unit type (PU Types 1, 2, 4, and 5) that VTAM is to communicate with over this nonswitched SDLC line. We may intermix PU Types 1 and 2 on the same line, creating a multipoint channel-attached link. But PU Type 4 or 5 must be coded as point-to-point lines; any other configuration for these PU types will result in a VTAM definition error. The format of the PU statement is as shown in Figure 12.3.

```
name     PU          ADDRESS=hex address
                     [,DISCNT=([YES|NO][,F|NF])
                     [,ISTATUS=ACTIVE|INACTIVE]
                     [,MAXDATA=size|261|265]
                     [,MAXOUT==n|1]
                     [,PASSLIM=n|MAXOUT]
                     [,PUTYPE=1|2|3|4|5]
                     [,RETRIES=n|7]
                     [,SPAN=(NCCF or NetView spanname]
                     [,SUBAREA=n]
                     [,TADDR=hex address|C1]
```

Figure 12.3 PU definition statement format for SDLC nonswitched channel-attached devices.

The MAXDATA operand is the maximum size of a PIU or segment. The size operand is a value you code for the PU. This value can be found by consulting the documentation provided with the device. For PU Type 1 devices the default is 261; for PU Type 2, the default is 265. The size of the MAXDATA value is based on the request/response header of 3 bytes, a transmission header of 2 bytes for PU Type 1 and 6 bytes for PU Type 2. Thus the actual amount of user data transmitted is the maxdata value minus 5 bytes for PU Type 1 and minus 9 bytes for PU Type 2. The valid range of the MAXDATA value is from 5 to 65,535. The MAXOUT operand is the maximum number of PIUs that VTAM will send to the PU before requesting a receive ready response from the PU. The range is 1 to 7. The PASSLIM operand defines to VTAM the number of consecutive PIUs to send to the PU before servicing other PUs on the same line. This allows you to provide more service to the more heavily used PUs on the same nonswitched line. The PUTYPE operand defines the type of PU to which this definition pertains. A value of 1 is for an SNA terminal-type controller, such as the IBM 3276; a 2 defines a cluster controller, such as the IBM 3274; a 4 defines the communications controller with an NCP, such as the IBM 3725; and a value of 5 defines the SSCP of VTAM. The RETRIES operand is the number of times VTAM will try to recover transmission errors to or from the PU before inactivating the PU. The default is seven times. The valid range is from 0 to 255. If NCCF or NetView is installed and you are using the span of control facility, you must supply the spanname from NCCF or NetView if you want this device to be under specific control of the network operators. The SUBAREA operand is used for PU Type 4 and 5 only. The value coded here is the actual subarea of the VTAM or NCP you are connecting to over this line. The TADDR operand is the SDLC station address assigned to a PU Type 4 with an NCP. This is used by VTAM for communicating to the NCP because VTAM is always the secondary partner when communicating through a communications adapter.

12.1.4 The LU Definition Statement

Since we have previously discussed in detail the definition for a logical unit in Section 10.3.3, we will not discuss it here. All the operands from an MVS LU definition hold true for a VM or VSE operating environment.

12.2 SDLC SWITCHED CHANNEL-ATTACHED MAJOR NODE

The VM and VSE SDLC switched channel-attached major node is quite similar to the MVS switched major node. The VM and VSE switched definitions contain GROUP, LINE, and PU statements. The clear differences between the two switched definitions are: (1) VM and VSE do not use the VBUILD statement and (2) LUs are not defined in a VM or VSE switched channel-attached major node definition.

Since many of the operands have the same functions as those in an MVS/VTAM environment, we will discuss only those operands that are specific to VM and VSE.

12.2.1 GROUP Statement for SDLC Switched Line

As you can see from Figure 12.4, you must have the line control operand (LNCTL) specified as SDLC along with the DIAL operand specifying NO in order for this major node to be considered by VTAM as a channel-attached SDLC switched major node in a VM or VSE environment.

The DIALNO operand is applicable to VSE only. The value coded is the actual telephone number used to connect the modems on the line. You must code the DIALNO operand if the SHOLD operand is coded.

The SHOLD operand is for X.21 Short Hold Mode/Multiple Port Sharing (SHM/MPS). The default NO means this group is not defined for X.21 SHM/MPS. This feature is available to VTAM V3.1 and higher only. The operand X21SW must be set to YES if SHOLD is coded.

```
name        GROUP      LNCTL=SDLC
                       ,DIAL=YES
                       [,DIALNO=telephone number]
                       [,SHOLD=NO|(free,npoll)]
                       [,SPAN=(NCCF or NetView spanname)]
                       [,X21SW=YES|NO]
```

Figure 12.4 Format of the VM, VSE, SDLC switched GROUP statement.

```
name        LINE        [ACTIVTO=t]
                        [,ADDRESS=channel-unit address|030]
                        [,ANSWER=ON|OFF]
                        [,AUTO=address]
                        [,AUTODL=YES|NO]
                        [,CALL=IN|OUT|INOUT]
                        [,ISTATUS=ACTIVE|INACTIVE]
                        [,MAXBFRU=([norm|1] [,max|2])
                        [,PAUSE=t|0.1]
                        [,REPLYTO=t|1.0]
                        [,RETRIES=n|7]
                        [,RETRYTO=n|12]
                        [,SERVLIM=n|4]
                        [,SPAN=(NCCF or NetView spanname)
```

Figure 12.5 Format of the VM, VSE, SDLC switched LINE statement.

12.2.2 LINE Statement for SDLC Switched Line

The important considerations for coding a switched SDLC line statement concerns the procedural operands (Figure 12.5). The ANSWER
operand determines if a PU can dial to VTAM. The PU may dial
VTAM once the line is active if the default, YES, is taken. If NO is
coded, the PU may not dial VTAM no matter what the status of the
line.

The AUTO operand denotes the use of an autocall unit for this
line. The address of the automatic calling unit is the same as the
line address. If an X.21 switched interface is in use on a VSE system, code the AUTODL=YES operand to ensure X.21 connectivity.

The determination of whether VTAM and/or the remote station
can initiate calls is coded on the CALL operand. The default IN allows only incoming calls; hence, VTAM cannot initiate the calls. If
OUT is coded, only VTAM may initiate the calls. But if INOUT is
coded, either VTAM or the station can initiate the calls. The
RETRYTO operand is VSE specific and only the ID, the X21SW=YES
operand, had been coded.

12.2.3 PU Statement for SDLC Switched Line

As we pointed out earlier, there are no LU statements for a channel-
attached SDLC switched physical unit. The LUs are defined dynami-

```
name    PU ADDR = [,ISTATUS=ACTIVE|INACTIVE][,MAXLU=n|2]
        [,SPAN=(NCCF or NetView spanname)]
```

Figure 12.6 Format of the VM, VSE, SDLC switched PU statement.

cally. The number of LUs, and consequently the number of LU control blocks, supported is defined by the MAXLU operand (Figure 12.6). All the other PU definition operands have been previously dscussed.

12.3 BSC CHANNEL-ATTACHED MAJOR NODE

This major node defines to the VM/VTAM and VSE/VTAM all the characteristics, number of clusters, and terminals that are grouped into this major node.

12.3.1 The BSC GROUP Definition Statement

For BSC channel-attached devices, this GROUP statement defines line characteristics for the lines defined following the GROUP statement and, if you desire, cluster and terminal-specific operands for the clusters and terminals associated with this group. Figure 12.7 contains the operands used for the GROUP definition statement.

Figure 12.7 identifies only one required operand for the GROUP definition statement. As with SDLC group definition statements, the LNCTL operand identifies to VTAM the protocol used for this grouping. In this case, BSC is coded to denote this group as binary synchronous.

12.3.2 The BSC LINE Definition Statement

The BSC LINE statement describes the channel to which the cluster controllers are attached. A LINE statement is coded for each BSC nonswitched line in your VM/VTAM or VSE/VTAM channel-attached

```
name    GROUP    LNCTL=BSC
                 [,SPAN=(NCCF or NetView spanname)]
```

Figure 12.7 GROUP definition statement format for BSC channel-attached devices.

```
name      LINE      [ADDRESS=cua|030]
                    [,ISTATUS=ACTIVE|INACTIVE]
                    [,RETRIES=n|7]
                    [,SERVLIM=n|4]
                    [,SPAN=(NCCF or NetView spanname]
```

Figure 12.8 LINE definition statement format for BSC nonswitched channel-attached devices.

network. Figure 12.8 outlines the operands for the LINE definition statement.

ADDRESS and SPAN have the same function here for BSC as they do for SDLC. However, the RETRIES and SERVLIM operands vary from their SDLC counterparts.

The RETRIES operand for BSC determines the number of recovery attempts VTAM tries during transmission to or from the cluster. Remember that SNA deals with physical units for this operand and the SERVLIM operand.

Under BSC protocol, each terminal has a polling address. This address is used by the communications adapter in the front end during polling sequences. For BSC, the SERVLIM specifies the maximum number of WRITE output operations to the 3270 screen before soliciting 3270 operator input. The value should be small enough to allow the end user to supply input before screen overwrites. The value is also application dependent and value selection should be discussed with the application development team.

12.3.3 The CLUSTER Definition Statement

The CLUSTER statement is used to define the type of cluster controller, the cluster controller resource name, and the general polling address for the cluster controller (Figure 12.9).

```
name      CLUSTER   GPOLL=char
                    [,CUTYPE=3271|3275]
                    [,ISTATUS=ACTIVE|INACTIVE]
                    [,SPAN=(NCCF or NetView spanname)]
```

Figure 12.9 The CLUSTER statement format for BSC nonswitched channel-attached devices.

The GPOLL operand is a hexadecimal representation of this cluster controller's polling address. For example, if the cluster controller's polling address were defined as the letter B, you would code the characters C2 for the GPOLL value. This GPOLL value is used by the VTAM during polling operations for requests to send or receive data to or from the cluster controller.

The CUTYPE operand defines to VTAM the type of station control unit. Usually, the default 3271 is taken. This value covers the IBM 3174, 3274, 3276, and 5937 BSC cluster control units. The 3275 value is coded for the IBM 5375 BSC controller.

12.3.4 The TERMINAL Definition Statement

A TERMINAL statement must be coded for each BSC terminal that is to be attached to the defined cluster control unit. The TERMINAL statement supplies VTAM with the resource name for the terminal, the type of terminal and its features, and a device address to be used by VTAM for polling.

We will discuss the three operands unique to this TERMINAL definition statement, ADDR, TERM, and FEATUR2.

The ADDR operand is determined just like the GPOLL operand of the CLUSTER statement. However, here the characters represent the device address instead of the station address. Figure 12.10 contains a table to assist you in determining the ADDR value for BSC cluster controllers using nonswitched lines.

The TERM operand denotes the type of terminal attached to this device address for any IBM 3270-family-compatible display that is

```
name     TERMINAL   ADDR=character
                    ,TERM=3275|3277|3284|3286
                    [,ISTATUS=ACTIVE|INACTIVE]
                    [,DLOGMOD=default logmode entry]
                    [,FEATUR2=([MODEL1|MODEL2][,PRINTR|NOPRINTR])]
                    [,LOGAPPL=owning application program name]
                    [,LOGTAB=interpret table name]
                    [,MODETAB=logon mode table name]
                    [,SPAN=(NCCF or NetView spanname)]
```

Figure 12.10 TERMINAL statement format for BSC nonswitched channel-attached devices.

being defined with this TERM statement code 3277. For IBM 3287-family-compatible printers, code a value of 3286.

The FEATUR2 operand identifies the devices features. The MODEL1 | MODEL2 operand tells VTAM the default screen or buffer size for this device. MODEL1 denotes a screen or buffer default size of 480 bytes. The MODEL2 defines a screen or buffer default size of 1920. Usually, the default MODEL1 is not taken. Most interactive displays and printers have a buffer or screen size of 1920 bytes or more. The PRINTR | NOPRINTR option is valid for an IBM 3275-compatible terminal with an IBM 3284 MODEL3 compatible printer. This alleviates the need to code a separate TERM statement for the 3284 printer.

12.4 SUMMARY

This concludes our discussion of VM and VSE VTAM definitions that need special attention. As you have seen, VM and VSE are unique in the definition of locally attached devices. Actually, the code necessary for defining these components is similar to the code used in an NCP. You will see the similarity later in Part 4 when we deal with coding an NCP. By now you should be aware of the repetitiveness of operands between definition statements. Operands such as DLOGMOD, MODETAB, LOGAPPL, PACING, and VPACING are used again and again between the different resources. In the following chapters we will discuss these operands in depth and their relationship to VTAM and the network as a whole.

13

VTAM User Tables — USSTAB, MODETAB, and COSTAB

VTAM has been designed to allow communications systems programmers to customize VTAM for a network's specific needs. The default constants, tables, modules, and exit routines supplied by IBM will indeed be suitable for some networks, but most will need some degree of customization. The management of your network, performance, and availability of network resources may prompt you to investigate the customization possibilities provided by VTAM. In this chapter we will discuss some of the more widely used customization practices. We will also point out why these areas are customized more than others.

13.1 UNFORMATTED SYSTEM SERVICES TABLE (USSTAB)

A majority of SNA terminals need a character-coded command to be entered by the end user to request a LOGON or LOGOFF. Typically, the IBM 3270 family compatible displays require unformatted system services to interpret the logon or logoff request. VTAM has two levels of unformatted system services, session and operation.

The session-level service provides the command and message handling for logical units. The command handling is used when the end user issues a logon or logoff request. Message handling is used when VTAM sends a message to the logical unit. IBM has supplied a default table named ISTINCDT. This is the table that is used if the operand USSTAB= has not been coded. When customizing the USS table, copy the default table to a new name and customize the new table. Also included in the default ISTINCDT is an upper- and lower-case translation table. This allows the end user to enter the unformatted request in upper or lowercase. The name of the USS table you want the user to access first is coded on the USSTAB= operand of the LU or TERMINAL statements.

The operation level of USS handles VTAM operator requests and the messages generated from those requests. The IBM supplied default table is named ISTINCNO. The specification of a USSTAB for a VTAM operator is coded in the ATCSTR00 member of VTAMLST by providing the start option USSTAB=. Figure 13.1 contains a table of some of the possible commands that ISTINCNO can modify.

The USSTAB ISTINCNO for operation level also contains the VTAM operator messages. If you decide to change the default message format from this table, make a copy of the table before altering the messages. There are two reasons for this procedure. The first is to provide recovery if the new messages fail to display properly. The second reason is NCCF and NetView usage of the messages. Message routing and the automatic start of some NCCF command lists key on the message ID and the format for the message. Be sure to investigate the network management operations functions before modifying the table.

VTAM OPERATOR COMMAND	SYSTEM		
	MVS	VSE	VM
All DISPLAY Commands	*	*	
All MODIFY Commands	*	*	*
VARY TERM	*	*	*
DISPLAY NCPSTOR			*
DISPLAY STATIONS			*
DISPLAY PATHTAB			*
DISPLAY ROUTE			*

Figure 13.1 USS table ISTINCNO default commands.

IBM provides the source code for the default USSTABs that are supplied with VTAM. If your system is an MVS or MVS/XA operating system, the tables can be found in the SYS1.ASAMPLIB data set. For a VSE operating system, you may find the source code in the VSE B book. For a VM operating system, the tables are found in a file on the VTM191 disk with a file type of ASSEMBLE.

Once you have coded your own USSTAB, the source code must be assembled and then link-edited into the VTAM load library. The load library contains all the VTAM-executable modules. For an MVS or MVS/XA system, the USSTAB must be link-edited to the data set named on the VTAMLIB DD statement from the VTAM start procedure. For a VSE system, the USSTAB must be link-edited to the VSE core image library. In VM, a procedure tool named VMFLKED is provided to assemble and link-edit the USSTAB to the VTAMUSER LOADLIB of VM.

Finally, before getting into the actual coding and examples of a USSTAB, we should discuss the table search mechanism used to resolve the unformatted system services request. The search for command verb, translation table, and message always begins with the table named in the USSTAB= operand for the resource issuing the request, that is, an end user requesting a logon or a VTAM operator requesting VTAM information. If VTAM searches the supplied table name and the command verb and the translation table or the message is not found, it will search the IBM supplied default tables. If the request is not found in the default tables, an appropriate message is sent to the requester describing the error. The parameters associated with a command verb, however, must be found in the table named on the USSTAB= operand. No searching past the named table is done for parameter.

We have reviewed the major components and described the uses of the USS tables. Now, let's look at a coded example.

13.1.1 USSTAB Macro

Each USS definition table must begin with the USSTAB macro (Figure 13.2). This indicates to VTAM that this table can be used to supply unformatted system services requests.

```
[name]   USSTAB    [TABLE=name]
```

Figure 13.2 Format of USSTAB macro.

The name operand assigns a name to the assembled Control Section (CSECT) for this USS table. As you can see, the CSECT name is optional and therefore, if it's not supplied, there will be no CSECT name assigned to the table.

The other operand applicable to the USSTAB macro is the TABLE=name operand. This operand is also optional. The value coded here is the name of the translation table that you are supplying to VTAM for command translation. Since it is optional, if we let the translation table look up the default, VTAM will use the IBM supplied default translation table named STDTRANS from the IBM default USS table named ISTINCDT.

This describes the session-level USS table. If we code an operation-level USS table, the TABLE=name operand is ignored because command translation is not performed for the operation level.

13.1.2 USSCMD Macro

The USSCMD macro is used to specify the actual command that can be entered by the end user or VTAM operator (Figure 13.3). The CMD operand supplies the user-defined command name. This name must be unique within the USS table being defined.

The FORMAT operand specifies the interpreted format of the command. It is usually allowed to default to PL1 in the majority of VTAM installations. For more information see the IBM VTAM customization manual.

The REP operand specifies the valid USS command that this user-defined command is replacing. The five valid default VTAM terminal operator commands and how they are used are as follows:

1. LOGON. Used by the end user to request a session with a VTAM application.
2. LOGOFF. Used by the end user to request session termination with the current application session.
3. IBMTEST. Used by the end user to determine the physical connectivity between the terminal and VTAM. This command re-

```
[name]    USSCMD    CMD=name
                    [ ,FORMAT=BAL | PL1 ]
                    [ ,REP=name ]
```

Figure 13.3 Format of USSCMD macro.

```
USSSNA     USSTAB
LOGON      USSCMD   CMD=LOGON,FORMAT=PL1
CICSP01    USSCMD   CMD=CICSP01,REP=LOGON
```

Figure 13.4 Example of USSTAB and USSCMD macros.

turns to the terminal display test data. The display of the test data verifies the connectivity to VTAM.

4. UNDIAL. Allows the VM end user to disconnect the terminal from the VTAM virtual machine and return control to the VM control program. This allows the end user to DIAL another virtual machine under the VM control program.

5. VM. Allows a VTAM terminal to log onto the VTAM SNA Console Support (VSCS) facility of VM. This allows the end user to DIAL or logon to any virtual machine just as if the terminal were native to VM.

From Figure 13.4, we can see the immediate use of the USSCMD macro. In Chapter 10 we defined the applications that will be executing under VTAM. One of the applications is the CICS production region. The name that is assigned to this application is CICSP01. Remember that we discussed the importance of naming conventions and the continuity of those naming conventions throughout the network? Well, here is a prime example. By using the application program ID (APPLID) as the command to logon to the CICS application, we enhance the users' abilities to recognize what application they are logging onto, and this also assists in reporting problems with session establishment to the application.

13.1.3 USSPARM Macro

The USSPARM macro further enhances the informality of session establishment (Figure 13.5). This instruction provides default values for VTAM LOGON and operator commands. The USSPARM macro

```
[name]    USSPARM   PARM=name|Pn
                    [,DEFAULT=value]
                    [,REP=name][,VALUE=value]
```

Figure 13.5 Format of USSPARM macro.

must follow a USSCMD macro and more than one USSPARM macro may follow.

The PARM operand supplies a user-defined keyword or positional parameter that can be entered by the end user for the previously coded USSCMD. The name parameter of the PARM operand specifies the keyword for this USSCMD. You may also code Pn for this USSPARM parameter. The n is a decimal integer starting with 1; the P signifies that this parameter is positional, and the n value is the position of the parameter.

The DEFAULT operand value specifies the value for the PARM parameter. If either the keyword value or the positional parameter for the PARM is not entered by the end user, the value from the DEFAULT operand is used.

The REP operand value specifies a keyword that is found in the generated command. This allows you to replace the user entered keyword value of the PARM operand with the value for the REP keyword value.

The VALUE operand provides a default value for the keyword specified on the PARM operand if the keyword is entered without a value. VALUE and DEFAULT are mutually exclusive. If you want both operands to be used for the same PARM keyword, use two USSPARM macros, the first macro using the VALUE operand and the second using the DEFAULT operand. This allows the end user to enter the keyword without a value, which processes the command using the VALUE keyword first; or, the end user may not enter the keyword, in which case, the DEFAULT operand value will be used.

In Figure 13.6, the USSPARM operand is used in four of the five possibilities. Under the LOGON USSCMD definition, the PARM value is specified as the first positional parameter entered by the

```
USSSNA     USSTAB
LOGON      USSCMD  CMD=LOGON,FORMAT=PL1
           USSPARM PARM=P1,REP=DATA
           USSPARM PARM=APPLID
           USSPARM PARM=LOGMODE
CICSP01    USSCMD  CMD=CICSP01,REP=LOGON
           USSPARM PARM=APPLID,DEFAULT=CICSP01
           USSPARM PARM=LOGMODE
           USSPARM PARM=DATA
```

Figure 13.6 Example of USSTAB and USSPARM macros.

end user. The value entered will replace the value for the keyword parameter DATA. The remaining two USSPARM macros define keywords that the end user may enter for this VTAM command. Notice, there are no default values assigned to these keywords. The user must enter the keyword and a value for this USSCMD for VTAM to generate the proper formatted command.

In the second USSCMD definition, the first USSPARM supplies both the keyword and the default value for the keyword if it is not entered. This allows the end user to enter CICSP01 on the VTAM terminal. This command will be processed by VTAM to initiate a session between the VTAM terminal and the CICS region.

Now that we can assist the end user in session initiation, we must provide a means of communicating possible application selections, session establishment errors, and VTAM terminal information.

13.1.4 USSMSG Macro

VTAM provides informational messages to the terminal or network operator. These messages are called "USS" messages. The default messages can be modified to suit your network requirements. This is accomplished by using the USSMSG macro in the USSTAB definition table (Figure 13.7).

There are 14 possible USS messages. Each message is issued to the terminal when the corresponding error for the message has been encountered. We will discuss 3 of the 14 possible USS messages. MSG10, which is sent to an LU when the LU is activated and a SSCP-LU session is active, is often referred to as the VTAM logo. The second USS message we will discuss is MSG7, which is issued when the LU attempts to establish a session but an error has occurred which inhibits the session establishment. This session establishment is also referred to as "binding." The final message, MSG0,

```
[name]    USSMSG    MSG=n|(n1,n2,...)
                    [,BUFFER=buffer address]
                    [,TEXT='message text']
                    [,OPT=option]
                    [,SUPP=ALWAYS|NEVER]
```

Figure 13.7 Format of USSMSG macro.

```
USSSNA    USSTAB
LOGON     USSCMD  CMD=LOGON,FORMAT=PL1
          USSPARM PARM=P1,REP=DATA
          USSPARM PARM=APPLID
          USSPARM PARM=LOGMODE
CICSP01   USSCMD  CMD=CICSP01,REP=LOGON
          USSPARM PARM=APPLID,DEFAULT=CICSP01
          USSPARM PARM=LOGMODE
USSMSGS   USSMSG  MSG=10,TEXT='WELCOME TO THE NETWO        X
                  RK. YOUR SNA LU NAME IS @@LUNAME',        X
                  SUPP=NEVER
          USSMSG  MSG=0,BUFFER=MSG0
          USSMSG  MSG=7,TEXT='% SESSION NOT BOUND,          X
                  %(2), SENSE DATA %(3)',SUPP=NOBLKSUP
```

Figure 13.8 Example of USSTAB and USSMSG macros.

is issued to an LU when the USS command has been successfully executed.

As stated previously, USS MSG10 is VTAM's logo or greeting message. The IBM default table does not provide text for this message. This gives you the opportunity to create a message for the end user that can be useful to the terminal operator. You may elect to display logon selection options for the end user to choose or just a simple greeting. The information displayed is up to you. In our example, Figure 13.8, we have coded a simple greeting message. However, the display does describe to end users the name assigned to their LU.

In USS, a special substitutable parameter, @@LUNAME, can be used in the TEXT operand of the USSMSG macro. This parameter, if coded, notifies VTAM that the actual displayed message shall have the assigned LU name for this terminal (e.g., LS320T02) displayed on the screen. Figure 13.9 shows the processed message as it appears on the terminal screens.

The format for the TEXT operand is the standard national alphanumeric character set. The length of the displayed message may not exceed 255 characters. This includes all substituted strings. The percent (%) sign has special meaning when used in the TEXT operand.

```
WELCOME TO THE NETWORK. YOUR SNA LU NAME IS LS320T02.
```

Figure 13.9 USSMSG10 TEXT message translated.

```
The coded MSG 7 is:
%           SESSION NOT BOUND, %(2)          SENSE DATA %(3)
LS320T02 SESSION NOT BOUND, BIND FAILURE SENSE DATA 08010000
```

Figure 13.10 Using the % for VTAM variable string insertion.

It represents the location of variable data that VTAM can issue with a USS message. The percent signs can be numbered if several variable data strings are issued by VTAM.

In Figure 13.8, message 7 (MSG7) supplies a good example for using the % variable character string insert capability of VTAM with USS messages. Message 7 is issued when the LU attempts to bind with an application but the request is denied. By using the %, VTAM can display some information about the reason for the bind failure. Figure 13.10 shows the inserted values that may appear during a bind failure by using the % substitution.

The OPT and SUPP operands are used only in conjunction with the TEXT operand. They are ignored if coded with the BUFFER operand. The OPT operand specifies whether two or more blanks encountered will be suppressed into one blank. If the message coded contains spatial formatting on the display, code OPT=NOBLKSUP; otherwise code OPT=BLKSUP if you want two or more blanks compressed to one blank. The default is BLKSUP. The SUPP operand specifies whether the message is to be written to the terminal. If ALWAYS is specified, the message will not be written. The NEVER parameter indicates that the message shall be written. The default is the SUPP start option of the VTAM ATCSTR00 start list. It is best to code SUPP=NEVER to be on the safe side.

The last operand to be discussed, BUFFER, like the TEXT operand, can also be used to supply the USS message text to the terminal screen. Unlike the TEXT operand, the BUFFER operand cannot have variable data. VTAM will display the message text from the buffer just as it is coded. The parameter of the BUFFER operand is an assembler label for the storage area of the message text. The

```
  2 BYTE HEADER                 Message Text
MESSAGE TEXT LENGTH         Maximum length is:
  (Header + Message Text)   65,535 or X'FFFF'
```

Figure 13.11 Format of BUFFER storage area.

```
MSG0 DC   X'0063',X'15',C'The LOGON COMMAND entered has       X
          been successfully executed and sent to the app      X
          ropriate application'
```

Figure 13.12 The BUFFER operand storage area for MSG0.

message text must be coded according to the rules for an assembler DC statement using C-type constants. The format of the buffer is as given in Figure 13.11.

Although the maximum length of the message is 65,535 bytes, it is not feasible to send a message that large to the terminal screen. Since most 3270 display terminals have a buffer of 1920 bytes, it is good practice not to exceed this value. The BUFFER storage area also allows you to store device-dependent write and control characters. In our example USSTAB for USS message 0 (MSG0), we have used the BUFFER operand. USS MSG0 is issued when a USS command has been successfully processed. The first two bytes of the message storage area labeled MSG0 (Figure 13.12), contain the length of the message. The next byte contains the write-type command for a carriage return to a new line X'15' followed by the actual message.

After coding all the USSCMD, USSPARM, and USSMSG macros and their operands for the USS table, the USSEND macro must be coded.

13.1.5 USSEND Macro

The USSEND macro signifies the end of the code for the USSTAB being defined. It follows all the USS macros, including the buffer storage area for the BUFFER operand. Once you have finished coding the USSTAB, it must be assembled and link-edited into the proper VTAM executable library. Figure 13.14 documents the USSTAB that will be used throughout this book. This USSTAB definition contains the logon verbs for the applications that were defined in Chapter 10. The name of the USS table is USSSNA. This is the name that is used to link the USSTAB module to VTAMLIB and also

```
[name]  USSEND
```

Figure 13.13 Format of USSEND macro.

```
          USSSNA    USSTAB
  LOGON      USSCMD   CMD=LOGON,FORMAT=PL1
             USSPARM  PARM=P1,REP=DATA
             USSPARM  PARM=APPLID
             USSPARM  PARM=LOGMODE
  CICSP01    USSCMD   CMD=CICSP01,REP=LOGON
             USSPARM  PARM=APPLID,DEFAULT=CICSP01
             USSPARM  PARM=LOGMODE
  CICST01    USSCMD   CMD=CICST01,REP=LOGON
             USSPARM  PARM=APPLID,DEFAULT=CICST01
             USSPARM  PARM=LOGMODE
  IMSP01     USSCMD   CMD=IMSP01,REP=LOGON
             USSPARM  PARM=APPLID,DEFAULT=IMSP01
             USSPARM  PARM=LOGMODE
  IMST01     USSCMD   CMD=IMST01,REP=LOGON
             USSPARM  PARM=APPLID,DEFAULT=IMST01
             USSPARM  PARM=LOGMODE
  TSO01      USSCMD   CMD=TSO01,REP=LOGON
             USSPARM  PARM=APPLID,DEFAULT=TSO01
             USSPARM  PARM=LOGMODE
  USSMSGS    USSMSG   MSG=10,TEXT='WELCOME TO THE NETWO >
                      RK. YOUR SNA LU NAME IS @@LUNAME', >
                      SUPP=NEVER
             USSMSG   MSG=0,BUFFER=MSG0
             USSMSG   MSG=7,TEXT='% SESSION NOT BOUND, >
                      %(2), SENSE DATA %(3)',SUPP=NOBLKSUP
MSG0 DC  X'0063',X'15',C'The LOGON COMMAND entered has >
    been successfully executed and sent to the appropr >
    iate application'
          USSEND
```

Figure 13.14 USSTAB named USSSNA in its entirety.

the name that is coded for the USSTAB= operand for logical unit
and non-SNA terminal definitions.

13.2 LOGON MODE TABLE

In the previous section we introduced the term "BIND" as being a
request of an LU to establish a session with an application. The
BIND contains session protocol information for the application from

the LU. This session protocol information is also called the "BIND image." It consists of the session parameters that will be used between the LU and the application, that is, the protocol between the Primary Logical Unit (PLU) (e.g., application) and the Secondary Logical Unit (SLU) (e.g., LU). This protocol agreement will determine such factors as which LU can initiate a send or receive request, the size of the message, whether chaining or segmentation of message units is allowed, and more.

IBM has supplied a default logon mode table, ISTINCLM. The module can be found in the MVS or MVS/XA VTAMLIB library, SYS1.VTAMLIB, in the VSE core image library, and in the VM VTAMUSER LOADLIB. If you create your own LOGON mode table, it must be assembled and link-edited into the appropriate VTAM library. If you decide to modify or create a LOGON mode table and relink it with the same module name or a new name, the mode table will not be in effect until the major node for the resources that use the LOGON mode table has been inactivated and then reactivated. This is because VTAM loads the module into VTAM address space for the major node.

The modification and creation of LOGON mode tables is accomplished by using the VTAM macros MODETAB, MODEENT, and MODEEND. The mode table is assigned to an LU or TERMINAL by coding the table name on the MODETAB operand of the LU or TERMINAL definition statement.

13.2.1 MODETAB Macro

There are no operands for the MODETAB macro (Figure 13.15). Its sole purpose is to define the start of a logon mode table. The optional name operand can be used as an assembler CSECT name for the mode table.

13.2.2 MODEENT Macro

The format of the MODEENT macro is quite extensive (Figure 13.16). Each operand has a hexadecimal value that represents the

```
[name]   MODETAB
```

Figure 13.15 Format of MODETAB macro.

```
[name]    MODEENT  [,COMPROT=value|0]
                   [,COS=name]
                   [,ENCR=value|0]
                   [,FMPROF=value|0]
                   [,LOGMODE=name]
                   [,PRIPROT=value|0]
                   [,PSERVIC=value|0]
                   [,PSNDPAC=value|0]
                   [,RUSIZES=value]
                   [,SECPROT=value|0]
                   [,SRCVPAC=value|0]
                   [,SSNDPAC=value|0]
                   [,TSPROF=value|0]
                   [,TYPE=value|1]
```

Figure 13.16 Format of MODEENT macro.

bit settings for the session protocol. The research for each bit setting
for one device type can be exhausting. Luckily, IBM has supplied a
default mode table with entries for most of the IBM device types. We
will describe the type of protocol being defined for each operand, but
we will not go into the bit settings of each.

The mode entries in Figure 13.17 represent three typical display
terminal devices. The first entry, S32702X, is to be used with LU

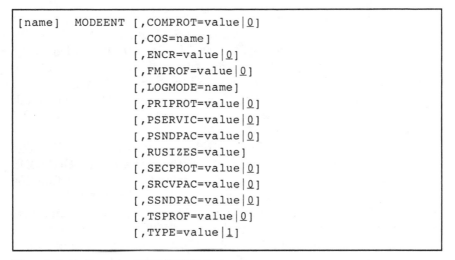

```
MT01       MODETAB
S32702X    MODEENT  LOGMODE=S32702X,FMPROF=X'03',               X
                    TSPROF=X'03',PRIPROT=X'B1',SECPROT=X'90',   X
                    COMPROT=X'3080',RUSIZES=X'87F8',            X
                    PSERVIC=X'028000000000185000007E00'
N32702X    MODEENT  LOGMODE=N32702X,FMPROF=X'02',               X
                    TSPROF=X'02',PRIPROT=X'71',SECPROT=X'40',   X
                    COMPROT=X'2000',RUSIZES=X'0000',            X
                    PSERVIC=X'008000000000185000007E00'
S32704X    MODEENT  LOGMODE=S32702X,FMPROF=X03',                X
                    TSPROF=X'03',PRIPROT=X'B1',SECPROT=X'90',   X
                    COMPROT=X'3080',RUSIZES=X'87F8',            X
                    PSERVIC=X'02800000000018502B507F00'
```

Figure 13.17 MODEENT macro coding example.

Type 2 devices that support the extended data stream feature. The second entry, N32702X, is used with non-SNA devices. Non-SNA display terminals are defined to SNA as LU Type 0. The third entry, S32704X, defines an IBM 3278 model 4 type of display terminal that supports both extended data stream and two screen sizes.

The LOGMODE operand specifies the name of the logon mode entry. In this mode table we have three entries defined, S32702X, N32702X, and S32704X.

The FMPROF operand defines the data flow control (DFC) protocols used for the LU-LU session. For both of the SNA LOGMODE entries, the value coded is X'03'. This value signifies that function management profile Type 3 will be used. The N32702X LOGMODE entry has a value of X'02'. This value shows that function management profile Type 2 is in effect. The FMPROF value specifies what DFC functions can be used during the session, which LU is responsible for recovery, and the type of response mode for the session, e.g., delayed or immediate.

The TSPROF operand defines the transmission services protocols. The SNA LOGMODEs defined above use a TS profile value of X'03' and the non-SNA LOGMODE uses a TS profile of X'02'. This profile defines the session rules for traffic flow PLU-SLU and SLU-PLU, pacing, and the size of the Request/Response Unit (RU) during normal traffic flow.

The PRIPROT operand describes the chaining usage and responses and immediate or delayed request mode and indicates compression of data and end bracket use. These usages pertain to the FM profile defined in FMPROF and particularly the primary half-session (PLU). For sessions between TSO and an LU, the value specified for chaining responses in the PRIPROT operand is used. For CICS and IMS, the chaining response is determined by the definition for the terminal in the application.

The SECPROT operand is also part of the FM usage information of the BIND image. This operand value defines the same session protocol parameters as the PROFPROT operand, except that they relate to the secondary half-session partner (SLU).

The final operand that is related to FM usage is the COMPROT. The value specified for this operand defines the common protocols that will be used between the primary and secondary half-session partners. This operand defines the use of Function Management Headers (FMH) and whether they can be exchanged; the use of brackets and the rules of their usage; the use of EBCDIC or ASCII code for the RU data; and the use of full-duplex (FDX), half-duplex flip-flop (HDX-FF), or contention protocol for normal send and receive flows for which LU is the contention loser and has recovery responsibility.

The SSNDPAC operand in our example is not coded. But a value is determined by the VPACING operand of the APPL definition statement which defines the primary logical unit. This operand defines inbound pacing from the SLU to the PLU. The VPACING value is used if the SSNDPAC value is not coded or a value of X'0000' is coded. Using this method provides greater flexibility for pacing modifications.

Outbound pacing is controlled by both the BIND image and another VTAM/NCP operand. The SRCVPAC operand defines the pacing count in the primary to secondary direction. If this value is not specified or coded with a value of X'0000', the value used in the PACING operand of the SLU will be used. The indication of one- or two-stage pacing is also important here. Two-stage pacing will take place

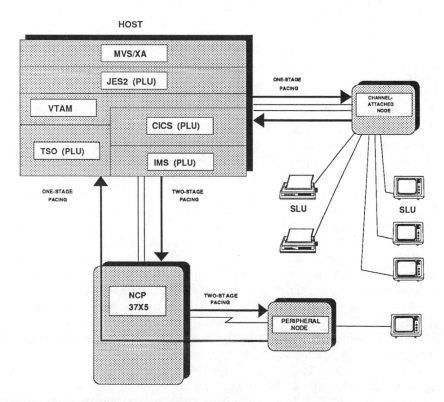

Figure 13.18 One-stage and two-stage pacing.

if the SLU is a resource of NCP. One-stage pacing is used when the SLU is a resource attached to the HOST. One- and two-stage pacing is diagrammed in Figure 13.18.

The RUSIZES operand defines the maximum size of the RU inbound and outbound to the PLU. The first byte defines the size of the RU inbound to the PLU from the SLU. For most LU Type 2 devices, the value is set at X'87', which equates to 1024 bytes. This equation is 8 x 2. The value coded here is used by the primary half-session if the PLU is TSO or IMS. If the PLU is CICS, the value coded in the CICS Terminal Control Table (TCT) operand RUSIZE for the entry that defines the LU secondary half-session partner is used. The second byte defines the maximum RU size outbound to the SLU. The peripheral node (e.g., cluster controller) will manage the buffers according to this value. In our example, the outbound RU size can be a maximum of X'F8' or 3840 bytes (15 x 2) in length. If IMS is the primary half-session partner, the value coded here is overridden with the IMS operand OUTBUF value. For CICS, it is application dependent. TSO will use the value specified in the RUSIZES operand.

The PSERVIC operand specifies the LU type, extended data stream support, and the screen sizes for the device. The LU type is the first byte of the PSERVIC. In our example, the first byte for the SNA device LOGMODEs specifies X'02', signifying that the LU being defined with this BIND is an LU Type 2. For N32702X, this value is X'00', which defines this BIND image for an LU Type 0 device. The following byte has a value of X'80' for all the defined LOGMODE entries. This value specifies support for extended data stream protocol. Finally, bytes 20 through 24 define the screen sizes for the device. The LOGMODE S32702X has the value X'1850' in bytes 20 and 21. The first byte defines the number of rows in the screen, the second byte the number of columns. For this value the screen size is 24 rows by 80 columns, or 1920. Bytes 22 and 23 for S32702X are X'0000' and therefore a secondary or alternate screen size is not supported. Byte 24 of the PSERVIC specifies whether the primary screen size is always used, static, or if the alternate size can be used as well. In LOGMODE S32704X, bytes 22 and 23 have the values X'2B50' coded. These values define an alternate screen size of 43 rows by 80 columns, or 3440. Byte 24 specifies that the screen size is dynamic, in accordance with the application.

The last operand to discuss is the TYPE operand. The value coded here defines the type of bind, negotiable or nonnegotiable. For LU-LU sessions with LU Type 2 devices, the default 1 is the only valid value. This default denotes a nonnegotiable bind. This value is used by the PLU when sending the bind to the SLU. In this case, the SLU

```
[name]   MODEEND
```

Figure 13.19 Format of MODEEND macro.

must accept the session parameters presented by the PLU. A value
of 0 requests a negotiable bind, but the application must also request
the negotiable bind in the OPNDST macro by specifying
PROC=NEGBIND. For more detailed information on the session parameters discussed above, consult the following IBM manuals:
VTAM Programming and *SNA — Sessions Between Logical Units.*

13.2.3 MODEEND Macro

The MODEEND macro indicates the end of the logon mode table and
follows the last MODEENT macro. There are no operands for the
MODEEND macro (Figure 13.19).

   After defining the logon mode table, you must assemble and link-
edit the load module into the VTAM's executable library as defined
in Section 13.2.

13.3 CLASS OF SERVICE TABLE

In Chapter 4 we discussed the routing capabilities of SNA in coordi-
nation with VTAM. The routes a PLU chooses for transmitting data
to the SLU were described to be both physical (explicit routes) and
logical (virtual routes). The ERs are mapped to the VRs, which define a specific route. In VTAM, priorities can be assigned to this
mapping for use by the communications systems programmer to assist in meeting the service level agreement for the application. This
prioritizing of routes is based on the VRs defined for the network.
Named entries are specified in a table to define a class of service.
The class can be identified as those PLUs that require a higher priority of transmission (e.g., CICS) versus PLUs that have a service
level agreement requiring a lower level of transmission priority (e.g.,
RJE). These class entries are placed in a Class Of Service (COS)
table. The entry name is associated with an SLU by using the COS
operand in the mode table.

   VTAM uses only one module name for the COS in a single network
configuration, ISTSDCOS. This is the name you must use in the
link-edit procedure when you want to add a COS table to VTAM
executable library.

```
name        COSTAB
```

Figure 13.20 COSTAB macro format.

In ISTSDCOS, there are two required COS entry names. The first
entry actually has no name. The name field consists of eight blanks.
This entry is the default COS entry if the COS operand is not coded
on the MODEENT macro that defines the LOGMODE for the SLU.
The second entry must be named ISTSVTCOS. This entry defines
the VRs and their priorities for the SSCP. This applies to all SSCP
sessions in a single network. Special consideration must be given to
the COS table for SNI.

13.3.1 COSTAB Macro

The COSTAB identifies the start of the COS table (Figure 13.20).
But, unlike the preceding tables, USSTAB and MODETAB, the
name operand is required. In a single network, this name must be
ISTSDCOS. Figure 13.21 defines the COS table that we will use as
an example for our discussion.

13.3.2 COS Macro

The name operand defines the COS name to be used on the COS
operand of the MODEENT macro of the LOGON mode table entry.
   In Figure 13.21, five COS entries are defined. ISTVTCOS will be
used by VTAM for SSCP sessions. The INTERACT COS name will
be assigned to LOGMODE entries that are used for interactive applications such as CICS and IMS. The DEVELOP COS name will be
used on the LOGMODE entries for application development PLUs
such as TSO, CICS, and IMS development. The BATCH COS name
will be used for JES/RJE and NJE sessions. The final COS entry
name is blank and defines the default COS name for all LOGMODE
entries for which the COS operand is not coded. The COS name
must be in each COS table of each VTAM in order for the name from
the LOGMODE entry to be used. This is because the LU's owning
SSCP will pass the logmode image along with the COS table name.
   The VR operand of the COS macro (Figure 13.22) defines the ordered pair or ordered pairs of virtual routes (vr#) and their assigned
transmission priority (tp#). As you know from Chapter 4 on SNA
routing, there is a maximum of eight virtual routes, numbered 0

```
ISTSDCOS COSTAB
ISTVTCOS COS VR=((0,2),(1,2),(2,2),(3,2),(4,2),(5,2),   X
             (6,2),(7,2),(0,1),(1,1),(2,1),(3,1),(4,1), X
             (5,1),(6,1),(7,1),(0,0),(1,0),(2,0),(3,0), X
             (4,0),(5,0),(6,0),(7,0))
INTERACT COS VR=((0,2),(1,2),(2,2),(3,2),(4,2),(5,2),   X
             (6,2),(7,2),(0,1),(1,1),(2,1),(3,1),(4,1), X
             (5,1),(6,1),(7,1),(0,0),(1,0),(2,0),(3,0), X
             (4,0),(5,0),(6,0),(7,0))
DEVELOP  COS VR=((0,1),(1,1),(2,1),(3,1),(4,1),(5,1),   X
             (6,1),(7,1),(0,2),(1,2),(2,2),(3,2),(4,2), X
             (5,2),(6,2),(7,2),(0,0),(1,0),(2,0),(3,0), X
             (4,0),(5,0),(6,0),(7,0))
BATCH    COS VR=((0,0),(1,0),(2,0),(3,0),(4,0),(5,0),   X
             (6,0),(7,0),(0,1),(1,1),(2,1),(3,1),(4,1), X
             (5,1),(6,1),(7,1),(0,2),(1,2),(2,2),(3,2), X
             (4,2),(5,2),(6,2),(7,2))
         COS VR=((0,0),(1,0),(2,0),(3,0),(4,0),(5,0),   X
             (6,0),(7,0),(0,1),(1,1),(2,1),(3,1),(4,1), X
             (5,1),(6,1),(7,1),(0,2),(1,2),(2,2),(3,2), X
             (4,2),(5,2),(6,2),(7,2))
         COSEND
```

Figure 13.22 Example of a COS table.

through 7. Each VR can have three transmission priorities assigned. Priority 0 assigns a low transmission priority, priority 1 assigns a medium transmission priority, and priority 2 assigns the highest transmission priority. This pairing allows for a maximum of 24 ordered pairs of VRs to TPs. The transmission priority is used by VTAM and NCP when transmitting data between subareas over a VR. Those SNA PIUs that display a higher TP number than others over the same VR will be serviced before PIUs on this same VR that have a lower TP. This means of prioritizing SNA data through the network has recently been extended to the peripheral SNA resources that are attached to NCP V4.3.1/V5.2.1. For more information on

```
[name]   COS VR=(vr#,tp#)|((vr#,tp#),...))
```

Figure 13.21 COS macro format.

VRs and their role in network performance consult *Advanced SNA Networking.*

13.3.3 COSEND Macro

The COSEND macro (Figure 13.23) identifies the end of the COS table. It must follow the last COS macro defined in the table.

Now that we have discussed the coding options for the COS table, there are some points we would like to bring to your attention about the usage of the COS table.

As we stated, the COS table assigns transmission priorities for PLUs when sending data to an SLU. By using this scheme, we can effectively throttle the transmission of data through the FEP, telecommunications lines, and cluster controllers.

In Figure 13.21, the COS name INTERACT has the same ordered pairs as the SSCP COS name ISTVTCOS. This is because interactive applications, such as CICS and IMS, that provide large databases of information require the requested data to be sent to the end user as fast as possible. By assigning the highest priority of transmission to these applications, we can ensure quick network retrieval time.

We have defined a class of service that provides a medial transmission priority to the COS name DEVELOP. This is accomplished by assigning a transmission priority of 1 to the first set of ordered pairs in the list. The second set in the list assigns a TP of 2. We chose this scheme because development work on TSO, CICS, and IMS, although important, is not in demand by the end-user community. Remember, overall, that it is the end user who must be supported.

The BATCH COS entry has been provided for applications that rely heavily on transmitting large amounts of print data over the network. Usually, this is aimed at JES/RJE and NJE facilities. But it can be of use for CICS or IMS background applications that also generate large amounts of data that must be transmitted over the network. Notice that the TPs for the BATCH COS entry are ordered from low priority in the first set of VRs to highest priority in the last set of VRs.

```
COSEND
```

Figure 13.23 COSEND macro format.

The last point concerns the actual assignment of COS names to the applications and SLUs. There is only one place where you can specify the COS name to use, on the MODEENT macro operand COS. The MODEENT macro defines a LOGMODE entry. There is only one operand that you can use to specify the default LOGMODE entry. That operand is the DLOGMOD and it can be coded on the APPL definition, the LU, LOCAL, and the TERMINAL statements, and as a parameter default in the USSTAB definition by using the USSPARM macro. With all these possibilities, where do you code the LOGMODE entry name so you can take advantage of the COS table? This is a very good question. The answer can only come from experience. Examine your network's session mapping. Most terminals will usually have a regular session with the same application. This may be a good starting point. You can assign the COS name according to the most used application for a specific terminal, thereby using the DLOGMOD operand on the LU, LOCAL, or TERMINAL definition statements.

13.4 SUMMARY

This concludes the chapter on VTAM user tables. We have discussed the three most commonly used tables. The USS table provides a user-friendly interface to VTAM for the end user to initiate a session with an application. The LOGON mode table provides the session parameters that are to be agreed upon between the PLU and the SLU. The class of service table allows the communications systems programmer to assign priorities to VRs and map this into a class that can be specified on the LOGMODE entry for a device.

Now that we have gone into the specifics of VTAM and modifying user tables that assist in the access to the network, we will turn our focus on generating connectivity to the network by discussing the Network Control Program (NCP).

NCP

14

NCP Macros — PCCU, BUILD, and SYSCNTRL

Now that the local domain has been defined to VTAM, we will describe the remote network. Its network is connected to the host processor via telephone circuits attached to a communications controller. In SNA, the communications controller is operated by a Network Control Program (NCP). This NCP is generated on the host processor. The NCP contains the definitions for the remote SNA resources of the VTAM domain. Figure 14.1 diagrams a sample single-domain network.

In this chapter we will concentrate on defining some of the more commonly used remote SNA resources found in today's SNA networks. Before we define resources in the NCP, you should have some understanding of the resources' physical and operational characteristics. The NCP must know its relationship to all SNA resources, which include the host VTAM, other communications controllers that are connected to this communications controller, the data links, and the resources that lie at the end of the data links. NCP definitions concerning LEN, enhanced subarea connectivity, dynamic table updates, and reconfiguration are discussed in detail in *Advanced SNA Networking*.

14.1 PCCU DEFINITION

Although the PCCU definition statement is a VTAM-related statement, it is placed in the NCP generation code. The PCCU definition

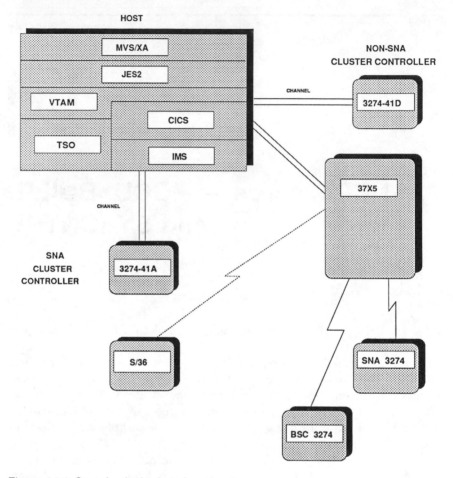

Figure 14.1 Sample single-domain network.

statement is the first statement found in the NCP generation code.

The PCCU definition statement describes the Programmed Communications Control Unit (PCCU) into which the NCP is loaded. This is a required definition statement. It defines the functions that VTAM is supplying for this NCP. At least one PCCU definition statement is required for an NCP. Figure 14.2 shows the format of the operands that we will discuss for the PCCU definition statement.

In Chapter 9 we reviewed and coded the VTAM start options list which defines VTAM's environment in the host processor. In the definitions we coded the HOSTPU operand. This operand defines to the SSCP the name of VTAM's physical unit. For consistency we will use the same name for the name of the PCCU definition statement. This

```
name       PCCU       [SUBAREA=n]
                      [,NEWPATH=(name1,name2,name3)]
                      [,AUTOIPL=YES|NO]
                      [,AUTOSYN=YES|NO]
                      [,VFYLM=YES|NO]
                      [,CUADDR=channel unit address]
                      [,MAXDATA=size|65535]
                      [,DUMPDS=dumpname]
                      [,DUMPSTA=link station name]
                      [,LOADSTA=link  station name]
                      [,INITEST=YES|NO]
```

Figure 14.2 PCCU definition statement and operands.

will assist you in locating the PCCU for a particular host VTAM
when multiple hosts can activate the NCP.

The first operand listed in Figure 14.2 is SUBAREA. The value
coded for this operand should match the HOSTSA operand value
supplied in the VTAM start options list. For our example, 01 is used.
This SUBAREA operand is used by VTAM to determine which
PCCU definition statement to process when activating the NCP. If
we were to omit the SUBAREA operand, this PCCU definition statement will be used by any VTAM that does not find a corresponding
SUBAREA operand that matches its HOSTSA operand. We have
chosen to code the SUBAREA operand because it also helps in docu-
menting the NCP, although in this case it is not necessary.

The NEWPATH operand is specific to VTAM V3.2 and NCP
V4.3/V5.2. These versions provide the means for dynamic path table
updates to occur in both VTAM and NCP. This path table update is
accomplished without executing the NCP generation procedure as is
required in earlier versions of VTAM and NCP. The names specified
on this parameter identify the names of the path table update members found in VTAMLST. You may define up to three names in this
NEWPATH parameter. Dynamic path table updates are discussed in
further detail in *Advanced SNA Networking*.

When a network operator issues the VARY NET,ACT,ID=NCP-
name VTAM command, VTAM will use the AUTOSYN and VFYLM
operands to determine if an NCP load module should be loaded in
the communications controller.

During the activate process for an NCP major node, VTAM tries to
match the NCP major node name specified on the VARY ACT command. By specifying AUTOSYN=YES, VTAM will immediately work

with the NCP found in the communications controller if the NCP major node name matches the NCP load module name found in the communications controller. If NO has been specified, VTAM will ask the operator whether the NCP requested on the VARY ACT command should be loaded or if the NCP in the communications controller should be used. We will specify YES on the AUTOSYN operand to allow automation of NCP activation to occur. If the NCP names do not match, the value of the VFYLM operand makes the determination.

The VFYLM operand adds one more criteria to the load module name comparison that AUTOSYN executes. The presence of the VFYLM operand directs NCP in the communications controller to identify not only the NCP name but also the NCP subarea. If the NCP name and subarea do not match those of the requested NCP major node, VTAM prompts the operator for a decision to load the communications controller with the requested NCP major node or stop the activation. This is specified by coding VFYLM=YES. If VFYLM=NO, the communications controller will be loaded with the requested NCP major node from the VARY ACT command. We have specified VFYLM=YES, which will help guard us from activating and consequently loading the wrong NCP major node.

Prior to the actual load process VTAM can request the communications controller to perform an initialization test and/or an Initial Program Load (IPL). The initialization test is performed before the IPL or before VTAM loads the communications controller.

The INITEST operand tells VTAM to run the initialization test if the value coded is YES. The test is not executed if you code NO for the INITEST operand. The initialization test performs diagnostics on the communications controller before it is loaded with an NCP. To run the INITEST program, a DD statement in MVS or a DLBL statement in VSE must be included in the VTAM start procedure. The name of the statement must be INITEST and the data set defined by the statement must contain the INITEST load module. In most cases this module is found in the SYS1.SSPLIB data set.

The AUTOIPL operand determines whether the initial program load procedure is to execute after an unrecoverable failure in the NCP or the communications controller or after a dump of the communications controller has occurred. By specifying YES, the contents of the communications controller are refreshed, cleared, and awaiting the new copy of the NCP load module. This only occurs during an error situation and should be coded on only one PCCU in the NCP.

VTAM knows the path to the communications controller from the channel unit address. The channel unit address is obtained from the

I/O GEN performed for the operating system. It can be specified with the U= parameter of the VARY NET,ACT command or it can be found on the CUADDR operand of the PCCU definition statement that corresponds to the requesting VTAM. This channel unit address is used in conjunction with the LOADSTA and DUMPSTA operands.

The LOADSTA operand defines the link station VTAM will use to perform the load procedure of the communications controller. The DUMPSTA operand defines the link station VTAM will use to perform the dump procedure for the communications controller.

In our example the channel unit address is A01. We have coded CUADDR=A01. Note that the address is in hexadecimal format. The LOADSTA and DUMPSTA operands do not have to be coded. These values will be defaulted to the value of the CUADDR operand with a suffix of -S. For documentation purposes, however, we have coded LOADSTA=A01-S and DUMPSTA=A01-S.

If a situation occurred in the NCP that created a need to dump the contents of the communications controller, the value coded for the DUMPDS operand will direct VTAM to the dump data set for that NCP. The value of the DUMPDS is the name of a DD or DLBL statement found in the VTAM start procedure. This statement defines a data set for receiving NCP dumps. This operand works with the AUTODMP operand. The AUTODMP operand specifies YES if the storage dump of the NCP is to be automated or NO if the operator is to have control of the dump procedure.

Lastly, the amount of data that can be transferred between the NCP and the VTAM represented by this PCCU definition statement cannot exceed the value of MAXDATA. The MAXDATA operand should be equal to the size of the largest PIU found in the network that may be transmitted between the NCP and VTAM. The default value is 65,535 and in most cases exceeds the largest PIU. It is best to determine the largest PIU by researching the applications and their output buffers used for transmitting data to a logical unit. As a guideline, the value coded here should not exceed the size of VTAM's IOBUF buffer pool in MVS and VM or the VFBUF buffer pool in VSE. Also, the product of the MAXBFRU and UNITSZ operand values of the NCP HOST definition statement should be less than or equal to the MAXDATA value on the PCCU. In addition the BFRS and TRANSFR operand values of the NCP BUILD definition statement also supply a check against the MAXDATA operand. We will discuss these operands in greater detail in the next section. Figure 14.3 shows the completed PCCU definition statement used for our single-domain example.

```
VTAM01    PCCU   CUADDR=A01,                                    X
                 AUTODMP=YES,                                   X
                 AUTOIPL=YES,                                   X
                 AUTOSYN=YES,                                   X
                 DUMPDS=NCPDUMP,                                X
                 MAXDATA=4096,                                  X
                 SUBAREA=01,                                    X
                 VFYLM=YES,                                     X
                 LOADSTA=A01-S,                                 X
                 INITEST=YES,                                   X
                 DUMPSTA=A01-S
```

Figure 14.3 Coded example of PCCU for a single-domain network.

14.2 BUILD DEFINITION STATEMENT

The BUILD definition statement is used to define to the NCP the physical make up of the communications controller, the NCP's ability to communicate with VTAM, and information about the NCP itself. The BUILD definition statement consists of some 63 operands and their associated parameters. Many of these operands are used to create the Job Control Language (JCL) procedure used to generate the NCP load module and will not be discussed here. Instead, we will focus our review on the BUILD definition statement operands that pertain to the NCP in the network control mode. The NCP in the communications controller is considered to be in network control mode when it performs dialing, answering, polling, and device addressing. This is in contrast to some of the other related software programs associated with a communications controller, such as Emulation Program (EP) or NCP Packet Switching Interface (NPSI). These programs and others are discussed in *Advanced SNA Networking*.

We will now define the communications controller to the NCP. In this example the communications controller is an IBM 3725. Figure 14.4 outlines the operands that define the physical make up of the 3725.

14.2.1 Defining Physical Characteristics to NCP

The format of the BUILD definition statement is as follows:

```
name    BUILD    operand,operand,...operand
```

```
NCP11BLD   BUILD       MODEL=3725,   comcontroller type     X
                       MEMSIZE=1024, installed memory        X
                       CA=(TYPE5,TYPE5-TPS)  CA types
```

Figure 14.4 Defining IBM 3725 physical characteristics to NCP.

The name operand is symbolic and is not used by NCP. It is basically used for documentation only. When defining the physical characteristics of the 3725, the MODEL operand specifies the communications controller model number to the NCP. Since we have a IBM 3725, we code 3725. Likewise, if the communications controller is an IBM 3720, code 3720 or for IBM 3745, code 3745. The MEMSIZE operand tells NCP the size of storage memory installed. We have coded it as 1024. This value is measured in kilobytes. The memory size is therefore 1024 kb, or 1 Mb. The NCP, however, will use the value of MEMSIZE or the actual physical installed storage found in the 3725, whichever is smaller. On an IBM 3720 the NCP will always use the installed memory size regardless of the value specified on the MEMSIZE operand. If your communications controller is an IBM 3745, the MEMSIZE value can be specified in megabytes. The range is then 1M to 8M. The letter M indicates to the NCP that the value is in megabytes. The CA operand defines to the NCP the number, position, and the presence of a two-processor switch for each channel adapter installed on the 3725. The channel adapter is the hardware interface between the mainframe and the communications controller. For a 3725 there is only one type of channel adapter. It is specified as TYPE5. The 3725 can have up to six installed channel adapters. The position of the TYPE5 parameter in the CA operand denotes the channel adapter position installed on the 3725. From Figure 14.4 we can see that the 3725 has two channel adapters installed. They occupy positions 1 and 2 of the available six positions. The second channel adapter also has the two-processor switch feature installed. For more information on the hardware and features of a 3725 refer to Chapter 2 or consult the appropriate IBM manual.

14.2.2 Defining NCP-to-VTAM Communications Characteristics

Now that the hardware characteristics of the 3725 that will contain this NCP are defined, NCP must be made aware of its relationship with VTAM. We will begin by defining the channel characteristics NCP will impose on VTAM.

```
NCP11BLD   BUILD       MODEL=3725,  comcontroller type          X
                       MEMSIZE=1024, installed memory            X
                       CA=(TYPE5,TYPE5-TPS), CA types            X
                       NCPCA=(ACTIVE,INACTIVE), active CAs       X
                       DELAY=(.2),  delay attn signal            X
                       TIMEOUT=420.0 default timeout/host
```

Figure 14.5 Operational operands for NCP to VTAM communications.

Figure 14.5 highlights the operands of the BUILD definition state-ment that define the channel between NCP and VTAM. The NCPCA operand specifies the status of the channel adapter's availability. For each channel adapter identified in the CA operand, the NCPCA oper-and will specify ACTIVE or INACTIVE. According to the configura-tion drawn in Figure 14.1, only one channel adapter is presently con-nected to the 3725. The NCPCA operand specifies that channel adapter position 1 is to be active. This is the channel adapter on the 3725 that will be used to load the NCP load module. Make sure that the physical channel connected to the 3725 is attached to the chan-nel adapter you specified as being active in the NCPCA operand. Another check on the physical connection is that the IO address for the channel adapter at both ends of the physical channel, the 3725 end and the host processor end, are equal to the CUADDR operand of the PCCU definition statement. Failure of either of these situa-tions will result in an error during NCP load attempts.

When the NCP has data (e.g., PIUs) to send to VTAM, it sends an attention interrupt signal to the host. VTAM will then read the data in the NCP buffers. This could cause serious performance problems if every read provided few PIUs in the NCP buffer retrieved. The DELAY operand is intended to assist in increasing the number of PIUs in the NCP buffer while reducing the number of reads for VTAM to perform when reading data from the NCP. The default value of 0 specifies that an attention interrupt will be issued to the host whenever there is a PIU queued in a buffer for a channel adapter. By specifying a larger value, the NCP can queue several PIUs destined for a host before issuing the attention interrupt. This saves the host and VTAM cycle time, which in turn helps perfor-mance. The DELAY value can be specified in tenths of a second be-tween 0 and 6553.5 for each active channel adapter. We have chosen .2 second for the active channel adapter. The attention interrupt will be issued before reaching the DELAY value if the amount of data queued in the NCP will fill the receive buffers allocated in the host according to the MAXBFRU value of the NCP HOST definition statement.

After the NCP issues the attention interrupt, it will wait for a response from VTAM. The TIMEOUT operand of the BUILD definition statement specifies the amount of time the NCP will wait for that response before disconnecting its link with VTAM. The range for this value is 0.2 to 840.0 seconds. The value for each channel adapter installed will default according to the value defined on the NCPCA operand. In our example, channel-adapter position 1 is active and will default to 420.0 seconds. Channel-adapter position 2 is inactive and defaults to 0, indicating immediate channel discontact. The implication is quite clear. If for some reason VTAM cannot send its response to an attention interrupt from NCP, all sessions on this NCP major node will be terminated. The default of 420.0 seconds for an active channel adapter should be sufficient. If timeouts with the NCP do occur, they may be caused by channel activity rather than VTAM being too busy to respond.

In the previous section we discussed the maximum amount of data that VTAM will accept from this NCP. This limit is coded on the MAXDATA operand of the PCCU definition statement. We picked the value of 4096 bytes in a single transfer of data as a suitable number based on research of network traffic message unit sizes. In the BUILD definition statement two operands reflect on the MAXDATA value, BFRS and TRANSFR (Figure 14.6).

14.2.3 NCP Buffer Allocation Operands

The BFRS operand tells NCP the size of the buffers in the buffer pool. These buffers will contain PIUs that pass through this NCP for resources in the network. The size should be a multiple of 4; other-

```
NCP11BLD   BUILD    MODEL=3725,  comcontroller type           X
                    MEMSIZE=1024, installed memory             X
                    CA=(TYPE5,TYPE5-TPS), CA types             X
                    NCPCA=(ACTIVE,INACTIVE), active CAs        X
                    DELAY=(.2),  delay attn signal             X
                    TIMEOUT=420.0, default timeout/host        X
                    BFRS=128,    NCP data buffer size          X
                    TRANSFR=32   # of BFRS xfrd to host
```

Figure 14.6 Buffer allocation operands for PIUs in the network.

wise, NCP will round the value up to a multiple of 4. The buffer size can range from 76 bytes to 240 bytes per buffer. The buffer pool in NCP is the remaining storage available after the NCP is loaded. Each buffer is formatted with a 12-byte management prefix. This buffer prefix is used by NCP to chain related buffers, and keep a data count and data offset of the PIU within the buffer. The default buffer size for the IBM 3725 and 3720 is 100 (88 + 12) and for the IBM 3745 it is 252 (240 + 12). For SDLC resources that support segmentation, a value of 128 is a good starting point.

The TRANSFR operand of the BUILD definition statement determines the maximum number of NCP buffers that can be transferred to the host at one time. Since the maximum amount of data in one PIU is 4096 bytes, as specified by the MAXDATA operand of the PCCU definition statement, the value for this TRANSFR operand times the BFRS value should not exceed the MAXDATA operand of the PCCU definition statement. In our example, a value of 32 buffers transferred in one read by VTAM will result in maximizing the data transfer to the host from NCP.

For the IBM 3720 and 3745 using NCP V5.1/V5.2 the value of TRANSFR times BFRS must be greater than 1296. The maximum value for TRANSFR is 255. The default for these NCPs is the number of NCP buffers required to hold a 4096-byte PIU. As you have probably surmised, the BFRS and TRANSFR operands play important management and performance roles in the network.

Prior to Extended Network Addressing (ENA) the MAXSUBA operand dictated the number of network addressable units available per subarea. The table in Figure 14.7 lists the possible values of MAXSUBA and the corresponding maximum number of resources per subarea prior to ENA. Our example supports ENA because VTAM and NCP are at version 3 and version 4 releases, respectively, which support ENA. Note that in the figure for NCP versions V4.3.1 and NCP V5.2.1 the number of subareas has been increased to 65,535, each with up to 32,768 elements. That allows for a mind boggling total of 2,147,450,880 addressable resources in one SNA network.

14.2.4 NCP Subarea Considerations

The specification of MAXSUBA (Figure 14.8) in the BUILD definition statement for a network that supports ENA is optional. However, until all nodes, including NCP and HOST nodes, in the network are ENA capable, the MAXSUBA operand must be coded. It must match the value of MAXSUBA in the ATCSTR00 start options list of VTAM and MAXSUBA operand in the BUILD of each NCP for every sub-

Pre-VTAM V3 and NCP V4 (NON-ENA)

# of Subareas	Max. # of Elements/Subarea
3	16,384
7	8,192
15	4,096
31	2,048
63	1,024
127	512
255	256

VTAM V3 and NCP V4 ENA

# of Subareas	Max. # of Elements/Subarea
3	32,768
7	32,768
15	32,768
31	32,768
63	32,768
127	32,768
255	32,768

VTAM V3.2 and NCP V4.3.1/V5.2.1 ENA

# of Subareas	Max. # of Elements/Subarea
65,535	32,768

Figure 14.7 The relation of the number of subareas (MAXSUBA) to the number of addressable elements in a subarea.

area node in the network. For more information on ENA and its effect on network addressing schemes refer to Chapter 7.

The SUBAREA (Figure 14.8) operand defines the subarea address assigned to this NCP. We have chosen subarea address 11. For an ENA networking scheme as in our example, the maximum subarea address can be 255 for this version of NCP. In a non-ENA networking scheme, the subarea address maximum value is limited to the value specified for the MAXSUBA of the BUILD definition statement. The SUBAREA operand is required for the BUILD definition statement.

```
NCP11BLD  BUILD      MODEL=3725,  comcontroller type      X
                     MEMSIZE=1024, installed memory        X
                     CA=(TYPE5,TYPE5-TPS), CA types        X
                     NCPCA=(ACTIVE,INACTIVE), active CAs   X
                     DELAY=(.2),  delay attn signal        X
                     TIMEOUT=420.0, default timeout/host   X
                     BFRS=128,     NCP data buffer size    X
                     TRANSFR=32,   # of BFRS xfrd to host  X
                     MAXSUBA=15,   maximum subareas         X
                     SUBAREA=11   Subarea of NCP
```

Figure 14.8 MAXSUBA and SUBAREA operand specifications.

14.2.5 Defining Concurrent Sessions Support for NCP

When an NCP is activated by VTAM, an SSCP-PU session is established. An NCP can have several sessions with different hosts in a network. In a single domain network the NCP has only controlling SSCP, hence, one SSCP-PU session. The MAXSSCP operand (Figure 14.9) defines to the NCP the number of SSCP-PU sessions that are conducted concurrently. The default and minimum value for MAX-SSCP is the number of channel adapters specified as being active in the NCPCA operand. The maximum value of MAXSSCP is 8 (16 for NCP V5 in an IBM 3745 Communications Controller). The SSCP-PU session includes sessions established over channel or link attachments. If the MAXSSCP is left to default to the active channel adapters specified in the NCPCA operand, no SDLC link-attached host can be in session with this NCP.

The number of host subareas that can activate this NCP is specified by the NUMHSAS operand (Figure 14.9). Formally stated, the NUMHSAS is the number of host subareas that have virtual routes ending in this NCP. This operand has a more important role in a multiple domain and in SNI. Since we have but one host and one virtual route, we can code the minimum value of 1.

The VRPOOL operand (Figure 14.9) specifies the number of virtual route and transmission priority number entries in the NCP virtual route pool. These entries are used during activation, restart, and VR clean-up after an ER failure. The value specified for VRPOOL should equal the number of virtual routes ending in this NCP. To ensure this, make the VRPOOL value equal to the NUMHSAS value. For more information on this, see the chapter on SNI for VRPOOL and NUMHSAS values concerning a gateway NCP in *Advanced SNA Net-*

```
NCP11BLD   BUILD      MODEL=3725,   comcontroller type      X
                      MEMSIZE=1024, installed memory         X
                      CA=(TYPE5,TYPE5-TPS), CA types         X
                      NCPCA=(ACTIVE,INACTIVE), active CAs    X
                      DELAY=(.2),   delay attn signal        X
                      TIMEOUT=420.0, default timeout/host    X
                      BFRS=128,     NCP data buffer size     X
                      TRANSFR=32,   # of BFRS xfrd to host   X
                      MAXSUBA=15,   maximum subareas         X
                      SUBAREA=11,   Subarea of NCP           X
                      MAXSSCP=1,    Concurrent SSCP-PU       X
                      NUMHSAS=1,    # of Host subareas       X
                      VRPOOL=1      # of VRs
```

Figure 14.9 Defining the number of concurrent sessions.

working. The default for the VRPOOL operand is 6 times the NUMHSAS value, but cannot exceed 5000. There is a second parameter for the VRPOOL operand that is used for reserving table entries for VRs that are dynamically added by NCP V4.3/V5. Dynamic path table updates are discussed in length in *Advanced SNA Networking*.

14.2.6 NCP Load Module Characteristics

The final operands of the BUILD definition statement specific to NCPV4.2 concern the characteristics of the NCP load module that are produced at the end of the generation process. In defining these characteristics we tell the NCP the host operating system environment that will load this NCP load module. The TYPSYS operand (Figure 14.10) provides this information. There is a value for each host operating system environment. The MVS value coded in Figure 14.10 specifies that the host operating system is MVS or MVS/XA. The default for the TYPSYS operand is OS. This also is interpreted by the NCP to mean an MVS or MVS/XA host environment.

The TYPGEN operand (Figure 14.10) defines to NCP the type of operational configuration; that is, it defines whether the communications controller this NCP will execute in is channel attached or link attached, if the emulation program is included, and if NCP V4 Subset is being used. In our example from Figure 14.1, we can see that the communications controller is channel attached only. In this case the TYPGEN operand will be set to NCP.

```
NCP11BLD   BUILD      MODEL=3725,   comcontroller type        X
                      MEMSIZE=1024, installed memory           X
                      CA=(TYPE5,TYPE5-TPS), CA types           X
                      NCPCA=(ACTIVE,INACTIVE), active CAs       X
                      DELAY=(.2),   delay attn signal           X
                      TIMEOUT=420.0, default timeout/host       X
                      BFRS=128,     NCP data buffer size        X
                      TRANSFR=32,   # of BFRS xfrd to host      X
                      MAXSUBA=15,   maximum subareas            X
                      SUBAREA=11,   Subarea of NCP              X
                      MAXSSCP=1,    Concurrent SSCP-PU          X
                      NUMHSAS=1,    # of Host subareas          X
                      VRPOOL=1,     # of VRs                    X
                      TYPSYS=MVS,   host operating system       X
                      TYPGEN=NCP,   operation configuration     X
                      VERSION=V4R2, version of NCP              X
                      NEWNAME=NCP11 NCP load module name
```

Figure 14.10 Defining NCP load module characteristics.

The NCP is made aware of the version of NCP you are defining by the VERSION operand (Figure 14.10). This operand assists the generation process in resolving default values for many of the NCP definition statements and their associated operands. The default for this operand is V3 for version 3. We have declared that the NCP in our scenario is version 4, release 2. Therefore, we have coded V4R2 for the VERSION operand. For NCP V4.3, code V4R3; for NCP V5.1, V5R1; and NCP V5.2, code V5R2.

There are two other operands for NCP V4.3 and V5.2.

The NETID operand of the BUILD definition statement identifies the owning network for this NCP. This name must match the NETID operand value specified on the VTAM start list statement NETID. The other operand for NCP V4.3 and V5.2 is the PUNAME operand. This operand allows you to assign a PU name to the NCP. In previous releases the NEWNAME operand is used as the NCP PU name. Since the NEWNAME value is also the name of the VTAM NCP major node, the name is usually changed any time a new NCP generation is performed, thus causing operation and configuration management confusion. The addition of the PUNAME operand allows for ease of operations by having the PU name value remain constant while the VTAM NCP major node name and the NEWNAME values can be changed with each new NCP generated. This is particularly useful for automating network operations.

Last, but not least, is the NEWNAME operand (Figure 14.10) of the BUILD definition statement. The value coded in this operand is the name of the NCP load module created at the end of the generation process. The name you specify cannot be greater than seven characters in length and must conform to the naming convention standards for partitioned data set members. This is because the resulting NCP load module will reside in a partitioned data set that is referenced by the NCPLIB DD statement in the VTAM start procedure. The name is limited to seven characters because the generation procedure will append the letter R to the name to create the NCP Resource Resolution Table (RRT). The default name chosen by the generation process is NCP001 for TYPGEN=NCP. We have coded NCP11 as the name of the NCP load module. This NEWNAME parameter is also the NCP PU name for NCP V4.2 and under.

The operands coded for the BUILD definition statement in our scenario provide NCP with the basis for communicating with VTAM and characteristic information about the NCP load module. BUILD definition statements concerning dynamic path updates are discussed in *Advanced SNA Networking*.

14.3 SYSCNTRL DEFINITION STATEMENT

Dynamic control facilities are included in the NCP with the SYSCNTRL definition statement. These facilities allow VTAM to issue requests to the NCP to modify specific BSC and S/S parameters defined in the NCP. The SYSCNTRL definition statement is required and must follow the BUILD definition statement even if there are no BSC or SS devices in your NCP. The format of the definition statement is:

```
[name]       SYSCNTRL  OPTIONS=(entry,...)
```

The name operand is a symbolic name for the definition statement and is optional. The OPTIONS operand is the only operand for the SYSCNTRL definition statement and is required. The entry parameters for VTAM are shown in Figure 14.11.

The sample single-domain network in Figure 14.1 shows that a BSC 3274 remote cluster controller is attached to the communications controller that will contain this NCP. The first two entries in the OPTIONS operand, MODE and RIMM, are required if BSC 3270 devices are included in the NCP.

The MODE parameter allows VTAM to set the destination mode of the BSC device. The RIMM parameter allows VTAM to reset the BSC device immediately after an error. The remaining parameters

```
SYSCNTRL   OPTIONS=(MODE,RIMM,NAKLIM,SESSION,    X
                    SSPAUSE,STORDSP,BACKUP,DLRID,X
                    BHSASS,DVSINIT,ENDCALL,       X
                    LNSTAT,RCNTRL,RCOND,RDEVQ,    X
                    RECMD,SESINIT,XMTLMT)
```

Figure 14.11 Dynamic control facility options for VTAM.

are used by VTAM for operator control functions. The NEGPOLL parameter allows VTAM to issue the MODIFY NEGPOLL command. This operator command modifies the NEGPOLL operand of a BSC LINE definition statement. The SESSION parameter supplies the code to VTAM for the MODIFY SESSION operator command. This command is used to modify the number of concurrent sessions on a BSC LINE. The SSPAUSE parameter provides VTAM with the ability to modify the service-seeking pause operand PAUSE of a BSC or SS LINE. The MODIFY POLL operator command is used for this dynamic change. The STORDSP parameter is required for VTAM to display the NCP storage using the operator command DISPLAY NCPSTOR. This allows viewing of the NCP storage without interrupting the NCP.

These entries are the basic SYSCNTRL options needed for VTAM for supporting BSC and SS devices. There are many more options that may be coded. During the NCP generation process, the options coded are compared with the NCP resource definitions for this NCP. If resources have not been defined that correlate with the SYSCNTRL option specified, the code for that dynamic control facility is not included in the NCP load module. Therefore, it is better to be on the safe side and code all the possible options for the SYSCNTRL definition statement.

14.4 SUMMARY

In this chapter, we discussed coding PCCU, BUILD, and SYSCNTRL macros of NCP. The PCCU macro defines the functions that VTAM is supplying for this NCP. Although it is a VTAM related statement, it is placed in the NCP code, the BUILD macro defines the physical make up of the communications controller and the information about the NCP itself. It also establishes NCP's ability to communicate with VTAM. The SYSCNTRL allows VTAM to issue requests to the NCP to modify specific BSC and SS parameters defined in the NCP. It is a required statement and must follow the BUILD macro.

15

NCP Macros — HOST, LUDRPOOL, PATH, and GROUP

15.1 HOST DEFINITION STATEMENT

The NCP must allocate buffers used in sending and receiving data between the host and the channel-attached communications controller. The HOST definition statement provides the number of buffers and the size of the buffers used for this communication. There must be one HOST definition statement for each VTAM that communicates to this NCP over a channel. The statement must also appear before any GROUP definition statements are encountered. The format of the HOST definition statement is:

```
[name]      HOST        operand[,operand,...operand]
```

The name operand is any symbolic name you choose to code. The remaining operands will be discussed in conjunction with Figure 15.1. The operands related to the buffers in VTAM and NCP play a major role in tuning your network.

When defining the buffer characteristics for the HOST definition statement, there are several factors to consider. One is the amount of storage required in the NCP buffer pool when allocating buffers for communications with the HOST. The INBFRS operand defines to the NCP the number of buffers that are initially required to handle data received from VTAM and is a required operand. If the data being received from VTAM is greater than this initial allocation, NCP will

```
HOST01          HOST        INBFRS=10,                              X
                            MAXBFRU=16,                             X
                            UNITSZ=256,                             X
                            BFRPAD=0,                               X
                            SUBAREA=1
```

Figure 15.1 HOST definition statement for a single-domain in NCP.

allocate more buffers in the multiple specified with the INBFRS operand. The BUFSIZE operand of the BUILD definition statement is used with the INBFRS value to allocate storage. The BUFSIZE we specified is 128 bytes. The amount of NCP storage used is BUFSIZE times INBFRS. We have allocated 10 buffers of the NCP buffer pool for the transfer of data from the host. Therefore the amount of storage initially allocated is 2560 bytes. This is an acceptable value until further analysis of message unit size can be determined.

In the PCCU definition statement we defined the size of the largest PIU that can be transmitted between this NCP and VTAM as 4096 bytes in length. Here in the HOST definition statement we define the amount of data VTAM can receive from this NCP. This value is determined by the MAXBFRU and UNITSZ operands. Their product is the largest amount of data this NCP will transfer to the host defined by this HOST definition statement. This does not mean the largest PIU but rather the largest amount of data in a single transfer of multiple PIUs. The product should not exceed the MAXDATA value coded on the PCCU definition statement that corresponds to this HOST definition statement.

The MAXBFRU operand value specifies the number of buffers allocated in VTAM to receive data from this NCP. This value cannot exceed the base number of IO buffers allocated by the IOBUF start option in ATCSTR00 of VTAMLST. Our IOBUF specified 32 buffers of 256 bytes each to be the base allocation of the IO buffer pool for this VTAM. We have coded a value of 16 based on the value specified for the operand UNITSZ.

The UNITSZ operand specifies the buffer size in the host. This value must match the IOBUF BUFSIZE operand in the ATCSTR00 start options list of VTAMLST. The UNITSZ operand is required and is compared by the NCP with the IOBUF BUFSIZE value passed to it in the XID format during activation. The NCP will not activate if these values do not match.

The BFRPAD operand is optional. This buffer pad is used by the access method to insert the message header and message text prefixes. VTAM under VSE uses a 15-byte buffer pad. TCAM uses a minimum of 17 bytes and VTAM under MVS and VM uses 0 bytes. We must specify the BFRPAD operand and assign a value of 0 because the default value is 28 bytes.

Each subarea in an SNA network must have a unique subarea address. The subarea of the host described by this HOST definition statement is supplied to the NCP by the SUBAREA operand. The subarea number assigned to the host according to the HOSTSA option of the start options list should be coded here. For our sample network the host subarea is 1.

15.2 LUDRPOOL DEFINITION STATEMENT

In our sample single-domain network we have configured a switched SDLC line. The switched line will connect a S/36 emulating a SNA/3770 RJE device. The LUDRPOOL operand is used to specify the number of LUs that are expected to have a session on this switched line. This allows NCP to allocate the appropriate number of LU control blocks in the LU pool for dynamic resources. The LUDRPOOL is also used in dynamic reconfiguration.

The LUDRPOOL definition statement is positional and must precede the first GROUP definition statement. Figure 15.2 details the usage of the LUDRPOOL definition statement.

The LUDRPOOL definition statement consists of two operands. The first operand, NUMTYP1, defines the number of expected LUs that are associated with a PU Type 1 SNA device. The switched line for our example is a PU Type 2 SNA device. In this case the NUMTYP1 operand could have been omitted since the default for the LUDRPOOL operands is 0. The NUMTYP2 operand specifies the number of expected LUs to be dynamically allocated in this NCP that are associated with a PU Type 2 SNA device. The value of 2 is coded here in accordance with the switched major node definition SWS36RJE that was previously defined in Chapter 11.

```
LUDR01          LUDRPOOL   NUMTYP1=0,                        X
                           NUMTYP2=16
```

Figure 15.2 Allocating LU pool entries for switched SDLC links.

15.3 PATH DEFINITION STATEMENT

Like VTAM the NCP has a routing capability for transmitting data through the network. In NCP, the PATH definition statement is used in the same manner as the PATH definition statement in VTAM. The destination subareas NCP can route data to and the control of the data flow can be defined in the PATH definition statement. By using the adjacent subarea and transmission group number pair associated with an explicit and virtual route, NCP can direct data to a destination subarea. The PATH definition statement is positional in the NCP. It must follow the GWNAU definition statements in a gateway NCP that defines the network addressable units of cross-network resources. In addition, the PATH definition statement must precede the first GROUP definition statement. Figure 15.3 outlines the coding of a PATH definition statement.

The label PATH1201 is a symbol defined for documentation purposes only. In this instance, it denotes the route table between subareas 11 and 01. The DESTSA operand can specify more than one destination subarea. The format for the DESTSA operand is:

```
DESTSA=(sa1[,sa2,sa3,...,sa255])
```

As you can see, DESTSA can range from 1 to 255 subarea addresses pre-VTAM V3.2 and NCPV4.3.1/V5.2.1. For these versions the maximum DESTSA value is 65,535. It is the only required operand of the PATH definition statement. At least one subarea address must be coded. Any subarea specified in this DESTSA operand cannot appear in any other DESTSA operand of this NCP. Therefore, it is best to code one PATH definition statement for each destination subarea to avoid routing discrepancies. The value coded for the DESTSA operand must be numeric.

In our sample single-domain configuration we are concerned with two subareas. The NCP must define a route to the only destination subarea possible with this configuration. That destination subarea is the controlling VTAM subarea 01. The Explicit Route (ER) between these subareas is defined in VTAM as ER0. The ER operand format for NCP is:

```
[ER0=(adjsa,[tgn],[lothresh],[medtrhesh],[hithresh],[totthresh])]
            1     5000       5000        5000      20000
```

The ER operand is optional but is usually coded. The default ER is ER0. You can code ER0 through ER7 for explicit routes to the desti-

```
PATH1201    PATH    DESTSA=1,      VTAM SUBAREA 01      X
                    ER0=(1,1),     ER0, ADJSA1, TG1     X
                    VR0=0          VR 0 MAPPED TO ER 0
```

Figure 15.3 Defining the route between subarea 01 and subarea 12.

nation subarea specified in the DESTSA operand for pre-VTAM V3.2 and NCPV4.3.1/V5.2.1. These versions will support ER8 through ER15 as well. The ER operand defines the adjacent subarea (*adjsa*) and transmission group number (*tgn*) pair used to map this explicit route. The *adjsa* is a subarea directly connected to this NCP that can be used to route data bound for the destination subarea(s) defined in DESTSA. The *adjsa* range permitted is 1 to 255. VTAM V3.2 and NCP V4.3.1/V5.2.1 support *adjsa* range of 1 to 65,535. For our scenario the only adjacent subarea is the destination subarea. So we code a 1 for the destination subarea.

The *tgn* is optional within the ER operand. It defines the transmission group that can be used to route the data to the adjacent subarea. The *tgn* defaults to 1 if it is not specified. Since the only route is a channel-attached host connection, the *tgn* must be defined as 1. If more ERs were to be specified in the PATH definition statement, this *tgn* could be used again. This *tgn* should be used in the adjacent subarea when defining the adjacent subarea's ER to this NCP.

The Transmission Group (TG) is the highway between subareas. During rush hour the highway may become congested. The ER operand allows us to control the data flow to avoid the congestion. These flow-control thresholds are optional within the ER operand. There are four threshold specifications possible. Each has a corresponding default value. The *lothreshold* value is the threshold used by NCP for low transmission priority traffic. The *medthreshold* value specifies the threshold for transmission priority 1 of the VR. The *hithreshold* value is the threshold for transmission priority 2 of the VR. Each threshold defaults to a value of 5000. The value represents the number of bytes queued for that transmission priority over the TG. The *totthreshold* is the total number of bytes that can be queued for that TG before NCP stops queuing PIUs for this TG. The queuing is ceased until the number of bytes falls below the threshold value.

The virtual route mapping is used here because NCP V4.2 supports activation of VRs to adjacent subareas. The VR format is:

```
[VR0=ern][,VR1=ern]...[,VR7=ern]
```

The VR operand is optional for the PATH definition statement. The VR operand maps the virtual route to the explicit route. This map is used by NCP when activating VRs. The Explicit Route Number (*ern*) must be an ER previously defined on an ER operand of this PATH definition statement. The VR mapping used in this NCP should agree with the VR mapping used in the destination subarea PATH table for the return explicit route.

Each VR defined has a corresponding pacing window. This pacing window is used to determine the number of PIUs that can be transmitted over the VR. The format of the VRPWS pacing window size operand is:

```
[VRPWS00=([min][,max]),...,VRPWS72=([min][,max])]
```

The VRPWS operand has two digits suffixed. The first represents the VR number and the second represents the transmission priority. There are three transmission priorities (TPs) for each VR. You can specify up to 24 VR pacing window size operands. The *min* and *max* values represent the minimum and maximum number of PIUs for this VR and the associated TP.

For the most part the threshold values of the ER operand and the VRPWS operands are not coded. Usually in-depth performance studies are needed to determine appropriate values. Performance implications of the thresholds and VR pacing window size are discussed in *Advanced SNA Networking*.

15.4 GROUP DEFINITION STATEMENT

Many of the data links and devices attached to the NCP have a common set of characteristics. These NCP resources can be grouped together by the GROUP definition statement. The operands used on the GROUP definition statement allow you to specify certain characteristic functions that are common to the group. Most of these common functions are determined by the communications protocol. BSC communications protocol over lines will have different characteristics and operational options than a line that uses SDLC protocol. Hence you will often hear that the GROUP definition statement describes the line group. The format of the GROUP definition statement is:

```
name      GROUP      [operand,operand...operand]
```

There is only one required operand for the GROUP definition statement, the LNCTL operand. LNCTL identifies the type of line control for all resources within this group. The name label is required and provides a symbolic name for the line group. A benefit of the GROUP definition statement is the ability to code several operands here that directly influence the capabilities of many of the resources defined under this group. This saves the communications systems programmer from repetitive coding for each resource. This is possible because the generation procedure uses the sift-down effect described in Chapter 9. For our sample single-domain configuration there will be three GROUP definition statements: a BSC group, SDLC non-switched group, and a switched SDLC group, each having a different characteristic flavor.

15.4.1 BSC GROUP Definition Statement

Line group definitions of BSC resources must be defined to the NCP before any SDLC line groups are defined. Operands coded in this GROUP definition statement reflect values for all lines under this group unless they are explicitly coded on successive LINE definition statements. We will discuss the group characteristics in three categories. The first will focus on the line characteristics of the group, the second will concern error recovery, and the third will center on servicing the data links defined for this group. Figure 15.4 details the BSC GROUP definition statement for our example.

```
BSC3270    GROUP    LNCTL=BSC,         BSC LINE CONTROL            X
                    TYPE=NCP,          LINE OPERATION MODE         X
                    DIAL=NO,           NON-SWITCHED LINK           X
                    CLOCKNG=EXT,       EXTERNAL CLOCKING/MODEM     X
                    DUPLEX=FULL,       4-WIRE CIRCUIT              X
                    SPEED=9600,        SPEED OF MODEM              X
                    CODE=EBCDIC,       EBCDIC CHARACTERS USED      X
                    RETRIES=(5,10,3),  3 RETRIES 5/10 SECS         X
                    REPLYTO=3,         3 S BEFORE POLL T.O.        X
                    TEXTTO=23.5,       23.5 S B4 MSG T.O.          X
                    PAUSE=1,           SERVICE PAUSE               X
                    POLLED=YES,        POLL ALL DEVICES            X
                    SERVPRI=OLD,       SESSION SERVICE PRIORITYX
                    SERVLIM=8,         SERVICE SEEK LIMIT          X
                    CUTOFF=1,          # OF TRANSFR SEQUENCE       X
                    TRANSFR=3          3 OF NCP BUFFERS XMIT
```

Figure 15.4 BSC group highlighting line characteristics.

When defining line groups, all lines under the group must use the same type of line control. BSC line groups must follow all SS line groups and precede all SDLC line group definitions. In the line group definition it is customary to code the line characteristics for the group. The LNCTL operand specifies the type of line control for this group. Figure 15.4 shows that the BSC line control is prevailing for all lines defined under this group. We code BSC because the devices at the end point of the physical link use BSC protocol for communicating with the host.

Because our configuration is a BSC 3270 family device, it is supported under SNA without the use of an emulation program. BSC 3270 family devices are the only non-SNA devices supported under SNA in their native mode. This permits the NCP to act in network control mode with this link. We specify this to NCP by coding the TYPE operand. The value NCP denotes the use of network control mode for the lines in this group.

To differentiate between switched and non-switched data links, the DIAL operand is coded. This operand specifies whether switched line control procedures are required for the lines in this group. By specifying NO, non-switched line control procedures are enforced.

Another characteristic of the links in this group is the responsibility for clocking the line speed. The CLOCKNG operand relays this information to NCP. The specification of CLOCKNG=EXT tells NCP that the modem attached to the link will supply the clocking. If CLOCKNG=INT is specified, the communication scanner for that line will provide the clocking within the communications controller if the proper business machine clock is installed. See Chapter 2 for more information on the IBM 3725 communications controller.

The physical medium of the link is also described to NCP. The DUPLEX operand specifies whether the facility is physically capable of half-duplex or full-duplex transmission. These are also referred to as "two-wire" or "four-wire" facilities. The NCP uses the value specified to control the Request-To-Send (RTS) signal to the modem. The specification of FULL keeps the RTS signal active whether the NCP is sending or receiving data. Specifying HALF activates the RTS signal only when the NCP is sending data. This operand should not be confused with half-duplex and full-duplex protocol, the transfer of data between session partners.

The speed of the link is specified on the SPEED operand. The SPEED operand is required when CLOCKNG=INT is coded. This is necessary because the communications scanner must know how to clock the data bits for sending and receiving data. By coding CLOCKNG=EXT, the generation procedure ignores the SPEED operand since the modem is responsible for the clocking. However, the speed operand is used by some network performance tools. It is also useful for documentation purposes.

The transmission code`is used by the NCP for communicating to the devices defined under this line group. Using the CODE operand, NCP can determine how the data destined for the device is to be translated. NCP's internal processing code is EBCDIC, and it translates the outgoing data to the code specified on the CODE operand. For BSC devices in network control mode the default is EBCDIC.

These line characteristic operands are the more widely used operands for BSC lines in conjunction with BSC 3270 devices. Let's now turn our attention to the operands concerned with error detection and recovery (Figure 15.5).

During the course of a session between two partners over the BSC link, NCP keeps a timer for response time to a poll of a device and a timer for measuring the time between message characters received from a device. For the latter, if the interval between two successive characters in a message received from a device exceeds the time specified in the TEXTTO operand, NCP will end the read or invite operation for the message with a text time-out error indication. Errors of this kind can lead to suspecting the cluster controller, modem, or line. The value coded is in seconds and is a nominal

```
BSC3270    GROUP      LNCTL=BSC,        BSC LINE CONTROL           X
                      TYPE=NCP,         LINE OPERATION MODE        X
                      DIAL=NO,          NON-SWITCHED LINK          X
                      CLOCKNG=EXT,      EXTERNAL CLOCKING/MODEM    X
                      DUPLEX=FULL,      4-WIRE CIRCUIT             X
                      SPEED=9600,       SPEED OF MODEM             X
                      CODE=EBCDIC,      EBCDIC CHARACTERS USED     X
                      RETRIES=(5,10,3), 3 RETRIES 5/10 SECS        X
                      REPLYTO=3,        3 S BEFORE POLL T.O.       X
                      TEXTTO=23.5,      23.5 S B4 MSG T.O.         X
                      PAUSE=1,          SERVICE PAUSE              X
                      POLLED=YES,       POLL ALL DEVICES           X
                      SERVPRI=OLD,      SESSION SERVICE PRIORITYX
                      SERVLIM=8,        SERVICE SEEK LIMIT         X
                      CUTOFF=1,         # OF TRANSFR SEQUENCE      X
                      TRANSFR=3         3 OF NCP BUFFERS XMIT
```

Figure 15.5 Error detection and recovery for BSC links.

value. The actual timed interval may be between the nominal value specified and twice the nominal value. The default 23.5 seconds is recommended for most BSC devices.

During a polling sequence the NCP will wait for a response to the poll, selection, or message text for the interval specified in the REPLYTO operand. If the response is not received in the time specified by the REPLYTO operand, the NCP will indicate to the host that a time-out error has occurred on this link. For BSC lines a default value of 3 seconds is recommended. The value may be coded to the nearest tenth of a second. If your BSC session is using conversational replies, ensure that the REPLYTO operand specifies a value large enough to accommodate the conversational text to be received.

Data link errors occurring during the transmission of data can be handled by the RETRIES operand. This operand defines a retry sequence to be used by NCP to recover from the transmission error. The first value is the maximum number of retries in the sequence. Our definition calls for five retries per sequence. This value can range from 0 to 255. The second parameter in the RETRIES operand is the number of seconds the NCP will pause between sequences. This value can range from 0 to 255 seconds. We have specified 10. The third parameter specifies the maximum number of times the retry sequence is executed. The range for this parameter is 1 to 255. If the maximum retry value is reached, the device is marked inoperative.

In the retry sequence during a send operation, NCP will retransmit the block of data in which the error occurred until it is successfully transmitted or until the maximum retry value is reached. If the error occurred during an NCP receive operation, the NCP will issue a negative response to the sending device. This causes the device to send the block in error until the NCP successfully receives it, the device sends an End-Of-Text (EOT) character, or the NCP has sent the device the number of negative responses that match the maximum number of retries. The values coded in Figure 15.5 are the recommended values.

When NCP services the lines defined in this group, it uses several operands. These operands determine the rate and type of service, which devices get service, and the amount of data the NCP will receive after servicing the line.

For BSC devices, the PAUSE operand (Figure 15.6) specifies the number of seconds for delaying successive service cycles when no sessions exist. The value can range from 0 to 255. The value must be an integer with no decimal extension. This operand saves the NCP cycles when sessions on a BSC line do not exist. The NCP will wait 1

```
BSC3270    GROUP      LNCTL=BSC,        BSC LINE CONTROL           X
                      TYPE=NCP,         LINE OPERATION MODE        X
                      DIAL=NO,          NON-SWITCHED LINK          X
                      CLOCKNG=EXT,      EXTERNAL CLOCKING/MODEM    X
                      DUPLEX=FULL,      4-WIRE CIRCUIT             X
                      SPEED=9600,       SPEED OF MODEM             X
                      CODE=EBCDIC,      EBCDIC CHARACTERS USED     X
                      RETRIES=(5,10,3), 3 RETRIES 5/10 SECS        X
                      REPLYTO=3,        3 S BEFORE POLL T.O.       X
                      TEXTTO=23.5,      23.5 S B4 MSG T.O.         X
                      PAUSE=1,          SERVICE PAUSE              X
                      POLLED=YES,       POLL ALL DEVICES           X
                      NEGPOLP=.2,       NEGATIVE POLL PAUSE        X
                      SERVPRI=OLD,      SESSION SERVICE PRIORITYX
                      SERVLIM=8,        SERVICE SEEK LIMIT         X
                      CUTOFF=1,         # OF TRANSFR SEQUENCE      X
                      TRANSFR=3         3 OF NCP BUFFERS XMIT
```

Figure 15.6 Line service operands for a BSC line group.

between each polling service cycle for each device on a line when no sessions exist. The PAUSE operand can only be coded for BSC devices when the line is in network control mode and the POLLED operand equals YES.

By specifying POLLED=YES, the NCP must poll and address each BSC device on the line individually. The default is NO. All lines in the line group must use the same POLLED operand. Both options cannot be included for different lines within the line group.

Non-productive polling performed by an NCP for devices of a line can create unnecessary overhead and can waste NCP cycles. The NEGPOLP operand for BSC lines provides a means for reducing the overhead. Nonproductive or negative polls are responses received from a device that has been polled by the NCP but does not have data to send to the NCP. The value specified on the NEGPOLP operand causes the NCP to wait before polling the device again for data. The range is 0.1 to 23.5. A large NEGPOLP value can increase the end user response time. The default is 0, but we have coded the recommended value of .2 second. This operand can also be changed by issuing the VTAM operator command MODIFY NEGPOLP. Section 15.3 further discusses modifying this operand.

When servicing a line, it is important to provide the best response available to existing sessions. This can be defined by the SERVPRI operand. The specification of OLD as seen in Figure 15.6 tells NCP to give priority service to existing sessions before establishing new sessions (SERVPRI=NEW).

The SERVLIM operand specifies the number of devices the NCP will check during service seeking of the service order table for a cluster on the line. An optimal value for this operand is half the entries in the largest service order table. NCP can then have more frequent opportunities to service existing sessions, hence better link response time; however, a higher value optimizes service seeking. Once a device has been serviced, the NCP can limit the amount of data it will receive from devices on the line with the CUTOFF and TRANSFR operands.

The CUTOFF operand defines the number of subblocks the NCP will accept from a device on this line. A subblock is the message text sent by the device that fills the number of NCP buffers specified in the TRANSFR operand for this line. If this number is reached before the NCP receives an end-of-block character from the device, the NCP breaks off the transmission. It is highly recommended that CUTOFF=1 and TRANSFR=3 be coded for BSC 3270 devices. Using these values avoids a "HOT I/O" situation that can bring down VTAM or NCP.

This ends our review of line characteristic definitions for a BSC line attached to this NCP. Now let's look at the definitions for an SDLC line group.

15.4.2 SDLC GROUP Definition Statement

Line group definitions of SDLC resources must be defined to the NCP after all BSC and SS line groups have been defined. Operands coded in this GROUP definition statement reflect values for all lines under this group unless they are explicitly coded on successive LINE definition statements. We will discuss the group characteristics in three categories. The first will focus on the line characteristics of the group, the second will concern error recovery, and the third will center on servicing the data links defined for this group. Figure 15.7 details the SDLC GROUP definition statement for our example.

The line group definitions for SDLC lines are quite similar to those of BSC lines. Many of the operands reviewed for BSC lines are used in the same fashion for SDLC lines. The LNCTL operand specifies the type of line control for this group. Figure 15.7 shows that the SDLC line control is prevailing for all lines defined under this group. SDLC is coded because devices at the end point of the physical link use SDLC protocol for communicating with the host.

```
SDLC3270 GROUP      LNCTL=SDLC,        SDLC LINE CONTROL          X

                    TYPE=NCP,          LINE OPERATION MODE        X

                    DIAL=NO,           NON-SWITCHED LINK          X

                    CLOCKNG=EXT,       EXTERNAL CLOCKING/MODEM    X

                    DUPLEX=FULL,       4-WIRE CIRCUIT             X

                    SPEED=9600,        SPEED OF MODEM             X

                    NRZI=NO,           NON-RETURN to ZERO MODE    X

                    RETRIES=(5,10,3),    3 RETRIES 5/10 S         X

                    REPLYTO=1,           1 S   BEFORE POLL T.O.X

                    TEXTTO=1,            1 S   B4 MSG T.O.         X

                    PAUSE=.2,          SERVICE PAUSE              X

                    SERVLIM=254        SERVICE SEEK LIMIT
```

Figure 15.7 SDLC group highlighting line characteristics.

Since the remote devices under this line group are using SDLC protocol, they are SNA resources; therefore, the NCP acts in network control mode with this link. We specify this to NCP by coding the TYPE operand. The value NCP denotes the use of network control mode for the lines in this group.

Just as in the BSC line group, the DIAL operand differentiates between switched and non-switched data links. This operand specifies whether switched line control procedures are required for the lines in this group. By specifying NO, non-switched line control procedures are enforced. For more information about switched line control procedures, consult *Advanced SNA Networking*.

As with the BSC line group, the responsibility for clocking the data falls under the jurisdiction of the modems. The CLOCKNG operand relays this information to NCP. The specification of CLOCKNG=EXT tells NCP that the modem attached to the link will supply the clocking. If CLOCKNG=INT is specified, the communications scanner for that line will provide the clocking within the communications controller if the proper business machine clock is installed.

The DUPLEX operand for SDLC links is dependent upon the ADDRESS operand of the LINE definition statement. If the second parameter of the ADDRESS operand specifies FULL, the DUPLEX operand has no effect on the SDLC link. On the other hand, if HALF is specified on the ADDRESS operand, the DUPLEX operand affects the RTS signal equal to that for a BSC line. The specification of FULL keeps the RTS signal always active. Specifying HALF activates the RTS signal only when the NCP is sending data. Again, this operand should not be confused with half-duplex and full-duplex protocol, the transfer of data between session partners.

The speed of the link is specified on the SPEED operand, which is required when CLOCKNG=INT is coded. This is necessary because the communications scanner must know how to clock the data bits for sending and receiving data. By coding CLOCKNG=EXT, the generation procedure ignores the SPEED operand since the modem is responsible for the clocking. However, the speed operand is used by some network performance tools. It is also useful for documentation purposes.

The NRZI operand is pertinent to SDLC lines only. This operand specifies the use on non-return-to-zero change-on-ones (NRZI) mode used by all SNA cluster controllers attached to this SDLC link. For the most part, the specification of NRZI=YES is dependent on the modems used for the SDLC line. This is because most SNA cluster controllers can support NRZI. The modems are in question because many modems are sensitive to the bit pattern used in NRZI and may lose synchronism. The guideline used for this operand is if the modem is a non-IBM modem, code NRZI=NO; if it is an IBM modem, code NRZI=YES. Your best bet is to consult the maker of the modem to get a definitive answer.

These line characteristic operands are the more widely used operands for SDLC lines. Let's now turn our attention to the operands concerned with error detection and recovery (Figure 15.8).

```
SDLC3270 GROUP      LNCTL=SDLC,        SDLC LINE CONTROL           X

                    TYPE=NCP,          LINE OPERATION MODE         X

                    DIAL=NO,           NON-SWITCHED LINK           X

                    CLOCKNG=EXT,       EXTERNAL CLOCKING/MODEM     X

                    DUPLEX=FULL,       4-WIRE CIRCUIT              X

                    SPEED=9600,        SPEED OF MODEM              X

                    NRZI=NO,           NON-RETURN TO ZERO MODE     X

                    RETRIES=(5,10,3),  3 RETRIES 5/10 SECS         X

                    REPLYTO=1,         1 S BEFORE POLL T.O.        X

                    TEXTTO=1,          1 S B4 MSG T.O.             X

                    PAUSE=.2,          SERVICE PAUSE               X

                    SERVLIM=254        SERVICE SEEK LIMIT
```

Figure 15.8 Error detection and recovery for SDLC links.

Time outs for polling responses and message text are also used for SDLC lines. If the interval between two successive characters in a message received from a device exceeds the time specified in the TEXTTO operand, NCP will end the read or invite operation for the message with a text time-out error indication. Errors of this kind can lead to suspecting the cluster controller, modem, or line. The value coded is in seconds and is a nominal value. The actual timed interval may be between the nominal value specified and twice the nominal value. In SDLC, the time out only occurs when the link station is the primary link station. The recommended value for SDLC lines is based on the line speed. In our case the recommended time-out value is 1 since the line speed is greater than 2000 bps. For line speeds between 0 and 1199 bps, the value is about 4. For line speeds between 1200 and 2000 bps, the recommended value is approximately 3 seconds. You will have to do some experimentation on your network to find the appropriate values for your SDLC lines.

The interval specified on the REPLYTO operand is the time NCP will wait for a response to a poll, selection, or message text response from a device on an SDLC line. The default for an SDLC line is 1 and is recommended. But again, realization of this value on your network must be determined by examining the configuration.

The RETRIES operand is used in the same manner as was previously discussed for the BSC GROUP definition. The difference is the range of values that can be coded for the parameters of the operand. The first value is the maximum number of retries in the sequence. Our definition calls for five retries per sequence. This value can range from 0 to 128. The second parameter in the RETRIES operand is the number of seconds the NCP will pause between sequences. This value can range from 1 to 255; we have specified 10. The third parameter specifies the maximum number of times the retry sequence is executed. The range for this parameter is 1 to 127. If the maximum retry value is reached, the device is marked inoperative.

In the retry sequence during a send operation, NCP will retransmit the block of data in which the error occurred until it is successfully transmitted or until the maximum retry value is reached. If the error occurred during an NCP receive operation, the NCP will issue a negative response to the sending device. This causes the device to send the block in error until the NCP successfully receives it, the device sends an End-Of-Text (EOT) character, or the NCP has sent the device the number of negative responses that match the maximum number of retries. The values coded in Figure 15.8 are the recommended values.

SDLC3270 GROUP	LNCTL=SDLC,	SDLC LINE CONTROL	X
	TYPE=NCP,	LINE OPERATION MODE	X
	DIAL=NO,	NON-SWITCHED LINK	X
	CLOCKNG=EXT,	EXTERNAL CLOCKING/MODEM	X
	DUPLEX=FULL,	4-WIRE CIRCUIT	X
	SPEED=9600,	SPEED OF MODEM	X
	NRZI=NO,	NON-RETURN TO ZERO MODE	X
	RETRIES=(5,10,3),	3 RETRIES 5/10 SECS	X
	REPLYTO=1,	1 S BEFORE POLL T.O.	X
	TEXTTO=1,	1 S B4 MSG T.O.	X
	PAUSE=.2,	SERVICE PAUSE	X
	PASSLIM=254,	max # of BLUs	X
	SERVLIM=4	# of SOT scans	

Figure 15.9 Line service operands for a SDLC line group.

When NCP services the lines defined in this group, it uses several operands. These operands determine the rate and type of service, which devices get service, and the amount of data the NCP will receive after servicing the line (Figure 15.9).

The PAUSE operand for an SDLC line is the polling interval of resources in the service order table. The value specified here is the amount of time NCP will wait before polling all resources in the service order table. That time includes the moment the NCP polls the first entry to the time the NCP services that first entry again. The cycle includes time for polling, reading, and writing to resources on the line. If the time spent in servicing all the active resources in the service order table equals or exceeds the values of PAUSE, the service cycle begins again. An advantage to this algorithm is that if the SDLC link is in a poll-wait state (i.e., waiting for the PAUSE value to elapse), any data ready for transmission to resources on the link is sent during the pause. The default value is 0.2 and is recommended.

The SERVLIM operand for SDLC line resources provides the NCP with the number of times it will scan the service order table for normal service before attempting to scan for special services. The maximum value for an SDLC link is 255. The default is 4 and is recommended. This means that the NCP will scan the service order table for normal service four times before scanning the table for special service. Normal service is that service required by existing active sessions. Special service includes those LUs and PUs seeking to establish a session or the issuance of activate and inactivate commands for PUs and LUs on this SDLC line.

To optimize the service received from the NCP, the PASSLIM operand is used to define the number of SDLC frames that the NCP can send to a PU in one service cycle. The default for this operand is 1 SDLC frame for a PU Type 2 device. The normal practice is to match the MAXOUT operand of the PU definition statement. For most PU Type 2 devices this is set to 7. Setting PASSLIM=7 for a PU Type 2 device is fine for a mixed message set and particularly for a multipoint line configuration. For performance considerations, on a point-to-point SDLC line with a PU Type 2 device, the value of 254 should be coded. As with most of the NCP operands and their parameters, analysis of your network's performance is the only real measure for defining these operands.

15.4.3 Switched SDLC GROUP Definition Statement

Applications executing under VTAM are unaware of the LU's link state. VTAM and NCP provide the capability of a remote SNA resource to use a nondedicated line to gain access to applications on the host. This switched connection is more often than not used for Remote Job Entry (RJE). Associated with switched lines is the VTAM switched major node definition. The switched major node defines the PUs and LUs that may access the network using a switched line.

RJE is used with most applications for batch processing. In our example, the IBM S/36 is used during the day for remote data entry processing. Interaction with the host is not necessary. However, at some point during the day, the information entered on the S/36 is needed for processing on the host. At this time, the S/36 can either dial in to gain access to the network or VTAM can initiate the connection by a dial-out procedure. The information from the S/36 is then transmitted to the host for processing by the appropriate application. Figure 15.10 details the switched SDLC GROUP definition statement for our example.

When defining switched line group definitions, the distinction between switched and dedicated is determined by the DIAL operand. By specifying DIAL=YES, the NCP generation process sets the lines defined under this GROUP definition statement for switched link procedures. Many of the operands coded on the SDLC GROUP definition statement are also used for a switched group. LNCTL, NRZI, CLOCKNG, and SPEED are also used and have the same implica-

```
SWSDLC    GROUP      LNCTL=SDLC,      SDLC LINE CONTROL           X
                     TYPE=NCP,        LINE OPERATION MODE         X
                     DIAL=YES,        SWITCHED LINK               X
                     CLOCKNG=EXT,     EXTERNAL CLOCKING/MODEM     X
                     DUPLEX=HALF,     2-WIRE CIRCUIT              X
                     SPEED=4800,      SPEED OF MODEM              X
                     NRZI=NO,         NON-RETURN TO ZERO MODE     X
                     RETRIES=(7,4,5), 5 RETRIES 7/4  S            X
                     REPLYTO=3,       1 S    BEFORE POLL T.O. X
                     TEXTTO=3,        1 S    B4 MSG T.O.          X
                     PAUSE=1,         SERVICE PAUSE               X
                     XMITDLY=2.2      delay xmiting XID
```

Figure 15.10 Switched SDLC GROUP definition.

tions on the line. Some of the operands are also used with the same context but with more consideration.

The DUPLEX operand for switched SDLC links is dependent upon the modems and the facility circuit. Recently switched lines have become able to use full-duplex transmission. New modems have allowed dial-up access to occur with full-duplex capabilities. But we have coded DUPLEX=HALF to show you the norm for a switched line.

In conjunction with full-duplex transmission, the SPEED operand has also recently been affected. Now with the newest modems, a dial-up line can run not only full duplex but at speeds up to 9600 bps. However, in keeping with the norm, we have defined the speed in the NCP SPEED operand to be 4800 bps.

During a dial-up connection, the facility being used is in the public networks. There is no special line conditioning performed over the circuits such as are found in most private and dedicated circuits. The lines used for transmission are the same telephone lines you and I use when talking on the phone. For this reason we should give special consideration to the time-out and polling operands.

Only real measurements can give you appropriate values. What we have done with the time-out operands is to give ample time for the slower transmission speed and lower circuit grade than that used for the non-switched SDLC lines (Figure 15.11). We have also reduced the polling rate by specifying the PAUSE operand value at 1. This may hinder response time performance, but if response time is a consideration, using a switched line for this resource is an error. Re-

```
SWSDLC     GROUP      LNCTL=SDLC,       SDLC LINE CONTROL           X
                      TYPE=NCP,         LINE OPERATION MODE         X
                      DIAL=YES,         SWITCHED LINK               X
                      CLOCKNG=EXT,      EXTERNAL CLOCKING/MODEM     X
                      DUPLEX=HALF,      2-WIRE CIRCUIT              X
                      SPEED=4800,       SPEED OF MODEM              X
                      NRZI=NO,          NON-RETURN TO ZERO MODE     X
                      RETRIES=(7,4,5),  5 RETRIES 7/4  SECS         X
                      REPLYTO=3,        1 S BEFORE POLL T.O.        X
                      TEXTTO=3,         1 S B4 MSG T.O.             X
                      PAUSE=1,          SERVICE PAUSE               X
                      XMITDLY=2.2       delay xmiting XID
```

Figure 15.11 Switched group operands of special consideration.

member, switched lines are primarily used for short access times to the host or for back-up procedures.

The XMITDLY operand is new in NCP V4.3/V5. During initial contact the two resources will exchange identification. In SNA the NCP link station is always the primary link station when the switched device is a peripheral node. The values can be NONE|n|2.2. Defining NONE will negate the XMITDLY function and the NCP will transmit its XID as soon as contact is made. This may cause XID collisions over the link, resulting in retransmissions of the XIDs. The n value is a number you specify in seconds that is used by the NCP to wait before sending an XID. The default value 2.2 is more than adequate for most dial-up circuits. By specifying a value other than NONE, the modems have a chance to equalize with each other before the NCP sends an XID. Again, this reduces the possibility of transmission errors. The XMITDLY value is also used as the reply-time-out value if (1) it is larger than the REPLYTO specification, (2) the line is a switched line, or (3) XIDs are being exchanged. The XMITDLY operand can also be defined on leased SDLC links. In particular it is used with T2.1 nodes using Low Entry Networking (LEN). LEN and T2.1 nodes are discussed in detail in *Advanced SNA Networking*.

15.4.4 Channel-Attached GROUP Definition Statement

In NCP V5.1 and NCP V5.2 an added feature of the NCP is the definition of a channel-attached HOST as a special line group. The IBM 3720 communications controller with this version of NCP can define the channel adapter in the traditional way in the BUILD statement or here in the CA group statement. If the CA line group is used, the HOST definition statement becomes a VTAM-only definition statement and is not used by the NCP. The IBM 3745 communications controller, however, defines all channel-attached nodes with the CA line group. As such, in an IBM 3745 the HOST definition statement is always a VTAM-only definition statement.

There are two flavors to channel-adapter links. A channel subarea link available with NCP V5.1 defines the channel between the NCP and a host access method, namely VTAM. The channel peripheral link attaches a T2.1 peripheral host node to the NCP through the channel. This node is seen by the SSCP as a peripheral T2.1 node attached to the NCP via an SDLC peripheral link in the NCP's subarea. Programs residing on System/370, 30XX, and 4300 IBM processors can function as the T2.1 peripheral node. One such program is the Transaction Processing Facility (TPF). This program can enter the NCP's subarea through the channel peripheral link as a T2.1 peripheral HOST node, but instead of utilizing LU6.2, TPF uses the standard LU2 session protocols.

15.5 SUMMARY

In this chapter we learned about HOST, LUDRPOOL, PATH, and GROUP macros of NCP. The HOST macro provides for defining buffers and buffer sizes. These buffers are used for sending and receiving data between the host and the channel-attached communications controller. The LUDRPOOL macro specifies the number of LUs that are expected to have a session on a line. The PATH macro uses the ER and VR statements to direct data to a destination subarea. It uses the adjacent subarea and the TG number pair associated with an ER and VR. The GROUP macro allows you to specify certain characteristic functions that are common to a group of links and devices attached to an NCP.

16

NCP Macros — LINE, SERVICE, CLUSTER, and TERMINAL

16.1 LINE DEFINITION STATEMENT

A LINE definition statement provides the NCP with information
about the functional characteristics of the link being defined. These
include the speed of the line, the type of facility (full or half-duplex),
and the recovery procedure for the link from transmission errors.
The characteristics just outlined have been discussed under the
GROUP definitions for BSC, nonswitched SDLC, and switched
SDLC.

The functional characteristics that we will discuss here are specific
to the type of line being defined, the assignment of an address in the
NCP, the type of attachment, and modems used for the link. We will
also begin to introduce to you the VTAM-only operands that are used
in an NCP for SNA resources. These operands are coded in the NCP
source generation deck and are ignored by the NCP generation process.

16.1.1 BSC LINE Definition Statement

The definition of the GROUP for the BSC line that we will describe
here contains many of the LINE operands that are common to all
lines regardless of their line control (e.g., BSC and SDLC). In this
section we will concentrate on operands specific to BSC line control
(Figure 16.1).

```
N11L000   LINE     ADDRESS=(000,HALF),  PORT 0, HDX PROTOCOL      X
                   ATTACH=MODEM,        MODEM ATTACHMENT          X
                   POLIMIT=(1,QUEUE),   MAX # -RSP/ACTION         X
                   AVGPB=256,           AVG # BYTES/POLL          X
                   PU=YES,              BSC 3270 = PU             X
                   ISTATUS=ACTIVE       INITIAL STATUS=ACTIVE
```

Figure 16.1 BSC LINE definition.

The one required operand of the LINE definition statement is the ADDRESS operand. This operand defines to NCP which Line Interface Coupler (LIC) port these definitions will affect. The description of the ADDRESS operand that follows is valid for all line definitions. The format of the ADDRESS operand is:

```
ADDRESS=[(lnbr,[HALF|FULL][sal,..san])]
        [channel adapter position]
```

The port parameter identifies the even or even/odd pair of ports that will be used by the NCP. The value is the position of the physical port of the LIC. The addresses assigned are logically defined within the NCP in accordance with the second parameter. See the Appendix for specifics about defining the *lnbr* parameter for the IBM 3720 and IBM 3745 communications controller using NCP V5.

By specifying HALF, NCP will assign a logical even-numbered address to the port. This value also defines the data transfer mode as half-duplex. This means that the data will travel over the assigned address for sending and receiving data. However, only one direction can operate at a time. If FULL is coded in this position, the data transfer mode uses full duplex, that is, the NCP can send and receive data over this port simultaneously. This occurs because the NCP logically associates an even/odd pair of addresses with the physical port. The even address is used for sending or transmitting data from the NCP and the odd address is used for receiving the data.

The sal through san parameter pertains to the use of this port in emulation mode. The *sal* through *san* corresponds to the Emulation Subchannel (ESC) address for the port. The ESC address is the hexadecimal digits specified in the Unit Control Block (UCB) of MVS or Physical Control Block (PCB) of VSE. Each ESC address is followed by the position of the channel adapter. The ESC address is the last two hexadecimal digits of the UCB. This type of address definition is used most often with the emulation program.

The usage of the channel-adapter position parameter comes into play when user-written channel-adapter code is loaded into the 3725. For an IBM 3725 this value ranges from 0 to 5; in an IBM 3720 the range is 0 to 1. Using the ADDRESS operand in this fashion is exemplified by the Non-SNA Interconnect (NSI) program from IBM.

In Figure 16.1 we see that line N11L000 is connected to port 0 of the IBM 3725 and transmits in half-duplex mode. The ATTACH operand tells NCP that the line attachment to the remote resource is through a modem. There are three other possibilities for this operand: DIRECT, LODIRECT, and DIR3275. Use the DIRECT parameter when the line is attached to the remote resources of this NCP without the use of modems. You must also specify DIAL=NO and CLOCKNG=EXT and omit the use of the SPEED operand. In this case, the clocking is performed by the remote resource. The LODIRECT parameter is used when the SPEED operand is coded for a remote resource attached to this NCP without modems. In addition the DIAL=NO and CLOCKNG=INT operands must be specified. This indicates that the communications scanner for the port to which this direct attachment is connected will provide the clocking. The final ATTACH parameter option is the DIR3725. This is specified on a LINE definition statement when the link is between two IBM 3725 communications controllers without modems.

When NCP polls devices, it expects the device to return a positive response to the poll whether or not the device has data to send to the host. POLIMIT (Figure 16.2) is used to tell the NCP the action it should take when receiving a negative response to a poll. Under VTAM, the only NCP action that is valid is to (1) break the logical connection to the device, (2) notify VTAM, and (3) queue the most current read request for the device at the top of the queue. The specification of the QUEUE parameter determines these events.

```
N11L000   LINE      ADDRESS=(000,HALF), PORT 0, HDX PROTOCOL     X
                    ATTACH=MODEM,     MODEM ATTACHMENT            X
                    POLIMIT=(1,QUEUE), MAX # -RSP/ACTION          X
                    AVGPB=256,        AVG # BYTES/POLL            X
                    PU=YES,           BSC 3270 = PU               X
                    ISTATUS=ACTIVE    INITIAL STATUS=ACTIVE
```

Figure 16.2 BSC LINE polling operands.

After receiving at least one message block from the device, the actions outlined above will go into effect after the NCP receives a specified number of consecutive negative responses to a poll. This number is assigned in the first parameter of the POLIMIT operand. Its value can range from 0 to 255. The default is 1 and is also the recommended value.

The receipt of data in NCP from a device in response to a poll can be governed by the AVGPB operand. For BSC or SS devices, the LINE definition statement is the lowest level definition statement that the AVGPB operand can be coded on. For an SDLC line, the PU definition statement can specify the AVGPB. The value specified here assists the NCP in determining if there is enough buffer space to receive the expected data transmitted from a device after a poll. This protects the NCP from an overrun error in the buffer pool. If the buffer space is not available, the NCP will delay polling the device until it can ensure that enough buffer space exists for receiving the data. The range for the value is 1 to 65,535 bytes. The default is the value specified on the BUILD BFRS operand of this NCP. The selection of the AVGPB value is most practical if the value reflects the link buffer of the device and is a multiple of the BFRS operand value. We have chosen the value 256 for two reasons: (1) the link buffer of an IBM 3274 is 256 bytes and (2) 256 is a multiple of 128 (size of NCP buffers).

In SNA the only non-SNA device that is supported without the use of an emulation program or line control program is the BSC 3270 device. The PU operand (Figure 16.3) on the LINE definition statement for a BSC line control protocol specifies to VTAM (not NCP) that this line contains BSC 3270 cluster controllers and BSC 3270 terminals that are to be treated as PUs and LUs, respectively. PU=YES is the default for a BSC 3270 device. For all other BSC devices, the default is PU=NO. In this case, the resources on this line must be supported by a line control program similar to IBM's

```
N11L000   LINE        ADDRESS=(000,HALF), PORT 0, HDX PROTOCOL      X
                       ATTACH=MODEM,    MODEM ATTACHMENT             X
                       POLIMIT=(1,QUEUE), MAX # -RSP/ACTION          X
                       AVGPB=256,        AVG # BYTES/POLL            X
                       PU=YES,           BSC 3270 = PU               X
                       ISTATUS=ACTIVE    INITIAL STATUS=ACTIVE
```

Figure 16.3 LINE VTAM operands.

Network Terminal Operator (NTO) program. The PU operand cannot be coded on the CLUSTER definition statement. It may be coded on the GROUP or LINE statement of the CLUSTER devices.

The ISTATUS operand performs the same function here as in the definitions for all SNA resources. In this statement we specify to VTAM that the line defined by this statement is to be activated whenever the NCP major node is activated. The activation pertains only to the LINE definition statement if the succeeding CLUSTER and TERMINAL definition statements have specified their own ISTATUS operand. However, the value specified here can sift down to the CLUSTER definitions for this line and in turn to the TERMINAL definitions associated with each cluster.

16.1.2 SDLC LINE Definition Statement

The definition of the GROUP for the SDLC line described here focuses on a nonswitched point-to-point SDLC line. Many of the operands coded on the GROUP definition statement are actually LINE operands and may also be coded on the LINE definition statement. Here in this section we will concentrate on prioritizing polling and transmission functions.

As in the BSC LINE definition, we must supply the physical port number of the IBM 3725 communications controller used to connect the physical line defined by this LINE definition. The ADDRESS operand in Figure 16.4 identifies port number 001 of the IBM 3725 as the attachment point for the physical line. It also defines the data transfer protocol as half duplex.

Here in the SDLC LINE definition for N11L001, modems are used on the facility to attach the remote resources to the IBM 3725 communications controller. This is specified on the ATTACH operand by the presence of the MODEM parameter.

When data arrives in the NCP with a destination for an LU off of the NCP, the NCP can expedite the delivery of the data to the LU.

```
N11L001   LINE      ADDRESS=(001,HALF),  PORT 1, HDX PROTOCOL     X
                    ATTACH=MODEM,        MODEM ATTACHMENT          X
                    HDXSP=NO,            SEND PRIORITY OVER POLL   X
                    AVGPB=256,            AVG # BYTES/POLL         X
                    ISTATUS=ACTIVE       INITIAL STATUS=ACTIVE
```

Figure 16.4 SDLC LINE definition statement for nonswitched resources.

```
N11L001   LINE      ADDRESS=(001,HALF), PORT 1, HDX PROTOCOL    X
                    ATTACH=MODEM,     MODEM ATTACHMENT           X
                    HDXSP=NO,         SEND PRIORITY OVER POLL    X
                    AVGPB=256,        AVG # BYTES/POLL           X
                    ISTATUS=ACTIVE    INITIAL STATUS=ACTIVE
```

Figure 16.5 Polling sensitive operands for the SDLC LINE definition.

This is determined by the value specified on the HDXSP operand (Figure 16.5). The operand is valid only if (1) LNCTL=SDLC, (2) PAUSE=0, and (3) the ADDRESS operand has HALF specified. If these requirements are met, this operand will go into effect when more than one device is active on the link. The specification of NO (the default) tells the NCP to send the data to the device during the polling service for that device. The NCP sends the data just prior to the actual polling sequence unless the link is in a poll-wait state. We have defaulted and coded HDXSP=NO because our PAUSE operand specifies PAUSE=.2 and therefore negates the use of HDXSP. The specification of YES on the HDXSP operand tells NCP that data destined for LUs on this link may be sent before the normal polling service of the destination device. However, if you have NCP cycles to burn, code PAUSE=0 and HDXSP=YES. This will increase end-user response time for the receipt of data.

The AVGPB operand for SDLC links has differing considerations if the link being defined is for Boundary Network Node (BNN) SDLC devices or for Intermediate Networking Node (INN) links. This discussion concerns BNN SDLC devices. The AVGPB operand for SDLC lines is really specific to PUs defined for this line. We have placed it in the LINE definition statement so that it may sift down to the PUs defined for this line. At the PU level we may override this value if measurements indicate that changing the value for a specific PU on the line warrants modification. Again, the appropriate value for PU Type 2 devices represented by an IBM 3274 cluster controller is optimized by the value 256. The default for this value is the BFRS value times 7. The minimum value is the BFRS value; the maximum value is 65,535. Usage for INN links will be discussed in *Advanced SNA Networking*.

16.1.3 Switched SDLC LINE Definition Statement

In defining the switched SDLC LINE definition many of the operands that are specific to the LINE definition statement have been

```
N11L002   LINE      ADDRESS=(002,HALF), PORT 2, HDX PROTOCOL      X
                    ATTACH=MODEM,     MODEM ATTACHMENT            X
                    ANSTONE=NO,       NCP SUPPLIES ANSWER TONE    X
                    ANSWER=ON,        ALLOW INCOMING CALLS        X
                    CALL=IN,          END-USER INITIATES CALL     X
                    ISTATUS=ACTIVE      INITIAL STATUS=ACTIVE
```

Figure 16.6 Switched SDLC LINE definition statement.

coded on the GROUP definition statement in Section 15.4.3. Here we
will concentrate on the dial procedure. Figure 16.6 contains the outline of the switched SDLC LINE definition statement used for our
sample single-domain network.

The physical port number of the IBM 3725 communications controller used that will accept the switched facility link is designated
by the ADDRESS operand. The ADDRESS operand in Figure 16.6
identifies port number 002 of the IBM 3725 as the switched facility
entry point into the SNA network. It also defines the data transfer
protocol as half duplex.

Since this is a switched LINE definition, N11L002 must use modems to gain access to the network. These modems must be capable
of handling a switched facility. Most modems have an auto-answer
feature or generate the answer tone to the calling modem. If, however, the modem does not provide this feature, the NCP can supply
the answer tone. The operand ANSTONE allows for this specification
by coding the YES parameter. We have auto-answer capable modems
and therefore have coded the default value of ANSTONE=NO.

Figure 16.7 highlights two VTAM-only operands that affect the
switched SDLC line dial capabilities. The CALL operand is valid
only if the DIAL=YES operand is specified on the GROUP definition
statement. The function of this operand is to notify VTAM whether

```
N11L002   LINE      ADDRESS=(002,HALF), PORT 2, HDX PROTOCOL    X
                    ATTACH=MODEM,     MODEM ATTACHMENT          X
                    ANSTONE=NO,       NCP SUPPLIES ANSWER TONE  X
                    CALL=IN,          END-USER INITIATES CALL   X
                    ANSWER=ON,        NCP ALLOWS DIAL IN CALL    X
                    ISTATUS=ACTIVE      INITIAL STATUS=ACTIVE
```

Figure 16.7 VTAM-only operands that affect switched SDLC LINE definitions.

the end user, VTAM, or both can create the switched link connection for the line being defined. The specification of CALL=IN identities the end user as the initiator of the connection. Specifying CALL=OUT notifies VTAM that it can initiate the connection in accordance with the switched major node definition for this switched SDLC line. If CALL=INOUT is coded, either the end user or VTAM can establish the connection.

The ANSWER operand is valid for dial-in capability of switched SDLC lines only. The end user can dial into the NCP over this switched line definition only if the line is active. To allow this we have coded ANSWER=ON and ISTATUS=ACTIVE. You can also specify ANSWER=OFF, which prohibits the dial-in capability for a connection regardless of the active or inactive status of the line. You may want to use this for security purposes. The ANSWER=OFF operand can be modified by the VTAM operator command VARY ANS. This command gives the VTAM operator or network manager the ability to enable or disable the dial-in capability.

16.1.4 Channel-Adapter LINE Definition

As you can see from Figure 16.8, the parameters used in the CA LINE definition are the same as those used in the BUILD definition statement. In fact they are all used and defined in the same manner by the NCP. The CA line group is always used for the IBM 3745 and is optionally used in the IBM 3720 when executing NCP V5. If you define your channel link on the IBM 3720 in a CA line group, be sure to remove the channel link definitions from the BUILD definition statement. Channel links defined in the line group must be defined in ascending order according to the channel adapter logical address specified on the ADDRESS operand.

```
HOST01CA LINE      ADDRESS=0,      CA position 0              X
                   CA=TYPE6,       3745 CA TYPE 6             X
                   DELAY=0.2,      WAIT .2 S B4 ATTN          X
                   TIMEOUT=440,    TIME CA OUT AFTER 440 S    X
                   NCPCA=ACTIVE,   CA COMES UP ACTIVE         X
                   CASDL=10,       CA SLOW DOWN LIMIT         x
                   TRANSFR=32,     # OF-ncp BUFFERS 2 SEND    x
                   INBFRS=16       # OF ncp BUFFERS 2 RECEIV
```

Figure 16.8 Sample CA LINE definition for a channel-adapter link on an IBM 3745.

The ADDRESS operand defines the logical address of the channel adapter by specifying the CA position on the controller rather than the UCB address for the channel. The value for the channel adapter for the IBM 3720 is either 0 or 1; for the IBM 3745 the value range is 0 through 15. See Appendix D for a table on assigning the physical channel-adapter position to the value specified on the ADDRESS operand.

The CASDL is used by the NCP to block inbound traffic to the NCP before indicating that the station has gone inoperative. The value specified is in seconds. The lowest possible value is 10.0 seconds and the highest is 840.0 seconds. The default is the TIMEOUT value specified for this line. If TIMEOUT is NONE, the CASDL operand is invalid. A low value will reduce the amount of lost data.

The INBFRS operand is usually defined on the HOST definition statement. Since the HOST definition statement is now a VTAM-only statement, post-NCP V4.2, the INBFRS value is now specified here on the CA LINE definition statement. Recall that the INBFRS value indicates to the NCP the number of NCP buffers that must be available to receive data from VTAM. The remaining parameters have been discussed in the BUILD definition statement and are used in the same manner.

16.2 SERVICE DEFINITION STATEMENT

Nonswitched data link devices attached to your NCP must be serviced by the NCP to send and receive data. The SERVICE definition statement causes the generation procedure to create a service order table for the resources associated with this line. The SERVICE definition statement must immediately follow the LINE definition statement and is valid for nonswitched links only. Each link must have a corresponding SERVICE definition statement. If the statement is omitted, a default service order table is created for a line operating in network control mode. The service order table is serviced by the NCP in accordance with the SERVLIM operand defined in the previous GROUP definition statements.

16.2.1 BSC Service Order Table

For each BSC device associated with the LINE definition this SERVICE definition statement belongs to an entry and must be included in the service order table. The service order table is defined on the

SERVICE definition statement by coding the ORDER operand. Figure 16.9 contains the service order table for the devices associated with the BSC line N11L000.

In the service order table you can specify up to 255 entries. The name of the SERVICE definition statement is required for BSC and SS definitions. In Figure 16.9 the name is defined as L000SOT. Each entry can be unique or a resource name can be specified several times within the service order table. The ORDER operand gives us this option. The specification of a resource several times in the service order table provides more service for that resource. If you choose to take advantage of this capability, review performance statistics relating to this cluster and its devices. You may wish to code the terminals that have a high access to high priority interactive applications on the host rather than those terminals that primarily use batch and print applications.

Each device defined under a LINE definition statement must be included in the service order table at least once. The generation procedure checks each resource name against the service order table to make sure that (1) the association with the LINE this SERVICE definition statement is coded for and (2) each resource name defined under this LINE definition statement is included in the service order table.

From Figure 16.9 we can see that there are nine entries in the service order table for this SERVICE definition statement. The table is scanned according to the value specified on the SERVLIM operand. See the BSC GROUP definition statement in Section 15.4.1 for a description of the SERVLIM operand as it relates to a BSC line.

16.2.2 SDLC Service Order Table

The service order table definition for SDLC lines needs only the PU names of the clusters that are associated with the LINE definition

```
L000SOT   SERVICE   ORDER=(N11BC01,B1101T00,B1101T01,B1101T02,   X
                     B1101T03,B1101T04,B1101T05,B1101T06,B1101T07,   X
                     B1101T08,B1101T09,B1101T10,B1101T11,B1101T12,   X
                     B1101T13,B1101T14,B1101T15,B1101T16,B1101T17,   X
                     B1101T18,B1101T19,B1101T20,B1101T21,B1101T22,   X
                     B1101T23,B1101T24,B1101T25,B1101T26.B1101T27,   X
                     B1101T28,B1101T29,B1101T30,B1101T31)
```

Figure 16.9 Service order table for BSC line N11L000.

```
L001SOT   SERVICE   ORDER=(N11SCC1)
```

Figure 16.10 Service order table for a dedicated SDLC line.

for which this service order table is created (Figure 16.10). Each PU
name associated with the LINE definition statement must be coded
in the service order table. The importance of order in the table is
greater because the PUs are obtaining the service from the NCP and
not the individual LUs.

The service order table can specify up to 255 entries. Each entry
can be unique or a resource name can be specified several times
within the service order table. In a point-to-point configuration such
as ours, there is only one possible entry. It does not buy you or the
resource additional service to replicate the resource name in the
service order table. Including a PU name several times in the service
order table is feasible for a multipoint configuration. Refer to Section
15.4.2 for the SERVLIM impact on an SDLC service order table definition.

16.3 CLUSTER DEFINITION STATEMENT

For each BSC cluster controller representing an IBM 3270 series
type of controller you must code a CLUSTER definition statement
(Figure 16.11). The definition is valid only if the DIAL=NO and
POLLED=YES operands are coded on the GROUP definition statement of the LINE definition statement this cluster controller is attached to. The CLUSTER definition must be coded directly after the
SERVICE definition statement, if it is coded, and must precede any
TERMINAL or COMP definition statements that pertain to this cluster controller.

```
N11BC01   CLUSTER   GPOLL=40407F7F,        GENERAL POLLING        X
                    CUTYPE=3271,           CONTROL UNIT TYPE      X
                    FEATUR2=(MODEL2),      BUFFER SIZE OF 1920    X
                    DLOGMOD=R3270,         LOGMODE ENTRY          X
                    MODETAB=MT01,          MODE TABLE NAME        X
                    USSTAB=USSNSNA,        NON-SNA USSTAB         X
                    ISTATUS=ACTIVE
```

Figure 16.11 BSC 3274 cluster controller definition.

Remember that earlier we stated that VTAM supports BSC 3270-type devices such as PUs and LUs by coding the PU=YES operand on the GROUP or LINE definition statement for a BSC line discipline. This treatment for a PU is made possible by the use of the GPOLL operand. The BSC 3270 cluster controller examines the status of all attached resources upon receiving a general poll.

The GPOLL operand provides the cluster control units with a unique station address on the line. This address is directly related to the cluster's position on the line. The first cluster attached to (or dropped off) the line is considered to be position 0. Position 0 is represented in the GPOLL operand as the hexadecimal value 40. A general poll is composed of two fields, a station address and a general poll character of hexadecimal 7F. Together they are coded on the GPOLL operand of the CLUSTER definition statement as 40407F7F.

The CUTYPE operand identifies the control unit as an IBM 3271 or 3275 cluster controller. The IBM 3X74 cluster controller series is classified as CUTYPE=3271. This is also the default value for the CUTYPE operand.

The remaining operands for the cluster N11BC01 are VTAM-only operands. These are used in the same manner as described in Section 10.2.3 and will not be reviewed at this time.

16.4 TERMINAL DEFINITION STATEMENT

A TERMINAL definition statement must be coded for each terminal or printer attached to a BSC cluster controller. This statement allows you to specify the name of the terminal, the type of terminal, and the polling and address characters used by the NCP to contact the device (Figure 16.12). For the TERMINAL definition statements coded in this discussion, all the VTAM-only operands coded on the CLUSTER definition are sifted down to the TERMINAL definitions.

The name of each TERMINAL definition statement is required. This name can be any valid assembler-language name. However, the

```
B1101T00   TERMINAL  POLL=40404040,      POLLING ADDRESS      X
                     ADDR=60604040,      SELECTION ADDRESS    X
                     TERM=3277           DEVICE TYPE
```

Figure 16.12 Sample TERMINAL definition statement for the BSC 3270 cluster controller.

name must be unique within this SNA network. The name assigned to the device in Figure 16.12 is B1101T00. The convention used for this name is as follows. The B identifies the device as a BSC device. The next four characters specify the subarea of the NCP for this cluster (11) and the cluster control unit station address (01) that owns this terminal. The last three characters identify the class of device (T for display terminal and P for printer) and the physical port number (00) used to attach the device to the cluster controller.

The POLL operand is used to define the polling characters that are assigned to this device. These characters are made up of the GPOLL control unit position character and the device position on the cluster controller. Using the GPOLL and device addressing table for BSC devices in Figure 16.13 we can equate the control unit position on

Control Unit or Device Position	Control Unit GPOLL or Device POLL Character	Control Unit Selection Character
0	4040	6060
1	C1C1	6161
2	C2C2	E2E2
3	C3C3	E3E3
4	C4C4	E4E4
5	C5C5	E5E5
6	C6C6	E6E6
7	C7C7	E7E7
8	C8C8	E8E8
9	C9C9	E9E9
10	4A4A	6A6A
11	4B4B	6B6B
12	4C4C	6C6C
13	4D4D	6D6D
14	4E4E	6E6E
15	4F4F	6F6F
16	5050	F0F0
17	D1D1	F1F1
18	D2D2	F2F2
19	D3D3	F3F3
20	D4D4	F4F4
21	D5D5	F5F5
22	D6D6	F6F6
23	D7D7	F7F7
24	D8D8	F8F8
25	D9D9	F9F9
26	5A5A	7A7A
27	5B5B	7B7B
28	5C5C	7C7C
29	5D5D	7D7D
30	5E5E	7E7E
31	5F5F	7F7F

Figure 16.13 GPOLL and device address table for BSC 3270 cluster controller.

the line and the device position on the cluster to the proper EBCDIC polling characters. The polling characters must be repeated for BSC protocol.

In Figure 16.12 we have assigned the value 40404040 to the POLL operand. The first set of numbers, 40, represents the cluster control unit's position on the line. Looking at the GPOLL and device addressing table we see that position 0 (actually the first cluster position) is equated to a 40. The second set of 40 in the POLL operand identifies the specific address for the device on the cluster controller. Here again the device is the first terminal on the cluster. The position of the terminal is directly related to the physical port used for

```
B1101T00  TERMINAL  POLL=40404040,ADDR=60604040,TERM=3277,VPACING=0
B1101T01  TERMINAL  POLL=4040C1C1,ADDR=6060C1C1,TERM=3277,VPACING=0
B1101T02  TERMINAL  POLL=4040C2C2,ADDR=6060C2C2,TERM=3277,VPACING=0
B1101T03  TERMINAL  POLL=4040C3C3,ADDR=6060C3C3,TERM=3277,VPACING=0
B1101T04  TERMINAL  POLL=4040C4C4,ADDR=6060C4C4,TERM=3277,VPACING=0
B1101T05  TERMINAL  POLL=4040C5C5,ADDR=6060C5C5,TERM=3277,VPACING=0
B1101T06  TERMINAL  POLL=4040C6C6,ADDR=6060C6C6,TERM=3277,VPACING=0
B1101T07  TERMINAL  POLL=4040C7C7,ADDR=6060C7C7,TERM=3277,VPACING=0
B1101T08  TERMINAL  POLL=4040C8C8,ADDR=6060C8C8,TERM=3277,VPACING=0
B1101T09  TERMINAL  POLL=4040C9C9,ADDR=6060C9C9,TERM=3277,VPACING=0
B1101T10  TERMINAL  POLL=40404A4A,ADDR=60604A4A,TERM=3277,VPACING=0
B1101T11  TERMINAL  POLL=40404B4B,ADDR=60604B4B,TERM=3277,VPACING=0
B1101T12  TERMINAL  POLL=40404C4C,ADDR=60604C4C,TERM=3277,VPACING=0
B1101T13  TERMINAL  POLL=40404D4D,ADDR=60604D4D,TERM=3277,VPACING=0
B1101T14  TERMINAL  POLL=40404E4E,ADDR=60604E4E,TERM=3277,VPACING=0
B1101T15  TERMINAL  POLL=40404F4F,ADDR=60604F4F,TERM=3277,VPACING=0
B1101T16  TERMINAL  POLL=40405050,ADDR=60605050,TERM=3277,VPACING=0
B1101T17  TERMINAL  POLL=4040D1D1,ADDR=6060D1D1,TERM=3277,VPACING=0
B1101T18  TERMINAL  POLL=4040D2D2,ADDR=6060D2D2,TERM=3277,VPACING=0
B1101T19  TERMINAL  POLL=4040D3D3,ADDR=6060D3D3,TERM=3277,VPACING=0
B1101T20  TERMINAL  POLL=4040D4D4,ADDR=6060D4D4,TERM=3277,VPACING=0
B1101T21  TERMINAL  POLL=4040D5D5,ADDR=6060D5D5,TERM=3277,VPACING=0
B1101T22  TERMINAL  POLL=4040D6D6,ADDR=6060D6D6,TERM=3277,VPACING=0
B1101T23  TERMINAL  POLL=4040D7D7,ADDR=6060D7D7,TERM=3277,VPACING=0
B1101T24  TERMINAL  POLL=4040D8D8,ADDR=6060D8D8,TERM=3277,VPACING=0
B1101T25  TERMINAL  POLL=4040D9D9,ADDR=6060D9D9,TERM=3277,VPACING=0
B1101T26  TERMINAL  POLL=40405A5A,ADDR=60605A5A,TERM=3277,VPACING=0
B1101T27  TERMINAL  POLL=40405B5B,ADDR=60605B5B,TERM=3277,VPACING=0
B1101T28  TERMINAL  POLL=40405C5C,ADDR=60605C5C,TERM=3277,VPACING=0
B1101T29  TERMINAL  POLL=40405D5D,ADDR=60605D5D,TERM=3277,VPACING=0
B1101T30  TERMINAL  POLL=40405E5E,ADDR=60605E5E,TERM=3277,VPACING=0
B1101T31  TERMINAL  POLL=40405F5F,ADDR=60605F5F,TERM=3277,VPACING=0
```

Figure 16.14 TERMINAL definitions for BSC 3274 cluster controller.

attachment. In BSC 3274 cluster controllers the port numbers range from 0 to 31. Looking at the GPOLL and device addressing table we see that port 0 is also represented by the character 40. The values together detail the NCP-specific poll address for the device.

The ADDR operand specifies the selection address for the device. This address is formulated by replacing the GPOLL characters of the POLL operand with the selection character of the control unit. This character is also based on the position of the control unit on the line. In our sample configuration, the line is point to point and therefore there is only one drop off of the line, the first drop. The selection character for the first drop off of a line is 60 as determined in the GPOLL and device address table. By replacing the first set of 4040 of the POLL operand value with 6060, we can specify the selection address of the ADDR operand as 60604040 for the terminal.

The TERM operand specifies to the NCP the type of device this TERMINAL definition represents. This is a required operand for the TERMINAL definition statement. If the line this terminal attaches to operates in emulation and network control modes, the TERM operand must also be specified on the LINE or GROUP definition statement. For the IBM 3X78 and 3X79 display stations, code TERM=3277. Figure 16.14 contains the entire code for the full 32-port BSC cluster controller.

16.5 SUMMARY

In this chapter, we learned about LINE, SERVICE, CLUSTER, and TERMINAL macros of NCP. A LINE macro defines the functional characteristics of a link such as line speed, duplex, and recovery procedure from transmission errors. The SERVICE macro causes the generation procedure to create a service order table for the resources associated with a line. This macro must follow a LINE macro and is applicable for nonswitched links only. The CLUSTER macro defines a BSC cluster controller. The TERMINAL macro defines each terminal or printer attached to a BSC cluster controller.

17

NCP Macros — PU, LU, and SDLCST

17.1 PU DEFINITION STATEMENT

The definition of an SNA resource must have a physical unit definition that defines several characteristics and functions. Among these are the name of the device, its address, the maximum amount of data the device can receive in one PIU or PIU segments, and the maximum number of PIUs the NCP will send to the device before servicing other devices in the service order table for this SDLC link. PUs are also coded for link stations when the SDLC link connects two NCPs. PU definitions for multipoint subarea links, switched subarea links, and T2.1 nodes are discussed in *Advanced SNA Networking*.

At least one PU definition statement must follow the SERVICE definition statement for an SDLC line. The PU definition statement may also follow an LU definition statement for a multipoint SDLC line configuration. When the line is an SDLC link between two NCPs, the PU definition statement must follow the LINE definition statement.

17.1.1 Nonswitched PU Definition Statement

The name for the PU definition statement is required. The ADDR operand (Figure 17.1) of the PU definition statement assigns the SDLC station address of the cluster controller for use in polling by

```
N11SCC1    PU      ADDR=C1,              STATION ADDRESS        X
                   MAXDATA=265,          MAX PIU SIZE           X
                   MAXOUT=7,             MAX # OF FRAMES        X
                   PASSLIM=7,            MAX FRAMES / SERVICE   X
                   DLOGMOD=SNA3278,      DEFAULT LOGMODE ENTRY  X
                   MODETAB=MT01,         MODE TABLE NAME        X
                   USSTAB=USSSNA,        NON-SNA USSTAB         X
                   ISTATUS=ACTIVE
```

Figure 17.1 Nonswitched SDLC 3274 cluster controller definition.

the NCP. This station address should match the station address specified on the cluster controller during the configuration process of the cluster controller. If the addresses do not match, the device will never be activated. The value for ADDR is an 8-bit address in hexadecimal representation ranging from 01 to FE. It is a required operand if the line is nonswitched and the PU type is PU Type 1 or PU Type 2 device. If LPDA compatible modems are used on this SDLC line, the value FD for the ADDR operand cannot be coded.

An IBM 3274 cluster controller has a receive buffer size of 256 bytes in length. This is the maximum amount of data the cluster can receive in one data transfer. The data is the information that is destined for the end user. This data plus the Transmission Header (TH) and Request/Response Header (RH) make up the total amount of data that can be transferred on one PIU or PIU segment. For a PU Type 2 device the TH and RH overhead is 9 bytes. The value for the MAXDATA operand is therefore 9 + 256 = 265 bytes. This value is the largest PIU or PIU segment that the cluster represented by this PU definition statement will accept in one data transfer. This MAXDATA value is truly device dependent and you should consult the device publication for the appropriate value.

Transmission of SDLC frames to a device is governed by the MAXOUT operand (Figure 17.2) of the PU definition statement. The value specified on this operand determines the number of SDLC frames that will be sent to the device before requesting a response from it. For IBM 3274 cluster controllers the value coded is usually the maximum allowed for the cluster, which is MAXOUT=7. After sending seven SDLC frames to the PU, the NCP will send a request to the PU to ensure that the data has arrived intact. The value of 7 is based on the modulus of modulo 8 for the link. We have not coded the MODULO operand of the LINE definition statement because the default of 8 is most commonly used. Modulo 8 indicates to NCP that up to seven SDLC frames can be sent to a PU before a response from

```
N11SCC1    PU      ADDR=C1,                STATION ADDRESS         X
                   MAXDATA=265,            MAX PIU SIZE            X
                   MAXOUT=7,               MAX # OF FRAMES         X
                   PASSLIM=7,              MAX FRAMES / SERVICE    X
                   DLOGMOD=SNA3278,        DEFAULT LOGMODE ENTRY   X
                   MODETAB=MT01,           MODE TABLE NAME         X
                   USSTAB=USSSNA,          NON-SNA USSTAB          X
                   ISTATUS=ACTIVE
```

Figure 17.2 Data transfer performance operands of the PU definition statement.

the PU is required. The other option for this operand is 128. This means that 127 SDLC frames will be transmitted to the PU before the NCP requests a response from the PU. This modulus is commonly used for satellite link connections.

The scan of the service order table is controlled by the SERVLIM operand. For each scan of the table the NCP must know how many PIUs can be sent when servicing a PU. The PASSLIM operand provides this value. For a point-to-point line configuration it is advisable to code the maximum value allowed for the PASSLIM operand. The maximum is 254 PIUs per service. If the line configuration is multipoint, a PASSLIM operand is the determining factor in the amount of service a PU can receive from the NCP.

The remaining operands in Figure 17.2 are VTAM-only operands. The DLOGMOD, MODETAB, USSTAB, and ISTATUS operands will sift down to the following LU definition statements. All of these operands are discussed in great detail in Chapter 11 and will not be reviewed here.

17.1.2 Switched PU Definition Statement

For the switched SDLC line a PU definition statement is required (Figue 17.3) to specify the type of PUs allowed to connect to this dial-up line and the number of LUs that can be expected to have sessions. The PUTYPE operand specifies the PU type that can access this switched line. You may code PUTYPE=1 for PU Type 1 devices only; for PU Type 2 devices, only code PUTYPE=2. For PU Type 4 devices, code PUTYPE=4, and if both PU Type 1 and PU Type 2 devices can use this switched line, code PUTYPE=(1,2). When the PU definition is for a switched line, the MAXLU operand is required. The MAXLU operand specifies the number of LUs that can have active sessions at any one time. We have coded MAXLU=2 to match the switched major node defined in Chapter 11.

```
┌─────────────────────────────────────────────────────────────────────┐
│  N11SWS36   PU     PUTYPE=2,              PU TYPE ALLOWED          X   │
│                    MAXLU=2                MAX # OF LUS                 │
└─────────────────────────────────────────────────────────────────────┘
```

Figure 17.3 Switched PU definition statement.

Note that there is no service order table for a switched line since a switched connection can only be point to point.

17.1.3 CA PU Definition Statement

Previously we introduced the two types of CA links available in NCP V5.1/V5.2. The PU definitions required for these links are quite simple (Figure 17.4). When defining the channel-subarea link, the PU-TYPE parameter must indicate a PU Type 5. No LU definition statements may follow the PU Type 5 definition. When defining a channel-peripheral link, the PUTYPE parameter is specified as PU-TYPE=2. At least one LU definition statement must follow the PU definition statement. In both cases the PU definition statement is defining a host link station.

17.2 LU DEFINITION STATEMENT

Devices attached to an SNA cluster controller gain access to the network through a Logical Unit (LU). Each LU is assigned a local address for use by the PU of the cluster controller and the NCP. The LU definition statement supplies the name of the logical unit, its logical address, control of data transmission to the LU, and the LU's dispatching priority in relation to the other LUs associated with the PU (Figure 17.5).

When defining LUs for an SNA 3274 cluster controller, the LOCADDR operand specifies the local address for each LU. It is the only required operand of the LU definition statement. The sequence

```
┌─────────────────────────────────────────────────────────────────────┐
│  For Channel-Subarea links code:                                      │
│  H01PUCA    PU     PUTYPE=5,         CHANNEL-SUBAREA LINK          X   │
│                    NETID=NETA            NETWORK ID                    │
│                                                                       │
│  For Channel-Peripheral links code:                                   │
│  H02PUCA    PU     PUTYPE=2          CHANNEL-PERIPHERAL LINK           │
│  H02LUCA    LU     LOCADDR=1                                          │
└─────────────────────────────────────────────────────────────────────┘
```

Figure 17.4 Channel-adapter link PU definitions.

```
S11C1T00  LU      LOCADDR=02,      1ST AVAILABLE LOG. ADDR.      X
                  BATCH=NO,        HIGH DISPATCHING PRIORITY     X
                  PACING=0,        NO PACING TO LU               X
                  VPACING=0        NO PACING TO NCP FOR THIS LU
```

Figure 17.5 LU definition statement.

for defining the LUs is dependent upon the local address. You must code the LUs in ascending local address order. For an SNA 3274 cluster controller the local address value begins at 2. The range for a PU Type 2 device is 1 to 255. A PU Type 1 device range for LOCADDR is 0 to 63. You should consult the cluster controllers' manuals for the valid local address range of that device.

The LU defined by this LU definition statement can be prioritized for dispatching to receive service from the NCP according to its primary use. The BATCH operand allows you to assign a low priority (BATCH=YES) or a high priority (BATCH=NO); the default value is NO. If an LU is representing a graphics printer, it may be worthwhile to assign a low priority to the printer. This will prohibit the large amount of data used for printing graphs from monopolizing the line and will allow interactive LUs to receive a greater portion of the service.

The BATCH operand has been removed from NCP V4.3/V5. This is because these versions support virtual route transmission priority between the NCP and the peripheral node. This will prohibit print output from other data-intensive LUs from monopolizing the peripheral SDLC link as well as the INN links between subareas.

Performance of an LU-LU session is greatly influenced by the PACING and VPACING operands (Figure 17.6) of the LU definition statement. The PACING operand specifies the number of SDLC frames that the NCP may send to the LU before it must wait to receive a pacing response. The pacing response is used by the LU to signal to the NCP that it is ready to receive more data during this service time. The range of the pacing value is 0 to 255. The specification of 0 indicates that no pacing between the LU and the NCP occurs; the default value is 1; the VPACING operand defines the number of PIUs destined for this LU that VTAM can send to the NCP before requesting a pacing response from the NCP; the default value here is 2. The specification of 0 for this operand indicates that no pacing responses are necessary between the NCP and VTAM for the transmission of data destined to the LU defined by this LU definition statement.

```
S11C1T00   LU      LOCADDR=02,    1ST AVAILABLE LOG. ADDR.     X
                   BATCH=NO,      HIGH DISPATCHING PRIORITY    X
                   PACING=0,      NO PACING TO LU              X
                   VPACING=0      NO PACING TO NCP FOR THIS LU
```

Figure 17.6 Flow control operands of the LU definition statement.

These session-pacing indicators prohibit the higher-level node from sending data to the lower-level node until a pacing response has been received from the lower-level node. As you may have guessed, these parameters play an important role for session performance. Further information on performance can be found in *Advanced SNA Networking*. Figure 17.7 contains the full definition for all the LUs associated with PU N11SCC1.

17.3 GENEND DEFINITION STATEMENT

After all the resources attached to the NCP have been defined, the GENEND definition statement is coded. This statement must follow the last resource definition statement of the NCP and is required.

The GENEND definition statement allows you to define user-written code characteristics and options that are to be included with the NCP load module. The statement is used in conjunction with supplementary programs such as IBM's Non-SNA Interconnection, NCP Packet Switched Interface, and Network Terminal Operator, to name a few.

17.4 MULTIPLE NCPs IN A SINGLE DOMAIN

Theoretically, in a single domain, 254 PU Type 4 nodes can be attached to a single VTAM host in a pre VTAM 3.2 network. This is not advisable in practice; however, several single-domain networks do have more than one attached NCP. In this section we will discuss the NCP statements needed to define NCP-NCP communications.

17.4.1 SDLCST Definition Statement

In a single-domain network it is not uncommon for NCP subareas to be connected by an SDLC link. In fact, most large networks have several SDLC subarea links between NCPs. This configuration allows for multiple paths between subareas. When these paths are activated, the NCPs must determine their roles and the subarea links' characteristics according to their roles. The role and link characteris-

```
S11C1T00 LU LOCADDR=02,PACING=0,VPACING=0
S11C1T01 LU LOCADDR=03,PACING=0,VPACING=0
S11C1T02 LU LOCADDR=04,PACING=0,VPACING=0
S11C1T03 LU LOCADDR=05,PACING=0,VPACING=0
S11C1T04 LU LOCADDR=06,PACING=0,VPACING=0
S11C1T05 LU LOCADDR=07,PACING=0,VPACING=0
S11C1T06 LU LOCADDR=08,PACING=0,VPACING=0
S11C1T07 LU LOCADDR=09,PACING=0,VPACING=0
S11C1T08 LU LOCADDR=10,PACING=0,VPACING=0
S11C1T09 LU LOCADDR=11,PACING=0,VPACING=0
S11C1T10 LU LOCADDR=12,PACING=0,VPACING=0
S11C1T11 LU LOCADDR=13,PACING=0,VPACING=0
S11C1T12 LU LOCADDR=14,PACING=0,VPACING=0
S11C1T13 LU LOCADDR=15,PACING=0,VPACING=0
S11C1T14 LU LOCADDR=16,PACING=0,VPACING=0
S11C1T15 LU LOCADDR=17,PACING=0,VPACING=0
S11C1T16 LU LOCADDR=18,PACING=0,VPACING=0
S11C1T17 LU LOCADDR=19,PACING=0,VPACING=0
S11C1T18 LU LOCADDR=20,PACING=0,VPACING=0
S11C1T19 LU LOCADDR=21,PACING=0,VPACING=0
S11C1T20 LU LOCADDR=22,PACING=0,VPACING=0
S11C1T21 LU LOCADDR=23,PACING=0,VPACING=0
S11C1T22 LU LOCADDR=24,PACING=0,VPACING=0
S11C1T23 LU LOCADDR=25,PACING=0,VPACING=0
S11C1T24 LU LOCADDR=26,PACING=0,VPACING=0
S11C1T25 LU LOCADDR=27,PACING=0,VPACING=0
S11C1T26 LU LOCADDR=28,PACING=0,VPACING=0
S11C1T27 LU LOCADDR=29,PACING=0,VPACING=0
S11C1T28 LU LOCADDR=30,PACING=0,VPACING=0
S11C1T29 LU LOCADDR=31,PACING=0,VPACING=0
S11C1P30 LU LOCADDR=32,PACING=1,VPACING=2,BATCH=YES,DLOGMOD=PRT
S11C1P31 LU LOCADDR=33,PACING=1,VPACING=2,BATCH=YES,DLOGMOD=PRT
```

Figure 17.7 LU definitions for SDLC 3274 cluster controller.

tics are determined by the SDLCST definition statement. The SDLCST definition statement must appear in the NCP source before any GROUP definition statement does.

As you can see from Figure 17.8, there are only two required operands of the SDLCST definition statement. The name operand is coded as any valid assembler-language symbol and is used by the SDLCST operand of the LINE definition statement that defines the SDLC subarea link.

The GROUP operand of the SDLCST definition statement is also required. The value coded here identifies the GROUP definition statement that defines the subarea link parameters associated with this SDLC selection table (SDLCST) definition.

The MAXOUT operand specifies the number of SDLC frames the NCP can receive on the line before issuing a response. This is specific to the NCP when operating in secondary mode. The MAXOUT value specified on the PU definition statement for this subarea link is the value that the primary-mode NCP will use for sending frames to the secondary-mode NCP before requesting an acknowledgment. The value for MAXOUT is determined by the modulus being enforced by the NCPs. If modulus 8 is being used, MAXOUT can range from 1 to 7. If modulus 128 is in use, MAXOUT can range from 8 to 127. The MODE operand specifies if this SDLCST definition describes functional characteristics for the NCP when it is in primary (polling responsibility and error recovery) or in secondary mode. The value coded here must be the same as the MODE operand of the associated GROUP definition statement pointed to by the GROUP operand of this SDLCST definition statement. Figure 17.9 outlines the procedure for determining which NCP of a subarea link is to act in primary or secondary mode.

The PASSLIM operand is functionally equivalent to the PASSLIM operand discussed for the SDLC LINE definition, except that here in the SDLCST definition the PASSLIM value can affect the mode of transmission on the subarea link (e.g., full or half duplex). Usually, SDLC subarea links are defined with a send and receive address on the LINE definition statement to facilitate the transmission of data in both directions. If, however, the PASSLIM value specified for the SDLCST definition is less than the MAXOUT value specified for this SDLCST definition, the line will operate in half-duplex transmission mode. It is best to take the default for this operand to ensure full-duplex transmission when the LINE definition for the subarea link is assigned two addresses.

```
name        SDLCST      GROUP=group name,
                        [,MAXOUT=n|7]
                        [,MODE=PRI|SEC]
                        [,PASSLIM=n|254]
                        [,RETRIES=NONE|(m[,t[,n]])]
                        [,SERVLIM=n|4]
                        [,TADDR=chars]
```

Figure 17.8 SDLCST definition statement format.

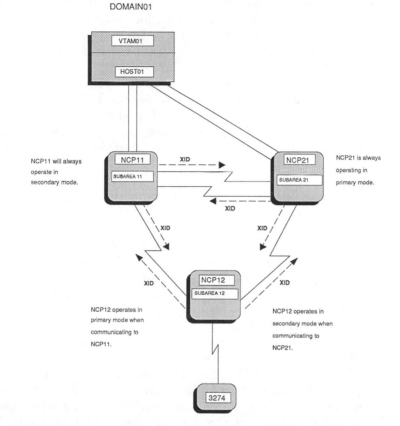

DOMAIN01

NCP11 will always operate in secondary mode.

NCP21 is always operating in primary mode.

NCP12 operates in primary mode when communicating to NCP11.

NCP12 operates in secondary mode when communicating to NCP21.

Figure 17.9 Primary and secondary mode is determined by the higher subarea number found in the exchange identification (XID) between NCPs in pre NCP 4.3 networks.

The RETRIES operand acts in the same manner here as the RETRIES operand for error recovery to peripheral nodes. However, ample time should be given to allow a link-attached NCP subarea to access its dump data sets on disk. Therefore, we suggest a minimum retry time for the RETRIES and REPLYTO values of 60.

The SERVLIM operand here also functions in the same manner as the SERVLIM operand of the LINE definition statement. Remember that the SERVLIM value determines the number of scans through the Service Order Table (SOT) to complete normal service of resources on the link before performing special services to the resources, that is, activation and deactivation or status requests from the SSCP for a resource on the link. The value for SERVLIM is dependent upon the number of status commands and activation and deactivation of devices on this link. If the commands are frequent, a low SERVLIM value is justifiable to avoid queuing of the status commands. However, for an SDLC subarea link, few status commands should traverse the link, and in most cases the subarea link is point-to-point and not multipoint, so the SERVLIM value can be set to 254 for optimal service to the INN link.

Finally the TADDR operand of the SDLCST definition statement specifies a unique SDLC station address for the NCP operating in secondary mode and may be specified on the SDLCST definition describing secondary mode. The default is the hexadecimal representation of the NCP's subarea address. Figure 17.10 shows the SDLCST definitions for NCP11.

17.4.2 SDLCST GROUP Definition Statements for Single-Domain NCP

Two GROUP definition statements must be defined for an SDLC subarea link when using the SDLCST definition statement. One group will specify the characteristics for the link during the primary mode of operation and the second will define the characteristics of the link during the secondary mode of operation. A GROUP definition statement must still be defined just before the LINE definition statement that defines the actual SDLC subarea link. All in all, three GROUP definition statements must be defined for one SDLC subarea link. However, the GROUP definition statements that reflect the mode of operation identified by the SDLCST definition statement for primary and secondary modes need only be defined once. Let's look at the coded example of the GROUP definition statements for the SDLC subarea links between NCP11 and NCP21 in Figure 17.11.

In Figure 17.11 we have defined the LINE characteristics that will be enforced by the NCP when the SDLC subarea link is operating in

```
PRISTE    SDLCST    GROUP=PRINCP,    NCP IN PRIMARY MODE           X
                    MAXOUT=127,      USING MODULO128               X
                    MODE=PRI,        PRIMARY MODE                  X
                    PASSLIM=254,     ENSURE FULL DUPLEX            X
                    SERVLIM=254      MAX SERVICE FOR INN LINK
SECSTE    SDLCST    GROUP=SECNCP,    NCP IN SECONDARY MODE         X
                    MAXOUT=127,      USING MODULO128               X
                    MODE=SEC,        PRIMARY MODE                  X
                    PASSLIM=254,     ENSURE FULL DUPLEX            X
                    SERVLIM=254      MAX SERVICE FOR INN LINK
```

Figure 17.10 SDLCST definitions for NCP NCP11.

```
PRINCP    GROUP    MODE=PRI,          NCP IN PRIMARY MODE          X
                   LNCTL=SDLC,        SDLC LINE CONTROL            X
                   TYPE=NCP,          NETWORK CONTROL MODE         X
                   DIAL=NO,           DEDICATED LINK               X
                   REPLYTO=(,60),     60-S REPLY TIME OUT          X
                   TEXTTO=3           3-S TEXT TIME OUT
SECNCP    GROUP    MODE=SEC,          NCP IN SECONDARY MODE        X
                   LNCTL=SDLC,        SDLC LINE CONTROL            X
                   TYPE=NCP,          NETWORK CONTROL MODE         X
                   DIAL=NO,           DEDICATED LINK               X
                   REPLYTO=(NONE,NONE),  NO REPLY TIME OUT         X
                   TEXTTO=NONE,       NO TEXT TIME OUT             X
                   ACTIVTO=420.0      MAX SERVICE FOR INN LINK
```

Figure 17.11 GROUP definition statements for primary and secondary mode.

primary and secondary modes. It is these values and not those defined on the GROUP, LINE, and PU definitions for the SDLC subarea link that will be used.

The first GROUP definition statement defines the characteristics
of the SDLC subarea link when the NCP is in the primary state. The
name PRINCP is the same name defined in the SDLCST definition
statement operand GROUP of the statement that defines the primary mode of operation. The MODE operand of the GROUP statement in Figure 17.11 defines to NCP that the operands defined here
are to be used when the NCP is in primary mode of operation with
the SDLC subarea link.

The LNCTL, TYPE, and DIAL operand values are all typical for a
dedicated SDLC link. The LNCTL operand specifies the usage of
SDLC as the link protocol. The TYPE operand specifies that the
lines in this group operate in network control mode. The DIAL oper-
and identifies this link as a dedicated nonswitched line.

The REPLYTO operand of the PRINCP group specifies the number
of seconds the primary NCP will wait for a response to a poll, selection, or message text that was sent to the secondary NCP before
issuing a time-out error for the secondary NCP. The range is .1 to 60
for a link in network control mode. The comma in the value defined
in Figure 17.11 indicates that the default for SDLC links in modulus
8 mode is taken. The default is 1. The 60 indicates that 60 must
expire for SDLC links in modulus 128 mode between receipt of a
response to a poll from the secondary NCP before issuing a time-out
error.

The TEXTTO operand defines the amount of time in seconds the primary NCP will wait between receipt of text messages from the secondary NCP before issuing a text time-out error. Barring problems with the link, 3 is sufficient for this type of condition.

The group that defines the secondary-mode characteristics for SDLC subarea links in this NCP is labeled SECNCP. Again, this must match the GROUP operand of the SDLCST definition statement that defines the link characteristics for the NCP operating in secondary mode. The MODE operand of the GROUP definition statement SECNCP identifies this group for use in defining the link characteristics when the NCP is in secondary mode of operation.

The LNCTL, TYPE, and DIAL operands have the same meaning here as in the definition for the group PRINCP. The time-out operands are defined differently and we have added a new time-out value, ACTIVTO.

The REPLYTO value for the SECNCP group specifies that the NCP will not keep elapsed time counts on this link. This prevents the link from becoming inoperative by the secondary NCP because of an error on the link from the primary NCP. The value REPLYTO=(NONE,NONE) is required when the group being defined describes the secondary mode of operation (e.g., MODE=SEC).

The same logic can be applied to the TEXTTO operand of the group SECNCP. In fact, if MODE=SEC for an SDLC subarea link group definition, the TEXTTO value must be equal to NONE. This makes sense since the NCP in secondary mode is acting in a passive state and the primary NCP controls the error recovery on the link.

The ACTIVTO operand is pertinent to the NCP in secondary mode only. It specifies the time-out value, in tenths of a second, that the secondary NCP will wait for a response from the primary NCP before entering shutdown mode. The range is from 60 to 420. The default if ACTIVTO is not specified is 60 in an IBM 3725 or 3720 for both modulus 8 and modulus 128 links. The IBM 3705 defaults to 420. You do not want to have to go through the process of reactivating NCPs and subarea links if ACTIVTO has been reached and the secondary NCP goes into shutdown mode. Therefore, it is to your advantage to have the secondary NCP wait as long as possible for communication to be reestablished by the primary NCP. Hence we have coded the maximum value of 420.0.

17.4.3 GROUP, LINE, and PU Definition Statements for SDLC Subarea Links

The LINE definition statements for an NCP SDLC subarea link are the same for peripheral LINE definitions. There are, however, three operands that are specific to an SDLC subarea link: SDLCST, MONLINK, and MODULO. Figure 17.12 contains the GROUP, LINE, and PU definitions for the SDLC subarea links in NCP11.

On the LINE definition statement for each subarea link defined, we have specified the same values for the SDLCST, MONLINK, and MODULO operands. The SDLCST operand on the LINE definitions

```
SALINKS   GROUP   LNCTL=SDLC,        SDLC IS LINE PROTOCOL        X
                  CLOCKNG=EXT,       MODEMS DO CLOCKING           X
                  NRZI=NO,           NO NONRETURN TO ZERO         X
                  PAUSE=0,           DO NOT WAIT TO POLL          X
                  SERVLIM=254,       MAXIMIZE SERVICE TO LINKS X
                  SPEED=56000,       LINE SPEED IS 56 KPS         X
                  ISTATUS=ACTIVE
SA113221  LINE    ADDRESS=(32,FULL), SEND/RECEIVE XMIT            X
                  ATTACH=MODEM,         MODEM ATTACHES LINK       X
                  SDLCST=(PRISTE,SECSTE), PRI & SEC SDLCST        X
                  MONLINK=NO,           MONITOR FOR ACTPU         X
                  MODULO=128            USE MODULUS 128
PU2132    PU      PUTYPE=4,       PU T.4 DEVICE (NCP)             X
                  MAXOUT=127,     USE MODULUS 128                 X
                  TGN=21,         TG NUMBER FOR LINK              X
                  ANS=CONTINUE    KEEP X-DOMAIN SESSIONS
SA113421  LINE    ADDRESS=(34,FULL),  SEND/RECEIVE XMIT           X
                  ATTACH=MODEM,         MODEM ATTACHES LINK       X
                  SDLCST=(PRISTE,SECSTE), PRI & SEC SDLCST        X
                  MONLINK=NO,           MONITOR FOR ACTPU         X
                  MODULO=128            USE MODULUS 128
PU2134    PU      PUTYPE=4,       PU T.4 DEVICE (NCP)             X
                  MAXOUT=127,     USE MODULUS 128                 X
                  TGN=21,         TG NUMBER FOR LINK              X
                  ANS=CONTINUE    KEEP X-DOMAIN SESSIONS
SA113612  LINE    ADDRESS=(36,FULL),  SEND/RECEIVE XMIT           X
                  ATTACH=MODEM,         MODEM ATTACHES LINK       X
                  SDLCST=(PRISTE,SECSTE), PRI & SEC SDLCST        X
                  MONLINK=NO,           MONITOR FOR ACTPU         X
                  MODULO=128            USE MODULUS 128
PU1236    PU      PUTYPE=4,       PU T.4 DEVICE (NCP)             X
                  MAXOUT=127,     USE MODULUS 128                 X
                  TGN=21,         TG NUMBER FOR LINK              X
                  ANS=CONTINUE    KEEP X-DOMAIN SESSIONS
```

Figure 17.12 GROUP, LINE, and PU definitions for SDLC subarea links in NCP11.

statement for subarea links tells NCP which SDLCST definition to use when the NCP is in primary or secondary mode. The first parameter specifies the name of the primary mode definitions. In this case we have NCP using the parameters specified on the SDLCST statement labeled PRISTE. The second parameter tells NCP to use the characteristics identified in the SDLCST statement defined for secondary mode of operation. In this instance the parameter points to the label SECSTE that identifies the SDLCST definitions for secondary mode. Used in this fashion, the link stations are considered "configurable."

NCP V4.3 and higher support pre-defined link station roles. This is accomplished by specifying either the primary or secondary SDLCST definition statement name on the LINE SDLCST operand. Used in this manner, the link station role is determined at NCP generation and is said to be a "pe-defined" link station. For pre-defined link stations the XID sent indicates that this link station can be *only* primary or secondary. In this case, the receiving link station must be *either* configurable or pre-defined as the opposite link station role. For example, if in Figure 17.13 the SDLCST operand of the LINE definition statement named INNLINK were specified as:

   SDLCST=(,SECSTE)

then this link station will always operate in a secondary link station role. Hence, the opposite link station to which the line attaches must be pre-defined as a primary link station or be defined as a configurable link station. Likewise, if the SDLCST operand of the LINE definition statement named INNLINK in Figure 17.13 were specified as:

   SDLCST=(PRISTE)

then this link station will always operate in a primary link station role. The opposite link station to which this line attaches must be pre-defined as a secondary link station or be defined as a configurable link station. One more note on pre-defined link stations: if you pre-define a link station as primary, then it is not necessary to define secondary SDLCST GROUP definitions for secondary. The opposite holds true if the link station is pre-defined as secondary.

The MONLINK operand is used on subarea link definitions by the NCP to actively monitor the link address for an ACTPU command from an SSCP when the NCP is not in session with an SSCP on this link. The code in Figure 17.12 is for the channel-attached NCP11 and therefore the SSCP-PU session is established via the channel

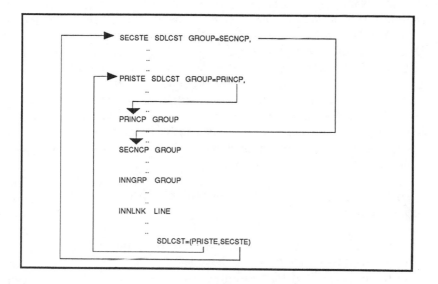

Figure 17.13 Diagram outlining the use of the SDLCST definition statement.

and not the defined subarea links. For NCPs such as NCP12 in Figure 17.12, remotely loaded and activated NCPs should have MONLINK=YES specified on all their SDLC subarea links to turn the activation process around quickly. However, if NCP11 were defined to be activated by VTAM01 through NCP21, MONLINK=YES should also be specified. The default value for MONLINK is NO if the TYPGEN operand of the BUILD definition statement is equal to NCP (channel attached). If the TYPGEN operand of the BUILD definition statement specifies NCP-R, the MONLINK operand defaults to YES (link attached).

The MODULO operand of the LINE definition statement specifies the use of modulus 8 or modulus 128. We stated on the SDLCST definitions that MAXOUT=127; therefore, we must code MODULO=128 in order for the NCP to handle the amount of frames that the link-attached subarea can send or receive. Remember that the equivalent definition on the attached NCP must also specify MODULO=128.

The PU definitions under each subarea link define the link station in the attached NCP. PU2132 defines the characteristics of the link station for this subarea link that terminates in NCP21. The PUTYPE operand identifies the PU at the end of this link as a PU Type 4 device. Again, the MAXOUT operand defines the number of frames that can be sent before a response is requested. It is best for both documentation and implementation purposes that this value match the MAXOUT value specified on the MAXOUT operand of the SDLCST definition statement.

The TGN operand identifies the transmission group number assigned to the subarea link. This number is used in correlation with the PATH statements when defining explicit routes to the link-attached NCPs. The ANS operand tells the NCP whether to keep active cross-domain sessions enabled if the NCP loses contact with the owning SSCP. For the most part ANS=CONTINUE is always coded to avoid a complete session outage.

17.4.4 PATH Statement Updates for Multiple NCPs in a Single Domain

The final step and probably the most confusing one is the definition of the routes between the NCP subareas.

Again we go back to that old question, "How can I get there from here?" Figures 17.14, 17.15, and 17.16 contain routing charts for the three NCPs involved with the example. For each row in each chart ask yourself the above question and see if it helps you understand the path defined. Then when you have completed that, look at Figure

OSA	DSA	ADJSA	TG	ER	VR
11	1	1	1	0	0
		21	11	1	1
		21	11	3	3
		1	1	4	4
		1	1	5	5
		21	11	6	6
	21	21	11	1	1
		21	11	2	2
		21	11	3	3
		12	12	4	4
	12	12	12	0	0
		21	11	2	2
		12	12	3	3
		12	12	1	1

Figure 17.14 Routing chart for NCP11 paths to other subareas.

OSA	DSA	ADJSA	TG	ER	VR
21	1	1	1	1	1
		1	1	0	0
		1	1	3	3
		11	11	4	4
		12	21	5	5
		1	1	6	6
	11	11	11	1	1
		11	11	2	2
		12	21	4	4
	12	12	21	1	1
		12	21	2	2
		11	11	3	3
		12	21	0	0

Figure 17.15 Routing chart for NCP21 paths to other subareas.

OSA	DSA	ADJSA	TG	ER	VR
12	1	11	12	5	5
		11	12	0	0
		21	21	1	1
		21	21	4	4
		11	12	6	6
	11	11	12	0	0
		11	12	4	4
		21	21	2	2
		11	12	1	1
		11	12	3	3
	21	21	21	4	4
		21	21	2	2
		21	21	1	1
		21	21	0	0
		11	12	3	3

Figure 17.16 Routing chart for NCP12 paths to other subareas.

```
NCP11:
    PATH TABLE:
        PATH1101 PATH  DESTSA=01,ER0=(1,1),ER1=(21,11),          X
                       ER3=(21,11),ER4=(1,1),                    X
                       ER5=(1,1),ER6=(21,11),VR0=0,              X
                       VR1=1,VR3=3,VR4=4,VR5=5,VR6=6
        PATH1121 PATH  DESTSA=21,ER1=(21,11),ER2=(21,11),        X
                       ER3=(21,11),ER4=(12,12),                  X
                       VR3=3,VR1=1,VR2=2,VR4=4
        PATH1112 PATH  DESTSA=12,ER0=(12,12),ER2=(21,11),        X
                       ER3=(12,12),ER1=(12,12),VR2=2,            X
                       VR1=1,VR3=3,VR0=0
NCP21:
    PATH TABLE:
        PATH2101 PATH  DESTSA=01,ER1=(1,1),ER3=(1,1),            X
                       ER0=(1,1),ER4=(11,11),                    X
                       ER5=(12,21),ER6=(1,1),VR1=1,              X
                       VR3=3,VR0=0,VR4=4,VR5=5,VR6=6
        PATH2111 PATH  DESTSA=11,ER1=(11,11),ER2=(11,11),        X
                       ER4=(12,21),VR1=1,VR2=2,VR4=4
        PATH2112 PATH  DESTSA=12,ER1=(12,21),ER2=(12,21),        X
                       ER3=(11,11),ER0=(12,21),                  X
                       VR1=1,VR2=2,VR3=3,VR0=0
NCP12:
    PATH TABLE:
        PATH1201 PATH  DESTSA=01,ER5=(11,12),ER0=(11,12),        X
                       ER1=(21,21),ER4=(21,21),                  X
                       ER6=(11,12),VR0=0,                        X
                       VR1=1,VR4=4,VR5=5,VR6=6
        PATH1211PATH   DESTSA=11,ER0=(11,12),ER4=(11,12),        X
                       ER2=(21,21),ER1=(11,12),ER3=(11,12),      X
                       VR0=0,VR4=4,VR2=2,VR1=1,VR3=3
        PATH1221 PATH  DESTSA=21,ER4=(21,21),                    X
                       ER2=(21,21),ER1=(21,21),ER0=(21,21),      X
                       ER3=(11,12),                              X
                       VR4=4,VR0=0,VR1=1,VR2=2,VR3=3
```

Figure 17.17 PATH statements for each NCP in the sample network.

17.17 for the completed PATH statements for each of the three
NCPs. Note that the three route charts have had their routes combined by using the adjacent subarea, explicit route, and transmission
group parities. The final figure (Figure 17.18) diagrams this sample
network with the transmission groups labeled. You may want to copy
it and go through the path statements to trace some of the routes to
help visualize the routes defined for each NCP subarea.

It is important to remember that when defining path tables in the
NCP, the order in which you define the ERs for each DESTSA de-

notes the hierarchical search that is performed. Note that only in NCP12 did we combine DESTSAs for the PATH statements. This is because both DESTSAs share the same primary route for the destination of the data. However, this was not true for NCP11 and NCP21. In those path tables we defined each DESTSA with its own PATH statement. This allows for direct path selection for each destination subarea defined. Figure 17.18 diagrams TGs used through the network.

Now that the NCP paths have been defined, a good exercise for you is to define the VTAM path statements. Remember VTAM must also know how to get to the destination subareas through its adjacent subareas.

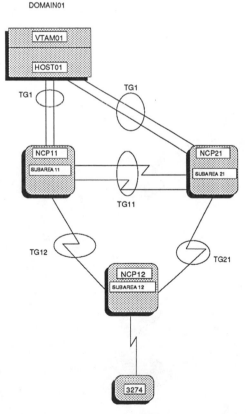

Figure 17.18 Diagram of single-domain network with multiple NCPs and their transmission groups.

17.5 SUMMARY

In this chapter we learned about PU, LU, and SDLCST macros of NCP. The PU macro gives the physical unit definition for an SNA resource. Such a definition includes the name of the device, its address, the maximum amount of data the device can receive in one PIU or PIU segments, and the maximum number of PIUs the NCP will send to the device before servicing other devices for an SDLC link. The LU macro defines a logical unit attached to a physical unit. The SDLCST macro defines the link characteristics when multiple number, of paths exist between NCP subareas.

The following table is the IBM-supplied default logon mode table for VTAM V3R2. You may use the entries in the table for your definitions. If you elect to create your own logon mode table, be sure to link-edit your table under a name other than ISTINCLM.

```
ISTINCLM MODETAB
IBM3767  MODEENT LOGMODE=INTERACT,FMPROF=X'03',TSPROF=X'03',PRIPROT=X'B*
             1',SECPROT=X'A0',COMPROT=X'3040'

         TITLE 'TWXDEVPT'
***********************************************************************
*                                                                     *
*            TWX DEVICE WITH THE DCODE SET TO KEYBOARD                 *
*            AND PRINTER.  THIS IS THE DEFAULT SETTING.                *
*                                                                     *
***********************************************************************
TWXDEVPT MODEENT LOGMODE=TWXDECPT,FMPROF=X'03',TSPROF=X'03',PRIPROT=X'B*
             1',SECPROT=X'A0',COMPROT=X'3040',DCODE=X'00'

         TITLE 'TWXDEVDP'
***********************************************************************
*                                                                     *
*            TWX DEVICE WITH THE DCODE SET TO KEYBOARD                 *
*            AND DISPLAY.                                              *
*                                                                     *
***********************************************************************
TWXDEVDP MODEENT LOGMODE=TWXDEVDP,FMPROF=X'03',TSPROF=X'03',PRIPROT=X'B*
             1',SECPROT=X'A0',COMPROT=X'3040',DCODE=X'80'
```

```
IBM3770  MODEENT LOGMODE=BATCH,FMPROF=X'03',TSPROF=X'03',PRIPROT=X'A3',*
                 SECPROT=X'A3',COMPROT=X'7080'

IBMS3270 MODEENT LOGMODE=S3270,FMPROF=X'02',TSPROF=X'02',PRIPROT=X'71',*
                 SECPROT=X'40',COMPROT=X'2000'

IBM3600  MODEENT LOGMODE=IBM3600,FMPROF=X'04',TSPROF=X'04',PRIPROT=X'F1*
                 ',SECPROT=X'F1',COMPROT=X'7000'

IBM3650I MODEENT LOGMODE=INTRACT,FMPROF=X'04',TSPROF=X'04',PRIPROT=X'B1*
                 ',SECPROT=X'90',COMPROT=X'6000'

IBM3650U MODEENT LOGMODE=INTRUSER,FMPROF=X'04',TSPROF=X'04',PRIPROT=X'3*
                 1',SECPROT=X'30',COMPROT=X'6000'

IBMS3650 MODEENT LOGMODE=IBMS3650,FMPROF=X'04',TSPROF=X'04',PRIPROT=X'B*
                 0',SECPROT=X'B0',COMPROT=X'4000'

IBM3650P MODEENT LOGMODE=PIPELINE,FMPROF=X'04',TSPROF=X'04',PRIPROT=X'3*
                 0',SECPROT=X'10',COMPROT=X'0000'

IBM3660  MODEENT LOGMODE=SMAPPL,FMPROF=X'03',TSPROF=X'03',PRIPROT=X'A0'*
                 ,SECPROT=X'A0',COMPROT=X'0081'

IBM3660A MODEENT LOGMODE=SMSNA100,FMPROF=X'00',TSPROF=X'00',PRIPROT=X'0*
                 0',SECPROT=X'00',COMPROT=X'0000'
         TITLE 'D6327801'
***********************************************************************
*                                                                     *
*              3276 SNA WITH 3278 MODEL 1 SCREEN                       *
*              PRIMARY SCREEN 12 X 40 (480)                            *
*              ALTERNATE SCREEN 12 X 80 (960)                          *
*                                                                     *
***********************************************************************
D6327801 MODEENT LOGMODE=D6327801,FMPROF=X'03',TSPROF=X'03',PRIPROT=X'B*
                 1',SECPROT=X'90',COMPROT=X'3080',RUSIZES=X'88F8',PSERVIC*
                 =X'0200000000000C280C507F00'
         TITLE 'D6327802'
***********************************************************************
*                                                                     *
*              3276 SNA WITH 3278 MODEL 2 SCREEN                       *
*              PRIMARY SCREEN 24 X 80 (1920)                           *
*              NO ALTERNATE SCREEN DEFINED                             *
*                                                                     *
***********************************************************************
D6327802 MODEENT LOGMODE=D6327802,FMPROF=X'03',TSPROF=X'03',PRIPROT=X'B*
                 1',SECPROT=X'90',COMPROT=X'3080',RUSIZES=X'88F8',PSERVIC*
                 =X'020000000000185000007E00'
         TITLE 'D6327803'
***********************************************************************
*                                                                     *
```

```
*              3276 SNA WITH       MODEL 3 SCREEN                    *
*              PRIMARY SCREEN 24 X 80 (1920)                         *
*              ALTERNATE SCREEN 32 X 80 (2560)                       *
*                                                                    *
**********************************************************************
D6327803 MODEENT LOGMODE=D6327803,FMPROF=X'03',TSPROF=X'03',PRIPROT=X'B*
               1',SECPROT=X'90',COMPROT=X'3080',RUSIZES=X'88F8',PSERVIC*
               =X'020000000000185020507F00'
        TITLE 'D6327804'
**********************************************************************
*                                                                    *
*              3276 SNA WITH       MODEL 4 SCREEN                    *
*              PRIMARY SCREEN 24 X 80 (1920)                         *
*              ALTERNATE SCREEN 43 X 80 (3440)                       *
*                                                                    *
**********************************************************************
D6327804 MODEENT LOGMODE=D6327804,FMPROF=X'03',TSPROF=X'03',PRIPROT=X'B*
               1',SECPROT=X'90',COMPROT=X'3080',RUSIZES=X'88F8',PSERVIC*
               =X'02000000000018502B507F00'
        TITLE 'D6327805'
**********************************************************************
*                                                                    *
*              3276 SNA WITH       MODEL 5 SCREEN                    *
*              PRIMARY SCREEN 24 X 80 (1920)                         *
*              ALTERNATE SCREEN 27 X 132 (3564)                      *
*                                                                    *
**********************************************************************
D6327805 MODEENT LOGMODE=D6327805,FMPROF=X'03',TSPROF=X'03',PRIPROT=X'B*
               1',SECPROT=X'90',COMPROT=X'3080',RUSIZES=X'88F8',PSERVIC*
               =X'02000000000018501B847F00'
        TITLE 'D6328904'
**********************************************************************
*                                                                    *
*              3276 SNA WITH 3289 MODEL 4 PRINTER                    *
*                                                                    *
**********************************************************************
D6328904 MODEENT LOGMODE=D6328904,FMPROF=X'03',TSPROF=X'03',PRIPROT=X'B*
               1',SECPROT=X'90',COMPROT=X'3080',RUSIZES=X'8787',PSERVIC*
               =X'03000000000018502B507F00'
        TITLE 'D6328902'
**********************************************************************
*                                                                    *
*              3276 SNA WITH 3289 MODEL 2 PRINTER                    *
*                                                                    *
**********************************************************************
D6328902 MODEENT LOGMODE=D6328902,FMPROF=X'03',TSPROF=X'03',PRIPROT=X'B*
               1',SECPROT=X'90',COMPROT=X'3080',RUSIZES=X'8787',PSERVIC*
               =X'030000000000185018507F00'
        TITLE 'D4A32781'
**********************************************************************
*                                                                    *
```

```
*                 3274 MODEL 1A WITH MODEL 1 SCREEN (LOCAL SNA)          *
*                 PRIMARY SCREEN 12 X 40 (480)                           *
*                 ALTERNATE SCREEN 12 X 80 (960)                         *
*                                                                        *
*************************************************************************
D4A32781 MODEENT LOGMODE=D4A32781,FMPROF=X'03',TSPROF=X'03',PRIPROT=X'B*
               1',SECPROT=X'90',COMPROT=X'3080',RUSIZES=X'87C7',PSERVIC*
               =X'0200000000000C280C507F00'
         TITLE 'D4A32782'
*************************************************************************
*                                                                        *
*                 3274 MODEL 1A WITH MODEL 2 SCREEN (LOCAL SNA)          *
*                 PRIMARY SCREEN 24 X 80 (1920)                          *
*                 NO ALTERNATE SCREEN DEFINED                            *
*                                                                        *
*************************************************************************
D4A32782 MODEENT LOGMODE=D4A32782,FMPROF=X'03',TSPROF=X'03',PRIPROT=X'B*
               1',SECPROT=X'90',COMPROT=X'3080',RUSIZES=X'87C7',PSERVIC*
               =X'020000000000185000007E00'
         TITLE 'LSK32782'
*************************************************************************
*                                                                        *
*                 3274 MODEL 1A WITH MODEL 2 SCREEN (LOCAL SNA)          *
*                 PRIMARY SCREEN 24 X 80 (1920)                          *
*                 NO ALTERNATE SCREEN DEFINED                            *
*                 KATAKANA                                               *
*                                                                        *
*************************************************************************
LSK32782 MODEENT LOGMODE=LSK32782,FMPROF=X'03',TSPROF=X'03',PRIPROT=X'B*
               1',SECPROT=X'90',COMPROT=X'3080',RUSIZES=X'87C7',PSERVIC*
               =X'020000000000185000007E00',LANG=X'11'
         TITLE 'D4A32783'
*************************************************************************
*                                                                        *
*                 3274 MODEL 1A WITH MODEL 3 SCREEN (LOCAL SNA)          *
*                 PRIMARY SCREEN 24 X 80 (1920)                          *
*                 ALTERNATE SCREEN 32 X 80 (2560)                        *
*                                                                        *
*************************************************************************
D4A32783 MODEENT LOGMODE=D4A32783,FMPROF=X'03',TSPROF=X'03',PRIPROT=X'B*
               1',SECPROT=X'90',COMPROT=X'3080',RUSIZES=X'87C7',PSERVIC*
               =X'020000000000185020507F00'
         TITLE 'D4A32784'
*************************************************************************
*                                                                        *
*                 3274 MODEL 1A WITH MODEL 4 SCREEN (LOCAL SNA)          *
*                 PRIMARY SCREEN 24 X 80 (1920)                          *
*                 ALTERNATE SCREEN 43 X 80 (3440)                        *
*                                                                        *
*************************************************************************
D4A32784 MODEENT LOGMODE=D4A32784,FMPROF=X'03',TSPROF=X'03',PRIPROT=X'B*
```

```
                 1',SECPROT=X'90',COMPROT=X'3080',RUSIZES=X'87C7',PSERVIC*
                 =X'02000000000018502B507F00'
         TITLE 'D4A32785'
*********************************************************************
*                                                                   *
*             3274 MODEL 1A WITH MODEL 5 SCREEN (LOCAL SNA)          *
*             PRIMARY SCREEN 24 X 80 (1920)                          *
*             ALTERNATE SCREEN 27 X 132 (3564)                      *
*                                                                   *
*********************************************************************
D4A32785 MODEENT LOGMODE=D4A32785,FMPROF=X'03',TSPROF=X'03',PRIPROT=X'B*
                 1',SECPROT=X'90',COMPROT=X'3080',RUSIZES=X'87C7',PSERVIC*
                 =X'02000000000018501B847F00'
         TITLE 'D4A32XX3'
*********************************************************************
*                                                                   *
*             3274 MODEL 1A (LOCAL SNA)                              *
*             PRIMARY SCREEN 24 X 80 (1920)                          *
*             ALTERNATE SCREEN TO BE DETERMINED BY APPLICATION       *
*                                                                   *
*********************************************************************
D4A32XX3 MODEENT LOGMODE=D4A32XX3,FMPROF=X'03',TSPROF=X'03',PRIPROT=X'B*
                 1',SECPROT=X'90',COMPROT=X'3080',RUSIZES=X'87C7',PSERVIC*
                 =X'02800000000000000000000300'
         TITLE 'D4A32771'
*********************************************************************
*                                                                   *
*             3274 MODEL 1A WITH 3277 MODEL 1 SCREEN                 *
*                                                                   *
*********************************************************************
D4A32771 MODEENT LOGMODE=D4A32771,FMPROF=X'03',TSPROF=X'03',PRIPROT=X'B*
                 1',SECPROT=X'90',COMPROT=X'3080',RUSIZES=X'87C7',PSERVIC*
                 =X'02000000000000000000000100'
         TITLE 'D4A32772'
*********************************************************************
*                                                                   *
*             3274 MODEL 1A WITH 3277 MODEL 2 SCREEN                 *
*                                                                   *
*********************************************************************
D4A32772 MODEENT LOGMODE=D4A32772,FMPROF=X'03',TSPROF=X'03',PRIPROT=X'B*
                 1',SECPROT=X'90',COMPROT=X'3080',RUSIZES=X'87C7',PSERVIC*
                 =X'02000000000000000000000200'
         TITLE 'D4C32781'
*********************************************************************
*                                                                   *
*             3274 MODEL 1C WITH MODEL 1 SCREEN(REMOTE SNA)          *
*             PRIMARY SCREEN 12 X 40 (480)                           *
*             ALTERNATE SCREEN 12 X 80 (960)                         *
*                                                                   *
*********************************************************************
D4C32781 MODEENT LOGMODE=D4C32781,FMPROF=X'03',TSPROF=X'03',PRIPROT=X'B*
```

```
                   1',SECPROT=X'90',COMPROT=X'3080',RUSIZES=X'87F8',PSERVIC*
                   =X'0200000000000C280C507F00'
          TITLE 'D4C32782'
**********************************************************************
*                                                                    *
*          3274 MODEL 1C WITH MODEL 2 SCREEN(REMOTE SNA)             *
*          PRIMARY SCREEN 24 X 80 (1920)                             *
*          NO ALTERNATE SCREEN DEFINED                               *
*                                                                    *
**********************************************************************
D4C32782 MODEENT LOGMODE=D4C32782,FMPROF=X'03',TSPROF=X'03',PRIPROT=X'B*
                   1',SECPROT=X'90',COMPROT=X'3080',RUSIZES=X'87F8',PSERVIC*
                   =X'020000000000185000007E00'
          TITLE 'RSK32782'
**********************************************************************
*                                                                    *
*          3274 MODEL 1C WITH MODEL 2 SCREEN(REMOTE SNA)             *
*          PRIMARY SCREEN 24 X 80 (1920)                             *
*          NO ALTERNATE SCREEN DEFINED                               *
*          KATAKANA                                                  *
*                                                                    *
**********************************************************************
RSK32782 MODEENT LOGMODE=RSK32782,FMPROF=X'03',TSPROF=X'03',PRIPROT=X'B*
                   1',SECPROT=X'90',COMPROT=X'3080',RUSIZES=X'87F8',PSERVIC*
                   =X'020000000000185000007E00',LANG=X'11'
          TITLE 'D4C32783'
**********************************************************************
*                                                                    *
*          3274 MODEL 1C WITH MODEL 3 SCREEN(REMOTE SNA)             *
*          PRIMARY SCREEN 24 X 80 (1920)                             *
*          ALTERNATE SCREEN 32 X 80 (2560)                          *
*                                                                    *
**********************************************************************
D4C32783 MODEENT LOGMODE=D4C32783,FMPROF=X'03',TSPROF=X'03',PRIPROT=X'B*
                   1',SECPROT=X'90',COMPROT=X'3080',RUSIZES=X'87F8',PSERVIC*
                   =X'020000000000185020507F00'
          TITLE 'D4C32784'
**********************************************************************
*                                                                    *
*          3274 MODEL 1C WITH MODEL 4 SCREEN(REMOTE SNA)             *
*          PRIMARY SCREEN 24 X 80 (1920)                             *
*          ALTERNATE SCREEN 43 X 80 (3440)                          *
*                                                                    *
**********************************************************************
D4C32784 MODEENT LOGMODE=D4C32784,FMPROF=X'03',TSPROF=X'03',PRIPROT=X'B*
                   1',SECPROT=X'90',COMPROT=X'3080',RUSIZES=X'87F8',PSERVIC*
                   =X'02000000000018502B507F00'
          TITLE 'D4C32785'
**********************************************************************
*                                                                    *
*          PRIMARY SCREEN 24 X 80 (1920)                             *
```

```
*              NO ALTERNATE SCREEN DEFINED                           *
*                                                                    *
**********************************************************************
D4C32782 MODEENT LOGMODE=D4C32782,FMPROF=X'03',TSPROF=X'03',PRIPROT=X'B*
              1',SECPROT=X'90',COMPROT=X'3080',RUSIZES=X'87F8',PSERVIC*
              =X'020000000000185000007E00'
         TITLE 'RSK32782'
**********************************************************************
*                                                                    *
*              3274 MODEL 1C WITH MODEL 2 SCREEN(REMOTE SNA)          *
*              PRIMARY SCREEN 24 X 80 (1920)                          *
*              NO ALTERNATE SCREEN DEFINED                            *
*              KATAKANA                                               *
*                                                                    *
**********************************************************************
RSK32782 MODEENT LOGMODE=RSK32782,FMPROF=X'03',TSPROF=X'03',PRIPROT=X'B*
              1',SECPROT=X'90',COMPROT=X'3080',RUSIZES=X'87F8',PSERVIC*
              =X'020000000000185000007E00',LANG=X'11'
         TITLE 'D4C32783'
**********************************************************************
*                                                                    *
*              3274 MODEL 1C WITH MODEL 3 SCREEN(REMOTE SNA)          *
*              PRIMARY SCREEN 24 X 80 (1920)                          *
*              ALTERNATE SCREEN 32 X 80 (2560)                        *
*                                                                    *
**********************************************************************
D4C32783 MODEENT LOGMODE=D4C32783,FMPROF=X'03',TSPROF=X'03',PRIPROT=X'B*
              1',SECPROT=X'90',COMPROT=X'3080',RUSIZES=X'87F8',PSERVIC*
              =X'020000000000185020507F00'
         TITLE 'D4C32784'
**********************************************************************
*                                                                    *
*              3274 MODEL 1C WITH MODEL 4 SCREEN(REMOTE SNA)          *
*              PRIMARY SCREEN 24 X 80 (1920)                          *
*              ALTERNATE SCREEN 43 X 80 (3440)                        *
*                                                                    *
**********************************************************************
D4C32784 MODEENT LOGMODE=D4C32784,FMPROF=X'03',TSPROF=X'03',PRIPROT=X'B*
              1',SECPROT=X'90',COMPROT=X'3080',RUSIZES=X'87F8',PSERVIC*
              =X'02000000000018502B507F00'
         TITLE 'D4C32785'
**********************************************************************
*                                                                    *
*              3274 MODEL 1C WITH MODEL 5 SCREEN(REMOTE SNA)          *
*              PRIMARY SCREEN 24 X 80 (1920)                          *
*              ALTERNATE SCREEN 27 X 132 (3564)                       *
*                                                                    *
**********************************************************************
D4C32785 MODEENT LOGMODE=D4C32785,FMPROF=X'03',TSPROF=X'03',PRIPROT=X'B*
              1',SECPROT=X'90',COMPROT=X'3080',RUSIZES=X'87F8',PSERVIC*
              =X'02000000000018501B847F00'
```

```
        TITLE 'D4C32XX3'
************************************************************************
*                                                                      *
*                3274 MODEL 1C (REMOTE SNA)                            *
*                PRIMARY SCREEN 24 X 80 (1920)                         *
*                ALTERNATE SCREEN TO BE DETERMINED BY APPLICATION      *
*                                                                      *
************************************************************************
D4C32XX3 MODEENT LOGMODE=D4C32XX3,FMPROF=X'03',TSPROF=X'03',PRIPROT=X'B*
               1',SECPROT=X'90',COMPROT=X'3080',RUSIZES=X'87F8',PSERVIC*
               =X'028000000000000000000300'
        TITLE 'D4C32771'
************************************************************************
*                                                                      *
*                3274 MODEL 1C WITH 3277 MODEL 1 SCREEN                *
*                                                                      *
************************************************************************
D4C32771 MODEENT LOGMODE=D4C32771,FMPROF=X'03',TSPROF=X'03',PRIPROT=X'B*
               1',SECPROT=X'90',COMPROT=X'3080',RUSIZES=X'87F8',PSERVIC*
               =X'020000000000000000000100'
        TITLE 'D4C32772'
************************************************************************
*                                                                      *
*                3274 MODEL 1C WITH 3277 MODEL 2 SCREEN                *
*                                                                      *
************************************************************************
D4C32772 MODEENT LOGMODE=D4C32772,FMPROF=X'03',TSPROF=X'03',PRIPROT=X'B*
               1',SECPROT=X'90',COMPROT=X'3080',RUSIZES=X'87F8',PSERVIC*
               =X'020000000000000000000200'
        TITLE 'D4B32781'
************************************************************************
*                                                                      *
*        3274 MODEL 1B/1D WITH MODEL 1 SCREEN (LOCAL NON-SNA)          *
*        3274 1C BSC WITH MODEL 1 SCREEN                               *
*        3276 BSC WITH MODEL 1 SCREEN                                  *
*        PRIMARY SCREEN 12 X 40 (480)                                  *
*        ALTERNATE SCREEN 12 X 80 (960)                                *
*                                                                      *
************************************************************************
D4B32781 MODEENT LOGMODE=D4B32781,FMPROF=X'02',TSPROF=X'02',PRIPROT=X'7*
               1',SECPROT=X'40',COMPROT=X'2000',RUSIZES=X'0000',PSERVIC*
               =X'0000000000000C280C507F00'
        TITLE 'D4B32782'
************************************************************************
*                                                                      *
*        3274 MODEL 1B/1D WITH MODEL 2 SCREEN (LOCAL NON-SNA)          *
*        3274 1C BSC WITH MODEL 2 SCREEN                               *
*        3276 BSC WITH MODEL 2 SCREEN                                  *
*        PRIMARY SCREEN 24 X 80 (1920)                                 *
*        NO ALTERNATE SCREEN DEFINED                                   *
*                                                                      *
```

```
****************************************************************
D4B32782 MODEENT LOGMODE=D4B32782,FMPROF=X'02',TSPROF=X'02',PRIPROT=X'7*
              1',SECPROT=X'40',COMPROT=X'2000',RUSIZES=X'0000',PSERVIC*
              =X'000000000000185000007E00'
         TITLE 'LNK32782'
****************************************************************
*                                                              *
*    3274 MODEL 1B/1D WITH MODEL 2 SCREEN (LOCAL NON-SNA)       *
*    3274 1C BSC WITH MODEL 2 SCREEN                            *
*    3276 BSC WITH MODEL 2 SCREEN                               *
*    PRIMARY SCREEN 24 X 80 (1920)                              *
*    NO ALTERNATE SCREEN DEFINED                                *
*    KATAKANA                                                   *
*                                                              *
****************************************************************
LNK32782 MODEENT LOGMODE=LNK32782,FMPROF=X'02',TSPROF=X'02',PRIPROT=X'7*
              1',SECPROT=X'40',COMPROT=X'2000',RUSIZES=X'0000',PSERVIC*
              =X'000000000000185000007E00',LANG=X'11'
         TITLE 'D4B32783'
****************************************************************
*                                                              *
*    3274 MODEL 1B/1D WITH MODEL 3 SCREEN (LOCAL NON-SNA)       *
*    3274 1C BSC WITH MODEL 3 SCREEN                            *
*    3276 BSC WITH MODEL 3 SCREEN                               *
*    PRIMARY SCREEN 24 X 80 (1920)                              *
*    ALTERNATE SCREEN 32 X 80 (2560)                            *
*                                                              *
****************************************************************
D4B32783 MODEENT LOGMODE=D4B32783,FMPROF=X'02',TSPROF=X'02',PRIPROT=X'7*
              1',SECPROT=X'40',COMPROT=X'2000',RUSIZES=X'0000',PSERVIC*
              =X'000000000000185020507F00'
         TITLE 'D4B32784'
****************************************************************
*                                                              *
*    3274 MODEL 1B/1D WITH MODEL 4 SCREEN (LOCAL NON-SNA)       *
*    3274 1C BSC WITH MODEL 4 SCREEN                            *
*    3276 BSC WITH MODEL 4 SCREEN                               *
*    PRIMARY SCREEN 24 X 80 (1920)                              *
*    ALTERNATE SCREEN 43 X 80 (3440)                            *
*                                                              *
****************************************************************
D4B32784 MODEENT LOGMODE=D4B32784,FMPROF=X'02',TSPROF=X'02',PRIPROT=X'7*
              1',SECPROT=X'40',COMPROT=X'2000',RUSIZES=X'0000',PSERVIC*
              =X'00000000000018502B507F00'
         TITLE 'D4B32785'
****************************************************************
*                                                              *
*    3274 MODEL 1B/1D WITH MODEL 5 SCREEN (LOCAL NON-SNA)       *
*    3274 1C BSC WITH MODEL 5 SCREEN                            *
*    3276 BSC WITH MODEL 5 SCREEN                               *
*    PRIMARY SCREEN 24 X 80 (1920)                              *
```

```
*       ALTERNATE SCREEN 27 X 132 (3564)                              *
*                                                                     *
**********************************************************************
D4B32785 MODEENT LOGMODE=D4B32785,FMPROF=X'02',TSPROF=X'02',PRIPROT=X'7*
             1',SECPROT=X'40',COMPROT=X'2000',RUSIZES=X'0000',PSERVIC*
             =X'00000000000018501B847F00'
         TITLE 'D4B32XX3'
**********************************************************************
*                                                                     *
*       3274 MODEL 1B/1D (LOCAL NON-SNA)                              *
*       3274 1C BSC                                                   *
*       3276 BSC                                                      *
*       PRIMARY SCREEN 24 X 80 (1920)                                 *
*       ALTERNATE SCREEN TO BE DETERMINED BY APPLICATION              *
*                                                                     *
**********************************************************************
D4B32XX3 MODEENT LOGMODE=D4B32XX3,FMPROF=X'02',TSPROF=X'02',PRIPROT=X'7*
             1',SECPROT=X'40',COMPROT=X'2000',RUSIZES=X'0000',PSERVIC*
             =X'0080000000000000000000300'
         TITLE 'SCS'
**********************************************************************
*                                                                     *
*       PRINTER WITH SNA CHARACTER SET                                *
*                                                                     *
**********************************************************************
SCS      MODEENT LOGMODE=SCS,FMPROF=X'03',TSPROF=X'03',PRIPROT=X'B1',  *
             SECPROT=X'90',COMPROT=X'3080',RUSIZES=X'87C6',            *
             PSERVIC=X'01000000E1000000000000000',                    *
             PSNDPAC=X'01',SRCVPAC=X'01'
         TITLE 'DSC4K'
**********************************************************************
*                                                                     *
*       PRINTER WITH 4K BUFFER                                        *
*                                                                     *
**********************************************************************
DSC4K    MODEENT LOGMODE=DSC4K,FMPROF=X'03',TSPROF=X'03',PRIPROT=X'B1',*
             SECPROT=X'90',COMPROT=X'3080',RUSIZES=X'8787',           *
             PSERVIC=X'03000000000018502B507F00'
         TITLE 'DSC2K'
**********************************************************************
*                                                                     *
*       PRINTER WITH 2K BUFFER                                        *
*                                                                     *
**********************************************************************
DSC2K    MODEENT LOGMODE=DSC2K,FMPROF=X'03',TSPROF=X'03',PRIPROT=X'B1',*
             SECPROT=X'90',COMPROT=X'3080',RUSIZES=X'8787',           *
             PSERVIC=X'03000000000018501B507F00'
         TITLE 'BAT13790'
**********************************************************************
*                                                                     *
*       3790 BATCH                                                    *
```

```
*                                                                      *
**********************************************************************
BAT13790 MODEENT LOGMODE=BAT13790,FMPROF=X'03',TSPROF=X'03',          *
            PRIPROT=X'00',SECPROT=X'00',COMPROT=X'0000',              *
            RUSIZES=X'0000'
         TITLE 'EMU3790'
**********************************************************************
*                                                                      *
*    3790 IN DATA STREAM COMPATIBILITY MODE                           *
*                                                                      *
**********************************************************************
EMU3790  MODEENT LOGMODE=EMU3790,FMPROF=X'03',TSPROF=X'03',           *
            PRIPROT=X'B1',SECPROT=X'B0',COMPROT=X'3080',              *
            RUSIZES=X'85C7',PSERVIC=X'020000000000000000000200'
         TITLE 'RJE3790A'
**********************************************************************
*                                                                      *
*    3790 RJE                                                          *
*                                                                      *
**********************************************************************
RJE3790A MODEENT LOGMODE=RJE3790A,FMPROF=X'03',TSPROF=X'03',          *
            PRIPROT=X'A3',SECPROT=X'A1',COMPROT=X'7080',              *
            RUSIZES=X'8585',PSERVIC=X'01106000F100800000010040'
         TITLE 'RJE3790B'
**********************************************************************
*                                                                      *
*    3790 RJE                                                          *
*                                                                      *
**********************************************************************
RJE3790B MODEENT LOGMODE=RJE3790B,FMPROF=X'03',TSPROF=X'03',          *
            PRIPROT=X'A3',SECPROT=X'A1',COMPROT=X'7080',              *
            RUSIZES=X'8585',PSERVIC=X'01102000F100800000010040'
         TITLE 'BAT23790'
**********************************************************************
*                                                                      *
*    3790 BATCH                                                        *
*                                                                      *
**********************************************************************
BAT23790 MODEENT LOGMODE=BAT23790,FMPROF=X'03',TSPROF=X'04',          *
            PRIPROT=X'B1',SECPROT=X'B0',COMPROT=X'7080',              *
            RUSIZES=X'8585',PSERVIC=X'0131000000000000000000000'
         TITLE 'BLK3790'
**********************************************************************
*                                                                      *
*    3790 BULK PRINT                                                   *
*                                                                      *
**********************************************************************
BLK3790  MODEENT LOGMODE=BLK3790,FMPROF=X'03',TSPROF=X'03',           *
            PRIPROT=X'B1',SECPROT=X'B0',COMPROT=X'3080',              *
            RUSIZES=X'8585',PSERVIC=X'0300000000000000000000000'
         TITLE 'SCS3790'
```

```
***********************************************************************
*                                                                     *
*       3790 WITH SNA CHARACTER SET                                   *
*                                                                     *
***********************************************************************
SCS3790   MODEENT LOGMODE=SCS3790,FMPROF=X'03',TSPROF=X'03',          *
                  PRIPROT=X'B1',SECPROT=X'B0',COMPROT=X'3080',        *
                  RUSIZES=X'8585',PSERVIC=X'010000000000000000000000'
          TITLE 'EMUDPCX'
***********************************************************************
*                                                                     *
*       3790 IN DPCX EMULATION MODE                                   *
*                                                                     *
***********************************************************************
EMUDPCX   MODEENT LOGMODE=EMUDPCX,FMPROF=X'03',TSPROF=X'03',          *
                  PRIPROT=X'B1',SECPROT=X'B0',COMPROT=X'3080',        *
                  RUSIZES=X'85C7',PSERVIC=X'020000000000000000000200'
          TITLE 'DSILGMOD'
***********************************************************************
*                                                                     *
* DSILGMOD  LOGMODE TABLE FOR BSC,LOCAL,SDLC 3275,3277,3278,3279      *
*           MODEL 2 OR 12, 24 X 80 SCREEN. MAY BE USED TO RUN         *
*              MODELS 3, 4, 5, 2C OR 3C AS MODEL 2                    *
*           ALSO FOR 3284, 3286, 3287, 3288, 3289 PRINTERS           *
*           THROUGH A 3271, 3272, 3274, 3275, OR 3276 CONTROLLER      *
*                                                                     *
***********************************************************************
DSILGMOD MODEENT LOGMODE=DSILGMOD,FMPROF=X'02',TSPROF=X'02',          *
                 PRIPROT=X'71',SECPROT=X'40',COMPROT=X'2000',         *
                 RUSIZES=X'0000',PSERVIC=X'000000000000000000000200'
          TITLE 'ISTNLDM'
***********************************************************************
*         NLDM LOGMODE FOR LU - LU SESSION WITH NCCF                  *
***********************************************************************
ISTNLDM   MODEENT LOGMODE=ISTNLDM,FMPROF=X'02',TSPROF=X'03',          *
                  PRIPROT=X'30',SECPROT=X'40',COMPROT=X'0000',        *
                  SSNDPAC=X'02',RUSIZES=X'0000',                      *
                  PSERVIC=X'000000000000000000000000'
          TITLE 'D329001'
***********************************************************************
*         LOGMODE TABLE ENTRY FOR THE 3290 TERMINAL                   *
*             OR EXTENDED DATA STREAM TERMINAL OFF 3274-1A            *
*             PRIMARY SCREEN SIZE 24 X 80                             *
*             ALTERNATE SCREEN SIZE 62 X 160                          *
***********************************************************************
D329001   MODEENT LOGMODE=D329001,FMPROF=X'03',TSPROF=X'03',          *
                  PRIPROT=X'B1',SECPROT=X'90',COMPROT=X'3080',        *
                  RUSIZES=X'8787',                                    *
                  PSERVIC=X'02800000000018503EA07F00'
          TITLE 'NSX32702'
***********************************************************************
```

```
*         LOGMODE TABLE ENTRY FOR NON-SNA 3270 DEVICES WITH        *
*             EXTENDED DATA STREAMS (3278 OR 3279).                *
*             SCREEN SIZE IS 24 X 80.                              *
******************************************************************
NSX32702 MODEENT LOGMODE=NSX32702,FMPROF=X'02',TSPROF=X'02',          *
              PRIPROT=X'71',SECPROT=X'40',COMPROT=X'2000',            *
              RUSIZES=X'0000',                                        *
              PSERVIC=X'008000000000185000007E00'
         TITLE 'NSX32703'
******************************************************************
*         LOGMODE TABLE ENTRY FOR NON-SNA 3270 DEVICES WITH        *
*             EXTENDED DATA STREAMS (3278 OR 3279).                *
*             PRIMARY SCREEN 24 X 80                               *
*             ALTERNATE SCREEN 32 X 80                             *
******************************************************************
NSX32703 MODEENT LOGMODE=NSX32703,FMPROF=X'02',TSPROF=X'02',          *
              PRIPROT=X'71',SECPROT=X'40',COMPROT=X'2000',            *
              RUSIZES=X'0000',                                        *
              PSERVIC=X'008000000000185020507F00'
         TITLE 'NSX32704'
******************************************************************
*         LOGMODE TABLE ENTRY FOR NON-SNA 3270 DEVICES WITH        *
*             EXTENDED DATA STREAMS (3278 OR 3279).                *
*             PRIMARY SCREEN 24 X 80                               *
*             ALTERNATE SCREEN 43 X 80                             *
******************************************************************
NSX32704 MODEENT LOGMODE=NSX32704,FMPROF=X'02',TSPROF=X'02',          *
              PRIPROT=X'71',SECPROT=X'40',COMPROT=X'2000',            *
              RUSIZES=X'0000',                                        *
              PSERVIC=X'008000000000018502B507F00'
         TITLE 'NSX32705'
******************************************************************
*         LOGMODE TABLE ENTRY FOR NON-SNA 3270 DEVICES WITH        *
*             EXTENDED DATA STREAMS (3278 OR 3279).                *
*             PRIMARY SCREEN 24 X 80                               *
*             ALTERNATE SCREEN 27 X 132                            *
******************************************************************
NSX32705 MODEENT LOGMODE=NSX32705,FMPROF=X'02',TSPROF=X'02',          *
              PRIPROT=X'71',SECPROT=X'40',COMPROT=X'2000',            *
              RUSIZES=X'0000',                                        *
              PSERVIC=X'00800000000018501B847F00'
         TITLE 'SNX32702'
******************************************************************
*         LOGMODE TABLE ENTRY FOR REMOTE SNA 3270 DEVICES          *
*             WITH EXTENDED DATA STREAMS (3278 OR 3279).           *
*             SCREEN SIZE IS 24 X 80.                              *
******************************************************************
SNX32702 MODEENT LOGMODE=SNX32702,FMPROF=X'03',TSPROF=X'03',          *
              PRIPROT=X'B1',SECPROT=X'90',COMPROT=X'3080',            *
              RUSIZES=X'87F8',                                        *
              PSERVIC=X'028000000000185000007E00'
```

```
        TITLE 'SNX32703'
**************************************************************************
*         LOGMODE TABLE ENTRY FOR REMOTE SNA 3270 DEVICES              *
*            WITH EXTENDED DATA STREAMS (MOD3).                        *
*               PRIMARY SCREEN 24 X 80 (1920)                          *
*               ALTERNATE SCREEN 32 X 80 (2560)                        *
**************************************************************************
SNX32703 MODEENT LOGMODE=SNX32703,FMPROF=X'03',TSPROF=X'03',            *
              PRIPROT=X'B1',SECPROT=X'90',COMPROT=X'3080',              *
              RUSIZES=X'87F8',                                          *
              PSERVIC=X'028000000000185020507F00'
        TITLE 'SNX32704'
**************************************************************************
*         LOGMODE TABLE ENTRY FOR REMOTE SNA 3270 DEVICES              *
*            WITH EXTENDED DATA STREAMS (MOD4).                        *
*               PRIMARY SCREEN 24 X 80 (1920)                          *
*               ALTERNATE SCREEN 43 X 80 (3440)                        *
**************************************************************************
SNX32704 MODEENT LOGMODE=SNX32704,FMPROF=X'03',TSPROF=X'03',            *
              PRIPROT=X'B1',SECPROT=X'90',COMPROT=X'3080',              *
              RUSIZES=X'87F8',                                          *
              PSERVIC=X'02800000000018502B507F00'
        TITLE 'SNX32705'
**************************************************************************
*                                                                      *
*         LOGMODE TABLE ENTRY FOR REMOTE SNA 3270 DEVICES              *
*            WITH EXTENDED DATA STREAMS (MOD5).                        *
*               PRIMARY SCREEN 24 X 80 (1920)                          *
*               ALTERNATE SCREEN 27 X 132 (3564)                       *
*                                                                      *
**************************************************************************
SNX32705 MODEENT LOGMODE=SNX32705,FMPROF=X'03',TSPROF=X'03',            *
              PRIPROT=X'B1',SECPROT=X'90',COMPROT=X'3080',              *
              RUSIZES=X'87F8',                                          *
              PSERVIC=X'02800000000018501B847F00'
        TITLE 'LSX32702'
**************************************************************************
*                                                                      *
*            3274 MODEL 1A WITH MODEL 2 SCREEN (LOCAL SNA)             *
*            WITH EXTENDED DATA STREAMS (MOD2)                         *
*            PRIMARY SCREEN 24 X 80 (1920)                            *
*            NO ALTERNATE SCREEN DEFINED                              *
*                                                                      *
**************************************************************************
LSX32702 MODEENT LOGMODE=LSX32702,FMPROF=X'03',TSPROF=X'03',PRIPROT=X'B*
              1',SECPROT=X'90',COMPROT=X'3080',RUSIZES=X'87C7',PSERVIC*
              =X'028000000000185000007E00'
        TITLE 'LSX32703'
**************************************************************************
*                                                                      *
*            3274 MODEL 1A WITH MODEL 3 SCREEN (LOCAL SNA)             *
```

```
*              WITH EXTENDED DATA STREAMS (MOD3)              *
*              PRIMARY SCREEN 24 X 80 (1920)                  *
*              ALTERNATE SCREEN 32 X 80 (2560)                *
*                                                             *
***************************************************************
LSX32703 MODEENT LOGMODE=LSX32703,FMPROF=X'03',TSPROF=X'03',PRIPROT=X'B*
               1',SECPROT=X'90',COMPROT=X'3080',RUSIZES=X'87C7',PSERVIC*
               =X'028000000000185020507F00'
         TITLE 'LSX32704'
***************************************************************
*                                                             *
*              3274 MODEL 1A WITH MODEL 4 SCREEN (LOCAL SNA)   *
*              WITH EXTENDED DATA STREAMS (MOD4)              *
*              PRIMARY SCREEN 24 X 80 (1920)                  *
*              ALTERNATE SCREEN 43 X 80 (3440)                *
*                                                             *
***************************************************************
LSX32704 MODEENT LOGMODE=LSX32704,FMPROF=X'03',TSPROF=X'03',PRIPROT=X'B*
               1',SECPROT=X'90',COMPROT=X'3080',RUSIZES=X'87C7',PSERVIC*
               =X'02800000000018502B507F00'
         TITLE 'LSX32705'
***************************************************************
*                                                             *
*              3274 MODEL 1A WITH MODEL 5 SCREEN (LOCAL SNA)   *
*              WITH EXTENDED DATA STREAMS (MOD5)              *
*              PRIMARY SCREEN 24 X 80 (1920)                  *
*              ALTERNATE SCREEN 27 X 132 (3564)               *
*                                                             *
***************************************************************
LSX32705 MODEENT LOGMODE=LSX32705,FMPROF=X'03',TSPROF=X'03',PRIPROT=X'B*
               1',SECPROT=X'90',COMPROT=X'3080',RUSIZES=X'87C7',PSERVIC*
               =X'02800000000018501B847F00'
         TITLE 'LNK32782'
***************************************************************
*                                                             *
*      3274 MODEL 1B/1D WITH MODEL 2 SCREEN (LOCAL NON-SNA)    *
*      3274 1C BSC WITH MODEL 2 SCREEN                         *
*      3276 BSC WITH MODEL 2 SCREEN                            *
*      PRIMARY SCREEN 24 X 80 (1920)                           *
*      NO ALTERNATE SCREEN DEFINED                             *
*      KATAKANA                                                *
*                                                             *
***************************************************************
LNK32782 MODEENT LOGMODE=LNK32782,FMPROF=X'02',TSPROF=X'02',PRIPROT=X'7*
               1',SECPROT=X'40',COMPROT=X'2000',RUSIZES=X'0000',PSERVIC*
               =X'000000000000185000007E00',LANG-X'11'
         TITLE 'NED32702'
***************************************************************
*      LOGMODE TABLE ENTRY FOR NON-SNA 3270 DEVICES WITH       *
*         EXTENDED DATA STREAMS (3278 OR 3279).               *
*         SCREEN SIZE IS 24 X 80.                             *
```

```
*           LANGUAGE IS ENGLISH.                                      *
*           QUERY FOR DOUBLE BYTE CAPABILITY.                         *
***********************************************************************
NED32702 MODEENT LOGMODE=NED32702,FMPROF=X'02',TSPROF=X'02',          *
               PRIPROT=X'71',SECPROT=X'40',COMPROT=X'2000',           *
               RUSIZES=X'0000',                                       *
               PSERVIC=X'0080000000000185000007E00',LANG=X'81'
         TITLE 'NKD32702'
***********************************************************************
* NAME:  NON-SNA KATAKANA, DOUBLE BYTE CAPABLE, 3270-2                *
*        LOGMODE TABLE ENTRY FOR NON-SNA 3270 DEVICES WITH            *
*           EXTENDED DATA STREAMS (3278 OR 3279).                     *
*           SCREEN SIZE IS 24 X 80.                                   *
*           LANGUAGE IS KATAKANA.                                     *
*           QUERY FOR DOUBLE BYTE CAPABILITY.                         *
***********************************************************************
NKD32702 MODEENT LOGMODE=NKD32702,FMPROF=X'02',TSPROF=X'02',          *
               PRIPROT=X'71',SECPROT=X'40',COMPROT=X'2000',           *
               RUSIZES=X'0000',                                       *
               PSERVIC=X'0080000000000185000007E00',LANG=X'91'
         TITLE 'LED32702'
***********************************************************************
*                                                                     *
*        LOGMODE TABLE ENTRY FOR LOCAL SNA                            *
*           3274 MODEL 1A WITH MODEL 2 SCREEN (LOCAL SNA)             *
*           PRIMARY SCREEN 24 X 80 (1920)                             *
*           NO ALTERNATE SCREEN DEFINED                               *
*           EXTENDED DATA STREAMS                                     *
*           ENGLISH LANGUAGE                                          *
*           QUERY FOR DOUBLE BYTE CAPABILITY                          *
***********************************************************************
LED32702 MODEENT LOGMODE=LED32702,FMPROF=X'03',TSPROF=X'03',PRIPROT=X'B*
               1',SECPROT=X'90',COMPROT=X'3080',RUSIZES=X'87C7',PSERVIC*
               =X'0280000000000185000007E00',LANG=X'81'
         TITLE 'LKD32702'
***********************************************************************
*                                                                     *
*        LOGMODE TABLE ENTRY FOR LOCAL SNA                            *
*           3274 MODEL 1A WITH MODEL 2 SCREEN (LOCAL SNA)             *
*           PRIMARY SCREEN 24 X 80 (1920)                             *
*           NO ALTERNATE SCREEN DEFINED                               *
*           EXTENDED DATA STREAMS                                     *
*           KATAKANA LANGUAGE                                         *
*           QUERY FOR DOUBLE BYTE CAPABILITY                          *
***********************************************************************
LKD32702 MODEENT LOGMODE=LKD32702,FMPROF=X'03',TSPROF=X'03',PRIPROT=X'B*
               1',SECPROT=X'90',COMPROT=X'3080',RUSIZES=X'87C7',PSERVIC*
               =X'0280000000000185000007E00',LANG=X'91'
         TITLE 'SED32702'
***********************************************************************
*        LOGMODE TABLE ENTRY FOR REMOTE SNA 3270 DEVICES              *
```

```
*              WITH EXTENDED DATA STREAMS (3278 OR 3279).            *
*              SCREEN SIZE IS 24 X 80.                               *
*              LANGUAGE IS ENGLISH.                                  *
*              QUERY FOR DOUBLE BYTE CAPABILITY                      *
*********************************************************************
SED32702 MODEENT LOGMODE=SED32702,FMPROF=X'03',TSPROF=X'03',         *
             PRIPROT=X'B1',SECPROT=X'90',COMPROT=X'3080',            *
             RUSIZES=X'87F8',                                        *
             PSERVIC=X'028000000000185000007E00',LANG=X'81'
         TITLE 'SKD32702'
*********************************************************************
*       LOGMODE TABLE ENTRY FOR REMOTE SNA 3270 DEVICES             *
*            WITH EXTENDED DATA STREAMS (3278 OR 3279).             *
*            SCREEN SIZE IS 24 X 80.                                *
*            LANGUAGE IS KATAKANA.                                  *
*            QUERY FOR DOUBLE BYTE CAPABILITY                       *
*********************************************************************
SKD32702 MODEENT LOGMODE=SKD32702,FMPROF=X'03',TSPROF=X'03',         *
             PRIPROT=X'B1',SECPROT=X'90',COMPROT=X'3080',            *
             RUSIZES=X'87F8',                                        *
             PSERVIC=X'028000000000185000007E00',LANG=X'91'
         TITLE 'SNASVCMG'
*********************************************************************
*       LOGMODE TABLE ENTRY FOR RESOURCES CAPABLE OF ACTING         *
*                        AS LU 6.2 DEVICES                          *
*********************************************************************
SNASVCMG MODEENT LOGMODE=SNASVCMG,FMPROF=X'13',TSPROF=X'07',         *
             PRIPROT=X'B0',SECPROT=X'B0',COMPROT=X'D0B1',            *
             RUSIZES=X'8585',ENCR=B'0000',                           *
             PSERVIC=X'060200000000000000000300'
         MODEEND
```

B

IBM Default USS Table

The following table is an IBM-supplied default USS table for VTAM V3R2. If you plan to customize your own USS table, be sure to link-edit your table with a name other than ISTINCDT.

```
ISTINCDT USSTAB    TABLE=STDTRANS
LOGON    USSCMD    CMD=LOGON,FORMAT=PL1
         USSPARM   PARM=APPLID
         USSPARM   PARM=LOGMODE
         USSPARM   PARM=DATA
LOGOFF   USSCMD    CMD=LOGOFF,FORMAT=PL1
         USSPARM   PARM=APPLID
         USSPARM   PARM=TYPE,DEFAULT=UNCOND
         USSPARM   PARM=HOLD,DEFAULT=YES
IBMTEST  USSCMD    CMD=IBMTEST,FORMAT=BAL
         USSPARM   PARM=P1,DEFAULT=10
         USSPARM   PARM=P2,DEFAULT=ABCDEFGHIJKLMNOPQRSTUVWXYZ0123456789
MESSAGES USSMSG    MSG=1,TEXT='INVALID COMMAND SYNTAX'
         USSMSG    MSG=2,TEXT='% COMMAND UNRECOGNIZED'
         USSMSG    MSG=3,TEXT='% PARAMETER EXTRANEOUS'
         USSMSG    MSG=4,TEXT='% PARAMETER VALUE INVALID'
         USSMSG    MSG=5,TEXT='UNSUPPORTED FUNCTION'
         USSMSG    MSG=6,TEXT='SEQUENCE ERROR'
         USSMSG    MSG=7,TEXT='%(1) UNABLE TO ESTABLISH SESSION - %(2) F-
               AILED WITH SENSE %(3)'
         USSMSG    MSG=8,TEXT='INSUFFICIENT STORAGE'
         USSMSG    MSG=9,TEXT='MAGNETIC CARD DATA ERROR'
         USSMSG    MSG=11,TEXT='% SESSIONS ENDED'
         USSMSG    MSG=12,TEXT='REQUIRED PARAMETER OMITTED'
         USSMSG    MSG=13,TEXT='IBMECHO % '
         EJECT
```

```
STDTRANS DC       X'000102030440060708090A0B0C0D0E0F'
         DC       X'101112131415161718191A1B1C1D1E1F'
         DC       X'202122232425262728292A2B2C2D2E2F'
         DC       X'303132333435363738393A3B3C3D3E3F'
         DC       X'404142434445464748494A4B4C4D4E4F'
         DC       X'505152535455565758595A5B5C5D5E5F'
         DC       X'606162636465666768696A6B6C6D6E6F'
         DC       X'707172737475767778797A7B7C7D7E7F'
         DC       X'80C1C2C3C4C5C6C7C8C98A8B8C8D8E8F'
         DC       X'90D1D2D3D4D5D6D7D8D99A9B9C9D9E9F'
         DC       X'A0A1E2E3E4E5E6E7E8E9AAABACADAEAF'
         DC       X'B0B1B2B3B4B5B6B7B8B9BABBBCBDBEBF'
         DC       X'C0C1C2C3C4C5C6C7C8C9CACBCCCDCECF'
         DC       X'D0D1D2D3D4D5D6D7D8D9DADBDCDDDEDF'
         DC       X'E0E1E2E3E4E5E6E7E8E9EAEBECEDEEEF'
         DC       X'F0F1F2F3F4F5F6F7F8F9FAFBFCFDFEFF'
         END
```

C

Product Support of SNA Network Addressable Unit Types

The two tables provided in this appendix correlate IBM product types to SNA network addressable unit types. This is not a complete list but rather a list of the most widely used products that support the various SNA network addressable units.

NODE TYPES				
PU 1	PU 2	PU 2.1	PU 4	PU 5
3271	3174	S/36	NCP	VTAM
6670	3274	S/38	37X5	4300
3767	3276	PC	3720	308X
	PC	TPF		3090
	3770	AS/400		
	AS/400			

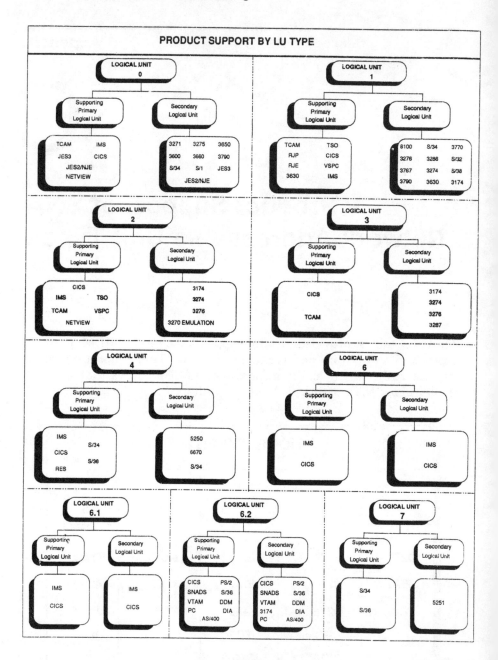

PRODUCT SUPPORT BY LU TYPE

D

IBM 3720 and 3745 Line and Channel-Adapter Considerations

These tables provide you with the line and channel-adapter definition values that require special attention for the IBM 3720 and 3745 communications controllers. This is partly because of the differences between the IBM 37X5 communications controllers and the added enhanced features of the IBM 3720 and 3745 communications controllers.

HISPEED=YES for 3720 LINE Definition		
Line Adapter Base	*lnbr* value for one scanner	*lnbr* value for two scanners
1	0	*
2	32	32 or 48

* Only one scanner is permitted on this line adapter base.
For highspeed lines on the IBM 3720, the lnbr value must be the lowest position on that scanner

lnbr value for IBM 3745		
Adapter Type	*lnbr* values	USGTIER Notes
LSS	0 - 511	
HSS	1024 - 1039	USGTIER1 & 2 do not support high speed scanners.
TRA	1088 - 1095	Only 1088 & 1089 are valid for USGTIER1 & 2. Only first TRA is supported.

channl adapt addr value for IBM 3745									
One CCU CCU A or B		Two CCUs CCU A and B			USGTIER Notes				
Physical Adapter Position	*channl adapt addr* value	CCU	Physical Adapter Position	*channl adapt addr* value	1	2	3	4	5
1	8	A	1	8	*	*	*	*	*
2	9	A	2	9			*	*	*
3	10	A	3	10			*	*	*
4	11	A	4	11			*	*	*
5	0	B	5	0	*	*	*	*	*
6	1	B	6	1			*	*	*
7	2	B	7	2			*	*	*
8	3	B	8	3			*	*	*
9	12	A	9	12				*	*
10	13	A	10	13				*	*
11	14	A	11	14				*	*
12	15	A	12	15				*	*
13	4	B	13	4				*	*
14	5	B	14	5				*	*
15	6	B	15	3				*	*
16	7	B	16	7				*	*

E

VTAM and NCP Performance Tuning Tables

The following tables have been supplied for your reference. They contain information on performance factors for VTAM, NCP, LU-LU flows, Network Data Flows, and communications links.

TUNING TABLE		
NETWORK COMPONENT	**PERFORMANCE FACTOR**	**SPECIFIED IN**
VTAM	Buffer Expansion	VTAM Start List
	Buffer Sizes	VTAM Start List
	ITLIM (Transient)	VTAM Start List
	EAS	VTAM Start List
	VTAMEAS	VTAM Start List
	VTAM Internal Trace (VIT)	VTAM Start List
	SONLIM (Transient)	VTAM Start List
	CSALIMIT/CSA24	VTAM Start List
	MAXPVT	Application Minor Node
	UNITSZ, MAXBFRU	NCP HOST Definition Statement
	DELAY, MAXBFRU	VTAM CTC Definition Statement
NCP	PAUSE	NCP Source LINE Definition
	NEGPOLP	NCP Source LINE Definition
	RETRIES	NCP Source LINE Definition
	ADDRESS=(n,FULL)	NCP Source LINE Definition
	NCP BUFFER size	NCP Source BUILD Definition
	MAXOUT (Modulus8|128)	NCP Source PU Definition
	MAXDATA (Segmentation)	NCP Source PU Definition
	PASSLIM	NCP Source PU Definition
	SERVLIM	NCP Source GROUP Definiton
	REPLYTO	NCP Source LINE Definition
	Service Order Table (SOT)	NCP Source SERVICE Definition
	DELAY	NCP Source BUILD Definition
	TG Activation Sequence	NCP Source TG Definitions

TUNING TABLE		
NETWORK COMPONENT	**PERFORMANCE FACTOR**	**SPECIFIED IN**
LU-LU Flows	Chaining	Application Definitions
	PACING, VPACING	LOGMODE Table, NCP Source, Appl. Definition
	Type of Response (Definite or Exception)	LOGMODE Table, Appl. Definition
	Compaction and Compression	Application Definitions
	Flip-Flop vs. Contention	Appl. Definitions, LOGMODE Table
Network Data Flows	INN Congestion Thresholds	NCP Source PATH Definition
	VR Window Sizes	VTAM/NCP Source PATH Definition
	VR Priority	LOGMODE Table COS Table
	Message Size	Application Definitions
	Alternate Routing	COS Table, PATH Tables
Links	Line Speed	Modem clocking, NCP clocking
	BSC vs. SDLC	NCP Source LINE Definition
	DUPLEX=FULL	NCP Source LINE Definition
	Point to point vs. Multi-point	NCP Source LINE and PU Definitions

F

Subsystem and Device Performance Considerations

This appendix contains several tables relating to network performance for subsystems and devices. The information in the tables does
not represent definitive values. These tables are provided as a reference. For accurate values consult the respective subsystem and device manuals.

SUBSYSTEM CONSIDERATIONS

CONSIDERATION	CICS	IMS	JES2	JES2/NJE
LU TYPE	DFHTCT TYPE = TERMINAL TRMTYPE= SESTYPE=	TYPE UNITYPE= SLUTYPEP SLUTYPE1 SLUTYPE2 SLUTYPE4 LUTYPE6	RMTnn LUTYPE1	INHERENTLY LU TYPE 0 i.e., NOT DEFINED USES FDX
TYPE OF RSP (PLU-TO-SLU)	DFHPCT TYPE=OPTGRP MSGOPT= (MSGINTEG)	NONREC NONREC - RQE RECOV - RQD	RQD	RQE
TYPE OF RSP (SLU-TO-PLU)	SESSION PARM. CODED RQD/RQE	(SEE IMS TABLE)	RQD	RQE
MAXRU (PLU-TO-SLU)	DFHTCT TYPE=TERMINAL BUFFER=	TERMINAL OUTBUF=	RMTnn BUFSIZE=	INIT. STATE & TPBUFSZ=nn i.e., NO LIMIT
MAXRU (SLU-TP-PLU)	DFHTCT TYPE=TERMINAL RUSIZE=	COMM RECANY=	RMTnn BUFSIZE=	see above
BID	ALWAYS	TERMINAL OPTION (SLUP)		NO BRACKETS
COMPRESSION	N/A	N/A	COMP / NOCOMP	STANDARD
COMPACTION	N/A	N/A	CMPCT / NOCMPCT	APPL COMPACT=
CHAIN SIZE	DEPENDS ON MSG SIZE & BUFFER	DEPENDS ON MSG SIZE & OUTBUF	Rnn.PRnn CKPTPGS= CKPTLNS=	USES SINGLE ELEMENT CHAINS

CICS LU TYPE DEFINITION EXAMPLES

DEVICE	LOGICAL UNIT	TRMTYPE=	SESTYPE=
3270	3270 - DS	3275	
		3270	
	3270 - PRT	3270P	
	LU 2	LUTYPE2	
	LU 3	LUTYPE3	
	SCS PR	SCSPRT	
3770	INTER-FLIP FLOP	3770I	
	INTER-CONTENTION	3770C	
	BATCH FLIP FLOP	3770	
		3770B	
		BCHLU	
	FULL FUNCTION	3770	USERPROG
		3770B	
	BATCH DATA INTER	3770	BATCHDI

IMS RESPONSE TYPES					
	UNITYPE=				
DATA TYPE	**SLUTYPE, 3600**		**3790**	**3767, 3770**	**SLUTYPE2**
	ACK	**OPTACK**		**SLUTYPE1**	
UPDATE TRANS	DRX	DRX/EXCP DRX	N/A	DR1/EXCP DR1	EXCP DR1
RECOV INQ TRANS	DRX	DRX/EXCP DRX	N/A	DR1/EXCP DR1	EXCP DR1
NONRECOV INQ TRANS	DRX/EXCP DRX	DRX/EXCP DRX	EXCP DRX	DR1/EXCP DR1	EXCP DR1
IMS MSG SWITCH	DRX	DRX/EXCP DRX	EXCP DRX	DR1/EXCP DR1	EXCP DR1
IMS COMMAND	DRX/EXCP DRX	DRX/EXCP DRX	EXCP DRX	DR1/EXCP DR1	EXCP DR1
SNA COMMAND	DR1	DR1	DR1	DR1	DR1
MFS CTL REQUEST	DRX/EXCP DRX	DRX/EXCP DRX	N/A	N/A	EXCP DR1
BROADCAST OUTPUT **MSG SWITCH** **REPLIES (RECOV)** **/FOR,/DIS,/RDIS** **LAST MFS PGED OUTPUT**	DR2	DR2	DR2	DR2	DR2
ALL OTHER IMS CMDS **REPLIES (NONRECOV)** **MFS PAGED OUTPUT**	EXCP DR2	EXCP DR2	EXCP DR2	EXCP DR2	EXCP DR2
SNA COMMANDS	DR1	DR1	DR1	DR1	DR1

SUBSYSTEM CONSIDERATIONS

CONSIDERATION	POWER	TSO	RES	BDT(MVS)
LU TYPE	PRMT TYPE = LUT1	BIND	TDESCR=	LU TYPE 0
TYPE OF RSP (PLU-TO-SLU)	RQD	RQD	RQD	RQE
TYPE OF RSP (SLU-TO-PLU)	RQD	BIND	RQD	RQE
MAXRU (PLU-TO-SLU)	FIXED 256	BIND	TERMINAL BUFSIZE=	4K MAX INIT. DECK
MAXRU (SLU-TP-PLU)	FIXED 256	BIND	TERMINAL BUFSIZE=	4K MAX
BID	N/A			
COMPRESSION	OUT - BIND IN - NO	N/A	RTAM SNACOMP=	YES
COMPACTION	PRMT CMPACT=name	N/A	RTAM CAPCT=	±NO
CHAIN SIZE	PRINT DATA SET	APPLICATION & MAXRU DEPENDENT	TERMINAL VBUF=	NO CHAINING

DEVICE CONSIDERATIONS

CONSIDERATION	3174	3274/3276	MLU 3770	3770
PU TYPE	2/2.1	2	2	2
NUMBER OF PUs	1	1	1	1
FDX or HDX PU	HDX	HDX	FDX	HDX
TYPE OF LOG ON	UNFORMATTED	UNFORMATTED	UNFORMATTED	UNFORMATTED
LU TYPES	1 - SCS PRTR. 2 - 3270 D.S. 3 - 3270 PRTR. 6.2 - DLU/ILU	1 - SCS PRTR. 2 - 3270 D.S. 3 - 3270 PRTR.	1	1
RJE (SINGLE OR MULTIPLE LUs)	N/A	N/A	MULTIPLE (1 - 6)	SINGLE
COMPRESSION	NO	NO	YES	YES
COMPACTION	NO	NO	YES	YES
CONTENTION or FLIP-FLOP	FLIP-FLOP	FLIP-FLOP	BOTH	BOTH
ENCRYPTION	YES	YES	YES	NO
NUMBER OF LUs	MULTIPLE	MULTIPLE	DEPENDS ON MAXRU & PACING	1
TS PROFILE	3	3	3	3
MAX. RUSIZE OUTBOUND FROM HOST	REMOTE - ANY LOCAL - 1536	REMOTE - ANY LOCAL - 1536	512	512
MAX. RUSIZE INBOUND TO HOST	1K or 2K	3274 - 1K 3276 - 2K	512	512

DEVICE CONSIDERATIONS

CONSIDERATION	3174	3274/3276	MLU 3770	3770
MAXDATA	265 or 521	265	265 or 521	265 or 521
SEGMENTATION	YES	YES	NO	NO
MAX. # SEGMENTS	NO LIMIT	NO LIMIT	N/A	N/A
MAXOUT	7	7	7	1
PACING TO DEVICE	LU 1 - ANY LU 2 - ANY LU 3 - RQD LU 6.2 - ANY	LU 1 - ANY LU 2 - ANY LU 3 - RQD	VARIABLE	1
PACING FROM DEVICE	ANY	ANY	VARIABLE	VARIABLE
LINE SPEED	T1 or 56 kbps	T1 or 56 kbps	19.2 bps	4.8 bps 3770 19.2 bps 3776, 3777
LU LOCADDR	2 - n	2 - n	1 - 6	1
ACTPU/ACTLU ERP	YES	YES	YES	YES
MULTIPLE ELEMENT CHAINS	YES	YES	YES	YES
SLU-PLU RSP DEFINITION	BIND	BIND	BIND	BIND
SLU-PLU RSP DEFAULT	RQE	RQE	RQD	RQD

G

Bibliography of Suggested IBM Manuals

VTAM

SC23-0111	VTAM Installation and Resource Definition
SC23-0112	VTAM Customization
GC31-6403	VTAM Directory of Programming Interfaces for Customers
SC23-0113	VTAM Operation
SC23-0114	VTAM Messages and Codes
SC23-0115	VTAM Programming
SC30-3400	VTAM Programming for LU 6.2

NetView

SK2T-0292	Learning About Netview
SC30-3476	NetView Installation and Administration Guide
SC30-3361	NetView Administration Reference
SC30-3462	NetView Customization
GC31-6005	NetView Directory of Programming Interfaces for Customers
SC30-3423	NetView Command Lists
SC30-3363	NetView Operation Primer
SC30-3364	NetView Operation
SC30-3365	NetView Messages
SC30-3376	NetView Operation Scenarios
SX27-3620	NetView Command Summary

SC30-3366   NetView Hardware Problem Determination Reference
SD21-0016   NetView 5822 Supplement

NetView/PC

SC30-3408   NetView/PC Planning and Operation Guide
SC30-3482   NetView/PC Installation Guide
SC30-3313   NetView/PC Application Program Interface/Communication
                         Services Reference

NCP

SC30-3348   NCP, SSP, and EP Generation and Loading Guide
SC30-3440   NCP Migration Guide
SC30-3447   NCP, SSP, and EP Resource Definition Guide
SC30-3448   NCP, SSP, and EP Resource Definition Reference
GC31-6202   NCP and Related Products Directory of
                         Programming Interfaces for Customers
SC30-3169   NCP, SSP, and EP Messages and Codes

Miscellaneous

Ranade, Jay and Sackett, George. *Advanced SNA Networking: A
  Professional's Guide to VTAM/NCP.*

H

List of Abbreviations

ACB	Access method control block or application control blocks.
ACF	Advanced Communications Function.
ACTLU	Activate logical unit.
ACTPU	Activate physical unit.
API	Application program interface.
APPL	Application program.
BIU	Basic information unit.
BSC	Binary synchronous communications.
BTU	Basic transmission unit.
CA	Channel adapter.
CDRM	Cross-domain resource manager.
CDRSC	Cross-domain resource.
CLSDST	Close destination.
CNM	Communications network management.
COS	Class of service.
CP	Control program.
CSP	Communications scanner processor.
CUA	Channel unit address.
CVT	Communications vector table.
DAF	Destination address field.
DFC	Data flow control.
DLU	Destination logical unit.
EBCDIC	Extended binary-coded decimal interchange code.
ER	Explicit route
EREP	Environmental recording editing and printing.
FID	Format identification.
GTF	Generalized trace facility.
INN	Intermediate networking node.
I/O	Input/Output.
IRN	Intermediate routing node.
LU	Logical unit.

MOSS	Maintenance and operator subsystem.
MVS	Multiple Virtual Storage.
MVS/XA	MVS for Extended Architecture.
MVS/370	MVS for System/370.
NAU	Network addressable unit.
NCB	Node control block.
NCCF	Network Communications Control Facility.
NCP	Network control program.
NIB	Node Identification Block.
NPDA	Network Problem Determination Application.
OAF	Origin address field.
OPNDST	Open destination.
OS	Operating system.
PEP	Partition emulation program.
PIU	Path information unit.
PLU	Primary logical unit.
PTF	Program temporary fix.
PU	Physical unit.
PUT	Program update tape.
RDT	Resource definition table.
RH	Request/response header.
RPL	Request parameter list.
RU	Request/response unit.
SBA	Set buffer address.
SDLC	Synchronous data link control.
SIO	Start I/O.
SLU	Secondary logical unit.
SMF	System management facilities.
SMP	System Modification Program.
SNA	Systems Network Architecture.
SNI	SNA network interconnection.
SSCP	System services control point.
SVA	Shared virtual area.
SVC	Supervisor call.
TAP	Trace Analysis Program.
TCB	Task control block.
TG	Transmission group.
TH	Transmission header.
TSO	Time-sharing option.
USS	Unformatted system services.
VM	Virtual machine.
VM/SNA	Virtual machine with SNA function.
VM/SP	Virtual Machine System Product.
VR	Virtual route.
VS	Virtual storage.
VSCS	VM SNA console support.
VSE	Virtual Storage Extended.
VTAM	Virtual Telecommunications Access Method.

Glossary

ACB. In context of VTAM, it refers to application control block or access method control block. In context of NCP, it refers to adapter control block.

ACB name. Name specified in the ACBNAME parameter of VTAM's APPL statement.

Access method. Software responsible for moving data between the main storage and I/O devices (e.g., disk drives, tapes, etc.) acquire. Process by which a VTAM application program (e.g., CICS) initiates and establishes a session with another LU.

adapter control block. A control block of NCP having control information and the current state of operation for SDLC, BSC, and start/stop lines.

Advanced Communications Function. A group of SNA-compliant IBM program products such as ACF/VTAM, ACF/TCAM, ACF/NCP, and ACF/SSP.

alert. Occurrence of a very high priority event that requires immediate attention and response.

alias name. A name defined in the name translation program when alias name does not match the real name. It is primarily used for an LU name, Logon mode table name, and class of service name in a different SNA network.

API. See application program interface.

application control block. A control block linking a VTAM application (e.g., CICS) to VTAM.

application program. A program (e.g., CICS) using the services of VTAM to communicate with different LUs and providing a platform for users to perform business-oriented activities.

application program identification. A name specified in the APPLID parametere of ACB macro. VTAM identifies to an application program by this name.

application program interface. Interface through which an application program interacts with VTAM.

application program major node. A group or collection of application program minor nodes. It is a partitioned data set (PDS) member of MVS containing one or more APPL statements.

ASCII. American Standard Code for Information Interchange.

automatic logon. A process by which VTAM automatically starts a session request between PLU and SLU.

begin bracket. An indicator in the request header (RH) indicating the first request in the first chain of a bracket. (See also end bracket.)

binary synchronous communications. A non-SNA link level protocol for synchronous communications.

bind. Request to activate session between a PLU and SLU.

BIU. A request header (RH) followed by all or part of a request/response unit (RU).

boundary function. Capability of a subarea node to provide support for adjacent peripheral nodes.

bracket. One or more RUs exchanged between two LU to LU half-sessions which must be completed before another bracket can be started.

BSC. See Binary Synchronous Communication.

buffer. A portion of main storage for holding I/O data temporarily.

CCP. Configuration Control Program.

CDRSC. Cross-domain resource.

chain. See RU chain.

Channel-attached. Attachment of a device directly to the computer's byte or block multiplexer channel.

CICS. Customer Information Control System.

class of service. Designation of transmission priority, bandwidth, and path security to a particular session.

cluster controller. A channel-attached or link-attached communications device (e.g., 3174) which acts as an interface between cluster of terminal devices and the CPU or communications controller.

CNM. Communications network management.

communications adapter. An optional hardware available on IBM 9370 and IBM 4331 that allows communications lines to be directly attached to it, thus alleviating need for a communications controller.

communications controller. Communications hardware that operates under the control of NCP and manages communications lines, cluster controllers, workstations, and routing of data through a network.

Configuration control program (CCP). An interactive application program used to define and modify configuration for an IBM 3710.

COS. See class of service.

cross-domain. Pertaining to more than one domain.

cross-domain resource (CDRSC). A resource owned and controlled by a cross-domain resource manager (CDRM) of another domain.

cross-network. Resources involving more than one SNA network.

Customer Information Control System (CICS). A database/data communications teleprocessing and transaction management system which runs as a VTAM application.

data link control (DLC) layer. A layer of SNA implemented in the SDLC protocol which schedules data transfer over a pair of links and performs error checking.

deactivate. To render a network resource inoperable by taking it out of service.

definite response. Value in the RH directing the receiver to respond unconditionally.

DFC. Data flow control.

disabled. An indication to SSCP that a particular LU is unable to establish an LU-LU session.

disconnected. Loss of physical connection.

domain. An SSCP and the PUs, LUs, links, and other resources that are controlled by that SSCP.

duplex. Capability to transmit in both directions simultaneously.

EBCDIC. Extended Binary Coded Decimal Interchange Code.

element. A resource in a subarea.

enabled. An indication to SSCP that a particular LU is ready to establish an LU-LU session.

end bracket. A value in the RH indicating an end of the bracket.

ER. See Explicit Route.

explicit route (ER). A set of one or more TGs that connect two subarea nodes.

FID. See Format identification.

FMH. Function Management Header.

format identification field (FID). A field in the TH indicating its format.

formatted system services. A segment of VTAM providing certain services that pertain to receiving field-formatted commands.

gateway NCP. An NCP connecting two or more SNA networks.

half-duplex. Ability to transmit data in one direction at a time only.

IMS/VS. Information Management System/Virtual Storage.

intermediate routing node (IRN). A subarea node with intermediate routing function. A subarea node may also be a boundary node.

local address. Address used by the peripheral node (e.g., cluster controller, terminals). Boundary function of a subarea node translates network address to local address and vice versa.

local attached. A channel-attached device.

logical unit. A port through which an end user accesses the SNA network and communicates with another logical unit.

logon mode table. A VTAM table containing one or many logon modes identified by a logon mode name.

LU. Logical Unit.

major node. A set of resources (minor nodes) that are given a unique name which can be activated or deactivated by a single command.

minor node. A resource within a major node.

multiple-domain network. A network with more than one SSCP.

Multiple Virtual Storage (MVS). An IBM mainframe operating system.

NAU. Network Addressable Unit.

NCCF. Network Communications Control Facility.

negotiable BIND. Capability of two LU-LU half-sessions to be able to negotiate parameters of a session.

NetView. An IBM network management product consisting of NCCF, NPDA, NLDM, and new enhancements.

network address. An address consisting of subarea and element fields.

network addressable unit (NAU). An SSCP or an LU or a PU.

Network Management Vector Table (NMVT). A record of information sent to a host by an SNA resource. It contains information about errors, alerts, and line statistics.

Network Terminal Option (NTO). A program product that runs in the communications controller and allows certain non-SNA devices to have sessions with VTAM application programs.

NMVT. Network Management Vector Table.

node name. A symbolic name for a major or minor node.

NTO. Network Terminal Option.

pacing. Pertaining to control of data transmission by the receiving station so that the sending station does not cause buffer overrun.

parallel sessions. Capability of having two or more concurrently active sessions between the same set of two LUs.

path information unit (PIU). A message consisting of TH and BIU.

physical unit (PU). A network addressable unit (NAU) that manages attached resources and acts as a routing node for communications between LUs. Examples of PUs are SSCP, Communications Controllers, and Cluster Controllers.

PIU. Path Information Unit.

PLU. Primary logical unit.

primary logical unit (PLU). In an LU-LU session, a PLU is the LU which is responsible for bind, recovery, and control.

PU. Physical unit.

request header (RH). Control information prefixed to the request unit (RU).

request parameter list (RPL). A control block containing parameters pertaining to a data transfer request or session initiation/termination request.

request unit (RU). A message unit containing user data or function management headers (FMH) or both.

return code. A code pertaining to the status of the execution of a particular set of instructions.

RH. Request/response header.

RPL. Request parameter list.

RU. Request/response unit.

SDLC. Synchronous Data Link Control.

session. A logical connection between two network addressable units (NAUs).

single-domain network. A network with one SSCP.

SLU. Secondary logical unit.

SMF. System management facility.

SSCP. System services control point.

System Support Program (SSP). An IBM program product to support NCP.

TAP. Trace analysis program.

TCAS. Terminal control address space.

terminal control address space (TCAS). The address space of TSO/VTAM that provides logon services for TSO user address spaces.

TG. Transmission group.

TH. Transmission header.

TIC. Token-Ring interface coupler.

Token-Ring interface coupler (TIC). An adapter to connect a communications controller to an IBM Token-Ring network.

trace analysis program (tap). A program service aid to help in analyzing trace data produced by VTAM and NCP.

transmission group (TG). A group of one or more links between two adjacent subarea nodes that appears as a single logical link.

transmission header (TH). Information created and used by path control and used as a prefix to a basic information unit (BIU).

transmission priority. Priority by which the transmission group control component of path control selects a PIU for transmission to the next subarea.

unbind. Request to terminate a session between two LUs.

unformatted system services (USS). An SSCP facility that translates a character coded request (e.g., logon or logoff) into a field formatted request for processing by formatted system services (FSS).

user exit. A user written program which can be given control at a determined point in an IBM program.

USS. Unformatted system services.

virtual route (VR). Logical connection between two subareas to provide for transmission priority and underlying explicit routes.

virtual route (VR) pacing. A technique used by the VR control component of path control to regulate PIU's flow over a virtual route.

VM SNA Console Support (VSCS). A VTAM component for VM providing SNA support and providing for SNA terminals to be VM consoles.

VM/SP. Virtual Machine/System Product.

VR. Virtual route.

VSCS. VM SNA console support.

VSE. Virtual Storage Extended operating system.

VTAM. Virtual Telecommunications Access Method.

VTAM application program. A program that can issue VTAM macro instructions and is known to VTAM through an ACB.

VTAM operator. A human being or a program authorized to issue VTAM operator commands.

XRF. Extended recovery facility.

X.21. CCITT's recommendations for an interface between the DTE and DCE for synchronous communications (e.g., HDLC) over a data network.

X.25. CCITT's recommendations for an interface between the DTE and packet switching networks.

X.25 NCP Packet Switching Interface (NPSI). A program product which runs in the communications controller that allows VTAM applications to communicate over an X.25-compliant network to SNA or non-SNA equipment or end users.

Index